"'R.C. Sproul,' someone said to me in the 1970s, 'is the finest communicator in the Reformed world.' Now, four decades later, his skills honed by long practice, his understanding deepened by years of prayer, meditation, and testing (as Martin Luther counseled), R.C. shares the fruit of what became perhaps his greatest love: feeding and nourishing his own congregation at St. Andrew's from the Word of God and building them up in faith and fellowship and in Christian living and serving. Dr. Sproul's expositional commentaries have all R.C.'s hallmarks: clarity and liveliness, humor and pathos, always expressed in application to the mind, will, and affections. R.C.'s ability to focus on 'the big picture,' his genius of never saying too much, leaving his hearers satisfied yet wanting more, never making the Word dull, are all present in these expositions. They are his gift to the wider church. May they nourish God's people well and serve as models of the kind of ministry for which we continue to hunger."

—Dr. Sinclair B. Ferguson
Teaching Fellow
Ligonier Ministries

"Dr. R.C. Sproul, well known as a master theologian and extraordinary communicator, showed that he was a powerful, insightful, helpful expository preacher. This collection of sermons is of great value for churches and Christians everywhere."

—Dr. W. Robert Godfrey
President emeritus and professor of church history emeritus
Westminster Seminary California, Escondido, California

"I tell my students again and again, 'You need to buy good commentaries and do so with some discernment.' Among them there must be preacher's commentaries, for not all commentaries are the same. Some may tell you what the text means but provide little help in answering the question, 'How do I preach this text?' Dr. R.C. Sproul was a legend in our time. His preaching held us in awe for half a century, and these pages represent the fruit of his exposition at the very peak of his abilities and insights. Dr. Sproul's expositional commentary series represents Reformed theology on fire, delivered from a pastor's heart in a vibrant congregation. Essential reading."

—Dr. Derek W.H. Thomas
Senior minister
First Presbyterian Church, Columbia, South Carolina

"Dr. R.C. Sproul was the premier theologian of our day, an extraordinary instrument in the hand of the Lord. Possessed with penetrating insight into the text of Scripture, Dr. Sproul was a gifted expositor and world-class teacher, endowed with a strategic grasp and command of the inspired Word. When he stepped into the pulpit of St. Andrew's and committed himself to the weekly discipline of biblical exposition, this noted preacher demonstrated a rare ability to explicate and apply God's Word. I wholeheartedly recommend Dr. Sproul's expositional commentaries to all who long to know the truth better and experience it more deeply in a life-changing fashion. Here is an indispensable tool for digging deeper into God's Word. This is a must-read for every Christian."

—Dr. Steven J. Lawson
Founder and president
OnePassion Ministries, Dallas

"How exciting! Thousands of us have long been indebted to Dr. R.C. Sproul the teacher, and now, through Dr. Sproul's expositional commentaries, we are indebted to Sproul the preacher, whose sermons are thoroughly biblical, soundly doctrinal, warmly practical, and wonderfully readable. Sproul masterfully presents us with the 'big picture' of each pericope in a dignified yet conversational style that accentuates the glory of God and meets the real needs of sinful people like us. This series of volumes is an absolute must for every Reformed preacher and church member who yearns to grow in the grace and knowledge of Christ Jesus. I predict that Sproul's pulpit ministry in written form will do for Christians in the twenty-first century what Martyn Lloyd-Jones' sermonic commentaries did for us last century. *Tolle lege*, and buy these volumes for your friends."

—Dr. Joel R. Beeke
President and professor of systematic theology and homiletics,
Puritan Reformed Theological Seminary, Grand Rapids, Michigan

ACTS

AN EXPOSITIONAL COMMENTARY

ACTS

AN EXPOSITIONAL COMMENTARY

R.C. SPROUL

 Ligonier Ministries

Acts: An Expositional Commentary
© 2019 by R.C. Sproul

Published by Ligonier Ministries
421 Ligonier Court, Sanford, FL 32771
Ligonier.org

Printed in China
RR Donnelley
0000522
First edition 2010
Ligonier Ministries edition, sixth printing

ISBN 978-1-64289-185-0 (Hardcover)
ISBN 978-1-64289-186-7 (ePub)
ISBN 978-1-64289-187-4 (Kindle)

Cover design: Ligonier Creative
Interior typeset: Katherine Lloyd, The DESK

Unless otherwise noted, all Scripture taken from the New King James Version®. Copyright © 1982 by Thomas Nelson. Used by permission. All rights reserved.

All emphases in Scripture quotations have been added by the author.

The Library of Congress has cataloged the Reformation Trust edition as follows:

Names: Sproul, R.C. (Robert Charles), 1939-2017, author.
Title: Acts: an expositional commentary / R.C. Sproul.
Description: Orlando: Reformation Trust, 2019. | Originally published: Wheaton, Ill.: Crossway, c2010. | Includes index.
Identifiers: LCCN 2019000146 | ISBN 9781642891850 (hardcover) | ISBN 9781642891867 (epub) | ISBN 9781642891874 (kindle)
Subjects: LCSH: Bible. Acts--Commentaries.
Classification: LCC BS2625.53 .S67 2019 | DDC 226.6/077--dc23
LC record available at https://lccn.loc.gov/2019000146

To Steve and Kathy Levee
lovers of God's truth

CONTENTS

SERIES PREFACE

When God called me into full-time Christian ministry, He called me to the academy. I was trained and ordained to a ministry of teaching, and the majority of my adult life has been devoted to preparing young men for the Christian ministry and to trying to bridge the gap between seminary and Sunday school through various means under the aegis of Ligonier Ministries.

Then, in 1997, God did something I never anticipated: He placed me in the position of preaching weekly as a leader of a congregation of His people—St. Andrew's in Sanford, Florida. Over the past twelve years, as I have opened the Word of God on a weekly basis for these dear saints, I have come to love the task of the local minister. Though my role as a teacher continues, I am eternally grateful to God that He saw fit to place me in this new ministry, the ministry of a preacher.

Very early in my tenure with St. Andrew's, I determined that I should adopt the ancient Christian practice of *lectio continua*, "continuous expositions," in my preaching. This method of preaching verse-by-verse through books of the Bible (rather than choosing a new topic each week) has been attested throughout church history as the one approach that ensures believers hear the full counsel of God. Therefore, I began preaching lengthy series of messages at St. Andrew's, eventually working my way through several biblical books in a practice that continues to the present day.

Previously, I had taught through books of the Bible in various settings, including Sunday school classes, Bible studies, and audio and video teaching series for Ligonier Ministries. But now I found myself appealing not so much to the minds of my hearers but to both their minds and their hearts. I knew that I was responsible as a preacher to clearly explain God's Word *and* to show how we ought to live in light of it. I sought to fulfill both tasks as I ascended the St. Andrew's pulpit each week.

What you hold in your hand, then, is a written record of my preaching labors amidst my beloved Sanford congregation. The dear saints who sit under my preaching encouraged me to give my sermons a broader hearing. To that end, the chapters that follow were adapted from a sermon series I preached at St. Andrew's.

Please be aware that this book is part of a broader series of books containing adaptations of my St. Andrew's sermons. This book, like all the others in the series, will *not* give you the fullest possible insight into each and every verse in this biblical book. Though I sought to at least touch on each verse, I focused on the key themes and ideas that comprised the "big picture" of each passage I covered. Therefore, I urge you to use this book as an overview and introduction.

I pray that you will be as blessed in reading this material as I was in preaching it.

—R.C. Sproul
Lake Mary, Florida
April 2009

PREFACE

It has been said that "the Holy Spirit leaves no footprints in the sand." Jesus likened the work of the Spirit to the wind, with a word play of the Greek word *pneuma* (breath, wind, spirit), saying, "The wind [*pneuma*] blows where it wishes . . . you hear the sound of it, but cannot tell where it comes from and where it goes" (John 3:8).

In the book of Acts we see the footprints of the Holy Spirit in and through the footprints of the Apostles. The sound of a mighty rushing wind introduces their work. As a sailing ship is carried about by the wind, so the apostolic mission in the early church was carried about by the Holy Spirit.

Acts does not present a perfect church, pristine and pure. No, it is an infant church, a nascent community. It is inspired, but not fully developed; alive with power and devotion, but not yet sanctified. All the problems addressed by Paul, Peter, John, James, et al. arise in the heat of the passion and struggles of the first decades of apostolic Christianity.

For Luke, Acts is his volume two. It flows naturally and irresistibly out of the gospel. It follows the accomplishment of redemption with the concrete application of redemption. Ultimately God is its author as well as its chief character. Here the invisible hand of Divine Providence becomes visible as the feet of the apostolic band, under the weight of the Holy Spirit, presses His imprint in the sand.

This book is not a technical commentary, though the technical analysis lies behind it and undergirds it. This is an expository commentary, drawn from real preaching to a real church in a real world of pain, sorrow, joy, and faith. May it be fodder for further preaching and nutrition for spiritual growth.

—R.C. Sproul
Orlando, Florida
2010

1

A SECOND ACCOUNT

Acts 1:1–3

The former account I made, O Theophilus, of all that Jesus began both to do and teach, until the day in which He was taken up, after He through the Holy Spirit had given commandments to the apostles whom He had chosen, to whom He also presented Himself alive after His suffering by many infallible proofs, being seen by them during forty days and speaking of the things pertaining to the kingdom of God.—Acts 1:13

Inasmuch as many have taken in hand to set in order a narrative of those things which have been fulfilled among us, just as those who from the beginning were eyewitnesses and ministers of the word delivered them to us, it seemed good to me also, having had perfect understanding of all things from the very first, to write to you an orderly account, most excellent Theophilus, that you may know the certainty of those things in which you were instructed.—Luke 1:1–4

During the apostolic age books were not typeset with machinery such as we are accustomed to in this day. Books were written by hand, usually on parchments made out of papyrus. In antiquity, the standard length of a book written in this manner was about 35 feet long. The scrolls were then rolled up and carefully preserved as they were read and passed from church to church.

Acts Overview

Initially Luke penned two volumes on separate scrolls: one, the gospel account of Christ, and the second, which was carried along with the first, the book of Acts. Very early on, it became the practice of the church to collect the four biographical sketches of Jesus that we call the four Gospels and keep them together in the church to be read and studied. As a result, the Gospel of Luke was separated from his volume two, the book of Acts. Sometimes these two books together are called Luke-Acts.

It was in the early church that this second portion of Luke's writings was given the title "Acts of the Apostles." Some saw the book as such an elaborate defense of the life and ministry of the Apostle Paul that they thought it ought to be titled "Acts of the Apostle Paul." However, Paul isn't even introduced until Acts 7, as we will see. There is also much attention given to the church in Jerusalem and to the ministries of Peter, John, Stephen, Philip, and others. Therefore, it would be a misnomer to call the book "The Acts of the Apostle Paul," although he emerges as the central figure.

Luke does not identify himself as the author, but if we look carefully at the "we" passages of Paul's missionary journey, we know that Luke was in that band of men with Paul. When he speaks in terms of "we," he is referring to himself as the writer of the book, so it is easy to deduce, as the church has, that Luke indeed was the author of both the Gospel attributed to him and this book of Acts.

An alternate title that could be given to the book, one that I favor, is "The History of the Acts of the Holy Spirit." Since it was inspired by the Holy Spirit and is a record of the outpouring of the Holy Spirit on the apostolic church and on the ministry of that church, one could even go so far as to call it "The Autobiography of the Holy Spirit." In any case, as we go through the narrative, let's not miss the power and presence of the third person of the Trinity, whom Jesus had promised so deeply and fervently in the Upper Room Discourse found in John's Gospel.

Certain similarities exist between the beginning of Luke's Gospel and the beginning of Acts. Both volumes are dedicated to a person named Theophilus. The name Theophilus, if we break it down linguistically, means "friend or lover of God." *Phileo* is a Greek word meaning "to love," and *theos* is the Greek word for "God." Theophilus can also mean "one who is loved by God." So, the name can mean either "one who loves God" or "one who is loved by God."

Because the name carries with it the concept of being either a lover of God or one loved by God, many have believed that the book is not addressed to one specific person but to all who are beloved of God or lovers of God. The case against that, however, is the addition in Luke's prologue of the title "most excellent."

That is significant because, in the ancient world, often major publications were dedicated to members of the nobility, and members of the nobility were often addressed with gracious titles such as "most excellent." Since Luke's Gospel is addressed not to just any Theophilus but to the most excellent Theophilus, many come to the conclusion that the book is ascribed to perhaps a Christian in high places in antiquity who was as devout as his name suggests. However, in the latter part of the first century and in the second century it was common for Christian apologists to address their defenses of the Christian faith to the emperor of Rome.

There is something else to note, briefly here, about the book of Acts. The book is a work of apologetics, a defense of the truth claims of the Christian faith. Along with that, conceivably, is a very important defense of the authenticity of the apostolic authority and office of Paul, because Paul was not one of the original twelve Apostles. Three times in this book there is an account of Paul's call and his conversion on the road to Damascus, which grants more and more credibility to this one to whom the Lord gave an apostolic mission to the Gentiles. We will look into that more as we encounter it from time to time in the text itself.

Luke the Historian

Luke knows that others had undertaken the task of writing down a history of the things that had gone on in the life of Jesus:

> Inasmuch as many have taken in hand to set in order a narrative of those things which have been fulfilled among us, just as those who from the beginning were eyewitnesses and ministers of the word delivered them to us, it seemed good to me also, having had perfect understanding of all things from the very first, to write to you an orderly account, most excellent Theophilus, that you may know the certainty of those things in which you were instructed. (Luke 1:1–4)

Luke, the beloved physician, was an educated man. His Greek is one of the highest in terms of literary quality to be found in the New Testament. He provides evidence of his academic credentials. He is writing not just as a believer but as a historian, basically saying, "I take great care to trace the story from the beginning, from those who were there, to include in my account things that either I saw or other people saw, whom I have interviewed." We get more information in the Gospel of Luke about the birth of Jesus than from any other source. According to tradition, Luke personally interviewed Mary, the mother of Jesus, to get her perspective on all the events surrounding the annunciation and the Nativity.

From the vantage point of the twenty-first century, we are dependent for our knowledge of antiquity on the historians who wrote the history of that time. We look to Tacitus, to Heroditus, to Suetonius, and to the Jewish historian Josephus. All these great historians of the ancient world have been subjected to the most rigorous scrutiny of critical scholarship. That is no less true of the Gospel writers. Because Luke wrote both a Gospel and a history of the apostolic outreach of the early church going into Gentile lands, there is a sense in which his work has been subjected to closer scrutiny from a secular perspective than any other biblical biographer.

I believe the Scriptures are the unvarnished Word of God, inspired by the Holy Spirit, infallible, inerrant in everything it says. I do not need the verification of a secular archaeologist to convince me that this is the Word of God, but (just as an aside, from a secular perspective) Luke has been esteemed as the most accurate historian of the ancient world. He enjoys a higher reputation than Suetonius, Heroditus, Tacitus, Pliny, Josephus, or any of the rest. His work has been checked more carefully than anybody else's.

How can we check out Luke's accuracy from the vantage point of the twenty-first century? When he talks about the appearance of an angel by the name of Gabriel to Zacharius or to Mary, it is hard to verify that story through the normal structures of scientific inquiry. Unless we were to find a petrified set of angel wings, we are not going to be able to do that. But there are many things included in this work that do have testability; that is, they can be verified or falsified by archaeological examination.

Early in the twentieth century a British scholar by the name of William Mitchell Ramsay, a skeptic about Christianity, traced the missionary journeys of the Apostle Paul as recorded in the book of Acts. He looked for evidence in the landscape and ruins and in the titles of the local rulers or magistrates in foreign cities that were not common knowledge to people who lived in Jerusalem. Ramsay started out a skeptic and ended up a believer because he was overwhelmed by the evidence he was able to uncover. The stones were crying out that every title of every magistrate Luke recorded in the book of Acts was verified by the turning over of the shovel. Likewise, the description and accounts of the towns were just as Luke had described them.

Twenty-five years ago or so I wrote a novel, and in that novel I included an episode in Tokyo. I had never been to Tokyo, and I knew very little about it, but all I had to do was go to the library to get manifold witnesses to street names, important buildings of commerce, and places of entertainment. I was able to reconstruct Tokyo in a fictional way without feeling that I would get caught with inaccuracies in describing the local scene. Today, with the Internet, writing that novel would be even easier. In the novel I also wrote in a detective scene. For background information I called someone from the FBI, and he explained how the organization works. Luke did not have that advantage. He had no library or Internet to find out how things were in Philippi, or Colosse, or Corinth, or Ephesus, yet the portrait he gives of those locations has been verified time and again. I mention this because Luke labors the point in the beginning of the Gospel of Luke and in the beginning of Acts that he was not writing a religious tract; he was writing history, one that has been corroborated by eyewitness testimony and by what he calls in his prologue to Acts "many infallible proofs."

Luke's Agenda

The former account I made, O Theophilus, of all that Jesus began both to do and teach, until the day in which He was taken up, after He through the Holy Spirit had given commandments to the apostles whom He had chosen (vv. 1–2). At Paul's conversion, after he had been knocked to the ground and blinded by the light and had heard a voice calling to him, Paul responded to Christ, "Lord, what do You want me to do?" (Acts 9:6). Years later, when Paul stood on trial before King Agrippa in chains and gave a defense of his ministry, he recounted that story of his conversion. On one occasion Agrippa said to Paul, "You almost persuade me to become a Christian" (Acts 26:28). Paul responded, "I would to God that not only you, but also all who hear me today, might become almost and altogether such as I am, except for these chains" (v. 29). As Paul made his defense, Festus interrupted and said, "Paul, you are beside yourself! Much learning is driving you mad!" (v. 24), and Paul replied, "I am not mad, most noble Festus, but speak the words of truth and reason" (v. 25). On that occasion, in the midst of the discussion he said to the king, "Therefore, King Agrippa, I was not disobedient to the heavenly vision" (Acts 26:19).

At the end of my life, I would love to stand before Christ and say, "Lord, I was not disobedient. I did everything you told me to do. I went everywhere you told me to go." The Lord and I both know that will not be true, so it would be foolish to claim it; but it was true of Paul. Paul's life and ministry are the paradigm of obedience in the apostolic church. He did do what Christ told him to do.

Luke's agenda was not only to verify that Paul was obedient to the heavenly vision but to remind his readers of the commandments that Jesus gave just before he ascended. What follows in the rest of Acts is a drama of the highest magnitude—the drama of the obedience of the early church to the mission that Christ had given to it. We have a record of the pristine apostolic community. We might be tempted to try to read Acts as the story of Christianity in its perfection, but if we read the New Testament epistles, we know that the early church was anything but perfect. Most of the apostolic letters were written to correct errors, heresies, abuses, and disobedient behavior among the people of the early church. That church was by no means perfect, but it is of vital importance to study because of its proximity to the foundation of the Christian church.

Years ago I was embroiled in a controversy on the doctrine of justification by faith alone, a controversy that never dies. During a meeting of theologians, someone was defending the Reformation doctrine of justification when another said to him, "Well, Luther may have been right in the sixteenth century, but it doesn't matter anymore." And the other theologian said, "It's not the sixteenth-century gospel I'm interested in defending; what concerns me is the first-century gospel." We must go back to the foundation of the Christian church, to the purity of the gospel as it was set forth by the Apostles, so that we can study the apostolic doctrine in that location. That is what Luke was doing, giving us an account of the obedience to the commandments of the Apostles whom Christ had chosen.

To whom He also presented Himself alive after His suffering by many infallible proofs, being seen by them during forty days and speaking of the things pertaining to the kingdom of God (v. 3). The prologue acts as a preface, and the preface is setting before us the purview of the author, the things he is going to select from the narrative of the early church. Through the rest of the book he talks about the apostolic witness to the kingdom of God. The theme of Acts is this: the church's obedience to Christ's commission and commandment to be His witnesses as the ascended King, the King of kings and the Lord of lords. If you wonder why the first-century church turned the world upside down and why we do not, it is because they preached the kingdom of God, and we do not. They believed that the kingdom burst in power at the appearance of the King, who came on the scene after John the Baptist, the forerunner who said, "Repent, for the kingdom of heaven is at hand!" (Matt. 3:2). Jesus came, saying, "The time is fulfilled, and the kingdom of God is at hand. Repent, and believe in the gospel" (Mark 1:15), and, "If I cast out demons with the finger of God, surely the kingdom of God has come upon you" (Luke 11:20).

A whole new chapter of world history began with the ministry of Christ and with His ascension to the right hand of the Father, where He is enthroned as the King. One of the worst distortions of theology that plagues the evangelical world is the idea that the kingdom of God is something completely future. That view completely destroys the biblical testimony of the breakthrough of the kingdom of God in the ministry of Jesus, especially in His ascension. Yes, the consummation of the kingdom is still in the future, but the reality of the kingdom is now. The mission of the early church was to bear witness to the reality of that kingdom in Jerusalem, Judea, Samaria, and the uttermost parts of the earth.

2

THE ASCENSION

Acts 1:4–11

And being assembled together with them, He commanded them not to depart from Jerusalem, but to wait for the Promise of the Father, "which," He said, "you have heard from Me; for John truly baptized with water, but you shall be baptized with the Holy Spirit not many days from now." Therefore, when they had come together, they asked Him, saying, "Lord, will You at this time restore the kingdom to Israel?" And He said to them, "It is not for you to know times or seasons which the Father has put in His own authority. But you shall receive power when the Holy Spirit has come upon you; and you shall be witnesses to Me in Jerusalem, and in all Judea and Samaria, and to the end of the earth." Now when He had spoken these things, while they watched, He was taken up, and a cloud received Him out of their sight. And while they looked steadfastly toward heaven as He went up, behold, two men stood by them in white apparel, who also said, "Men of Galilee, why do you stand gazing up into heaven? This same Jesus, who was taken up from you into heaven, will so come in like manner as you saw Him go into heaven."

Suppose our Lord were to manifest Himself visibly to us and invite us each to ask Him a question. What question would you ask? In Acts 1:1–14 we have the record of the last opportunity Jesus' disciples had to ask Him a question face-to-face. The disciples had studied at Jesus' feet for three years and surely during that time had peppered Him endlessly with theological questions, and now, before Jesus' departure, they have time for one more. **And being assembled together with them, He commanded them not to depart**

from Jerusalem, but to wait for the Promise of the Father, "which," He said, "you have heard from Me; for John truly baptized with water, but you shall be baptized with the Holy Spirit not many days from now." Therefore, when they had come together, they asked Him, saying, "Lord, will You at this time restore the kingdom to Israel?" (vv. 4–6).

The Disciples' Question

The question they asked concerned four things: time, kingdom, Israel, and restoration. They had all been advised of the prophecies of Old Testament Israel. They, like all pious Jews down through the centuries, looked forward to that day when the glory of Israel would be restored, when, as Amos had prophesied, the fallen booth of David would be righted anew. At the time of the disciples' question, David's kingdom was hidden under the suppression of the Roman government. There had been no restoration of the kingdom of Israel. That is why so many people were disappointed in Jesus—they had looked to Him to bring that kingdom to Israel, to bring the restoration.

Ephesus in Turkey and Corinth in Greece have the most comprehensive rebuilding and restructuring of ruins from antiquity that can be found anywhere in the world. Almost the whole town of Ephesus has been reconstructed from the ruins. Despite the comprehensive reconstruction, many pieces of buildings, pillars, and columns in these towns are still lying in the weeds, covered in moss. I visited these sites, and as I looked at the ruins I thought about the image that Amos had in his mind of the throne of David, he who had once reigned in glorious splendor but whose throne had been overturned (Amos 9:9). It had been smashed into pieces, and weeds were growing all around it. It was covered with moss and dirt. Amos said that someday God would restore the throne of David, and for centuries hope for that historic moment burned in the breasts of the Jewish people.

As Jesus was on the Mount of Transfiguration, the disciples said, "Why then do the scribes say that Elijah must come first?" (Matt. 17:10). In other words, "Are you going to restore the throne to David? Are you going to restore the kingdom to national ethnic Israel?" They were still thinking of the kingdom in terms of earthly, national boundaries, restricted to the borders of Israel itself. They hadn't grasped the central teaching of Jesus during His lifetime, when He proclaimed the kingdom of God that would go far beyond the boundaries of Israel and that the greater Son of David would initiate a kingdom with no end, a spiritual kingdom with earthly implications. They forgot what Jesus had taught them to pray in the Lord's Prayer: "Our Father in heaven, hallowed be Your name. Your kingdom come. Your will be done on earth as it is in heaven" (Matt. 6:6–10).

The Lord Jesus reigns right now as the King of kings and the Lord of lords in heaven. That is what the ascension is all about. But in the meantime, like the disciples, we yearn for the day when that kingdom will be manifest, when at the end of His reign He brings the new heaven and the new earth, the kingdom in its fullest consummation. We still look forward to that.

Jesus' Answer

How did Jesus answer their question? He did not rebuke His disciples, saying, "How many times do I have to tell you that I'm not going to restore the kingdom of Israel? How many times do I have to tell you that My kingdom is completely spiritual? What He said was this: **"It is not for you to know times or seasons which the Father has put in His own authority. But you shall receive power when the Holy Spirit has come upon you; and you shall be witnesses to Me in Jerusalem, and in all Judea and Samaria, and to the end of the earth"** (vv. 7–8). If there is a thematic passage for the book of Acts, one that defines the whole scope of the book, it is that.

For centuries, the church has recognized this passage as the Great Commission, the passage in which our Lord gave His marching orders to His church. He told His disciples, in effect, that it was none of their business when the kingdom will be consummated. That is in the Father's hands and under the Father's authority. Rather, they were to concern themselves with being the Lord's witnesses in His absence.

Jesus went on to say that as soon as He received His crown, He would declare the sending of the Holy Spirit upon them, upon His church, to empower their mission. The mission of the church, the reason we exist, is to bear witness to the present reign and rule of Christ, who is at the right hand of God. If we try to do it in our own power, we will fail. The reason for the outpouring of the Spirit is not to make us feel spiritual. It is not to give us a spiritual high. It is so that we can do the job that Jesus gave the church to do.

I had lunch with an extraordinary man who ministers in the Sudan. As we were eating, he showed me a picture of his family, and in it the children were carrying guns. When I asked him about that, he explained that they carry guns when they go to church because the church had been bombed ten times by Muslims. This man is on the front line of mission work every day. That is what we need—to be in touch with people like that. We are to live by this same Great Commission. It is our responsibility to make sure that Christ's kingdom is being witnessed to throughout the world. We are called to be a missionary church.

One of the great books of our time is Elisabeth Elliot's *Through Gates of Splendor*, which chronicles the slaughter of her husband and four other missionaries, including Nate Saint, at the hands of the Auca Indians in Ecuador. The five missionary martyrs made the front page of *Life* magazine. Afterward Elisabeth

Elliot went back to Ecuador and continued to minister to the Auca Indians who had killed her husband, and she raised her daughter in the midst of that group. Some who converted through her ministry babysat her daughter, the same people who had killed her father. Rachel Saint was seen there too, worshiping in a church with some of the very ones who murdered her brother. That is the Great Commission, the church being obedient to the instructions that Christ gave at the moment of His departure. Calvin said that it is the task of the visible church to make the invisible kingdom of Christ visible, to manifest to people what it would be like to live in a commonwealth ruled by Jesus. We are called to bear witness to a reign based on righteousness, truth, mercy, and charity.

I believe that within thirty years the largest and strongest branch of Christendom will be in Africa and that it is absolutely critical that the church in the United States right now pour as many resources as possible into the emerging churches of the Third World, particularly in Africa. We have the materials; we have things that these people need, to be grounded and strengthened for future generations. They cannot provide it, but we can. As we continue studying the book of Acts, we are going to see the first-century church in action, crawling over glass and pouring out blood—giving their lives—to obey Jesus' last command to be His witnesses to the uttermost parts of the earth.

The Ascension

Now when He had spoken these things, while they watched, He was taken up, and a cloud received Him out of their sight (v. 9). This was the Shekinah cloud predicted in the book of Daniel, where the Son of Man appeared before the Ancient of Days, arriving on the Shekinah cloud of glory. This was Jesus' return to heaven from whence He had come in the first place. He came in humiliation and returned on the glory cloud, being elevated into heaven to the right hand of God. The disciples stood there transfixed and watched until the ascending Jesus was nothing more than a speck on the horizon.

We live in central Florida, not very far from Cape Kennedy, where there are periodic rocket launches. The roads become jammed with cars of tourists who want to see the liftoff of one of these rockets. But we know a secret. We do not have to drive over there; we just keep the television on. As soon as an upcoming liftoff is announced, we walk outside and watch it from the front yard. That's what the disciples did; only it wasn't a rocket ship they were watching but the King of kings going to His coronation.

As they were watching it, the angels appeared to them with a question: **"Men of Galilee, why do you stand gazing up into heaven? This same Jesus, who was taken up from you into heaven, will so come in like manner as you saw Him go into heaven"** (v. 11). He will return in glory. In the meantime, it is time to go to work, fulfilling the Great Commission.

3

A NEW APOSTLE

Acts 1:12–26

Then they returned to Jerusalem from the mount called Olivet, which is near Jerusalem, a Sabbath day's journey. And when they had entered, they went up into the upper room where they were staying: Peter, James, John, and Andrew; Philip and Thomas; Bartholomew and Matthew; James the son of Alphaeus and Simon the Zealot; and Judas the son of James. These all continued with one accord in prayer and supplication, with the women and Mary the mother of Jesus, and with His brothers. And in those days Peter stood up in the midst of the disciples (altogether the number of names was about a hundred and twenty), and said, "Men and brethren, this Scripture had to be fulfilled, which the Holy Spirit spoke before by the mouth of David concerning Judas, who became a guide to those who arrested Jesus; for he was numbered with us and obtained a part in this ministry." (Now this man purchased a field with the wages of iniquity; and falling headlong, he burst open in the middle and all his entrails gushed out. And it became known to all those dwelling in Jerusalem; so that field is called in their own language, *Akel Dama*, that is, Field of Blood.) "For it is written in the Book of Psalms: 'Let his dwelling place be desolate, and let no one live in it'; and, 'let another take his office.' Therefore, of these men who have accompanied us all the time that the Lord Jesus went in and out among us, beginning from the baptism of John to that day when He was taken up from us, one of these must become a witness with us of His resurrection." And they proposed two: Joseph called Barsabas, who was surnamed Justus, and Matthias. And they prayed and said, "You, O Lord, who know the hearts of all, show which of these two You have chosen to take part in this ministry and apostleship from which Judas by transgression fell, that he might go to his own place." And they cast their lots, and the lot fell on Matthias. And he was numbered with the eleven apostles.

When we looked in our last study at the ascension, we considered the mandate that Christ gave to the disciples He left behind, when He instructed them to return to Jerusalem and to wait. The waiting period lasted some ten days. It is significant that we have this little pericope, this passage of ten days, in which we get a brief description of the behavior and activity of the nascent church of Christ. What were they doing while they were waiting, and in what way does that instruct us even now?

They returned to Jerusalem from the mount called Olivet, which is near Jerusalem, a Sabbath day's journey (v. 12). Vesta and I once stayed at a hotel on the slope of the Mount of Olives overlooking the city of Jerusalem. One night we sat and listened to the **Hallelujah Chorus** emanating from the old section of the city. It was a spectacular moment in our lives. I have that vision in my mind when I picture the disciples returning to Jerusalem from the Mount of Olives to obey the instructions that Jesus had given them. When they entered, they went into the upper room where they were staying. The eleven Apostles that were left after the death of Judas are named in the text, and we are told, **these all continued with one accord in prayer and supplication, with the women and Mary the mother of Jesus, and with His brothers** (v. 14).

With One Accord

We see already two things about how the church behaved in its first week of existence. The first thing that characterized the church in the early days was obedience. Who, having witnessed Christ, wouldn't be eager to go out and spread the news everywhere? They were biting at the bit, eager to go; nevertheless, they stayed where they were told to stay. They waited, and they waited obediently. Second, we are told that when they came back to the upper room, they came as a group, as a body.

No one has ever been saved by somebody else's faith. We all belong to groups. We are part of a family, or a school class, or a football team; we are all part of a community, a state, and a nation; we have memberships in a host of corporate organizations. But in the final analysis, when we stand before God, we stand or fall on the basis of our faith in Christ or our lack of it. In that sense, redemption is personal and individual. However, when Christ established His church, though He saved individuals one at a time, every person He has ever brought to Himself, He has placed in a body—His church.

I once heard of a minister who visited with a parishioner who had been derelict in his duty to participate in the life of the church. The minister asked him, "Why is it that you are never in church? Why aren't you involved in any of the programs? I know you're on our rolls. I remember the day you joined. You've been baptized and you've made a profession of faith, but you're never around."

The fellow replied, "Well, I don't need the church. My faith is private and personal. I don't need the rituals and trappings of religion. I can worship God by myself. I can get by just fine on my own."

They were having a picnic while this discussion was going on, and the minister walked over to a charcoal grill where there was a heap of white burning coals prepared for the cooking of the hamburgers. With the tongs he took one of the coals off the pile and moved it out to the side, away from the center of the fire, and continued to converse with this church member. After a few minutes, he pointed to that coal and said, "Ten minutes ago that coal was white hot, but now it's cold." Once it was removed from the support system of the rest of those burning coals, it lost its heat, its capacity to be productive in the purpose for which it was made.

We cannot stand alone. We need each other. We need the support of fellowship, the mutual encouragement, the strength, and the prayers of the community in which we are involved. I get excited when people join St. Andrew's and become part of the congregation. It tremendously strengthens who we are as a body. There are that many more people to pray, encourage, and offer mutual support. That is what happened in the early church. The Apostles went back to the upper room. Later 120 gathered there as a group—the very beginning of the church. What did they do? How did they spend their time? "These all continued with one accord in prayer and supplication." They gathered together for prayer.

When the Lord cleansed the temple from its commercialism, He reminded the people that His Father's house was to be a house of prayer (Matt. 21:13). The church, during the first week of its existence, was united together in prayer. Luke does not tell us what they were praying about, but there was plenty about which to pray. They could have been offering thanksgiving for what they had witnessed and experienced. They might have spent time in confession as well as praying for the burgeoning expansion of the church that was going to come in the near future. Whatever might have comprised those prayers, they stayed together, praying with one another.

We are told in passing that the Apostles were there with the women and Mary the mother of Jesus and with His brothers. This is the last reference to Mary that we have anywhere in the New Testament, but we see Mary as a member of the first church. I can't help but think of Mary's Magnificat: "My soul magnifies the Lord, and my spirit has rejoiced in God my Savior" (Luke 1:46–47). Her Son was her redeemer. She wasn't co-redemptrix with Him. She was there with the rest of the disciples as part of the gathered church, praying for and to her own Son. Along with Mary, the mother of Jesus, were His uterine brothers. We know from other indications in the text that during the earthly ministry of Jesus, His brothers were skeptics. They did not buy into His messianic claims; they were unbelievers. James, the brother of Jesus, who wrote the epistle of James, was converted by His brother's resurrection. So even the family members who had been skeptical were persuaded and converted by the resurrection of Christ.

Apostles Commissioned

In those days Peter stood up in the midst of the disciples (altogether the number of names was about a hundred and twenty) (v. 15). We see here a gathering of 120 disciples. We typically speak of the twelve disciples or Apostles, as if the terms *disciple* and *Apostle* are interchangeable; but when we look at the Gospel record, we realize that Jesus had many more disciples than just twelve. There were the seventy that on one occasion He sent out on a mission. Here Luke mentions 120. Paul talks about five hundred who were witnesses of the resurrection. The term disciple, *mathates* in Greek, simply means "student" or "learner." Jesus had been a rabbi who gathered a following of students as He traveled around the countryside. Anyone in that group was a disciple; they were following His discipline. From this larger group of disciples, Jesus chose twelve who would be Apostles. The disciple is a student. The Apostle is an ambassador commissioned by a king or a ruler and given designated authority to speak in his name and with his power. In the ancient world, if a king sent an Apostle, an *apostolos*, as his emissary, his word was the word of the king. It carried the authority and weight of the word of the king. So before Jesus left this planet, He commissioned twelve men to be His emissaries, His ambassadors, and He gave them the right to speak with His authority. That is why He said to them, "He who receives you receives Me, and he who receives Me receives Him who sent Me" (Matt. 10:40).

We hear people saying, "Jesus I like, but Paul I can't stomach." However, what we read in the New Testament is not what Jesus wrote; it is only what was written about Him by His Apostles. If we reject the apostolic witness, we reject the One who commissioned them as Apostles. We cannot have it both ways. We cannot have Christ and not Paul, just as we cannot embrace Paul without embracing the One who granted him that authority.

There is a certain symmetry, a parallelism, between the Old Testament twelve tribes of Israel and the twelve Apostles of the New Testament. However, one of the Apostles was lost because he was not a believer from the beginning. Judas Iscariot had betrayed Jesus and was now dead, so they gathered by the instruction of God to select a new Apostle. This narrative is important not just for historical interest but for its profound theological content—it gives us the criteria for apostleship. There are people today who claim for themselves nothing less than apostolic authority; however, there are no Apostles in the world today because no one can meet the criteria established here in the New Testament for apostolic succession, as we will see.

Peter's Speech

Peter stood up and gave a speech. **"Men and brethren, this Scripture had to be fulfilled, which the Holy Spirit spoke before by the mouth of David"** (v. 16). Note that David did not write on his own impulse but under the supervision of God the Holy Spirit. Peter continues, **". . . concerning Judas, who became a guide to those who arrested Jesus; for he was numbered with us and obtained a part in this ministry." (Now this man purchased a field with the wages of iniquity; and falling headlong, he burst open in the middle and all his entrails gushed out)** (vv. 16–18). The gory details of the end of Judas's life are not something we want to dream about or to talk about in any great detail with our children, but I have to mention them in passing because there is a possible discrepancy between Luke's and Matthew's accounts of the death of Judas. In Matthew's account we are told that after Judas had received the thirty pieces of silver in exchange for delivering Jesus to the officials, he was stricken with remorse, went back and threw the coins to the leaders, and went out and hanged himself (Matt. 27:5). The discrepancy is that tradition holds that Judas was buried in a field purchased by the blood money he got for betraying Jesus. The authorities used the money Judas threw at their feet to purchase his burial plot in a place they called the Field of Blood.

Matthew said he died by hanging himself, and Luke gives the detail here that Judas's entrails burst apart as he fell down. The suggestion is that he hanged himself in a rather violent manner, and as a result of that hanging, he fell headlong so that his internal organs ruptured. We have a grim reminder of the end of the life of Judas.

Peter shows us what else the disciples were doing in those first ten days of waiting: they came together to focus their attention on the teaching of the Scriptures. That is how the early church was born. The disciples were trying to understand all that had transpired before them, probably remembering the discussion Jesus had with those on the way to Emmaus, when He began with Moses and went through the whole Old Testament and showed them how the things that they had witnessed in Jerusalem had to happen. They came to pass because each detail had been predicted centuries before by the Old Testament prophets. After Jesus ascended, the Apostles went back to the upper room and searched through the Scriptures to see if they could find anything about Judas, and they read David's prophetic writing about the one who would betray the Messiah and how that one would have to be replaced. **"For it is written in the Book of Psalms: 'Let his dwelling place be desolate, and let no one live in it'; and, 'Let another take his office'"** (v. 20).

Criteria for Apostleship

Following instructions from the Old Testament, they decided to fulfill the text: **"Therefore, of these men who have accompanied us all the time that the Lord Jesus went in and out among us, beginning from the baptism of John to that day when He was taken up from us, one of these must become a witness with us of His resurrection"** (v. 21). If we look carefully at this we can see three basic criteria for apostleship before Pentecost. First, a candidate had to have been a member of Jesus' band of disciples from the beginning, from the days of His baptism at the Jordan by John the Baptist. He had to have been with Jesus for the three years of Jesus' public ministry in order to qualify for selection to the rank of Apostle. Second, he had to have been an eyewitness of the resurrection. These criteria are why none today can be Apostles. None living today was numbered among those who followed after Jesus in the first century, and none was an eyewitness of the resurrection.

The third criterion for apostleship, far and away the most important, is the direct and immediate commissioning to the office by Christ Himself. In the Old Testament, true prophets were called by God. That is why prophets such as Amos, Jeremiah, and Isaiah provide in their books the circumstances of their call, the occasions at which God directly and immediately set them apart as prophets. But Jesus was gone, so how could He choose a new Apostle? According to Acts, they used nominations. They went through their group and selected two possible candidates, and then they chose lots to decide between the two. In choosing lots, they were following an ancient tradition in the Old Testament involving the use of the Urim and the Thummim. When Old Testament priests were unable to discern the will of God, they prayerfully cast lots, the outcome of which was determined by the providence of God. Here, the lot fell upon Matthias, and we hear no more about him afterward. We have only the record of his selection to apostleship, which completed the Twelve. James was martyred shortly thereafter, but he was not replaced.

Then we come to Paul. One of the earliest controversies that faced the original Christian community was how Paul could be an Apostle. He hadn't been a disciple of Jesus, nor had he been an eyewitness to the resurrection. He saw the glorified vision of Christ on the road to Damascus, but that was after the ascension. Paul missed the first and second criteria for apostleship, but he met the third one. There's a reason why Paul's call to be an Apostle is recited three times in Acts, when Christ directly and immediately called Paul to the role. Despite that, people today claim that if Paul could become an Apostle while lacking two of the three criteria, then all the criteria aren't necessary, so people today can be Apostles too. People claim all the time that they have the credentials of an Apostle today because God called them, or God spoke to them, and God said, "You shall be my Apostle to this generation." Paul did not have the first two criteria, so he was instructed to go back to Jerusalem to be confirmed in the apostolic office by those whose credentials were beyond a shadow of a doubt.

I could say I have a call to be an Apostle today, but there is no one left to confirm me. By the end of the first century, the sub-apostolic fathers clearly understood the difference between their authority in the church and the authority of the original Apostles. After the last Apostle died, there were still teachers, ministers, preachers, and evangelists, but there were no more Apostles.

From the outset of the book of Acts we are provided a glimpse of the life of the early church in its pristine purity—obedient, unified, praying, searching the Scriptures, and submissive to apostolic authority. That should be in front of us all the time as we seek to build the church today.

4

PENTECOST

Acts 2:1–12

When the Day of Pentecost had fully come, they were all with one accord in one place. And suddenly there came a sound from heaven, as of a rushing mighty wind, and it filled the whole house where they were sitting. Then there appeared to them divided tongues, as of fire, and one sat upon each of them. And they were all filled with the Holy Spirit and began to speak with other tongues, as the Spirit gave them utterance. And there were dwelling in Jerusalem Jews, devout men, from every nation under heaven. And when this sound occurred, the multitude came together, and were confused, because everyone heard them speak in his own language. Then they were all amazed and marveled, saying to one another, "Look, are not all these who speak Galileans? And how is it that we hear, each in our own language in which we were born? Parthians and Medes and Elamites, those dwelling in Mesopotamia, Judea and Cappadocia, Pontus and Asia, Phrygia and Pamphylia, Egypt and the parts of Libya adjoining Cyrene, visitors from Rome, both Jews and proselytes, Cretans and Arabs we hear them speaking in our own tongues the wonderful works of God." So they were all amazed and perplexed, saying to one another, "Whatever could this mean?"

One of the most difficult virtues to acquire in life is the ability to handle disappointment and the frustration that inevitably comes with unfulfilled expectations. A friend once told me, "Everybody has land mines in their personality, and land mines are hidden bombs under the surface.

Some have wall-to-wall land mines, and you have to tiptoe around them carefully because at the slightest irritation, they explode. The more easygoing may have only one or two bombs planted in their field, but woe to the person who steps on them."

Well, one of my land mines is a lost reservation. When I have traveled all day and finally get to a hotel at which I know a reservation has been made in my name, only to find that there is no record of it, my land mine is triggered. It shouldn't be a big deal, but somehow, for me, it is.

We can observe something similar with children and their playschool benches. They take a mallet and a square peg and try to pound it into a round hole. For the first few minutes they are patient as they try, but the result is predictable. Pretty soon the screaming starts and the mallet is thrown across the room.

It is hard to deal with disappointments. We purchase something we have always wanted, but when we get it, it just isn't what we thought it would be. We work to get a degree, a position, or a promotion, but when we acquire it, it is not anything like we imagined. Particularly hard to handle are disappointments that result after we have waited a long time for something that never comes.

In the Old Testament, the prophet Habakkuk complained about all the misery going on in the midst of the people. God spoke to him and talked about His promises, and in the midst of the promises God said to His prophet, "Though it tarries, wait for it; because it will surely come, it will not tarry" (Hab. 2:3). That's the hardest thing for the Christian, waiting for God to keep His promises.

Jesus' last instruction to the Apostles concerned waiting: "He commanded them not to depart from Jerusalem, but to wait for the Promise of the Father, 'which,' He said, 'you have heard from Me; for John truly baptized with water, but you shall be baptized with the Holy Spirit not many days from now'" (Acts 1:4–5). That was His last promise. They were going to receive power such as they had never imagined, a heavenly power, because the Holy Spirit was going to come upon them. It was not going to happen that day or the next, but soon, and they were to wait for it.

A Promise Fulfilled

Acts 2 tells of the fulfillment of the promise. The day of Pentecost on the Jewish calendar was the day of an annual feast called the Feast of Harvests, the Feast of Ingathering, or sometimes the Feast of Weeks. A week has seven days, so a week of weeks is seven times seven, which is forty-nine days. After those forty-nine days are accomplished, the fiftieth day is Pentecost, so fifty days after the great celebration of Passover is this feast. It was the Jewish Thanksgiving of the Old Testament. It was also called the Feast of Firstfruits because, since the arid climate of Palestine has two rainy seasons, they had two growing seasons, a former season and a latter season. They would celebrate at the former rains and again at the later rains. People gathered for the Thanksgiving event of Pentecost at the central sanctuary in Jerusalem to thank God for the harvest.

When the Day of Pentecost had fully come, they were all with one accord in one place. And suddenly there came a sound from heaven, as of a rushing mighty wind, and it filled the whole house where they were sitting (vv. 1–2). Suddenly—instantly—something radical happened. John Sartelle tells the story of a hundred-mile-an-hour wind that once blew through his neighborhood in Memphis, Tennessee. It wasn't a tornado, but the winds were hurricane force. He said the winds sounded like a roaring train. It was so loud that his family was terrified, and they went into the center part of the house and sheltered themselves as best they could. He said it was a perfect storm except for the fact that there has been only one perfect storm in all of history—the one seen in the second chapter of Acts. The Apostles were gathered in the house, and all of a sudden the sound of a mighty, powerful, overwhelming, rushing wind filled the place where they were sitting.

When Nicodemus came to Jesus by night and inquired about salvation, Jesus said, "Most assuredly, I say to you, unless one is born of water and the Spirit, he cannot enter the kingdom of God" (John 3:5). In other words, a necessary condition for becoming a Christian is being born of the Spirit. The Greek word for "spirit" is *pneuma*, from which we get terms such as pneumatic drills and pneumatic forces. Air-driven machines are called pneumatic. Jesus played with words on that occasion because Nicodemus said, "How can a man be born when he is old? Can he enter a second time into his mother's womb and be born?" (v. 4). Jesus said, "The wind blows where it wishes, and you hear the sound of it, but cannot tell where it comes from and where it goes. So is everyone who is born of the Spirit" (v. 8).

The Greek word *pneuma* not only means "spirit," but it also means "wind" and "breath." We find the same meanings in the Hebrew word *ruah*. At creation God breathed into man His own *ruah*, His breath, and man became a living spirit, a living *ruah*. From the beginning of the Scriptures in the Old Testament, the breath of God is associated with His life-giving Spirit. It is associated with the power of creation, the energy of divine operation. In the Greek New Testament, another word used to describe the work of God's Spirit is *dunamis*, from which we get "dynamite," an explosive power.

The Apostles had waited, and if ever expectations were exceeded, it was in this perfect storm. They had waited with no idea of what was going to happen, and suddenly, out of nowhere, the sound of a mighty, rushing wind came roaring into the room. In addition to the sound it made, there was also a visual dimension to it. **There appeared to them divided tongues, as of fire, and one sat upon each of them. And they were all filled with the Holy Spirit and began to speak with other tongues, as the Spirit gave them utterance** (vv. 3–4). People were gathered in Jerusalem from the provinces, and even from outside of Palestine, who did not speak the local language; yet all of a sudden, after the Holy Spirit came, the Apostles began preaching in other languages. People from different parts of the world were hearing the Word of God proclaimed in their own language.

Wind and Fire

When we look at this text of what happened at Pentecost, particularly in light of Pentecostalism in our day, almost all the attention goes to the phenomenon of *glossolalia*, the speaking in tongues, which I do not want to minimize or underestimate, but I want us to focus on two other dimensions, the sound and the sight of what happened on Pentecost, because therein we see its great significance.

What happened on Pentecost was the rushing *pneuma* of God. The mighty power of the Holy Spirit came roaring through a room filled with people whom Jesus had selected to be there to receive power from heaven to fulfill their mission in this world, and they heard the wind. What they saw was fire, tongues of fire, appearing over each one's head. This was no ordinary wind. This was the wind of God, a theophany, a visible manifestation of the invisible God. The most common visible manifestation of God in the Old Testament was through fire. In the Midianite wilderness, the theophany was a bush burning but not consumed, and out of that fire God spoke to Moses and changed the course of history. When God led the children of Israel through the wilderness, He did so through a pillar of cloud and a pillar of smoke, or fire. The judgment throne of God that went across the sky, the whirlwind into which people were caught up, was a chariot of fire, so much so that the New Testament tells us, "Our God is a consuming fire" (Heb. 12:29). When God gave the law to the people at Mount Sinai, flames were visible on the mountain, symbolizing the power of the transcendent majesty of God.

The fire was symbolic of two things. First, fire is a source of light. Today we do not think much of fire as a source of light because we use candles only for decoration, but for most of human history, homes were illumined by some kind of flame. Our days, then and now, are illumined by a star that is a ball of fire in the heavens. In that sense, we do see the connection between light and fire, and one of the most important operations of God the Holy Spirit is to illumine the truth of God, to put a searchlight on it for our understanding.

Not only does the fire symbolize the heavenly presence, the source of light and truth, but it also symbolizes (in biblical language) ardor, warmth, and affection. When Jesus rebuked the church at Laodicea in the book of Revelation, he said, "I know your works, that you are neither cold nor hot. I could wish you were cold or hot. So then, because you are lukewarm, and neither cold nor hot, I will vomit you out of My mouth" (Rev. 3:15–16). He does not want lukewarm Christians. He wants Christians who are on fire, burning with a passion for the things of God. When the Spirit comes upon a person, He kindles that spark. He starts a flame that consumes the heart and soul so that the affection born that hour will increase in intensity as we grow in Christ, and the fuel for that fire is the Word, prayer, and the sacraments.

Archie Perish, St. Andrew's prayer mentor, said that most Christians look at the day of Pentecost as something marvelous that happened once in the past but has no current significance. He pointed out that others, such as Pentecostals, seek an almost constant renewal of Pentecost. He concluded by saying that the church fails to understand the ongoing, lasting significance of that moment.

When the Jews were delivered from bondage in Egypt and the angel of death passed over the firstborn because blood was on the door, God said, "You shall observe this thing as an ordinance for you and your sons forever . . . And it shall be, when your children say to you, 'What do you mean by this service?' that you shall say, 'It is the Passover sacrifice of the LORD, who passed over the houses of the children of Israel in Egypt when He struck the Egyptians and delivered our households'" (Ex. 12:24, 26–27). The significance of the Passover did not end after that first event.

We understand this a little bit when we talk about the cross. The consequences of the death of Christ were not just for the eyewitnesses of that day. The atonement He made for the sins of those who were there that day is applied every day to every person who puts their trust and hope in Him. The atonement's efficacy, strength, application, and consequence go on and on. Was the resurrection significant only for Jesus? On Easter Sunday do we celebrate the fact that one day a man rose from the dead, or do we believe that He was the firstborn of many brethren and that His victory over death goes on and applies to you and me and all who are in Christ?

Pentecost was a watershed moment in the history of the church. The day of Pentecost was that moment in redemptive history when God unlocked the power of the Holy Spirit and gave it to His church, not just for those who were gathered there, but to the church of every age and to every Christian throughout time. That wind, that fire, is as much for us today as it was for those gathered in the upper room. We are to be people of the Holy Spirit, as well as of the Son and the Father.

5

PETER'S SERMON, PART 1

Acts 2:13–21

Others mocking said, "They are full of new wine." But Peter, standing up with the eleven, raised his voice and said to them, "Men of Judea and all who dwell in Jerusalem, let this be known to you, and heed my words. For these are not drunk, as you suppose, since it is only the third hour of the day. But this is what was spoken by the prophet Joel:

'And it shall come to pass in the last days, says God,
That I will pour out of My Spirit on all flesh;
Your sons and your daughters shall prophesy,
Your young men shall see visions,
Your old men shall dream dreams.
And on My menservants and on My maidservants
I will pour out My Spirit in those days;
And they shall prophesy.
I will show wonders in heaven above And signs in the earth beneath:
Blood and fire and vapor of smoke.
The sun shall be turned into darkness,
And the moon into blood,
Before the coming of the great and awesome day of the LORD.
And it shall come to pass
That whoever calls on the name of the LORD
Shall be saved.'"

I n this study we are going to look at the record of the first sermon preached in the apostolic community after the ascension of Christ. The Gospels, of course, record for us the sermons delivered by Jesus Himself, but what we see in the second chapter of Acts is the first recorded sermon from one of the band of Jesus' disciples and Apostles, on this occasion from the Apostle Peter. The sermon was delivered in its entirety on the day of Pentecost, but we are going to divide it in thirds and examine it in three separate studies. The initial preaching of this sermon yielded a response of three thousand converts on the day of Pentecost.

As we begin our study, I ask you to exercise your imagination in a departure from our normal approach to a text of Scripture. Try to imagine that you were a bystander, an eyewitness, to the events that transpired in Jerusalem when God opened the heavens and poured out the Spirit upon the 120 people gathered there on that occasion, where God, through the Holy Spirit, enabled the Apostles to speak in languages in which they were unskilled, so that people from all over the region, and even outside of Palestine, heard their proclamation in their native tongue.

A False Assumption

When we hear stories like this, or read of them in the text of Scripture, it is our tendency as Christians to identify with the good guys, to see ourselves as among those who received this outpouring of the grace of God and welcomed it, rather than among those who remained skeptics and cynics. Unbelievers who were there that day did not hear the message of God in their own language but heard instead a cacophony. They heard gibberish and could make no sense of it whatsoever. Their first assumption was that the Jewish men assembled in that place were completely drunk, intoxicated beyond all measure, and were babbling in their drunken incoherence. When that charge was made, Peter stepped up and defended the truth of the gospel and of what had been taking place.

He began by answering the charge, **"They are full of new wine"** (v. 13). For those of you who have been taught that real wine is not found in the New Testament, but only unfermented grape juice, this is just one text of many that indicates that the wine used by Jews in the Old and New Testaments was real wine and had the power to intoxicate. That is why the unbelievers assumed that this was an occasion at which wine had been overindulged, and not only that, but with new wine, which was not even the most powerful wine of the day.

Peter stood up with the eleven, raised his voice, and said, **"Men of Judea and all who dwell in Jerusalem, let this be known to you, and heed my words.**

For these are not drunk, as you suppose, since it is only the third hour of the day" (vv. 14–15). He did not go into an elaborate defense against the charge of drunkenness; he simply mentioned in passing how ridiculous it would have been to see 120 pious Jewish men assembled at nine o'clock in the morning, all of them drunk. In a sense, Peter was saying in his opening salvo, "You must be drunk to assume that so many people here are drunk out of their minds. That's not what's happening." He did not spend much time on what was *not* the cause of the phenomenon; rather, he took them immediately to a biblical explanation of the phenomenon that had just occurred.

Four Characteristics

In dealing with this text James Montgomery Boice made note of four things that happened throughout Peter's sermon. First, this first-recorded apostolic sermon was biblical throughout; fundamentally, Peter's sermon was expository. He did not stand up and give his latest views of public opinion or a psychology lesson, nor did he scratch the itches of the people by giving them something to lay their fascination upon. He took his hearers immediately to the Word of God, which is the only kind of authentic preaching there can ever be in the church.

Second, in the course of this sermon, the Apostle Peter took people inexorably to the person and work of Christ. Christ is at the center of the preaching of the Apostles. It was Christocentric.

Third, it was preached fearlessly. It is easy to be bold when preaching to the choir. It is easy for a preacher to be bold when he is in his own pulpit, among friends. But when there are manifestly hostile people breathing out fire, as Stephen was soon to find out, a bold preacher takes a great risk. That is why Martin Luther said that in every generation there will be the threat of the gospel going into eclipse. Every time the gospel is proclaimed, clearly and boldly, opposition arises and conflict comes. A minister has never mounted a pulpit anywhere in the world who has not been absolutely aware of how dangerous it is to be bold. So when preachers are fearful, they have to come back to this text and look at the way the Apostles, without respect for their lives or their worldly goods, would say, like Luther, "Let goods and kindred go, this mortal life also," and then preach with boldness.

Fourth, Peter's sermon was preached reasonably. The Apostle did not simply play on the emotions of his hearers, but he reasoned with them, showing them the rational character of the truth of the proclaimed Word of God.

When I was a young Christian, a nationally famous faith-healer was touring the United States, and he came into our area. I went to see him, fascinated by this phenomenon. When I got there, I saw two large tents. I walked into the first tent and saw spread out on the sawdust-covered floor a shooting gallery, amusements, and food stands. That was my first clue that there was something different about this from church. Then I went into the main tent to hear the evangelist, but before he started his sermon, the warm-up act came on, which was a man with a tambourine. I could sense the release of emotion as he played and people getting whipped up as he said to the crowd, "Turn around and tell your neighbor that the Devil is a liar." A lady in front of me turned around and said, "The Devil is a liar." I stood there, sort of stunned, watching it, so one of the ushers came over to me and said, "What's the matter, son? Don't you feel the Holy Spirit?" I looked at him and replied, "If this is the Holy Spirit, I'm going to sleep in tomorrow morning." If ever a service was held in the flesh, I was in the middle of it. When Peter proclaimed with boldness and in the power of the Holy Spirit, he did not leave his brain in the parking lot. He did not ask people to circumvent their intelligence, because the gospel that moves the heart gets to the heart through the mind. That is how apostolic preaching is manifested.

Pentecost and the Old Testament

Peter then cites from the book of Joel, **"It shall come to pass in the last days, says God, that I will pour out of My Spirit on all flesh; your sons and your daughters shall prophesy, your young men shall see visions, your old men shall dream dreams. And on My menservants and on My maidservants I will pour out My Spirit in those days; and they shall prophesy"** (vv. 17–18). The events of the day of Pentecost were tied into an Old Testament experience. Moses' father-in-law, Jethro, saw all that Moses was doing to lead the people, and he asked him, "What is this thing that you are doing for the people? Why do you alone sit and all the people stand before you from morning until evening?"

Moses replied, "Because the people come to me to inquire of God. When they have a difficulty, they come to me, and I judge between one and another, and I make known the statutes of God and his laws" (Ex. 18:14–16).

So Jethro told him, "The thing that you do is not good. Both you and these people who are with you will surely wear yourselves out. For this thing is too much for you; you are not able to perform it by yourself. Listen now to my voice; I will give you counsel, and God will be with you: Stand before God for the people, so that you may bring the difficulties to God. And you shall teach them the statutes and the laws, and show them the way in which they must walk and the work they must do. Moreover you shall select from all the people able men, such as fear God, men of truth, hating covetousness; and place such over them to be rulers of thousands, rulers of hundreds, rulers of fifties, and rulers of tens" (vv. 17–21).

Moses did, and in Numbers we read, "The LORD said to Moses: 'Gather to

Me seventy men of the elders of Israel, whom you know to be the elders of the people and officers over them; bring them to the tabernacle of meeting, that they may stand there with you. Then I will come down and talk with you there. I will take of the Spirit that is upon you and will put the same upon them; and they shall bear the burden of the people with you, that you may not bear it yourself alone'" (11:16–17). God did take of the Spirit that was upon Moses and give it to seventy elders, and they began to prophesy.

They spoke in ecstatic utterances, and two of them wandered outside the boundaries of the camp. One of them was named Eldad and the other Medad. Then Joshua, the chief lieutenant of Moses, was upset when he saw Eldad and Medad manifesting the power of the Holy Spirit that, up until that moment, had been reserved for Moses. He thought that Eldad and Medad were participating in a revolt against the leadership. Moses said to Joshua, "Are you zealous for my sake? Oh, that all the LORD's people were prophets and that the LORD would put His Spirit upon them!" (Num. 11:29). That is my dream—a laity empowered by God, one that is not satisfied with hiring professionals to do the work of ministry but will come when their neighbor is in need and pray as priests for their friends.

The prayer of Moses became a prophecy later on in Jewish history at a time of terrible crisis. The land had been ravaged by a plague of locusts, which had come through the land and eaten all that was green and completely destroyed the crops of the people of Israel. It was calamitous. God spoke judgment to the people through Joel, because the people had turned away from the Lord. However, He tempered His message of judgment with hope:

It shall come to pass afterward
That I will pour out My Spirit on all flesh;
Your sons and your daughters shall prophesy,
Your old men shall dream dreams,
Your young men shall see visions.
And also on My menservants and on My maidservants
I will pour out My Spirit in those days.
And I will show wonders in the heavens and in the earth:
Blood and fire and pillars of smoke.
The sun shall be turned into darkness,
And the moon into blood,
Before the coming of the great and awesome day of the LORD.
And it shall come to pass
That whoever calls on the name of the LORD
Shall be saved. (Joel 2:28–32)

Peter said in his sermon that the fulfillment of what Joel had prophesied was what they had just witnessed. The Holy Spirit had been poured out, not on seventy, not on 140, not just on men, but on women, servants, and everybody in the flock of God. God has poured out His Spirit upon all of us. There is no such thing as a Christian who has not been anointed by the Holy Spirit for ministry. Paul will say later, "For by one Spirit we were all baptized into one body" (1 Cor. 12:13). We do not all have the same gifts, but we have the same Spirit, and we are all called to be deeply involved in the ministry of the kingdom of God.

If we consider the church today as a set of concentric circles, the center circle comprises the core of the church, the people who attend every Sunday morning and are involved in every aspect of church life. The next circle represents those who are somewhat regular in church attendance. We might see them once a year at some other function besides a Sunday morning service. The third level represents those who come on Christmas, Easter, and maybe Thanksgiving. Those in the two outer circles are denying Pentecost, because the whole life of the church is to involve the whole people of the church because every Christian has received the same power that the seventy elders received in Israel and that the people assembled at the day of Pentecost received.

Peter includes this portion of Joel's prophecy: **"I will show wonders in heaven above and signs in the earth beneath: blood and fire and vapor of smoke. The sun shall be turned into darkness, and the moon into blood, before the coming of the great and awesome day of the LORD"** (vv. 19–20). People claim that disturbances in the sky are what Jesus described as the signs of His final coming, so wasn't Peter speaking a bit prematurely, saying that the text of Joel was fulfilled in his own day? Some commentators say that the last days began with the advent of Christ into the world and that these kinds of spectacular signs did occur, literally, on Good Friday, when apparently a solar eclipse turned all Jerusalem into darkness in the middle of the afternoon. Others look to A.D. 70, when astronomical disturbances were reported, both by Josephus and Tacitus, at the time of the destruction of Jerusalem, which was the climactic judgment that fell upon Old Testament Israel. Another interpretation is based on prophetic words used during times of judgment in the Old Testament. The language of doom was used concerning Tyre and Sidon and Sodom and Gomorrah. It is a poetic form of expressing the radical judgment of God.

Peter is saying, however, that we are in the last days. We are in the day of the Lord that every Jew in the Old Testament looked forward to, the day on which they saw all hope of messianic fulfillment and about which Amos warned, "Is not the day of the LORD darkness?. . . But let justice run down like water, and righteousness like a mighty stream" (Amos 5:20–24). The crisis moment in world history was the coming of Christ into the world. For those who were being redeemed, the day of the Lord was a day of light and brightness and joy, but for those who were perishing, it was a day of unspeakable darkness, as predicted by Joel.

Ministry of the Holy Spirit

Peter ends the quote from Joel with this: **"Whoever calls on the name of the Lord shall be saved"** (v. 21). Peter was not concerned about the meaning of the tongue-speaking, the *glossolalia*; he was concerned about the significance in redemptive history of the outpouring of the Holy Spirit to the whole community. He went on to proclaim the life and ministry of Christ, as we will see in our next study. There were three thousand on that day whose hearts were moved by the Word of God, who put their trust in Christ.

A lot of churches today are excited about the Holy Spirit, and that is fine; but the danger of that is to misunderstand the mission of the Holy Spirit. The Holy Spirit always points beyond Himself to Christ. If you are in a Spirit-filled church that does not focus on the ministry of Christ, you are not in a Spirit-filled church. It is that simple. The Holy Spirit is sent to empower the church to bear witness to Christ, to apply the work of Christ on the cross in terms of its redemptive significance to all who believe. The Father sends, the Son accomplishes, and the Spirit applies the work of Christ. On the day of Pentecost, the Spirit was poured out without measure, and the focus was on Christ.

6

PETER'S SERMON, PART 2

Acts 2:22–33

"Men of Israel, hear these words: Jesus of Nazareth, a Man attested by God to you by miracles, wonders, and signs which God did through Him in your midst, as you yourselves also know—Him, being delivered by the determined purpose and foreknowledge of God, you have taken by lawless hands, have crucified, and put to death; whom God raised up, having loosed the pains of death, because it was not possible that He should be held by it. For David says concerning Him:

> 'I foresaw the LORD always before my face,
> For He is at my right hand, that I may not be shaken.
> Therefore my heart rejoiced, and my tongue was glad;
> Moreover my flesh also will rest in hope.
> For You will not leave my soul in Hades,
> Nor will You allow Your Holy One to see corruption.
> You have made known to me the ways of life;
> You will make me full of joy in Your presence.'

"Men and brethren, let me speak freely to you of the patriarch David, that he is both dead and buried, and his tomb is with us to this day. Therefore, being a prophet, and knowing that God had sworn with an oath to him that of the fruit of his body, according to the flesh, He would raise up the Christ to sit on his throne, he, foreseeing this, spoke concerning the resurrection of the Christ, that His soul was not left in Hades, nor did His flesh see corruption. This Jesus God has raised up, of which we are all witnesses. Therefore being exalted to the right hand of God, and having received from the Father the promise of the Holy Spirit, He poured out this which you now see and hear."

I n our last study we began to look at Peter's sermon on Pentecost, and we will continue to examine it in this study.

In the realm of theology we make a distinction between two Greek words, *kerygma* and *didache*. What is meant by scholars when they speak of the *kerygma* is the essential message preached by the Apostles in the early church. That *kerygma* always pointed out that Old Testament prophecy had been fulfilled in the person and work of Jesus. We have already seen an example of this with Peter's application of the prophet Joel to the day of Pentecost. Also essential to the *kerygma* was a brief recap of the life and ministry of Christ—His birth from the seed of David, the miracles He performed through the power of God, and His crucifixion, burial, resurrection, and ascension into heaven. Those were part and parcel of the essential ingredients of the apostolic preaching, or the *kerygma*. The *didache* refers to the teaching that would follow the preaching of the gospel. After people responded positively to the gospel and entered into the church, they received instruction, what we call the didactic part of the Christian experience. In this study we will focus primarily on the *kerygma*.

We ended our last study with Peter's reference to the prophecy of Joel concerning the day of the Lord, when "the sun shall be turned into darkness and the moon into blood, before the coming of the great and awesome day of the LORD. And it shall come to pass that whoever calls on the name of the LORD shall be saved" (Joel 2:31–32). Jonathan Edwards made the point that the gospel is never truly proclaimed unless it is done against the backdrop of the serious warning that God Almighty gives of His judgment upon all who cling to their impenitent ways and never acknowledge their sin and come to the cross. In this day and age, we look down on any preaching that smells of brimstone, that suggests hell, and that communicates the idea that God will give an everlasting judgment against unrepentant people. However, every page of the New Testament gives that warning. Therefore, the final verse of Joel's prophecy, "Whoever calls on the name of the LORD shall be saved," is not an insignificant postscript but an invitation made against the backdrop of the promise of a future calamity that will befall the human race at the time of the day of the Lord.

Word to the Jews

After recalling Joel's warning and plea, Peter addresses himself to those from the Jewish community: **"Men of Israel, hear these words: Jesus of Nazareth, a Man attested by God to you by miracles, wonders, and signs which God did through Him in your midst, as you yourselves also know"** (v. 22). So often we miss the central significance of the miracles performed by Jesus in the New Testament. To be sure, there was an immediate need that our Lord compassionately addressed by giving sight to the blind and hearing to the deaf, but beyond the local and immediate work of compassion there was a far deeper significance, something that the philosopher John Locke called "the credit of the proposer." The claims that Jesus made to being the Son of God were verified, authenticated, and demonstrated to be genuine by the miracles that God performed in and through Him. Nicodemus came to Jesus at night and said, "Rabbi, we know that You are a teacher come from God; for no one can do these signs that You do unless God is with him" (John 3:2). The primary point of a miracle is God's giving His sign of approval, His attestation, that this one is speaking the truth. So, in this sermon, Peter appeals to the miracles of Jesus, which were well known to his audience.

"Him, being delivered by the determined purpose and foreknowledge of God, you have taken by lawless hands, have crucified, and put to death" (v. 23). Here we see another marvelous example of the doctrine of concurrence, which is critical to our understanding of the providence of God, or how God rules over the world. We are told in the Westminster Confession, "God from all eternity, did, by the most wise and holy counsel of His own will, freely, and unchangeably ordain whatsoever comes to pass." If He didn't, He wouldn't be God. If He didn't, He wouldn't be sovereign. However, His sovereign foreordination of all things, says the Confession, is not carried out in such a way as to eliminate secondary causes or do violence to the will of the creature. That is, when God brings His will to pass, He works in, through, and by the real decisions of real people. The classic example is Joseph before his brothers at the time of their reunion. They were terrified that Joseph would wreak revenge against them, but Joseph put them at ease. He said of their atrocious act of betrayal against him, "You meant evil against me; but God meant it for good" (Gen. 50:20). Joseph's brothers acted treacherously and delivered Joseph into slavery, but God was working through it for His own good purposes. It is difficult to conceive of the greatness and majesty of His sovereignty, that God can bring His goodness to pass even through wretched sin.

At the same time we cannot say, "Look at the good that God has brought out of my sin," nor could Judas go and boast before the throne of God's judgment and say, "Were it not for my act of betrayal, there would have been no cross, and without the cross, there would be no redemption. So you owe it all to me for my wonderful work of bringing to pass your salvation." No, the only intention Judas had was to get his hands on the thirty pieces of silver; but God trumped Judas's desires and brought to pass the cross.

This is what Peter was saying here. The men of Israel meant to destroy Jesus of Nazareth, but in the process they were working out nothing less than the eternal will of God. Nevertheless, Peter said, their work was lawless, and they were culpable for that.

The Resurrection

"**. . . whom God raised up, having loosed the pains of death, because it was not possible that He should be held by it**" (v. 24). Jesus was delivered by them to the Romans and condemned by every earthly court and killed, but the verdict of the courts was trumped by the heavenly court when the heavenly Judge responded to the greatest injustice in the history of the world by raising Jesus from the dead.

How many times in my life have I heard skeptics say, "How can you, if you're in your right mind, believe in the resurrection of Christ?" The resurrection of Christ is at the heart and soul of the Christian faith. As the Apostle Paul said to the Corinthian church: "If Christ is not risen, your faith is futile; you are still in your sins!" (1 Cor. 15:17). That is why I say to hostile unbelievers, "Don't be mad at us. Pity us because we are investing all our hope in this single tenet: that a man in Jerusalem was killed, and the grave couldn't hold Him." The skeptics say, "That's impossible! If we know anything, we know that when people die they stay dead."

David Hume argued against the miracles of Scripture on the basis of probabilities, saying that the probabilities against the real resurrection would always outnumber the probability for it. All things being equal, Hume was right, but all things were not equal. We are dealing here with One who is sinless, and the Scriptures tell us that it is through sin that death came into the world. The really astonishing statistic is not that one should rise from the dead but that one should remain sinless throughout his life. If that is true, then it would be morally unjust for God to allow a sinless man to suffer the curse that He assigned to sin.

Maybe that is what Peter had in mind when he said that not only was it possible for Jesus to be raised from the dead, but it was impossible for Him not to be raised from the dead. However, maybe what he had in mind was that from all eternity, as the Old Testament predicted again and again, the Messiah of Israel would not be conquered by death, and that it is impossible for anyone or anything to prevent the determinate will of almighty God.

When people stumble before the resurrection, we can ask them, "What kind of a God do you believe in?" They will likely reply, "I don't believe in God. I believe that life, motion, and power happen by that transcendent power we call chance." That is superstition and nonsense. People today try to convince the whole world that there was once a time when there was nothing—absolutely nothing—and then poof! Out of nothing came not just something, but everything. Those who propose that deny not only religion but every article of science. The very fact of being, that anything is at all, screams of a transcendent being who alone has the power of life in His hands. Job understood that when he said, "The LORD gave, and the LORD has taken away; blessed be the name of the LORD" (Job 1:21). So here is Peter in front of the mob, saying in essence, "You think it's incredible that this Jesus was raised from the dead? How could it be otherwise, considering who He is? It was impossible for death to hold Him."

The Prediction of David

Peter then turned his attention to David in the Psalms: **"I foresaw the LORD always before my face, for He is at my right hand, that I may not be shaken. Therefore my heart rejoiced, and my tongue was glad; moreover my flesh also will rest in hope. For You will not leave my soul in Hades, nor will You allow Your Holy One to see corruption. You have made known to me the ways of life; You will make me full of joy in Your presence"** (vv. 25–28). About whom was David speaking? Many of David's psalms were prophetic, as every Jew in Israel knew. Many of David's psalms were coronation psalms that predicted the coming Messiah and what He would be like. Peter quotes one of them, in which David rejoices in a promise to the Holy One of Israel, who will not be abandoned to hell and whose soul will not suffer corruption.

Peter wanted the people to consider who David was speaking about. Was he referencing himself or another? **"Men and brethren, let me speak freely to you of the patriarch David, that he is both dead and buried, and his tomb is with us to this day"** (v. 29). This is as if we were to say to Muslims today, "Muhammad is dead and buried," or to Buddhists, "Buddha died, and he stayed dead," or to Confucians, "Confucius died, and he's still dead." That is the point Peter is making here, that David died and is still dead, as his tomb will attest.

"Therefore, being a prophet, and knowing that God had sworn with an oath to him that of the fruit of his body, according to the flesh, He would raise up the Christ to sit on his throne, he, foreseeing this, spoke concerning the resurrection of the Christ, that His soul was not left in Hades, nor did His

flesh see corruption" (vv. 30–31). This prediction had been made a thousand years before, a time before anybody had ever heard of Jesus of Nazareth, but whom God had attested in their midst.

"This Jesus God has raised up, of which we are all witnesses. Therefore being exalted to the right hand of God, and having received from the Father the promise of the Holy Spirit, He poured out this which you now see and hear" (vv. 32–33). Peter was explaining Pentecost. God had taken the Spirit that was upon Christ and given it to the whole body of believers, the church. In explaining the significance of the outpouring of the Holy Spirit, Peter took his listeners right back to the life and ministry of Jesus, who was raised from the dead and exalted to the right hand of the Father, and after His ascension into heaven, this Jesus, along with the Father, poured out the Spirit on that day.

7

PETER'S SERMON, PART 3

Acts 2:34–39

"For David did not ascend into the heavens, but he says himself:

'The LORD said to my Lord,
"Sit at My right hand,
Till I make Your enemies Your footstool."'

"Therefore let all the house of Israel know assuredly that God has made this Jesus, whom you crucified, both Lord and Christ." Now when they heard this, they were cut to the heart, and said to Peter and the rest of the apostles, "Men and brethren, what shall we do?" Then Peter said to them, "Repent, and let every one of you be baptized in the name of Jesus Christ for the remission of sins; and you shall receive the gift of the Holy Spirit. For the promise is to you and to your children, and to all who are afar off, as many as the Lord our God will call."

During the first century, the cult of emperor worship spread throughout the entirety of the Roman Empire. The most powerful, perhaps, of the Caesars who reigned during that first century, Octavian, took upon himself the title Caesar Augustus. Octavian was a powerful ruler and was worthy of the titles that befit kings and emperors. Indeed, he was mighty and authoritative, but one thing he was not was *august*. *Augustness* is an attribute that belongs to God alone, for it denotes His transcendent majesty and eternal glory.

During the first and second centuries, citizens of Rome were required to take a loyalty oath and say publicly, "*Caesar curios*," which means "Caesar is lord." The Christian community, however, would not say it. They were willing, as civil servants of Rome, to offer the emperor honor and obedience, but they could not take the loyalty oath, even if the refusal cost them their lives, because their confession was "Jesus is Lord." The first creed of the first-century church was short and simple: "*Jesus ho kurios*," Jesus is Lord, and we see that startling confession at the conclusion of Peter's sermon at Pentecost.

Peter had been speaking about prophecies. In our last study we looked at his treatment of a psalm of David, and in the preceding lesson, we examined his treatment of passages from the book of the prophet Joel. Here Peter turns his attention to another Old Testament text, Psalm 110. **"David did not ascend into the heavens, but he says himself, 'The LORD said to my Lord, "Sit at My right hand, till I make Your enemies Your footstool"'"** (vv. 34–35).

Psalm 110

This passage from Psalm 110 is quoted repeatedly in the New Testament. During Jesus' life, the Pharisees of His day were embattled over His claim to lordship. Their question was, "How can someone of the seed of David, a son of David, also be the Lord of David?" In Jewish categories, the father always had dominance over the son. So, since David preceded Jesus by one thousand years, it was inconceivable to the Jew that David would look to Jesus as his Lord. That is why this text became so central to the early Jewish community. They were reminded to go back to Psalm 110, an enthronement psalm, in which David himself said, "The LORD said to my Lord . . ." God's sacred name, Yahweh, was given by God to Moses in the Midianite wilderness, out of the burning bush. Jews protected this name by means of creative circumlocution, lest they be guilty of profaning it. They heaped up titles for God, the most sacred of which was *Adonai*, "Lord." Psalm 110 reads, "*Yahweh* said to my *Adonai*," or, "God said to my Sovereign One, 'Sit at My right hand.'" The content of this discussion within the Godhead is between God Himself and the One whom He has appointed to be David's Lord, his *Adonai*, which translates the New Testament, *kurios*, or Lord.

Essential to the Apostles' Creed, after the confession of the life, death, and resurrection of Jesus, is the affirmation that He ascended into heaven where He is seated at the right hand of God, which means He has been placed in the seat of cosmic authority. God has elevated Christ to His right hand and given Him all authority on heaven and earth. This is a political statement with a vengeance, a statement of cosmic authority. Above every emperor, governor, king, and president is the One whom God has placed at His right hand, calling Him not just King, but King of kings, and not just Lord, but Lord of lords. That is what was prophesied by David in the Old Testament a thousand years before Jesus. He said in essence, "God is going to take His Messiah and elevate Him to His right hand, to the seat of cosmic authority." Too often we reduce the significance of that affirmation. The theology that is prevalent today presents a sweet and blessed Jesus who saves us from our sin but does not reign.

Savior and Lord

Extremely divisive over the last twenty-five years has been the Lordship-Salvation Controversy, which became popularized by the idea of the carnal Christian. Some time ago I talked to a young man who said he was a Christian, but he was using and selling illegal drugs. He was also living with a girl not his wife. His hedonistic lifestyle gave no manifestation whatsoever of godliness. When I questioned the discrepancy between his profession of faith and his lifestyle, he said, "I'm a carnal Christian. I've received Jesus as my Savior, but I'm going to wait awhile before I submit to him as my Lord."

The recent disjunction between Christ as Savior and Christ as Lord is foreign and antithetical to the New Testament. At the heart of this text where the *kerygma* is being preached is the affirmation of the lordship of Christ. I get terrified when I listen to the jargon of Christians who say, "I asked Jesus into my heart, and I invited Him to be the Lord of my life." What was He before that invitation? Christianity can be a "religion" that has nothing to do with the truth content of the biblical message. The message is far more radical than this. Peter is saying that it is a matter of objective reality. God, who created heaven and earth, has made Christ the Lord of the universe. He rules; He does not wait for us to invite Him. He rules us whether or not we want Him to rule. We can be hostile to His reign; we can be renegades in His dominion; we may fight against His just empowerment as the King of kings and Lord of lords, but all that does not reduce Him to impotency. Our attempts to supplant Him as Lord are impotent because God has decreed His lordship.

The metaphor of bowing the knee is used again and again in the Old Testament with respect to the coming Messiah of Israel, and we—even to this day—bow the knee as a gesture indicating worship. The Scriptures tell us that there will be a day when every human being on the face of the earth will bow his knee to Christ as Lord. People ask, "How can that be? Most of the people in the world do not embrace the Christian faith." In the final analysis that does not matter. What matters is who God declares to be Lord, and God said, "I make Your enemies Your footstool" (Ps. 110:1). David said, "You shall break them with a rod of iron; you shall dash them to pieces like a potter's vessel" (Ps. 2:9). Many people come willingly and prostrate themselves before the King of kings. Others flee from the King of kings. God says that all at some point will bow down whether they want to or not, even if it means God has to break their knee. That is far different from modern evangelism that issues an invitation to people. God does not invite people to come to Christ; He commands it. He requires it because He has put Christ at His right hand.

Hard Hearts

Peter continued on, and we well wonder how he survived the day. **"Therefore let all the house of Israel know assuredly that God has made this Jesus, whom you crucified, both Lord and Christ." Now when they heard this, they were cut to the heart** (vv. 36–37). The last thing I am interested in doing when I preach is to make people feel guilty, but I also know that our heart is made of calcium. Our heart is stone, and it takes nothing less than the power of God to cut through it. The people listening to Peter were just like us. They did not want someone making ultimate demands upon their lives, and their hearts had become hardened. Their necks had become so stiff and hard that they crucified the Son of God. You cannot get more recalcitrant than that, but God was pleased that day, by His Word, to cut into that stone and to pierce the heart.

Has that ever happened to you? Has the Word of God ever come to you so that, when you heard it, you knew the arguments were over, and you cried out, "What can I do?" If that has not happened to you, then you have missed the Redeemer. Genuine repentance is provoked when the excuses and rationalizations go, and the self-applause is silenced, and we say, "Oh God, my God, what have I done?" That is what happened that day. **"Men and brethren, what shall we do?"** (v. 37). Peter told them what to do. He said, **"Repent, and let every one of you be baptized in the name of Jesus Christ for the remission of sins, and you will receive the gift of the Holy Spirit"** (v. 38).

Peter had been speaking to a group of guilty people. Part of what I do is the work of an apologist; I try to deal with the intellectual questions that arise about the truth-claims of Christianity. Many times I have talked to people and dealt with their philosophical objections for hours, patiently, until finally I have come to a place in the conversation where I say, "'Just a minute. Can we lay aside those questions? Let me ask you this: What do you do with your guilt?" Every time I have done that, the discussion stops because nobody can look me in the eye and say, "I don't have any guilt."

We can have guilt feelings when we should not feel guilty. We are so easily manipulated by guilt. Sometimes we carry burdens of guilt that have nothing to do with the things of God. They are culturally imposed. There is a difference between false guilt and real guilt. There really is such a thing as guilt; real guilt takes place when we disobey the law of God. When we transgress the law of God, we are guilty, even though we may not feel guilty. Imagine going on trial for armed robbery, a crime for which there is irrefutable proof, and the judge asks, "What's your defense?" and you say, "My defense is that I don't feel guilty." The judge would think you were a fool. Guilt is not measured by guilt feelings. The worst thing that could happen to us is to actually have guilt yet not feel it. That is what happened to the people in Jerusalem. They had the worst of all possible guilt—they had crucified the Son of God—but they did not feel it until the Word came to them and cut them to the heart.

Since the garden of Eden human beings have tried every conceivable method to eradicate guilt and ease the pangs of conscience, but the only thing that will do it is an authentic treatment for authentic guilt—real forgiveness. We are debtors who cannot pay our debts. We cannot live well enough today and tomorrow to atone for the past. The only thing that will take care of real guilt is real forgiveness.

The price tag for forgiveness is repentance. When we repent, we pray, "God, I am heartily sorry that I have offended You. I acknowledge my sin, which is ever before me, and my only hope in life and death is a redeemer." That is the message that the Apostle Peter preached that day, and he extended the application beyond the crowd. He said, **"The promise is to you and to your children, and to all who are afar off, as many as the Lord our God will call"** (v. 39). We come to the One who gives to us the remission of sins.

8

LIFE IN THE EARLY CHURCH

Acts 2:42–47

⁌⁌⁌

And they continued steadfastly in the apostles' doctrine and fellowship, in the breaking of bread, and in prayers. Then fear came upon every soul, and many wonders and signs were done through the apostles. Now all who believed were together, and had all things in common, and sold their possessions and goods, and divided them among all, as anyone had need. So, continuing daily with one accord in the temple, and breaking bread from house to house, they ate their food with gladness and simplicity of heart, praising God and having favor with all the people. And the Lord added to the church daily those who were being saved.

Some time ago I read the results of a poll conducted among those who label themselves "born-again Christians." The appellation "born-again" set before the word "Christian" is not a designation that many churchgoers in the United States like to use for themselves. I also fuss a bit about its being a manifest redundancy. There is no other kind of Christian possible except a born-again Christian, and no one can be born again without being a Christian. Those who have been born again do not have to say they are "Christian," and if they are true Christians, they don't have to say they are "born again." The two are synonymous; but because there are so many schools of thought within the visible church and because of the widespread growth of nineteenth-century liberalism, which denies the essential truths of the Christian faith while simultaneously claiming to be Christian, some have an aversion to using terms such as *regeneration or rebirth* to define a true Christian. In any case, the results of this particular poll were terrifying. The majority of those who identified themselves as born-again Christians said that they believe one gets into heaven through good works. A vast number of them affirmed the reality of reincarnation. More than half argued that there are several ways to God apart from Christ. I do not see how we could be more optimistic than to assume that maybe 10 percent of those who identified themselves as regenerate Christians were, in fact, converted people.

I might have a rather dismal view of the matter through eyes jaundiced by too much theology, but it reminded me of our Lord's warning that His church will always contain tares along with the wheat. A ditty I learned the first year I was a Christian goes something like this: "Wherever God erects a house of prayer, the Devil builds a chapel there, and 'twill be found upon examination that the latter has the largest congregation."

Revival

I mention all this because, in the record of what happened on the day of Pentecost after Peter's sermon, we are told that an astonishing revival took place right there in Jerusalem. Three thousand were added to the church that day. By today's standards of mass evangelism, that kind of response does not seem all that great. A member of St. Andrew's told me that several years earlier he had gone to a Billy Graham crusade, and when the altar call was given, he went forward, but there was no change in his life. He lived away from the Lord for the next thirty years until he finally came to Him. He asked me if I thought he had been truly converted at the time of the crusade or if his conversion had come later. I told him that I cannot know for sure. Someone can be converted and then fall into serious sin for a season, but thirty years is a long season. So, I said, in all likelihood, it is much more probable that what he did originally was make a false profession of faith, something that occurs whenever there is such an evangelistic meeting with a call to conversion. So often this is produced by our dependence upon human techniques and methods to prime the pump and get people to convert through the power of our program. Though many real conversions take place, the statistics cannot be trusted. In fact, evangelistic statistics are often inflated. If as many people in this country were, in fact, converted who claim to be born again, it would mean that America is in the greatest period of revival in the history of the church, one that would make the Reformation pale into insignificance. Not only would this be the third Great Awakening, but it would dwarf the first and second Great Awakenings. The reality is actually quite different.

I labor this point for a reason. In the revival that took place on the day of Pentecost it was the Lord who added to the church three thousand people. Therefore, I assume that every last one of those added to the church that day was converted and regenerated by God the Holy Spirit. God built His church initially with people that He converted, that were the fruit of His action in their lives, not as a result of the things that people do to try to prime the pump. That is significant, because what we get now is a bird's-eye view of how this group of people in the early church behaved and of their pattern of Christian activity.

Steadfast

The first thing said of them is this: **"They continued steadfastly in the apostles' doctrine and fellowship, in the breaking of bread, and in prayers"** (v. 42). They did not stop studying the Word of God, but they continuously and in a diligent manner applied themselves to doctrine, which is one of the most politically incorrect words in the church today. "Don't talk to me about doctrine," people say. "I don't need any doctrine. All I need to know is Jesus." That is how far we have come from the first-century church, which focused its attention steadfastly and continuously on coming together to study the doctrine of the Apostles. They did not study the inventions of the Gnostics or of those outside the heart and soul of the orthodox Christian community; they studied apostolic doctrine. Today that apostolic doctrine is in the Scriptures. The early church was a Bible-studying church, steadfastly, continually devoted to devouring the Word of God that came from the Apostles.

In the sixties the charismatic movement exploded on center stage. Sudden revival broke out at Notre Dame, at Duquesne University, and in mainline churches, including Lutheran, Episcopal, Methodist, and Presbyterian. When I began teaching ministerial students at a Presbyterian college, the students wanted to talk about nothing but charismatic gifts. Ever since those days I have said that if I want to find somebody who loves to pray, I will look for a charismatic. Those students would come to our house every night, and we would pray for hours, sometimes all night long. I was involved in that for a little while, but the charismatics were so focused on getting Spirit-filled and manifesting the gift of tongues and other such phenomena that it was taking them away from the Scriptures. I have heard at least a hundred specific prophecies uttered under the so-called influence of the Holy Spirit that have never come to pass. People became so excited about experience, about the gifts of the Spirit and being Spirit-filled, that they didn't want to hear anything about doctrine.

Once, about thirty charismatic Christians from every conceivable denomination came from France to our study center in Pennsylvania. They were excited about the fellowship they were enjoying in the Spirit. I asked their leader, "Given the diverse denominational backgrounds represented by your group, how can you have unity and lay aside issues such as justification and the atonement of Christ?" Five minutes later they were arguing vigorously. The only way they could keep their unity was to lay aside doctrine, so they began to enjoy a fellowship without doctrine or the Word, and they called their fellowship Spirit-filled.

There is no such thing as a Spirit-filled Christian who neglects the study of the Word of God. There is no such thing as a Spirit-filled church that does not give itself continually and steadfastly to the study of sacred Scripture. The first sign of a Spirit-filled church is one in which the Spirit-filled people do not flee from Scripture and seek a substitute for it but are driven to it to have their spiritual lives rooted and grounded in the Word of God.

Those in the early church, we are told, continued steadfastly in fellowship. You might have heard the saying, "The family that prays together, stays together." I like to change it a bit and say: "The family that prays and plays together, stays together." That is one of the things the early Christians did. In addition to their diligent study of the things of God, they had a tremendous time of fellowship. They experienced *koinonia*, in which the people became close-knit friends, enjoying the love of God and the peace of Christ and sharing in the joy and delight of what they were learning in the apostolic teaching. There is no reason for any group of Christians ever to be known as "the frozen chosen." Jim Baker, before he got in trouble, once said on television, "Some Christians are the worst thieves in the world because they steal the joy of the Lord." Joy should be the possession of every Christian, and we should be excited in getting together for fellowship.

A word of caution: the primary reason we are to come to church on Sunday morning is to worship God. However, we are told by the polls that the primary reason people come to church on Sunday morning is to enjoy fellowship with their Christian friends. What motivates people to come to church is not worship but fellowship. Maybe, if we are going to be truly Christian, we ought to do away with fellowship, since it competes so strongly with worship. However, that would be an error in the opposite direction. We see in the early church the model of how church should function. They came to hear and study the Word of God, but they also came to enjoy the friendship and camaraderie in the fellowship of believers in the church.

They continued also in the breaking of bread and in prayers. The breaking of bread has two significances here. On the one hand, this breaking of bread refers simply to mealtime and not always exclusively to the Lord's Supper; on the other hand, church dinners were a big part of the early church. There really is no warmer experience of friendship than sharing meals. Whether sitting around a table, or going out to dinner, or inviting people into our homes, warmth and intimacy are experienced when people gather together around a meal. So they ate a lot of meals together, but incorporated in those meals was the celebration of the Lord's Supper.

We see in the early church the study and proclamation of the Word, the enjoyment of fellowship, the breaking of bread, and the sacrament of the Lord's Supper. We also see prayer. Jesus himself designated His Father's house as a house of prayer, and the first-century community was a praying church. At St. Andrew's we have just scratched the surface on learning how to pray. In the years to come we want to emphasize even more strongly ways in which we can become prayer warriors, ways in which we can band together as a fellowship of believers who corporately and privately bring their prayers before the Lord our God.

All Things in Common

Then fear came upon every soul, and many wonders and signs were done through the apostles. Now all who believed were together, and had all things in common, and sold their possessions and goods, and divided them among all, as anyone had need (vv. 43–45). These are some of the most controversial verses in the whole New Testament. Everyone who has ever argued the case for communism has used these verses to support it. They claim that communism echoes true Christianity, where no one has private property or the ownership of personal goods, despite the fact that the law of God in the Old Testament and elsewhere in the New Testament is designed to protect and endorse the legitimacy of private property. Distinctly absent from this description is government, either secular or ecclesiastical, to enforce this activity in the early church. This was not an economic necessity for the Christian. Nowhere does the New Testament require that everybody have their goods in common. The Lord gives us prosperity that we can enjoy beyond our needs. Who is it that determines what we need? What determines how we should desire to use our earthly resources? Totalitarian governments that impose communism bring great affliction on people. Another affliction is government-imposed socialism in which wealth is redistributed by government coercion. Both communism and socialism are far removed from the New Testament principle.

Some in the early church were living in desperate poverty while others were prospering under the hand of Providence. The sharing and distribution was driven by something that should drive the church of every century—generosity. Christians are not required to give up all their private property, but we are required to be generous because we live under the hand of the most generous God.

The Old Testament principle of giving was the tithe. Everybody in Israel had the same proportionate responsibility. If ever there was a flat tax, this was it. Wealthy men had to give 10 percent of their wealth to the work of God, and the poor had to give 10 percent of their poverty to the work of God. Not everybody gave the same amount of money. The wealthy gave much more than the poor, but everybody gave the same percent. Everybody had the same responsibility. That is not the way we do it in the United States. The government forces us to operate under what they call "social justice," but there is nothing just about it, and it is not driven by generosity. In fact, forms of socialism undermine the principle of what we see in the early church because the giving of the early Christians was voluntary. They gave because they wanted to give.

The Lord loves a cheerful giver. He doesn't just love givers—anybody can be a giver. He loves *cheerful* givers. He loves people who love to express their gratitude to Him by building the kingdom of God. One of the greatest legacies my father left with me was his overwhelming generosity. I watched the joy and delight that filled his life with that spirit of generosity, but I have also seen the stark contrast of the spirit of selfishness that rules the hearts of so many. Let it never be said of us that our hearts are cold or turned inward and our eyes turned away from those in need. Let us be known for our generosity as Christians, as the first-century church was known.

In Church

So continuing daily with one accord in the temple, and breaking bread from house to house, they ate their food with gladness and simplicity of heart, praising God and having favor with all the people. And the Lord added to the church daily those who were being saved (vv. 46–47). They did not hold their gatherings in the temple, but they went from house to house. The first Christians had *ekklesiola*, that is, house churches. They did not have a building big enough to house the three thousand, so they went from house to house at different times in different homes, where they shared their faith together.

In this brief glimpse of life in the early church, we have a model of what the church is supposed to look like. We are two thousand years removed from the apostolic church, but we need to have the vision of that church blowing assumptions from our minds so that when we come together, we do so with delight and rejoicing and praising God for what He has done for us in Christ.

9

HEALING AT THE GATE BEAUTIFUL

Acts 3:1–10

Now Peter and John went up together to the temple at the hour of prayer, the ninth hour. And a certain man lame from his mother's womb was carried, whom they laid daily at the gate of the temple which is called Beautiful, to ask alms from those who entered the temple; who, seeing Peter and John about to go into the temple, asked for alms. And fixing his eyes on him, with John, Peter said, "Look at us." So he gave them his attention, expecting to receive something from them. Then Peter said, "Silver and gold I do not have, but what I do have I give you: In the name of Jesus Christ of Nazareth, rise up and walk." And he took him by the right hand and lifted him up, and immediately his feet and ankle bones received strength. So he, leaping up, stood and walked and entered the temple with them—walking, leaping, and praising God. And all the people saw him walking and praising God. Then they knew that it was he who sat begging alms at the Beautiful Gate of the temple; and they were filled with wonder and amazement at what had happened to him.

The city of Amsterdam in the Netherlands got its name because of a dam built along the Amstel River. Around this dam in concentric circles the city was built, a major European metropolis to this day. Some years ago I journeyed to Holland for my graduate work, and I lived twenty-five miles outside the city in a small Dutch village. It was my custom to commute to the

University of Amsterdam by train from the outskirts of the little village to the city hub called Central Station. In those days the free University of Amsterdam was located downtown. As I would get off the train in Amsterdam, I would walk down the main street, first across a bridge and then down toward the dam, and from there I would make a turn toward the university. Every day when I crossed that bridge, I passed a beggar. He was seated on the side of the bridge with his little collection basket, and I could not pass him without dropping in some coins.

Years later I went back to Holland and traversed that same route I had walked each day all those years ago. The beggar was still there begging, and I gave him some coins. On that trip I purchased a big picture book of Amsterdam, and as I was going through the pages I saw a photograph of the bridge, and, sure enough, there was that same beggar, sitting there with his hands out waiting for alms. He was a fixture of the city. His story is similar to one we read in Acts about a man, a fixture by the Gate Beautiful, who encountered Peter and John.

Together at the Temple

Now Peter and John went up together to the temple at the hour of prayer (v. 1). One of the things that jumps out at me as I read this text is the company that was being kept there. Peter, the one who had betrayed Jesus only a few weeks earlier, was now going side by side with his companion John, whom we know stayed with Jesus during the ordeal of the execution because he was at the foot of the cross when Jesus commended the care of His mother, Mary, into his hand. So the one who fled is now working together with the one who remained loyal to Jesus at the time of His death.

The second thing we see here is that they went to the temple. The separation of the Christian community from the Jewish community took many years. In fact, it wasn't finalized until the year A.D. 70, with the destruction of the temple and of Jerusalem. As we read further in the book of Acts, we will see that when Paul went on his missionary journeys, it was his custom to go first into the synagogue and engage in relationships there.

In the first-century church, before the Judaizing heresy threatened the very life of Christendom, the early Apostles went to the temple to pray. There were different times of the day established for prayers. This time it was the ninth hour, the time for evening prayers, at three o'clock in the afternoon. We get the details from Luke about where they were at what time and what was going on.

And a certain man lame from his mother's womb was carried, whom they laid daily at the gate of the temple which is called Beautiful (v. 2). Luke gives us a description of the sight and situation of the person involved in the narrative. First, he describes the man himself. Luke, as a physician, was careful to give significant details about this occasion. There are many ways in which people can become lame, such as through disease or accidents, and many of the lame can remember what it was like to walk. They can remember what it was like to run and to leap with joy, but those days are gone, as they are now confined to wheelchairs or worse. But this man's lameness was congenital. He was born lame. Never in his entire life had he stood on his own two feet unaided. Never in his life had he had the experience that we take for granted of walking down the street. This man had never stood, walked, run, or jumped. He had been carried, and every day his friends or family (we are not told who) carried this man in his helpless condition to the gate that separated the court of the Gentiles from the court of the Jews and sat him by it. It had to take some effort because not only was the temple elevated, but the stairs from the first court to the second court made the court of the Jews even higher. Carrying someone up there was a difficult task. They carried this man and put him by the Gate Beautiful.

Josephus tells us in vivid terms what the second temple, the one built by Herod, looked like. It was one of the wonders of the ancient world. All the doors and gates within the temple complex were huge and beautiful, but this particular gate was called the Beautiful Gate or the Gate Beautiful because, though made of bronze in its interior, it was covered completely with silver and gold. It was a portico of magnificent opulence. Next to that symbol of wealth they laid this poor beggar so that people who walked past him, entering through the Gate Beautiful into the inner courtyard of the Jews, would be moved to compassion by his pitiable condition and give him alms.

The giving of alms in Old Testament Israel and in New Testament Christianity was a practice expected by God of His people. One of the surviving documents from the second century, the short book called the *Didache*, or the "Teaching of the Apostles," gives us a summary of Christian duty and obligation and obedience, and stressed in the *Didache* is the generous giving of alms.

"Rise Up and Walk"

The man saw Peter and John about to come into the temple, and he asked for alms. **And fixing his eyes on him, with John, Peter said, "Look at us"** (v. 4). Imagine that you are in that man's place, and in your pain and debilitated state, two strangers come by and make eye contact. That in itself is significant. Watch what people do with their eyes when they see a beggar on the street. The most normal human reaction to the presence of a beggar is to look the other way, as if the person doesn't exist. If any man was accustomed to watching people approach him and look the other way, it was this poor beggar. But when Peter and John came, they did not avert their gaze. They looked directly at him. They made eye contact with him, and they emphasized that eye contact by saying to him, "Look at us."

So he gave them his attention, expecting to receive something from them (v. 5). The man looked at Peter and John, watching their hands, watching for the wallet, watching for the money that was about to come, in a state of eager anticipation. On this occasion Peter expressed the immortal words, **"Silver and gold I do not have, but what I do have I give you: In the name of Jesus Christ of Nazareth, rise up and walk"** (v. 6).

What? The man's heart sank at the first portion of what Peter said: "Silver and gold I do not have." The man was likely thinking, "Well, then, why are you looking at me, and why did you ask me to look at you? You filled my heart with expectation only to tell me you have no money. What help can you possibly give?" Peter did not have money to give, but he did have something for the man: "In the name of Jesus Christ of Nazareth, rise up and walk."

Then an astonishing event took place. **He took him by the right hand and lifted him up, and immediately his feet and ankle bones received strength** (v. 7). Peter reached down and took him by the hand and helped him to his feet, and where moments before his legs had been useless limbs, now he could stand. **So he, leaping up, stood and walked and entered the temple with them— walking, leaping, and praising God** (v. 8). What an incredible moment. He was no staged plant for a healing service. This man was known by everyone in the temple complex because, like the beggar on the road from the Central Station in Amsterdam, he was there every day, and everybody knew he could not walk.

Centuries later the great theologian Thomas Aquinas visited Rome and had an audience with Pope Innocent II. Aquinas was somewhat amazed by the opulence of the Vatican in that day. This was prior to the building of St. Peter's, but even then it was a glorious headquarters for the church, filled with riches, and the pope was somewhat proud of the riches of the church, and he said to Aquinas, "No longer do we say, 'Silver and gold have we none.'" Thomas looked at the pope and said, "Maybe that is why we can no longer say, 'Rise up and walk.'" However, the church's riches were not why the church lost its power to heal people. The reason is that the power evidenced in the early days of the church was given by Christ to His Apostles to establish the church. Aquinas knew that, but I guess he did not want to miss the opportunity to chide the pope for the opulence of the church.

All the people saw him walking and praising God. Then they knew that it was he who sat begging alms at the Beautiful Gate of the temple; and they were filled with wonder and amazement at what had happened to him (vv. 9–10). That event became the provocation for Peter's second famous sermon.

10

PETER'S SECOND SPEECH

Acts 3:11–21

Now as the lame man who was healed held on to Peter and John, all the people ran together to them in the porch which is called Solomon's, greatly amazed. So when Peter saw it, he responded to the people: "Men of Israel, why do you marvel at this? Or why look so intently at us, as though by our own power or godliness we had made this man walk? The God of Abraham, Isaac, and Jacob, the God of our fathers, glorified His Servant Jesus, whom you delivered up and denied in the presence of Pilate, when he was determined to let Him go. But you denied the Holy One and the Just, and asked for a murderer to be granted to you, and killed the Prince of life, whom God raised from the dead, of which we are witnesses. And His name, through faith in His name, has made this man strong, whom you see and know. Yes, the faith which comes through Him has given him this perfect soundness in the presence of you all. Yet now, brethren, I know that you did it in ignorance, as did also your rulers. But those things which God foretold by the mouth of all His prophets, that the Christ would suffer, He has thus fulfilled. Repent therefore and be converted, that your sins may be blotted out, so that times of refreshing may come from the presence of the Lord, and that He may send Jesus Christ, who was preached to you before, whom heaven must receive until the times of restoration of all things, which God has spoken by the mouth of all His holy prophets since the world began."

Wᵉ turn our attention to a sermon of Peter's, which is the second recorded sermon by this Apostle in the book of Acts. The first thing to notice about the sermon is the lack of political correctness and sensitivity in which it was delivered to its hearers. It is the kind of sermon that would cast people in jail if they preached it today.

"Why Do You Marvel?"

It begins with Luke's record: **Now as the lame man who was healed held on to Peter and John, all the people ran together to them in the porch which is called Solomon's, greatly amazed** (v. 11). We know that he was not holding on to Peter and John because he needed their physical support to stand. That was already established in the marvel of his miracle that we looked at in the last study. This man, who had been congenitally crippled and had never stood on his own two feet in his entire life, was so miraculously healed by the touch of the Apostles that he not only stood, but he walked, jumped, and leapt for joy without any assistance or handholding. Yet we are told that this man, after running and praising God, came back to Peter and John and held onto them for dear life. Wouldn't you? If someone had just cured you of a malady that had afflicted you for so many years, you wouldn't want those people out of your sight. So he came and held on tightly.

All the people gathered together in Solomon's porch, greatly amazed. **So when Peter saw it, he responded to the people: "Men of Israel, why do you marvel at this?"** (v. 12). If we examine the miracles as recorded in the Gospels, we see that it is almost as if the Gospel authors had a literary formula whereby they told first the circumstances of the affliction, then the miraculous power of Christ in healing that affliction, then the astonished response of the people. Because of its frequent use in the New Testament, one of the first verbs people learn when they study Greek is the word *thoumazo*, which indicates astonishment.

Peter asked a question here that comes across like the truck driver whose truck was stuck under an overpass. A policeman came to him and said, "Did you get your truck stuck?" The man had a tremendous grasp of the obvious. Without batting an eyelash the truck driver said, "No. I was delivering the overpass and I ran out of gas." Just so, Peter asks why the people are amazed. It is a wonder someone in the crowd didn't say, "Are you crazy? Why wouldn't we be amazed? We've been walking past this crippled man every day, and now he is walking and leaping and jumping and praising God. How else should we be but in a state of absolute amazement?"

Peter was not being facetious, because he added to the question: **"Why look so intently at us, as though by our own power or godliness we had made this**

man walk?" (v. 12). The implication is that what would be truly amazing is if the Apostles had been able to make the man walk by means of their own strength and power. Instead, Peter was saying, nobody should be amazed, because they had raised the man in the name of Jesus. At that point, Peter gave the sermon of all sermons.

"The God of Abraham, Isaac, and Jacob, the God of our fathers, glorified His Servant Jesus" (v. 13). There is something different about this sermon from the first one we looked at on the day of Pentecost. On the day of Pentecost there were three different sections to Peter's sermon, and in each one he gave an exposition of an Old Testament passage. In this sermon he did not do that. It is not as if he was now abandoning the Scriptures; rather, he was compacting them, choosing his words carefully. There is a summation of Old Testament prophecy about the Messiah who was to come. Peter started off by saying, in essence, "You are looking at us as if we had the power and godliness to heal this man but where you ought to look is at God."

Notice that Peter did not say that God glorified His *Son* Jesus or His *prophet* Jesus, though He was that, or His *Prince of Peace.* The language that Peter used here took them squarely back to the Old Testament. This miracle was done by the One who "glorified His Servant Jesus," identifying Christ with the promised Messiah of the latter portion of the book of Isaiah, the "*ebed Yahweh,*" the servant of the Lord, the One whose exploits are set forth in Isaiah 53—the "Man of sorrows and acquainted with grief" (v. 3), the One who would bear the sins of His people. That is the servant of the Lord that every Jew expected to appear on the scene of history, and now Peter was saying, "Don't look at me. Don't look at John. Look at the God of our fathers, who in this act glorifies His servant, the servant of the Lord."

The Crucified One

Peter then issued a sharp contrast: **"But you denied the Holy One and the Just, and asked for a murderer to be granted to you, and killed the Prince of life, whom God raised from the dead, of which we are witnesses"** (vv. 14–15). Another prophecy from the Old Testament was that the Messiah would be known as the Holy One of Israel. The first to recognize the identity of Christ in the Gospel record were the demons who screamed out at Jesus, "What have we to do with You, Jesus, You Son of God? Have You come here to torment us before the time?" (Matt. 8:29). They knew who He was. Peter tried to communicate to the people something about the One they had crucified. He is the servant of the Lord, the Holy One of Israel, the Righteous One who is to come, who is our righteousness. They had delivered, denied, and killed the very Prince of life.

We can easily recall the name of the person who shot John Fitzgerald Kennedy on November 22, 1963, but can we recall as easily the name J.D. Tippet, the police officer the assassin allegedly shot on the same day? We remember the details of the death of John Kennedy, but we forget the name of the other man who was killed by the same assassin on the same day in the same city. Why is murdering a policeman such a terrible crime? It is a crime to commit homicide at all, but the higher the office of the one killed, the greater the significance it holds for us. When a president is murdered, it is an assassination. It becomes an unforgettable moment in a nation's history. Yet the assassination of a president is nothing compared to the murder of the Prince of life Himself.

John wrote of Him, "In Him was life" (John 1:4); and, "I am the way, the truth, and the life" (John 14:6); and, "I am the Alpha and the Omega" (Rev. 1:8). Here in Acts Jesus is called the Prince of life, and Peter told the people they had murdered Him. That is preaching for conviction. Peter was saying, "You denied, delivered, and murdered the Holy One of Israel, yet now you marvel that He would be raised from the dead and that His power can raise people from a crippled state? What you ought to marvel at is that you are still alive."

When Jonathan Edwards preached his sermon "Sinners in the Hands of an Angry God," he said, "Oh sinner, you cannot give any sound reason why you have not dropped into the pit of hell since you rose from your bed this morning, except that the grace of God in His hand has held you up." Can we give any reason for God to keep us from everlasting destruction? Do we have any merit before which we can stand in front of God and say, "You owe it to me, God, to raise me up like you raised Jesus"? God forbid that we would ever talk like that before God; but we think it all the time.

"And His name, through faith in His name, has made this man strong, whom you see and know. Yes, the faith which comes through Him has given him this perfect soundness in the presence of you all. Yet now, brethren, I know that you did it in ignorance, as did also your rulers. But those things which God foretold by the mouth of all His prophets, that the Christ would suffer, He has thus fulfilled" (vv. 16–18). We see here an exceptive clause, something that the people were hoping they could latch on to, their ticket out of hell at the last judgment—that God would give them a free pass on the basis of their ignorance.

Without Excuse

Someone told me that he has a friend who is not an atheist but an agnostic. I told him that an agnostic is the worst kind of atheist. *Theism* is the affirmation of the existence of God or of gods. *Atheism* covers everything outside the category of theism, so the agnostic is outside the category of the theist because he will not affirm the existence of God, and then he blames God for it. He says that the reason he cannot affirm the existence of God is that he is *agnostos*. He is without knowledge. The Latin translation of *agnosis* or *agnostic* is "ignoramus," so the plea of the agnostic is this: "Oh, God, if you just would have made yourself known to me, if you had just shown me a miracle, if you had just given me sufficient data to make a rational judgment, I would have been your most faithful supporter." That, despite the fact that every moment of the supposed agnostic's existence, heaven is declaring the glory of God and God is manifesting Himself clearly before his very eyes and in the midst of his soul. Every human being that walks upon this earth knows with certainty that God exists. Our sin is not that we do not know Him; it is that we refuse to acknowledge Him, even though we do know Him.

Paul says in Romans that man is without excuse (1:20), so what excuse will an agnostic be able to rest on? The excuse of every self-proclaimed agnostic is, "If I had just known you were there, I would have repented and embraced the Savior, but I didn't get it. Please forgive me for my ignorance." Paul warns that ignorance is not going to be an excuse on the day of judgment because we are not ignorant. We are not without knowledge. We are not *agnosis*.

In the early days of Christendom, the reality of a certain kind of ignorance played a role on the cross. Our Lord cried out to the Father about His murderers, "Father, forgive them, for they do not know what they do" (Luke 23:34). Following on that, Peter was saying to this crowd, "You murdered Him. You killed Him. You betrayed Him. You denied Him. But I know you did it in ignorance." Then he went on to say, **"Repent therefore and be converted, that your sins may be blotted out, so that times of refreshing may come from the presence of the Lord, and that He may send Jesus Christ, who was preached to you before, whom heaven must receive until the times of restoration of all things, which God has spoken by the mouth of all His holy prophets since the world began"** (vv. 19–21). They were ignorant because they had ignored the plain teaching of the Word of God. Peter was saying that every recent happening there in Jerusalem had been predicted in detail in the Old Testament, and had they been diligent students of the Word of God, they would not have been surprised by the death of their Messiah, nor would they have participated in screaming for His blood.

God has shown us plainly what the truth is. He manifested the true identity of Jesus by raising Him from the dead, which, by the way, He never did for Muhammad, or Confucius, or Buddha, or anyone else. God raised Christ from the dead, certifying Him as His only Son, but in our ignorance we say that it does not matter what anyone believes. We can take hold of whatever religion we like, so long as we are good people following God to the best of our ability. People are running away from God as fast as they can run, into a religion of idolatry. Anything but the true God will satisfy the hearts of wicked people. Then when God shows plainly the truth of His Son, they are amazed. How could it be?

Peter could have said to the people, "Why aren't you in the temple jumping, leaping, and praising God? It is your God, the God of your fathers, the God of your heritage, who is glorifying His Son." Some might think that what Peter said to those people was insensitive or harsh or offensive, but they cannot say that it was false, because he spoke the unvarnished truth to those who had, in fact, denied the Son of God. We, by extension, are a part of that mob until we cling to Christ, like the healed man clung to Peter and John, praying that He will never let us go and that we will not lose our grip on Him. He alone is the Holy One, the Righteous One, the Prince of life itself.

11

SONS OF COVENANT

Acts 3:17–26

"Yet now, brethren, I know that you did it in ignorance, as did also your rulers. But those things which God foretold by the mouth of all His prophets, that the Christ would suffer, He has thus fulfilled. Repent therefore and be converted, that your sins may be blotted out, so that times of refreshing may come from the presence of the Lord, and that He may send Jesus Christ, who was preached to you before, whom heaven must receive until the times of restoration of all things, which God has spoken by the mouth of all His holy prophets since the world began. For Moses truly said to the fathers, 'The Lord your God will raise up for you a Prophet like me from your brethren. Him you shall hear in all things, whatever He says to you. And it shall be that every soul who will not hear that Prophet shall be utterly destroyed from among the people.' Yes, and all the prophets, from Samuel and those who follow, as many as have spoken, have also foretold these days. You are sons of the prophets, and of the covenant which God made with our fathers, saying to Abraham, 'And in your seed all the families of the earth shall be blessed.' To you first, God, having raised up His Servant Jesus, sent Him to bless you, in turning away every one of you from your iniquities."

The occasion for this second sermon of Peter's recorded in the book of Acts was the healing of a man who had been born unable to stand or walk. Peter and John encountered him by the Gate Beautiful as he was begging for alms. Peter said to him, "Silver and gold I do not have, but what I do have I give you: In the name of Jesus Christ of Nazareth, rise up and walk" (3:6). To the astonishment of all those assembled there in that portion of the temple, this man stood, walked, and began to leap and praise God while the crowd marveled and gathered around. Peter used that occasion to preach this sermon.

The sermon was a scorching denunciation of those who were gathered. Peter pointed a finger in their faces and said, "You are the very people who betrayed Christ, who delivered Him, screamed for His blood, and are guilty of His murder. By the power of that same Jesus, this man was made whole. It wasn't by my power or John's power. It was by the power of Jesus' name."

Ignorance

This was not the most politically correct, winsome, and persuasive sermon ever preached, but in the middle of this scathing denunciation of the people standing there, Peter mellowed for a moment and said, **"Yet now, brethren, I know that you did it in ignorance, as did also your rulers"** (v. 17). In other words, "I know that you murdered the Son of God, but I also know that you didn't know what you were doing." This brings to mind the prayer of our Lord in the very midst of His execution, when He prayed to the Father from the cross, "Father, forgive them, for they do not know what they do" (Luke 23:34). Elsewhere the Scriptures say, "Had they known, they would not have crucified the Lord of glory" (1 Cor. 2:8).

The Roman Catholic Church's historic moral theology distinguishes between two kinds of ignorance. One is called "vincible" ignorance and the other "invincible" ignorance. That which is vincible may be conquered or overpowered. That which is invincible cannot be defeated or overpowered. If I do something out of ignorance, in which I had no way of knowing what was right or wrong, that would be invincible ignorance, and that kind of ignorance would excuse me. On the other hand, if I did something out of ignorance for which there was plenty of knowledge or evidence available, but I ignored it, I cannot say, "I am sorry; I didn't know."

We can illustrate these two kinds of ignorance by means of traffic laws. Suppose I were to drive from Florida to Atlanta, Georgia, and while I am driving through the city of Atlanta, I fail to stop at a red light. A policeman pulls me over to issue me a ticket, and I ask, "Why did you pull me over?"

The policeman replies, "You went through a red light back there."

"What's wrong with that?" I ask.

"It's against the law to go through red lights. You have to stop at a red light."

I reply, "Well, I'm not from Georgia, so how would I know that? I didn't know that I had to stop for that red light."

The policeman notices from my driver's license that I reside in Florida, and he asks, "Don't you have to stop at a red light in Florida?"

"Yes," I answer, "but this isn't Florida; this is Georgia. How do you expect me to know the traffic laws here? I don't live here."

How will that excuse hold up when I go before the magistrate? The magistrate will say, "If you presume to drive your car in the state of Georgia, you are responsible to know the driving code, and it is readily available." I could claim ignorance in a case like that, but it would be vincible ignorance, which would not excuse me.

Conversely, suppose the city planners of Orlando are having a shortfall on their budget and they come up with a scheme to add a lot of revenue to the city treasury in a hurry. They decide that beginning tomorrow morning at 6 a.m. it is going to be illegal to proceed through a green light. Drivers have to stop on green and go on red, and there will be a fine for everybody caught going through a green light. The city planners decide to position traffic policemen at every intersection in Orlando to arrest everyone that goes through a green light. To ensure that they will rake in a lot of money, they decide not to publish the new law. So the next day I drive downtown and go through a green light, and I am pulled over and charged one hundred dollars for doing so. I go to the magistrate, who tells me I am guilty because the law says I have to stop at a green light. I had no idea about this secret law, and no possible way of knowing anything about it. In that case, my ignorance should excuse me. That kind of ignorance is what the church calls "invincible."

There are millions of people who are counting on their ignorance to get them past the judgment seat of God. "I never went to church. I never read the Bible. I never studied the things of God. How could you possibly hold me accountable?" That is vincible ignorance, which does not excuse, and it is the type of ignorance that characterized those who stood at the bottom of the cross and cried for the blood of Christ. Despite that, our Lord said, "Forgive them, for they do not know what they do" (Luke 23:34), and here in Acts Peter acknowledged that they had a chance to be forgiven if they would repent.

The Unforgivable Sin

I am asked frequently about the nature of the unforgivable sin. Many fear that they will commit this sin or that they might already have committed it. There is indeed an unforgivable sin, and our Lord warned His contemporaries about it. The occasion of that warning concerned those who had accused Jesus of being in league with the Devil (Matt. 12:22–32). Jesus put up with a lot of insults and hostility from His contemporaries, but at that point He drew a line in the sand and said, "Therefore I say to you, every sin and blasphemy will be forgiven men, but the blasphemy against the Spirit will not be forgiven men. Anyone who speaks a word against the Son of Man, it will be forgiven him; but whoever speaks against the Holy Spirit, it will not be forgiven him; either in this age or in the age to come" (vv. 31–32).

That is serious business, but why would Jesus say that sinning against Him is forgivable but sinning against the Holy Spirit is not? Is there something more egregious about sinning against the third person of the Trinity than against the second person or the first person? Almost everyone at some point in their life has blasphemed God by taking the Lord's name in vain. Blasphemy is something we do with our mouth; it is a verbal disrespect and dishonoring of Almighty God, whose name is protected in the Decalogue. If we have ever used the name of Christ or the Father as a curse word, flippantly, then maybe it is too late for us, because that is certainly blasphemy. Fortunately, Jesus makes a distinction between speaking against Him and speaking against the Holy Spirit.

There is a progression in redemptive history unfolded for us in Scripture. Later in the New Testament, particularly in the book of Hebrews, the distinction between sinning against the Son and sinning against the Spirit evaporates. When Jesus was killed, the people who were blaspheming Him really did not know what they were doing. That was Friday, but on Sunday, God raised Him from the dead. The point is this: if the Holy Spirit has convicted you of the truth of the identity of Jesus, you cannot call Him a devil with impunity.

I do not believe it is possible, because of the mercy of God, for any Christian ever to commit that sin, but here in Acts the crowd came perilously close to it. Peter took his listeners through the Scriptures, the Old Testament, reminding them of their heritage as Jews, children of Abraham, descendants of Moses, inheritors of the covenant. Nevertheless, Peter says, "I know that you did it in ignorance, as did also your rulers" (v. 17).

I listen to people blaspheme God every day, and I think, "If they only knew. If they had any idea how offensive this is to God, they would rather die than talk like this." They do not know. Should they know? Yes, they should know, but there is hope if they do not know. Our culture twists this truth to say that God loves everyone despite their ignorance and sin. That is the way we preach today, but it is not how Peter preached. **"But those things which God foretold by the mouth of all His prophets, that the Christ would suffer, He has thus fulfilled. Repent therefore and be converted, that your sins may be blotted out"** (vv. 18–19).

Aren't you glad that pencils come with erasers? Every morning I do two crossword puzzles, and I refuse to use anything but a pen. You ought to see the mess that I make out of the morning paper with my pen because I do not have anything to erase my errors. Can you imagine God erasing every sin that you have ever committed? If we are in Christ, we have found the place of forgiveness. We have found the One who will remove our sins, blot out our transgressions, and erase the writing on the wall against each one of us, but the only way those sins are erased is if we humble ourselves, acknowledge our sins, and turn from them. We must repent of our sins and come before God with a broken and contrite heart. Forgiveness by God is not automatic.

The grace taught in this day and age is cheap. People claim that God automatically forgives everybody; but so long as you remain impenitent, as long as you refuse to confess your sins before Him, He will not forgive you. That is why Peter said, "I know you didn't know it, but you should have known it because it was taught ages ago."

Conviction

Years ago I went with two elders of my church to an apartment in Cincinnati while I was working with Evangelism Explosion. A woman invited us in. One of the elders began to tell her the gospel, but she stopped him in mid-sentence and said, "I've heard that a thousand times, so please, don't waste my time or yours." I interrupted her and said, "I don't deny that you have heard this before, but could it possibly hurt you to hear it one more time?" She acquiesced, so I picked up where the elder had left off, and I finished the gospel presentation. I didn't ask her to make a response. I didn't do anything. I just thanked her for letting me finish and for being polite enough to let us in her house, and we left.

Six months later she appeared in the new members' class at my church. She recounted our visit to her apartment and then said, "As soon as those men walked out the door, I went to my bedroom and fell apart. I flooded the room with my tears because for the first time I really got it, and my sins were forgiven." She had heard the gospel, but she hadn't known it. She had never been brought to repentance and experienced the erasing of her sin. Many go faithfully to church and Bible study, and they hear the message, but it has never embedded in their soul. There is a price for forgiveness. We have to lay ourselves bare before God and say, "God, be merciful to me, a sinner." Then comes the promise of forgiveness.

Peter then quoted Moses: **"For Moses truly said to the fathers, 'The Lord your God will raise up for you a Prophet like me from your brethren. Him you shall hear in all things, whatever He says to you'"** (v. 22). This takes us to the Mount of Transfiguration, when Moses and Elijah appeared with Jesus. The glory of Christ shone through the veil of Jesus' humanity, and the disciples fell on their faces in terror before them. The glory cloud surrounded them, and they heard a voice from heaven, which said, "This is My beloved Son. . . . Hear Him" (Matt. 17:5). That was Peter's point in this sermon here in Acts: "This is the Son of God. Listen to Him, because if you don't, your sins will not be erased, and your ignorance will not save you."

In our next study we will see the response to Peter's sermon. Whenever the gospel is preached, the response is divided, and it was no different with Peter's audience. A mass of people fled to the gospel, embraced Christ, and had their sins forgiven, while the rulers arrested Peter and John.

12

NO OTHER NAME

Acts 4:1–12

Now as they spoke to the people, the priests, the captain of the temple, and the Sadducees came upon them, being greatly disturbed that they taught the people and preached in Jesus the resurrection from the dead. And they laid hands on them, and put them in custody until the next day, for it was already evening. However, many of those who heard the word believed; and the number of the men came to be about five thousand. And it came to pass, on the next day, that their rulers, elders, and scribes, as well as Annas the high priest, Caiaphas, John, and Alexander, and as many as were of the family of the high priest, were gathered together at Jerusalem. And when they had set them in the midst, they asked, "By what power or by what name have you done this?" Then Peter, filled with the Holy Spirit, said to them, "Rulers of the people and elders of Israel: If we this day are judged for a good deed done to a helpless man, by what means he has been made well, let it be known to you all, and to all the people of Israel, that by the name of Jesus Christ of Nazareth, whom you crucified, whom God raised from the dead, by Him this man stands here before you whole. This is the 'stone which was rejected by you builders, which has become the chief cornerstone.' Nor is there salvation in any other, for there is no other name under heaven given among men by which we must be saved."

I need to put a warning label on the bottle, as it were, because there are things in this passage that some might find jarring and others might even find offensive. If you come to the text assuming that what you are about to read is simply the ancient opinions of first-century Christians, which opinions may indeed be biased and not worthy of your consideration, you may easily dismiss these jarring portions. If, on the other hand, you come to the reading of this text already persuaded that it is nothing less than the unvarnished Word of God and yet you still find offense with it, then, of course, that would mean something quite different—it would be time for an urgent glance at the state of your soul. If we are offended by what the Lord God Almighty speaks, then certainly the problem is not with Him but with us.

Tolerance

It seems that every month or so a poll is released that tells us what contemporary Christians believe and what they are practicing. I am not always that impressed by these polls because the way in which people are identified as "evangelical" or as "born again" is usually quite loose and ambiguous, as is the way in which the inquiries are worded. In my estimation, many such polls are not bathed in precision by any means. Nevertheless, the general trends they indicate are of some interest to me. The net result of a recent survey was that the vast majority of people who call themselves evangelical Christians in our society do not embrace a Christian worldview; that is, they have a religious inclination toward the person of Jesus, but their thinking is not informed by what Jesus or the Apostles taught. Rather, their thinking and behavior have been saturated in the tenets of secularism.

There is no tenet more basic to contemporary secular culture than that of religious tolerance. Our country was based on the principle that people of all religious creeds and backgrounds are welcome on our shores and are to be accorded the freedom of religious expression so that all religions are equally tolerated under the law. Today, however, the assumption of the secularist is that all religions are not only to be equally tolerated under the law but are equally valid (or invalid). The American truth today is that what you believe does not matter so long as you are sincere, and there are many roads that go to heaven. Some go directly and some by a more circuitous route, but in the final analysis, all that God is really concerned about is that we be people of faith. I cannot think of a principle more plainly and categorically opposed to the universal teaching of sacred Scripture—both Old and New Testaments—than that idea.

If I know anything about the nature of God from the Scriptures, it is this: God hates religion, if what we mean by "religion" are the systems and practices that we invent with our own minds and hands. The primary sin of fallen humanity, as Paul tells us in Romans 1, is that we universally take the plain, manifest revelation of God and exchange that truth for a lie and turn our attention to idols. For that, we expose ourselves to God's unmitigated and just wrath, because to trade in His glory for an idol is the supreme insult to His holiness. The only other insult that comes close is to mention the name of His only begotten Son in the same breath with that of Buddha or Confucius or Muhammad, who are idols, not sons of the living God. Nevertheless, there is nothing in our culture today more intolerable than exclusivity, than to meet with the Christian assertion that there is only one way to God. Only a handful of professing Christians in our culture will stand up publicly and say there is only one way to God and that way is through Christ. The rest, by denying that principle, are guilty of nothing less than treason to the Son of God.

Only One Way

One of my college professors had been a war correspondent, and she was openly hostile against Christianity. She knew I was a Christian, and one day in the middle of class she said to me, "Mr. Sproul, do you think that Jesus is the only way to God?"

Everyone turned and looked at me; they couldn't wait to hear how I would answer.

I thought, "What do I do now? If I say, 'No, I don't believe that He is the only way,' I will publicly deny Him. If I say, 'Yes, He is the only way,' then the wrath of the teacher is likely to descend on me, and I'll know the scorn of my classmates." So, cleverly, I answered with my hand in front of my mouth, "Yes." I mumbled my reply, hardly like Luther at the Diet of Worms.

She said, "Speak up! I didn't hear what you said. Do you believe that Jesus is the only way to God?" I had to face the music. I said, "Yes, Ma'am, I do."

She looked at me and replied, "That's the most bigoted, outrageous, narrow-minded, arrogant statement I've ever heard in my life." I sank down into the chair in an attempt to find protection.

She finished the class, and as we were leaving she stood at the door. She had mellowed a bit after publicly humiliating me. As I passed, she said, "I guess I was a little rough on you today. It wasn't nice to do."

I said, "Yes, Ma'am, you were."

"I'm sorry," she said. "I just can't believe how any intelligent person could be so narrow and bigoted as you are."

I said, "Can you believe that I could be foolish enough, even though I'm educated, to come to the conviction that Jesus is at least one way to God?"

"Yes, I can understand that," she said.

I told her what Jesus said, "I am the way, the truth, and the life. No one comes to the Father except through me" (John 14:6), and then I asked her, "What could be more arrogant than a disciple of Jesus challenging his Lord's teaching on the way of salvation? I believe it because He said it."

"Yes, I see that," she said, "but I still don't get it. How can you believe in such a narrow God?"

I said, "For the sake of argument, suppose that once upon a time there was nothing, no universe; the only thing in existence was God Himself. So God created everything, and from all the creatures He made, He took one—man—and stamped Him with His divine image. He blessed mankind and called them to mirror His righteousness. Yet soon after, they believed the Serpent, who gave them the promise that they would be as great as God. They were involved in cosmic revolt from the outset. Wouldn't God have been perfectly just to simply destroy all of mankind?"

She said, "I suppose so."

"But He didn't do that," I continued. "Instead, He gave them a promise of mercy and forgiveness. He promised a Messiah who would come and bear their sins for them. Later He called the people out of darkness, out of slavery. They had become impotent before the mightiest ruler in the world, the pharaoh, but God made them His people and gave them His law, the first of which is exclusive: 'You shall have no other gods before me.' Later they bowed before the Baal and the Ashtoreth and all the rest of the pagan deities of their day, but still God didn't destroy them. Instead, He sent them His prophets and called them to come back to Him, as a father calls a wayward child to come back. But they greeted the prophets with stones, and they killed them. Finally, to show His great love, God sent the eternal second person of the Trinity, His only begotten Son, and let Him take on the cloak of human flesh and live in the midst of this corruption and endure the punishment on the cross that the whole world deserved. He offered His only Son to people who were hostile toward Him, and the people killed His Son. Nevertheless, God said that if you'll just put your trust in His Son and honor Him, then He will forgive every sin you have ever committed. He will give you everlasting life in a place where death is exiled, in a place where there is no night, no sin, no pain, and no harm. He will give you joy and happiness such as no creature has ever contemplated. All you have to do is honor His Son and Him alone."

I told all that to my teacher, and then I asked her, "After hearing all that, could you still stand before God and say, 'That's a very nice story, but what's the big deal about Jesus? You haven't done enough. Why didn't You give us twenty saviors? Why should it bother You whether I put my trust and devotion and admiration and adoration on Christ or on Muhammad?'"

Would any of us ever dare to say before Almighty God, "You haven't done enough"? This is what Peter's speech was about that day at the temple when the highest court of Israel sat in judgment on the Apostles and said, **"By what power or by what name have you done this?"** (v. 7). Peter replied, **"Rulers of the people and elders of Israel: If we this day are judged for a good deed done to a helpless man, by what means he has been made well, let it be known to you all, and to all the people of Israel, that by the name of Jesus Christ of Nazareth, whom you crucified, whom God raised from the dead, by Him this man stands here before you whole"** (vv. 8–10).

The Apostles had healed by the name of Jesus of Nazareth, the One whom the people had crucified but whom God had raised from the dead. Why? So that all Israel might know that this is the only name there is under heaven through which men may be saved. If you are a Christian, you should be prepared to die for that affirmation. If you are not, you are playing at religion, and you have missed the Son of God.

13

OBEYING GOD OR MAN

Acts 4:13–22

Now when they saw the boldness of Peter and John, and perceived that they were uneducated and untrained men, they marveled. And they realized that they had been with Jesus. And seeing the man who had been healed standing with them, they could say nothing against it. But when they had commanded them to go aside out of the council, they conferred among themselves, saying, "What shall we do to these men? For, indeed, that a notable miracle has been done through them is evident to all who dwell in Jerusalem, and we cannot deny it. But so that it spreads no further among the people, let us severely threaten them, that from now on they speak to no man in this name." So they called them and commanded them not to speak at all nor teach in the name of Jesus. But Peter and John answered and said to them, "Whether it is right in the sight of God to listen to you more than to God, you judge. For we cannot but speak the things which we have seen and heard." So when they had further threatened them, they let them go, finding no way of punishing them, because of the people, since they all glorified God for what had been done. For the man was over forty years old on whom this miracle of healing had been performed.

Anytime someone is introduced as famous, it seems to be unnecessary; if he is famous, he should not have to be introduced. Yet we never know how far our influence extends; sometimes we are surprised. One of the most shocking and surprising experiences of my life came on the day when Lech

Walesa, the leader of the Polish Solidarity Movement, was placed under house arrest by Soviet officials in Poland. The picture of his arrest was on the front page of every newspaper in America. When he was arrested, he was shaking his fists in defiance of the arresting authorities, and in his hand he was holding one of my books. I recall thinking how incredible that was. I later found out he had placed that same book in the casket of his father.

I never would have dreamed that anything I had written would find its way into the hands of Lech Walesa. It made me think about his position in modern history. "Why was the government at that time interested in arresting him? Why didn't they just execute him?" That is usually the way it works; tyrannical governments always have a secret police. They find a way to get rid of those in opposition to them, usually by some form of execution. I realized that the reason Lech Walesa was put under house arrest rather than executed was that he had already become too well known; to kill him would have made him a martyr, and the thing that every tyrannical regime fears more than anything else is a public uprising.

The Christian and the State

Back in the eighteenth century the philosopher Montesquieu, when he wrote his book *The Spirit of the Laws*, said that the maintenance of all forms of tyranny depends upon the ability of the government to keep the people afraid. That is why there are purges and secret police and mass executions in nations with that sort of regime. Montesquieu said that it only takes one person, one Lech Walesa with enough courage to withstand the tyrant, to bring down a powerful regime. Throughout history individuals have swum against the current and withstood powerful obstacles. Mahatma Gandhi was one. In our own country, Martin Luther King stood against the authorities of his day. He defied those authorities and raised questions about the legitimacy of civil disobedience.

In the middle of the eighteenth century in the little town of Northampton, Massachusetts, Jonathan Edwards was a preacher. The town was divided between loyalty to the crown and loyalty to their local magistrates. The division over those loyalties was felt all over New England. There were Christians on both sides of that debate.

Some insisted that it is never legitimate for anyone under any circumstance to disobey the civil magistrate. They felt exploited by the taxation coming from Parliament in England, but they refused to rebel or to join in the rebellion because the Bible teaches that it is the Christian's duty to submit to those in authority over us, whether children to their parents, students to their teachers, employees to their employer, or citizens to their government. Where we find levels of authority over us, the Bible calls us to be model citizens of submission. Out of that principle of submission to the civil magistrate, Mary and Joseph made the arduous journey to Bethlehem, risking the lives of both Mary and the unborn infant Jesus. In deep affliction and inconvenience they made the journey to obey the authorities. Repeatedly in Scripture we find the principle of submission to those in authority.

However, a question always arises: Is it ever legitimate to refuse to obey authorities? We are going to consider that in light of Acts 4:13–22. A man born unable to stand or walk had been healed by Peter and John by the Beautiful Gate, and many people, including those in authority, had witnessed it. **Now when they saw the boldness of Peter and John, and perceived that they were uneducated and untrained men, they marveled** (v. 13). They marveled, obviously, at the eloquence of Peter as he spoke on this occasion. This brings to mind the promise of Jesus to His disciples before He left this world: "When they arrest you and deliver you up, do not worry beforehand, or premeditate what you will speak. But whatever is given you in that hour, speak that; for it is not you who speak, but the Holy Spirit" (Mark 13:11). So these men believed that promise of God, and in the face of adversity and opposition, Peter spoke with boldness so that the whole Sanhedrin, seventy-one of them, along with the people were amazed.

And they realized that they had been with Jesus (v. 13). How many times have people said of you, "I can tell that you've been spending time with Jesus"? People talk about my connection to the Steelers or the Penguins or to the Irish, but nobody says, "Oh, he must have just been with Jesus." But they made that connection with Peter and John. The events that had transpired so recently in Jerusalem still resonated in their ears so that it was clear to them that these men belonged to the group that had followed Jesus.

And seeing the man who had been healed standing with them, they could say nothing against it (v. 14). Actually, they could have said anything they wanted to against it, but Luke is saying that they did not dare publicly say anything against it. No one from the Sanhedrin, the Scribes, the Pharisees, or the Sadducees was going to come out and say, "That's enough. Stop this healing. No more miracles!" They didn't dare say that because of the multitudes gathered there.

Holy Allegiance

But when they had commanded them to go aside out of the council, they conferred among themselves, saying, "What shall we do to these men?" (v. 15). The authorities had to do something because they saw the situation growing beyond their control, which is why they said, **"For, indeed, that a**

notable miracle has been done through them is evident to all who dwell in Jerusalem, and we cannot deny it" (v. 16). Here are the enemies of the Apostles, conferring among themselves and basically saying, "Well, what are we going to do now? The whole city knows that a miracle has taken place, and everybody is cheering them on." We see here the wickedness in the hearts of fallen people who, when they know that the manifest power of God has been given right before their very eyes, form a conspiracy to squelch it. That is what they were doing.

This is what they decided: **"So that it spreads no further among the people, let us severely threaten them, that from now on they speak to no man in this name." So they called them and commanded them not to speak at all nor teach in the name of Jesus** (vv. 17–18). Peter and John were in the worst possible ethical conflict, one between ruling authorities. Children ask their mother if they can go to a movie, and when the mother says no, they go ask the father instead. They attempt to set one authority against the other. It rarely works because the father usually says, "Go ask your mother."

Consider soldiers who had participated in genocide and later went on trial for their war crimes at Nuremberg. When the court interrogated them, they all said, "I was only obeying orders." The court refused to uphold that excuse and said the soldiers were required to disobey the magistrate rather than commit genocide.

Martin Luther King knew the law. He knew that any statute published by any state in the United States was challengeable by the Supreme Court if it violated constitutional rights, and so with passive resistance he went ahead and broke the law in order to get before the Supreme Court, a right provided to him by the higher magistrate with respect to the lesser magistrate.

The conflict of such situations at times can be unbearable. Here is how the Apostles handled it: **"Whether it is right in the sight of God to listen to you more than to God, you judge"** (v. 19). Only a few weeks had gone by since the Apostles had heard the words of Jesus that we call the Great Commission: "Go therefore and make disciples of all the nations, baptizing them in the name of the Father and of the Son and of the Holy Spirit" (Matt. 28:19). Jesus gave to Peter and to John and to the entire church of the first century a mandate. It is our mandate too. If any authority under heaven comes to the Christian and tells him he may not pray, or preach, or worship, or tithe, or do any of the things God commands, that Christian not only may disobey, but he must disobey.

In the ethics class offered at our seminary, we provide a simple principle. It is simple in the sense that anybody can understand it; however, the application of it to concrete circumstances is often excruciatingly difficult. The principle is this: we are always to obey those in authority over us, unless that authority commands us to do something that God forbids, or forbids us from doing something that God commands.

If a husband says to his wife, "I want you to earn some extra income for us by turning to prostitution," not only may she disobey him, but she must disobey him. Conversely, if a woman is married to an unbelieving man who says to her, "You may not go to church on Wednesday night and join the choir," what should the wife do? She should stay home, because God nowhere commands women to sing in the choir. I plead for it, but I cannot command it. But if the husband says to his wife, "You are not permitted to go to church on the Sabbath and join the corporate worship of the people of God," not only may she disobey him, but she must disobey him, because God commands her to be in the assembly of the saints.

Submission or Defiance?

As you can see, applying this principle can be painful and very costly when we are caught in this vice between two differing authorities. We can never use the excuse "I'm just obeying orders" as a license or an excuse for sin. The other side of it is this: just because God gives us the right and responsibility to disobey when an authority over us commands us to do something He forbids or forbids us from doing something He commands, that is not a license to be disobedient whenever we happen to disagree with the authority or whenever the authority is exploiting or afflicting us and bringing discomfort or inconvenience. Joseph and Mary were inconvenienced when making that arduous journey to Bethlehem, but they submitted, because God never commanded that Joseph and Mary be comfortable or wealthy or popular.

The general principle is that we bend over backwards to be submissive, but we stand with ramrod defiance when the magistrate commands disobedience to God. That is why it is very important for us to understand, in our daily lives, what God commands and what He forbids; otherwise, we are like sheep without a shepherd, and we go along with what Nietzsche called a "herd morality," doing whatever anybody tells us to do, when, in fact, there are times the Christian has to say no. There is a reason why the blood of the church became the seed of its growth in the first century—the many who would not submit to the tyrants who told them to deny faith in Christ. With Job we have to say, "Though He slay me, yet will I trust Him" (Job 13:15). I urge you to be prepared for that time when you have to choose obedience to those who command sin or obedience to Christ.

14

HOLY BOLDNESS

Acts 4:23–31

And being let go, they went to their own companions and reported all that the chief priests and elders had said to them. So when they heard that, they raised their voice to God with one accord and said: "Lord, You are God, who made heaven and earth and the sea, and all that is in them, who by the mouth of Your servant David have said:

'Why did the nations rage,
And the people plot vain things?
The kings of the earth took their stand,
And the rulers were gathered together
Against the Lord and against His Christ.'

"For truly against Your holy Servant Jesus, whom You anointed, both Herod and Pontius Pilate, with the Gentiles and the people of Israel, were gathered together to do whatever Your hand and Your purpose determined before to be done. Now, Lord, look on their threats, and grant to Your servants that with all boldness they may speak Your word, by stretching out Your hand to heal, and that signs and wonders may be done through the name of Your holy Servant Jesus." And when they had prayed, the place where they were assembled together was shaken; and they were all filled with the Holy Spirit, and they spoke the word of God with boldness.

I f you remember your grammar from elementary school, you know that we decline nouns, not personal adjectives, but I believe it was George Bernard Shaw who invented the idea of the declension of personal adjectives. Here is the way it works: "I am confident, you are cocky, and he is arrogant." Another way to do it is this: "I am bold, you are brash, and she is foolhardy." When we describe ourselves, we tend to choose adjectives that sound virtuous, but when the same property is manifested in somebody else, we tend to diminish the virtue of it. That is what Shaw had in mind.

Boldness

Thus far in our study of the book of Acts, an adjective repeated frequently has to do with the boldness of Peter and John and the early church. In the New Testament, boldness is an attribute of virtue, an attribute that is to mark the life of the church in every generation. We see that worked out in the text. **Being let go, they went to their own companions and reported all that the chief priests and elders had said to them** (v. 23). Peter and John had been commanded to speak no more in the name of Jesus, and they had responded by saying, "Whether it is right in the sight of God to listen to you more than to God, you judge" (v. 19). They made it clear that they were not going to submit to that ruling, but in fear of the people, the Sanhedrin let John and Peter go.

They went back to the early church and reported all that the chief priests and elders had said to them. **So when they heard that, they raised their voice to God with one accord and said: "Lord, You are God"** (v. 24). What could be more obvious than that, and why were they saying it? They were acknowledging that although they had just been before the highest authority in the land, the Lord is God, the One worthy of adoration and highest submission.

Psalm 2

"Who by the mouth of Your servant David have said: 'Why did the nations rage, and the people plot vain things? The kings of the earth took their stand, and the rulers were gathered together against the LORD and against His Christ'" (vv. 25–26). Immediately, in the midst of their prayer, they were reminded of the Word of God that came to Israel through the lips or the pen of David in Psalm 2. The psalm begins with a question: "Why do the nations rage, and the people plot a vain thing? The kings of the earth set themselves, and the rulers take counsel together, against the LORD and against His Anointed" (vv. 1–2). Described in Psalm 2 is a summit meeting of the most powerful rulers in the world about those who refused to submit to the dominion and reign of God. "Let us break Their bonds in pieces and cast away Their cords from us"

(v. 3). This was separation of state from God with a vengeance. David predicted that there would be an international conspiracy, one not limited to a particular country or group but one in which the rulers from all over the world would assemble together in defiance against the lordship of God Almighty and against His anointed Son.

When David describes this scene of the summit meeting of the enemies of God, we are told that the Lord sits in the heavens and laughs. He looks at the assembly of all the power and might of the kings of the world as they gather together and aim their arrows against Christ. He is amused at first with the power and the strength of these kings, and He makes fun of them. "The Lord shall hold them in derision" (v. 4), David said, but only for a moment, because God's amusement turns to wrath, and He says, "You shall break them with a rod of iron; You shall dash them to pieces like a potter's vessel" (v. 9). The latest generation of tanks will be scooped up by God in His hand, and He will turn it over and crush it against the ground. He warns them, "Kiss the Son, lest He be angry, and you perish in the way" (v. 12).

The Sovereign God

John and Peter went back to the people of God and told them what had happened, and they began to praise God, and they remembered what David had said about the rulers of the world taking counsel together. **"For truly against Your holy Servant Jesus, whom You anointed, both Herod and Pontius Pilate, with the Gentiles and the people of Israel, were gathered together to do whatever Your hand and Your purpose determined before to be done"** (vv. 27–28).

The early church had no debates about Calvinism and Arminianism. There wasn't an Arminian to be found in the early church. Every Christian believed in the sovereignty of God, and they believed in it absolutely. They never negotiated the sovereignty of God, because Jesus revealed exactly who God is and the power of the Almighty against all the machinations of the people of the world. The early church saw all the displays of power on the part of the ruling authorities as nothing. Just a few weeks before this, God's Son had been delivered into their hands for execution, but it had all been decreed beforehand by God. Our Lord Jesus would not have suffered a scratch through the conspiracy of human enemies against Him were it not for the determinant counsel of the Father, who ordained from all eternity that the Son should suffer at the hands of these wicked men for our sake.

Those in the early church understood that despite all the antagonistic actions of those authorities, God was still sovereign. God was still in control. That is why they said, **"Now, Lord, look on their threats, and grant to Your servants that with all boldness they may speak Your word, by stretching out Your hand to heal, and that signs and wonders may be done through the name of Your holy Servant Jesus." And when they had prayed, the place where they were assembled together was shaken; and they were all filled with the Holy Spirit, and they spoke the word of God with boldness** (vv. 29–31).

The character of the first-century Christian church was marked repeatedly with unparalleled boldness. Yet, just a matter of weeks before this moment, when the lanterns were appearing in the garden of Gethsemane as the soldiers came to arrest Jesus, His disciples fled in panic. At Calvary when Christ was being executed, John and Mary were there, but where were the rest of them? Peter had been huddling in a corner, cursing, denying that he ever met Jesus.

Resurrection Courage

When the book of Revelation speaks of the final judgment of God, it mentions those whom God will send into the lake of fire—murderers, adulterers, and cowards. If anything marks the church at the beginning of the twenty-first century, it is cowardliness. If anything describes the difference between us and the first-century church, it is our lack of boldness. Yet we see in Acts a sudden transformation. Just a few days before, the Apostles had been in the upper room hiding, cowering, terrified, locking the doors for fear of the Jews, and now here they are, standing up against the highest authority in the land without fear. Two things had happened: the resurrection and Pentecost.

The resurrection galvanized the faith of the early church. When they saw the risen Christ, when they saw His victory over death and over His enemies, when He burst alive from the tomb, a faith was born in the breasts of the Apostles and the disciples that the whole world could not extinguish. Adding to the power of that faith was the power of Pentecost, in which God the Holy Spirit came upon them, and they began to proclaim the Word of God fearlessly to the whole world.

I remember a time during my college days when it was announced on the Jack Paar television program that Billy Graham would be his guest. All the Christians on campus gathered to the one television set in the dorm where we could watch the late-night program. Jack Paar, in his inimitable fashion, wanted to speak frivolously and be silly with Billy and said, "I guess you're here tonight to try to save my soul and try to straighten my life out. You're probably going to try to get me to repent."

Billy smiled and said, "Well, Jack, have you thought about repenting? You know you need to, and, yes, I am concerned about your soul because without Jesus, Jack, you're going to perish." I could hardly believe what I was hearing.

Billy Graham wasn't nasty or insensitive, but he was bold before the whole nation. He wasn't going to be manipulated into being silent about the truth of Christ.

Where is that boldness among us? I am not advocating a brash, foolhardy, obnoxious, or offensive approach. I am saying that we need to be done with cowardliness and proclaim the gospel with the boldness that characterizes a Christian who has been persuaded of the resurrection of Christ and the defeat of death. We can have the same change in us that was in these men who went from fearful infidels to valorous saints.

15

LYING DONORS

Acts 4:32–5:11

Now the multitude of those who believed were of one heart and one soul; neither did anyone say that any of the things he possessed was his own, but they had all things in common. And with great power the Apostles gave witness to the resurrection of the Lord Jesus. And great grace was upon them all. Nor was there anyone among them who lacked; for all who were possessors of lands or houses sold them, and brought the proceeds of the things that were sold, and laid them at the Apostles' feet; and they distributed to each as anyone had need. And Joses, who was also named Barnabas by the Apostles (which is translated Son of Encouragement), a Levite of the country of Cyprus, having land, sold it, and brought the money and laid it at the Apostles' feet. But a certain man named Ananias, with Sapphira his wife, sold a possession. And he kept back part of the proceeds, his wife also being aware of it, and brought a certain part and laid it at the Apostles' feet. But Peter said, "Ananias, why has Satan filled your heart to lie to the Holy Spirit and keep back part of the price of the land for yourself? While it remained, was it not your own? And after it was sold, was it not in your own control? Why have you conceived this thing in your heart? You have not lied to men but to God." Then Ananias, hearing these words, fell down and breathed his last. So great fear came upon all those who heard these things. And the young men arose and wrapped him up, carried him out, and buried him. Now it was about three hours later when his wife came in, not knowing what had happened. And Peter answered her, "Tell me whether you sold the land for so much?" She said, "Yes, for so much." Then Peter said to her, "How is it that you have agreed together to test the Spirit of the Lord? Look, the feet of those who have buried your husband are at the door, and they will carry you out." Then immediately she fell down at his feet and breathed her last. And the young men came in and found her dead, and carrying her out, buried her by her husband. So great fear came upon all the church and upon all who heard these things.

The Bible says that "God loves a cheerful giver" (2 Cor. 9:7). We have heard that verse so many times that we have become inoculated to the weight of the insight. If we will but pause to reconsider it, we will see that God takes delight when He sees His people bringing their tithes and offerings to Him cheerfully. God is pleased when our giving is a response of indescribable gratitude for the good and perfect gifts we have received from Him. Everything we have comes from His hand, so how could we possibly be anything but cheerful givers? The fact that God loves the cheerful giver implies that He is not particularly pleased with the reluctant giver, and the text that we read in this study indicates that He is furious at the lying giver.

Ananias and Sapphira

To understand the text, we must read between the lines. As we learned in our study of Acts 2, in the early church there was a commonality of possessions, but the sharing was voluntary. People were excited to be caught up in the mission of the church and to be recipients of all God had poured out on them, which made them willing to part with anything they had in order to increase the kingdom. They sold their homes and lands and gave the proceeds to help the poor—anything to bear witness to Christ—but it wasn't required of any.

In the text before us now we see a man who sold his land, and he gave every cent of the profits for distribution among the people. His name was Barnabas, and he was called the Son of Encouragement. The New Testament paints a lovely portrait of Barnabas. He was quick to bring comfort and consolation to those in pain, and he did whatever was in his means to alleviate others' problems. He sold what he had and cheerfully laid it at the feet of the Apostles. In contrast to him we find the conspiracy of Ananias and Sapphira, who together contrived a scheme to sell their property and give part of the proceeds to the church but keep some for themselves.

Peter said to them, **"Ananias, why has Satan filled your heart to lie to the Holy Spirit and keep back part of the price of the land for yourself? While it remained, was it not your own? And after it was sold, was it not in your own control? Why have you conceived this thing in your heart? You have not lied to men but to God"** (vv. 3–4). Peter makes clear that they were not required to do what Barnabas had done, namely, to give all the proceeds from the sale of their property to the people of God. Therefore, their sin was not in holding back some of the funds but in the pretense, the hypocrisy. They lied to the church. They lied to God. They lied to the Holy Spirit. They pretended that they were giving the full amount when they were not. Giving gifts to God is sacred business, and to taint a gift to the Lord by concealing it in the package of a lie is a kind of blasphemy against the sanctity of God. So, again, Ananias and Sapphira were killed not because they failed to give everything to God but because they lied about their gift.

This raises a question about the concept of stewardship and tithing and the giving of gifts, a discussion I will begin with a story about two pieces of currency, a one-hundred-dollar bill and a one-dollar bill. The one-hundred- dollar bill said to the one-dollar bill, "You wouldn't believe the places I've been. I've been in five-star hotels all over the world. I've eaten in the finest restaurants. I've dined with kings and queens and prime ministers and presidents all around the world." The one-dollar bill was overwhelmed by all this and said, "I've never had the opportunity to be with kings and queens. I've never been in a five-star hotel. I've never eaten in a five-star restaurant, but I can tell you this: I'm in church every Sunday morning."

Myths about Tithing

There are a host of myths that surround the question of giving and tithing, and I want to mention three of them. The first myth, one I hear frequently in the church, is that tithing was an Old Testament principle that has no bearing upon the Christian community today. By divine mandate the people of Israel were required to bring to the Lord 10 percent of their annual earnings, their increase for the year, in addition to other offerings that were to be given from time to time. By divine law, every person in the community was expected to give 10 percent of their income cheerfully. Something beautiful about this system was that everyone was required to give not the same amount but the same percentage.

That is why we see Jesus speaking of the woman who gives the widow's mite (Mark 12; Luke 21). She had hardly two pieces of wood to rub together, but she made sure that she gave her penny to the work of God's kingdom. Jesus rebuked the Pharisees, who were so scrupulous about tithing. They gave their mint and cumin; if they found a dollar bill on the sidewalk, they would make sure to put a dime in the collection plate at the temple. But, Jesus said, "[You] have neglected the weightier matters of the law: justice and mercy" (Matt. 23:23). Jesus saw the tithe as part of the Law of God—not the most important part, but it was expected from everybody. Therefore, one's bringing his 10 percent was nothing to boast about because one was only doing his duty.

A poll taken a few years ago indicated that only 4 percent of Americans who call themselves "born-again Christians" are tithers. The other 96 percent may give but not to the level of the tithe. Many years ago I saw a campaign brochure designed to raise the level of giving in a particular church denomination. The campaign slogan was "Take a step toward tithing." What we ought to be saying is "Take a step *from* tithing." The tithe is indeed an Old Testament principle, but it is nowhere abrogated in the New Testament. Besides, the New Testament labors the point that the benefits of the new covenant are far greater than the benefits of the old covenant, so if people in the old covenant were required to give 10 percent back to God, how much greater is the responsibility of those who live under the benefits of the new covenant?

The principle of tithing should be a no-brainer for the Christian. It is something that all Christians ought to do, and if they are not doing it, they ought to move heaven and earth to start. If they are not tithing, as we are told in the book of Malachi, they are robbing God. They are stealing from God. So the first myth is that tithing does not apply to us today.

The second myth is that all one's tithe has to go to his or her local church. The idea comes from the Old Testament. When the tithes were brought in, they were brought into a central place, the storehouse, and then distributed to the Levites for the work of the temple and other ministries. Theirs was an agrarian society in which the tithe consisted of produce and livestock, all of which was brought to the storehouse for distribution. From that, the idea arose that the central place is now the local church. Why do it that way? If we are going to follow the pattern of Israel, where all the gifts come to one place, why don't we send our tithes and gifts to our denominational headquarters instead and let the monies be distributed from there? I have yet to hear a minister propose that.

Israel was a theocratic state. They had only one church, the temple, a central sanctuary. One tribe among them was consecrated to do both the worship and the teaching. All religious education and worship was undertaken by the Levites, and they were to be supported by the tithes of the other tribes. In keeping with that, maybe what we ought to do in America is to ask the federal government to create a new bureau where all Christian tithes and offerings will go, and the bureau can distribute the monies, some to Baptists, some to Pentecostals, some to independents, and some to Presbyterians. How many of us would vote for that?

Today, not all the ministry of the kingdom of God is done in the local church. We cannot have ministers ordained or educated without seminaries, Christian colleges, and other specified ministries that support them, and all such organizations are dependent upon the gifts of donors. Some suggest that churches should support seminaries and Christian colleges, but I cannot think of a single seminary in America that would continue to have its doors open if it depended solely upon gifts from churches.

I believe that the lion's share of our tithe should be given to our local church, but I also believe that it is perfectly legitimate to designate a portion of our tithe for the support of other Christian ministries that need our help. We find that principle set forth in the *Didache*, one of the earliest books of the Christian community. Some practical advice given in the *Didache* is this: "Let your donations sweat in your hand." It does not say, "Let your donation freeze in your hand so that you never give it." The point is, hold on to it until you have given careful scrutiny to where you are going to give the gift. But sooner or later it has got to come out of your hand and into the work of the Lord.

The third myth, the one you hear more than any other, is that some cannot afford to tithe. Yet the poorest among us is living at a higher standard than 99 percent of all people in every era since the beginning of the world. How can we, who have been blessed with so many creature comforts, stand up before God and say, "I can't afford it"?

Let me translate that myth into real terms. "I can't afford it" really means "I cannot tithe and still do all the things I am doing now." Yes, that is true. Obviously, if you are giving only 2 percent and you increase that giving by 8 percent, you are going to feel it. But when you say, "I can't afford it," what you mean is, "I can't afford to do everything else that I'm doing and move my giving up to 10 percent." However, God said, "Try Me now in this . . . if I will not open for you the windows of heaven and pour out for you such blessing that there will not be room enough to receive it" (Mal. 3:10).

David said: "I have been young, and now am old; yet I have not seen the righteous forsaken, nor his descendants begging bread" (Ps. 37:25). I am not appealing to people to tithe because God is going to out-give you, although He surely will. I have yet to hear a tither say, "I wish I had never decided to tithe. When I think of all the money I have given to the kingdom of God, it really adds up. If I still had that money, I'd have a hefty retirement account. I could have a condominium in Miami and a summer house in Paris if I just hadn't tithed." I have never met a tither who regretted tithing, because it is one of the greatest privileges that the Christian has.

Achan

We have to take seriously what happened to Ananias and Sapphira. There is some similarity to this occasion in Joshua 7. The Israelites were set to come up against Ai, a small, insignificant town, but the Israelites were defeated in the battle. Afterward Joshua said, "O Lord, what shall I say when Israel turns its back before its enemies? For the Canaanites and all the inhabitants of the land will hear it, and surround us, and cut off our name from the earth. Then what will You do for Your great name?" (Josh. 7:8–9). And God responded this way:

> Get up! Why do you lie thus on your face? Israel has sinned, and they have also transgressed My covenant which I commanded them. For they have even taken some of the accursed things, and have both stolen and deceived; and they have also put it among their own stuff. Therefore the children of Israel could not stand before their enemies, but turned their backs before their enemies, because they have become doomed to destruction. Neither will I be with you anymore, unless you destroy the accursed from among you. Get up, sanctify the people, and say, "Sanctify yourselves for tomorrow, because thus says the LORD God of Israel: 'There is an accursed thing in your midst, O Israel; you cannot stand before your enemies until you take away the accursed thing from among you." (Josh. 7:10–13)

So Joshua and his soldiers went through the camp and they found Achan, who had violated the commandment of God and taken the silver and gold for himself. He withheld it from God and buried it under the floor of his tent. Finally he confessed his crime, and Joshua said, 'Why have you troubled us? The LORD will trouble you this day.' So all Israel stoned him with stones; and they burned them with fire after they had stoned them with stones" (Josh. 7:25). Achan and his family were executed. They were not even buried according to Jewish custom but were burned instead.

God is gracious and patient with us, and He promises to bless us when we are cheerful and when we give the sacrifice of praise and bring our offerings to Him for the advancement of His kingdom. However, when we lie about it, if we pretend to be tithers when we are not, when we pretend to be giving all when we are holding back and burying it in our tents, we expose ourselves to His great displeasure. I think that most Christians who fail to tithe have done so not primarily due to avarice but because they do not really understand their responsibility. But we do know it.

16

IF IT IS GOD

Acts 5:12–41

And through the hands of the apostles many signs and wonders were done among the people. And they were all with one accord in Solomon's Porch. Yet none of the rest dared join them, but the people esteemed them highly. And believers were increasingly added to the Lord, multitudes of both men and women, so that they brought the sick out into the streets and laid them on beds and couches, that at least the shadow of Peter passing by might fall on some of them. Also a multitude gathered from the surrounding cities to Jerusalem, bringing sick people and those who were tormented by unclean spirits, and they were all healed. Then the high priest rose up, and all those who were with him (which is the sect of the Sadducees), and they were filled with indignation, and laid their hands on the apostles and put them in the common prison. But at night an angel of the Lord opened the prison doors and brought them out, and said, "Go, stand in the temple and speak to the people all the words of this life." And when they heard that, they entered the temple early in the morning and taught. But the high priest and those with him came and called the council together, with all the elders of the children of Israel, and sent to the prison to have them brought. But when the officers came and did not find them in the prison, they returned and reported, saying, "Indeed we found the prison shut securely, and the guards standing outside before the doors; but when we opened them, we found no one inside!" Now when the high priest, the captain of the temple, and the chief priests heard those things, they wondered what the outcome would be. So one came and told them, saying, "Look, the men whom you put in prison are standing in the temple and teaching the people!" Then the captain went with the officers and brought them without violence, for they feared the people, lest they should be stoned. And when they had brought them, they set them before the council. And the high priest asked them, saying, "Did we not strictly command you not to teach in this name? And look, you have filled Jerusalem with your doctrine, and intend to bring this Man's blood on us!" But Peter and the other apostles answered and said: "We ought to obey God rather than men. The God of our fathers raised up Jesus whom you murdered by hanging on a tree. Him God has exalted to His right hand to be Prince and Savior, to give repentance to Israel and forgiveness of sins. And we are His witnesses to these things, and so also is the Holy Spirit whom God has given to those who obey Him." When they heard this, they were furious and plotted to kill them. Then one in the council stood up, a Pharisee named Gamaliel, a teacher of the law held in respect by all the people, and commanded them to put the apostles outside for a little while. And he said to them: "Men of Israel, take heed to yourselves what you intend to do regarding these men. For some time ago Theudas rose up, claiming to be somebody. A number of men, about four hundred, joined him. He was slain, and all who obeyed him were scattered and came to nothing. After this man, Judas of Galilee rose up in the days of the census, and drew away many people after him. He also perished, and all who obeyed him were dispersed. And now I say to you, keep away from these men and let them alone; for if this plan or this work is of men, it will come to nothing; but if it is of God, you cannot overthrow it—lest you even be found to fight against God." And they agreed with him, and when they had called for the Apostles and beaten them, they commanded that they should not speak in the name of Jesus, and let them go. So they departed from the presence of the council, rejoicing that they were counted worthy to suffer shame for His name.

Through the hands of the apostles many signs and wonders were done among the people. And they were all with one accord in Solomon's Porch. Yet none of the rest dared join them, but the people esteemed them highly. And believers were increasingly added to the Lord, multitudes of both men and women, so that they brought the sick out into the streets and laid them on beds and couches, that at least the shadow of Peter passing by might fall on some of them** (vv. 12–15). So much power was invested in the Apostles in the first generation of the church that even the passing shadow of Peter and the handkerchief of Paul were used by God to manifest His power in order to bear witness to His chosen Messiah, Christ.

A multitude gathered from the surrounding cities to Jerusalem, bringing sick people and those who were tormented by unclean spirits, and they were all healed (v. 16). This is the first hint recorded for us in the book of Acts of the progress of the gospel that followed the Great Commission: "You shall receive power when the Holy Spirit has come upon you; and you shall be witnesses to me in Jerusalem, and in all Judea and Samaria, and to the end of the earth" (Acts 1:8). Everything recorded in the first part of the book of Acts takes place within Jerusalem, but now, for the first time, we begin to see growth. The church expanded as people from neighboring villages and towns outside Jerusalem began flocking to the city and joining the church of Jesus Christ. This only served to further antagonize the religious authorities of the day.

Growing Hostility

When we ask why these supposedly religious people were so hostile against the first-century church, the answer is clear: they were consumed by jealousy. The chief priests, the scribes, the Sadducees, and the Pharisees held the highest esteem in the community. Theirs was the highest rung of the social ladder, but an upstart itinerant preacher from Galilee had come and announced that He was the Messiah and exposed their hypocrisy. After that, the people began clamoring to hear about Jesus, forcing the Pharisees and the Sadducees into the background. By this time, the leaders had grown sick and tired of hearing the name of Jesus. They were so consumed by envy that they wanted to put an end to the clamor once and for all.

If we study church history, which we tend not to do, we will note a pattern: those most hostile to the purity of the gospel have been clergy. That is as true today as it ever was before. Most of the guns aimed against the Scriptures in our day do not come from secularists, who could care less. They come from unbelieving seminary professors and ministers who simply will not identify with the truth of the gospel. Has that not been the problem from the very beginning of the church? Was it not the problem in ancient Israel, when it was the priests of the nation who betrayed their covenant God? That is why we cannot assume that just because someone is an ordained minister or elder he is committed to the truth of the gospel. Here in Acts we see a record of the conflict between the genuine and the counterfeit.

Then the high priest rose up, and all those who were with him (which is the sect of the Sadducees), and they were filled with indignation, and laid their hands on the apostles and put them in the common prison (vv. 17–18). They were not merely issued a warning this time; they were locked up and guarded. **But at night an angel of the Lord opened the prison doors and brought them out, and said, "Go, stand in the temple and speak to the people all the words of this life"** (vv. 19–20). Just as the Lord had opened up the tomb of the risen Christ, so the angel of God was sent to this prison, the doors were opened, and the Apostles were set free. What did they do the first thing in the morning? **And when they heard that, they entered the temple early in the morning and taught** (v. 21). They were right back in the temple preaching and teaching. They continued the enterprise that had gotten them thrown in prison in the first place.

In the meantime, the officials in the Sanhedrin, unaware of the Apostles' release, came together for another meeting. They wanted to carry on with their interrogations so as to inflict more punishment on the Apostles, so they sent for the prisoners. **But when the officers came and did not find them in the prison, they returned and reported, saying, "Indeed we found the prison shut securely, and the guards standing outside before the doors; but when we opened them, we found no one inside!"** (vv. 22–23). Then someone else said, **"Look, the men whom you put in prison are standing in the temple and teaching the people!"** (v. 25).

By this time, the Sanhedrin was furious, and the officials sent the guards to arrest the Apostles again. **Then the captain went with the officers and brought them without violence, for they feared the people, lest they should be stoned** (v. 26). They arrested them, but they arrested them gently. They told them they were under arrest, and the Apostles came humbly. We are told why the officers didn't rough them up: they were afraid. The officials were not afraid for the Apostles; rather, the officials were afraid that if they were violent toward the Apostles publicly, the populous would stone them.

And when they had brought them, they set them before the council. And the high priest asked them, saying, "Did we not strictly command you not to teach in this name? And look, you have filled Jerusalem with your doctrine, and intend to bring this Man's blood on us!" (vv. 27–28). The reason the Apostles were in trouble was that they continued to preach Christian doctrine, which is the truth of God. If someone is not preaching doctrine, he is not preaching Christianity, yet many today are immersed in the pernicious idea that doctrine is not good for Christians.

Peter and the other Apostles gave the same answer they had given earlier: **"We ought to obey God rather than men"** (v. 29). Peter continued, **"The God of our fathers raised up Jesus whom you murdered by hanging on a tree. Him God has exalted to His right hand to be Prince and Savior, to give repentance to Israel and forgiveness of sins. And we are His witnesses to these things, and so also is the Holy Spirit whom God has given to those who obey Him"** (vv. 30–32). "The God of our fathers"—Peter is including the officials. God is not solely the father of the Apostles or of the people gathered in the streets, but of the Sanhedrin, the Pharisees, and the Sadducees. This was bold preaching, and it stands in sharp contrast to the style of preaching in our day.

After listening to a recording of Jonathan Edwards's famous sermon "Sinners in the Hands of an Angry God," I realized that Edwards was consumed by the fear that the people in his congregation would slip into everlasting damnation. His accent on the peril of hell is dominant in that sermon, which is surely why people fainted as they listened to it. As I listened to it, I was overcome with a dread and fear of the wrath of God, and I thought, "Have I fully repented of my sins? How would my congregation respond if a sermon like this were preached in their presence today?" Many contemporary preachers have done everything in their power to eclipse any idea of the judgment of God, of God's wrath and the notion of hell, ignoring the fact that our Lord Himself taught more about hell than He did about heaven. The issue before the people in Acts was the issue of the Christ. What do you do with this Christ, the One whom God has given for the remission of sins, whom God has raised from the dead, proving that He is the Messiah? He is the Deliverer of Israel, and if you continue to contend against that, you will indeed face the wrath of the Father. Jonathan Edwards did not preach his sermon in a spirit of hatred or meanness. It was preached out of love and compassion and care for his people.

Gamaliel's Advice

In the midst of the drama we are following, we are told that the hatred, the jealousy, and the anger against the church accelerated. The fury of the Sanhedrin escalated to such a degree that they plotted to kill the Apostles. In the midst of their discussion, one of the Pharisees stood up, the most respected rabbi of his generation, Gamaliel. He was tutor to a most brilliant student, Saul of Tarsus, who even at this moment was on the side of the Pharisees against the early church. Gamaliel, who was known for his sage advice, said, **"Men of Israel, take heed to yourselves what you intend to do regarding these men. For some time ago Theudas rose up, claiming to be somebody. A number of men, about four hundred, joined him. He was slain, and all who obeyed him were scattered and came to nothing. After this man, Judas of Galilee rose up in the days of the census, and drew away many people after him. He also perished, and all who obeyed him were dispersed. And now I say to you, keep away from these men and let them alone; for if this plan or this work is of men, it will come to nothing; but if it is of God, you cannot overthrow it—lest you even be found to fight against God"** (vv. 35–39). The officials thought this was sage advice.

I would say that half of Gamaliel's advice was good. He was half right and half wrong when he said, "If this plan . . . is of men, it will come to nothing." Islam is not of God, and it has not failed; it has been around for centuries. There are abundant evidences in history of false religions under the wrath of God that have not disappeared from the face of the earth. The Gnostic heresy that plagued the church in the second and third centuries is alive and well today and is being taught in the pages of the *Orlando Sentinel* by a theologian at Princeton University trying to revive, along with Dan Brown's *The Da Vinci Code*, the Gnostic literature of the early church. When Ligonier was at one point struggling to keep alive financially, one of my associates said to me, "We have worked so diligently to maintain this ministry on a sound financial basis and have made the right kind of administrative decisions. It scares me that we could succeed in spite of God." I replied, "That's true. We could succeed, in terms of the way success is measured in the world." Any of us can be successful for a season.

The right part of Gamaliel's advice, the true part, was this: "If it is of God, you cannot overthrow it." There is tremendous comfort in that. When we sing "The Church's One Foundation," or "A Mighty Fortress Is Our God," or "Glorious Things of Thee Are Spoken," we hear in our music the testimony that the church of Jesus Christ, though buffeted and assailed on every side and riddled by heresy and persecution, will not fail. It cannot fail. It is the only institution on the face of the earth that has an absolute, unconditioned guarantee for its future success—not every church or church member, but the true church of Christ will always be victorious, and it cannot be stopped by the conditions of human affairs. I wish that Gamaliel would have said, "Go back out in the marketplace and rethink, restudy, and reexamine what you have done. Why don't you examine the message of these men, because it just might be true? If it is true, you are enemies of God."

The officials followed Gamaliel's advice and let the Apostles go, but not before they commanded them to speak no more in the name of Jesus and then beat them unmercifully. **So they departed from the presence of the council, rejoicing that they were counted worthy to suffer shame for His name** (v. 41). They did not complain of ill treatment. There is no higher honor or glory for a human being to receive on this planet than that of partaking in the humiliation of Christ. That is the only part of His glory He will share with us in this world. In heaven, the rest of His glory will be showered upon us, but now we glory in His cross.

17

APOSTLES AND DEACONS

Acts 6:1–7

Now in those days, when the number of the disciples was multiplying, there arose a complaint against the Hebrews by the Hellenists, because their widows were neglected in the daily distribution. Then the twelve summoned the multitude of the disciples and said, "It is not desirable that we should leave the word of God and serve tables. Therefore, brethren, seek out from among you seven men of good reputation, full of the Holy Spirit and wisdom, whom we may appoint over this business; but we will give ourselves continually to prayer and to the ministry of the word." And the saying pleased the whole multitude. And they chose Stephen, a man full of faith and the Holy Spirit, and Philip, Prochorus, Nicanor, Timon, Parmenas, and Nicolas, a proselyte from Antioch, whom they set before the apostles; and when they had prayed, they laid hands on them. Then the word of God spread, and the number of the disciples multiplied greatly in Jerusalem, and a great many of the priests were obedient to the faith.

Some time ago I traveled to California for the annual Shepherds' Conference at John MacArthur's church. To the best of my knowledge, this is one of the largest pastors' conferences held in America. One of the most exciting things a minister can do is to have fellowship with other pastors. The night before I was scheduled to speak, I awoke feeling quite ill, and by morning I had lost my voice completely. As the time for my session grew near, I still could not speak, so John prayed with me before I began. I made it through, and afterward John told me that I had delivered the best message of my life. I saw afresh that day that our strength really is made perfect in weakness. When we are brought to a place where the only strength we have is that which is given to us by the Lord, it is when we are most used. That event had been the most difficult time of speaking I had ever experienced, yet it was also one of the most rewarding. One reason I was so grateful for the opportunity I had in California is that today it is very difficult to find pastors who will preach expository sermons, who break forth the text of Scripture and don't simply give psychological advice or insights on contemporary events. Pastors must be ministers of the Word because that is our mandate.

Widows in Need

In the early days of the church, the number of the disciples was multiplying, and a complaint arose in the congregation between the Jewish Christians and the Hellenistic Jewish Christians. There were the Hebrew-speaking Palestinian Jews and the Greek-speaking Jews of the Diaspora who had come back into Jerusalem and become part of the New Testament community. A debate arose between the Greek-speaking Jewish Christians and the Hebrew-speaking Jewish Christians about the distribution of money, time, and energy that the church was expending on the care of widows. This was the first crisis that infected that Christian community. Some among them felt neglected because their widows were not being ministered to. James wrote, "Pure and undefiled religion before God and the Father is this: to visit orphans and widows in their trouble, and to keep oneself unspotted from the world" (James 1:27).

The first year I was in seminary, I worked at a church of about one thousand members. I wanted to do the best job I could, so I got hold of the church's pictorial members' guide and tried to memorize the faces and names of everyone in the congregation. One morning after church, an elderly woman came to the back of the church. I had never seen her before, and I welcomed her and thanked her for visiting. She looked at me and said, "Young man, I'm a charter member of this church." I did not recognize her because she was unable to attend church on a regular basis. She was a frail widow alone in the world.

When a woman's husband dies, everybody weeps with her and displays some compassion at first, but soon into her widowhood, her whole life changes. She finds herself excluded from activities that she and her husband formerly attended together. Widows experience a kind of loneliness that none who are not widows or widowers can possibly understand. Every church has its proportionate number of those who have lost their mates.

Division of Labor

This happened in the early church. Both widows and widowers were being neglected, so the Twelve called a meeting. They summoned the whole church and said, **"It is not desirable that we should leave the word of God and serve tables"** (v. 2). Since the Apostles had been given a particular mandate by Christ, they could not be involved in the daily care of the lives of the people. In order to be effective in the job to which they had been called, they had to devote themselves to prayer and to the preaching of the Word of God.

The same applies in the church today. Every year, seventeen thousand ministers in America leave the ministry. A primary reason is that ministers in the modern church are not encouraged, equipped, enabled, or allowed to devote themselves to the preaching and teaching of the Word of God. Today a minister is expected to be the CEO of a corporation. He is expected to do the administration and the work of development; he is expected to be an expert in counseling and pastoral care. As a result, we have raised up generations of pastors who are jacks of all trades and masters of none, and one of the reasons why they do not open the Word of God for the congregation on Sunday morning is that they do not know how. They have spent their time learning everything else but the texts of Scripture.

The Apostles did not say, "We are going to forget about the orphans and widows." Rather, they summoned the people together and said, **"Therefore, brethren, seek out from among you seven men of good reputation, full of the Holy Spirit and wisdom, whom we may appoint over this business; but we will give ourselves continually to prayer and to the ministry of the word." And the saying pleased the whole multitude. And they chose Stephen, a man full of faith and the Holy Spirit, and Philip, Prochorus, Nicanor, Timon, Parmenas, and Nicolas, a proselyte from Antioch, whom they set before the apostles; and when they had prayed, they laid hands on them** (vv. 3–6). These seven men were obviously men of great faith, great ability, and great commitment, and they were set aside and consecrated by the laying on of hands to give themselves to service (*diakonia*), to minister to the needs of people in the church. This is how the diaconate was founded. Here they are simply called "the seven," but out of this group of seven the institution of deacons was established in the early church.

I came to St. Andrew's Chapel because some friends asked me one day, "How about starting a church and becoming its pastor?" I just laughed. "I already have a job," I replied. "I can't do that." They accepted my answer, but the next week they came back and said, "How about if we start a church, and you can just be our minister of preaching and teaching? That is all you will have to do." Vesta and I talked about it, and we prayed. I realized then that every one of my heroes from church history, theologians such as Augustine, Calvin, Luther, and Edwards, preached from a pulpit before his own congregation in addition to his daily teaching of theology. I told Vesta, "That's what's missing from my life." So I went back to those friends and said, "If you will let me devote my time to preaching and teaching, I will do it."

That is how St. Andrew's was established. As the church grows, there are more tables to serve, more widows to visit, and more orphans to care for, and we have grown our diaconate proportionately. The work of our deacons is indispensible. No matter how early I arrive at the church on a Sunday morning, the deacons are already there. They have already prepared the Table of the Lord for Communion. They have set up parking accommodations. There is no glamour in such work, just service, but that is how the church is supposed to operate. I thank God daily for the deacons of our church who are willing to give of themselves freely to these servant tasks and ministries of mercy that become increasingly more pressing in our midst. That is what makes it possible for me to study the Word of God and preach it, which is what God's people most need.

18

STEPHEN ON TRIAL

Acts 6:8–7:60

And Stephen, full of faith and power, did great wonders and signs among the people. Then there arose some from what is called the Synagogue of the Freedmen (Cyrenians, Alexandrians, and those from Cilicia and Asia), disputing with Stephen. And they were not able to resist the wisdom and the Spirit by which he spoke. Then they secretly induced men to say, "We have heard him speak blasphemous words against Moses and God." And they stirred up the people, the elders, and the scribes; and they came upon him, seized him, and brought him to the council. They also set up false witnesses who said, "This man does not cease to speak blasphemous words against this holy place and the law; for we have heard him say that this Jesus of Nazareth will destroy this place and change the customs which Moses delivered to us." And all who sat in the council, looking steadfastly at him, saw his face as the face of an angel. Then the high priest said, "Are these things so?" And he said, "Brethren and fathers, listen: The God of glory appeared to our father Abraham when he was in Mesopotamia, before he dwelt in Haran, and said to him, 'Get out of your country and from your relatives, and come to a land that I will show you.' Then he came out of the land of the Chaldeans and dwelt in Haran. And from there, when his father was dead, He moved him to this land in which you now dwell. And God gave him no inheritance in it, not even enough to set his foot on. But even when Abraham had no child, He promised to give it to him for a possession, and to his descendants after him. But God spoke in this way: that his descendants would dwell in a foreign land, and that they would bring them into bondage and oppress them four hundred years. 'And the nation to whom they will be in bondage I will judge,' said God, 'and after that they shall come out and serve Me in this place.' . . . You stiff-necked and uncircumcised in heart and ears! You always resist the Holy Spirit; as your fathers did, so do you. Which of the prophets did your fathers not persecute? And they killed those who foretold the coming of the Just One, of whom you now have become the betrayers and murderers, who have received the law by the direction of angels and have not kept it." When they heard these things they were cut to the heart, and they gnashed at him with their teeth. But he, being full of the Holy Spirit, gazed into heaven and saw the glory of God, and Jesus standing at the right hand of God, and said, "Look! I see the heavens opened and the Son of Man standing at the right hand of God!" Then they cried out with a loud voice, stopped their ears, and ran at him with one accord; and they cast him out of the city and stoned him. And the witnesses laid down their clothes at the feet of a young man named Saul. And they stoned Stephen as he was calling on God and saying, "Lord Jesus, receive my spirit." Then he knelt down and cried out with a loud voice, "Lord, do not charge them with this sin." And when he had said this, he fell asleep.

I n our last study we looked at the decision of the Apostles to set apart seven men for ministries of mercy and service, *diakonia*. They were chosen so that the Apostles would be free to fulfill their vocation to labor in the preaching and teaching of the Word. Luke tells us the names of those seven, and included in that list is Stephen. As Luke continues his narrative of the early church, he focuses on Stephen. **And Stephen, full of faith and power, did great wonders and signs among the people. Then there arose some from what is called the Synagogue of the Freedmen (Cyrenians, Alexandrians, and those from Cilicia and Asia), disputing with Stephen. And they were not able to resist the wisdom and the Spirit by which he spoke** (vv. 8–10). Stephen was doing marvelous things in the midst of this people, but there was a group from the Greek-speaking community among them that raised opposition against his teaching and preaching, and they entered into a dispute with him.

Luke tells us they were not able to resist his wisdom or the spirit by which he spoke. They started by engaging Stephen in honest debate, but their honesty was short-lived. When they were unable to stop his arguments, they turned to corrupt manners in order to silence him. They found some willing to bear false witness against Stephen. One by one the false witnesses came and accused him. They said, **"We have heard him speak blasphemous words against Moses and God"** (v. 11). They stirred up the people, the elders, and the scribes, and they came upon him, seized him, and brought him before the council. Again they set up false witnesses who said, **"This man does not cease to speak blasphemous words against this holy place and the law; for we have heard him say that**

this Jesus of Nazareth will destroy this place and change the customs which Moses delivered to us" (vv. 13–14).

Stephen's Face

Not a single word of what the false witnesses said was true, except that Jesus did indeed say He was going to destroy the temple. However, they twisted Jesus' words as part of their grand conspiracy against Stephen, this eloquent spokesman for Christ. Luke then gives a parenthetic footnote: **And all who sat in the council, looking steadfastly at him, saw his face as the face of an angel** (v. 15).

The French existential philosopher Jean-Paul Sartre described the destructive effects of becoming the object of people's stares. In polite society, there is only so long we can maintain eye contact with someone before making him or her very uncomfortable. When we see someone walking down the street and our eyes meet briefly, we say hello and then look away. People stare at paintings in art museums or at animals in zoos, but if we stare too long at a human being, we are likely to get a hostile reaction because, Sartre said, staring at others reduces them to the status of objects. Stephen had become the object of hostile stares, as his accusers and the court watched him as he was accused. We are told that they looked at him steadfastly. Then they began to see a certain radiance emanating from Stephen's face. He looked as if he had the face of an angel.

Something similar is recorded elsewhere in Scripture. We see it in the Old Testament when Moses went up the mountain and spoke with God and asked if he could see God's glory. God told him, "'You cannot see My face; for no man shall see Me, and live.' And the LORD said, 'Here is a place by Me, and you shall stand on the rock. So it shall be, while My glory passes by, that I will put you in the cleft of the rock, and will cover you with My hand while I pass by. Then I will take away My hand, and you shall see My back; but My face shall not be seen'" (Ex. 33:20–23). Moses got an instantaneous glance at the back of God, and suddenly Moses' face began to shine with such intensity that it was blinding to those who saw him. That light on the face of Moses did not come from inside of him; it was reflected glory that came from having been in the presence of God.

We see this also at the Mount of Transfiguration, where Christ was transfigured. The light that radiated from His garments and His face was not a reflection from outside Him but from within, as for a moment the divine burst through the veil of the human. Those in His presence fell on their faces at the sight. In Stephen's case the radiance is more like that which happened to Moses rather than to Jesus. Stephen was not at that moment reflecting the ugliness and horror reflected in the faces of his accusers but the grace and loveliness of God pouring forth.

Stephen's History Lesson

Then the high priest said, "Are these things so?" (7:1). You have heard the charges, Stephen. Are they correct? Are you speaking blasphemous things about Moses and about God and the law? Are you guilty or innocent? By way of reply, Stephen gave them a lesson in redemptive history. I cannot help but think that here in Acts, volume 2 of Luke's history, that Luke was reminiscing on what happened in volume 1 on the Emmaus road. There, some people fell in with Jesus along the road to Emmaus but did not recognize Him. They became involved in an animated conversation about all the events that had taken place so recently in Jerusalem. Jesus asked, "'What kind of conversation is this that you have with one another as you walk and are sad?' Then the one whose name was Cleopas answered and said to Him, 'Are You the only stranger in Jerusalem, and have You not known the things which happened there in these days?' And He said to them, 'What things?'" (Luke 24:17–19). And so they told Him about this Jesus whom many had thought was the Messiah, and how He had been killed, but now a rumor was running through the city that He had been raised from the dead. Then Luke tells us that Jesus, beginning with Moses, took them through the entire Old Testament and explained all that the Old Testament had taught regarding the Messiah. After listening to this history lesson, the identity of Jesus was suddenly clear to them. After Jesus left them, they realized that they had just heard a course in Old Testament history from the Messiah Himself. They said, "Did not our heart burn within us while He talked with us on the road, and while He opened the Scriptures to us?" (Luke 24:32).

How could Luke not have that in mind here, where he is setting down a similar kind of overview, a reconnaissance of the entire history of redemption, from the lips of Stephen? Stephen said, **"Brethren and fathers, listen: The God of glory appeared to our father Abraham when he was in Mesopotamia, before he dwelt in Haran, and said to him, 'Get out of your country and from your relatives, and come to a land that I will show you.' Then he came out of the land of the Chaldeans and dwelt in Haran. And from there, when his father was dead, He moved him to this land in which you now dwell"** (vv. 2–4). He reminds them that God had made a covenant with Abraham, and in Abraham's old age he had been blessed with a son, Isaac, and the covenant promise had been passed down through Isaac to Jacob and his sons. Stephen recounted how Jacob's sons had risen up against their brother Joseph and sold him into slavery. Finally, after his release, Joseph had been elevated to the position of prime minister in Egypt. Stephen reminded them that in those desperate times of famine, when Joseph was the prime minister, God had told Jacob to go down into Egypt with his family and reside there where there was plenty of food to eat, so they went and settled in the land of Goshen.

Stephen continued with how another pharaoh had come to power who did not know Joseph, and instead of treating the people of Israel graciously, he had enslaved them. The people groaned under a burden of oppression for many years until God heard their groanings. Then Stephen reminded them of Moses, who, in defending his own people, had become an outcast in the wilderness, but it was there that God had come to him in the burning bush and told Moses to go to Pharaoh with a message from God: "Let my people go." Stephen took his audience through the exodus and recounted that later, after the people had been liberated, they began to murmur and complain and desired to go back to Egypt. God then sent them the prophets, but they had killed the prophets.

Stephen's rehearsal of Jewish history was set before the leaders in his defense. We might think he would have concluded his overview by saying, "So, you see, I'm really just trying to follow in the tradition of our fathers. I'm trying to be an obedient Jew," but that is not what he said.

Provocative Words

Instead, his sermon took on an incendiary tone. **"You stiff-necked and uncircumcised in heart and ears! You always resist the Holy Spirit; as your fathers did, so do you"** (v. 51). Reformed theology holds to what is called *irresistible grace*, which is something of a misnomer. Irresistible grace does not mean that we are incapable of resisting the grace of God; we do that every day. What is meant by irresistible grace is that despite our resistance, the power of the Holy Spirit vanquishes our sinful rejection of Christ and gives us ears to hear and hearts to embrace Him. However, that was not the response of those present, which is why Stephen said, "You always resist the Holy Spirit."

Any time a large group gathers for worship, it is virtually inevitable that among their number there are some who are not true believers. They may be members of the church, but they still resist the Holy Spirit, and their necks have become stiff; they are set in their ways and their hearts have been calcified. They have no hearing in their ears for the things of God. Oh, they hear the sermons, but it never gets past the outer canal of their ears. There are people like that right now in all our churches.

Then Stephen asked them a question: **"Which of the prophets did your fathers not persecute?"** (v. 52). In other words, "Name one who was well received." They had killed those who foretold the coming of the Righteous One. Stephen had been giving them the history of themselves. They had received the law by the direction of angels and had not kept it. In a sense they were circumcised, but in a strange and different way: **When they heard these things they were cut to the heart, and they gnashed at him with their teeth** (v. 54). They were cut to the heart, but not in the sense that their hearts were opened to the Word of God. This is an example of how the Word of God, faithfully proclaimed, cuts between bone and marrow, flesh and tissue (Heb. 4:12). These were stinging words with barbs on them that cut to the very heart of the listeners, but instead of repenting, they gnashed at him with their teeth. They did not show their teeth by smiling. Rather, they gritted their teeth and clenched their jaws in anger. They were furious at this one who had just accused them of killing Jesus unjustly.

Stephen's Vision

But he, being full of the Holy Spirit, gazed into heaven and saw the glory of God, and Jesus standing at the right hand of God (v. 55). If I had a mob ready to kill me, so furious that they were advancing and gnashing their teeth, I would not be able to take my eyes off of them except to look around quickly for a way of escape. Stephen looked up, and God in His grace gave him a taste of heaven. God peeled back the curtain for just a moment and allowed this man, on trial for his life, to see His glory. The teeth of the men that were being gnashed at him were not worthy to be compared with the blessed vision that Stephen enjoyed as he looked up into heaven.

Stephen looked up and saw the glory of God, but Luke tells us that Stephen also saw Jesus. He had just been giving witness to Jesus. The Greek word for *witness* in the New Testament is *martyrea*, from which we get the English word "martyr." Stephen was the first to be martyred in the name of Jesus, and in the moment just preceding his martyrdom, he looked up and saw Jesus standing at the right hand of God.

Stephen was overcome by this, and he directed his gaze back to the group and told them what he was seeing. **"Look! I see the heavens opened and the Son of Man standing at the right hand of God!"** (v. 56). At St. Andrew's we cite the Apostles' Creed, which recounts the life of Jesus in summary form: "He was conceived by the Holy Spirit, born of the Virgin Mary, suffered under Pontius Pilate, was crucified, dead, and buried. On the third day, He rose again from the dead and ascended into heaven, where He is seated at the right hand of God the Father Almighty." That last part is called in theological terms the *sessio*. The great honor that the Father bestows upon Christ is that He goes to His coronation and is enthroned and given all authority in heaven and earth. He sits in the ruling position; the Son of Man is the heavenly Judge. We all someday will stand before the judgment seat of Christ. It is absolutely inescapable. Later in the book of Acts, Paul tells the Athenians that God has set a date on which

He will judge the world by Christ, and all are going to stand there. As believers, we have passed from condemnation, but we are still going to appear before the judgment seat of Christ.

In modern trials, only two people stand in the courtroom—the prosecutor and the defense attorney. The presiding judge sits on the bench, and he remains seated throughout the trial. Here in Acts, Stephen was on trial for his life before the highest earthly court of Israel, and he looked up and saw Jesus standing, not sitting, at the right hand of God, His customary place. Imagine for a moment that you are on trial for your life. You have come into the courtroom, made your plea of innocence, and sat down, and then comes the prosecutor's opening statement. He charges you with a heinous crime. When he has finished with his opening statement, he asks the defense attorney to give his opening statement, but as the prosecutor looks around, there is no defense counsel present. You would be quite frightened at that moment. But then imagine that the judge leaves the bench, comes down to the floor, and says, "I am the counsel for the defense." That would be the best-case scenario, having the judge as your defense attorney.

That is what Stephen saw. The heavens opened, and he saw the Judge of heaven and earth rising in his defense. Jesus had told His disciples before He left that He was going to send them another *paraclete*. The Holy Spirit is the other *paraclete*. The first one to be given the title *Paracletus* in the New Testament is Christ, who is our advocate with the Father, our defense attorney. God has appointed Him both judge and defense attorney. If you are in Christ, you have Christ as your advocate before the Father. If not, you will have Him simply as your judge.

Murder of Stephen

After Stephen told the people what he had seen, **they cried out with a loud voice, stopped their ears, and ran at him with one accord** (v. 57). Little children stop their ears when they do not want to hear something. Likewise, those in this crowd stopped their ears and rushed at Stephen. They grabbed him and took him outside the city. Most likely, Pilate had already been deposed and brought out of office, and we do not know if there was a Roman procurator there at this time. The crowd was not allowed to execute the death penalty under Roman rule, but they were so furious at that moment that the law did not matter. They grabbed Stephen and dragged him outside the city to the place of stoning, **and the witnesses laid down their clothes at the feet of a young man named Saul** (v. 58), who was complicit in this godless act. Saul, who became Paul, never got over it, as we will see.

This is the first we find of the Apostle Paul in all of history, and we are introduced to him as part of a murderous mob. The crowd grabbed rocks and stones, and with all their might they began to throw the rocks into Stephen's face, chest, and head. First, he was cut and marred and bruised. What a horrible way to be executed, one stone at a time. In the midst of his pain, he prayed. He called on God and asked for two things: **"Lord Jesus, receive my spirit"** and **"Lord, do not charge them with this sin"** (vv. 59–60). Both things Stephen said just like his Savior before him, and having said that, he breathed his last.

It has been said so many times that it is now almost trite: the blood of the martyrs is the seed of the church. This was the first seed sown in the apostolic community, and it was watched over by the Lord Jesus.

19

SAUL OF TARSUS

Acts 7:58–8:3

And they cast him out of the city and stoned him. And the witnesses laid down their clothes at the feet of a young man named Saul. And they stoned Stephen as he was calling on God and saying, "Lord Jesus, receive my spirit." Then he knelt down and cried out with a loud voice, "Lord, do not charge them with this sin." And when he had said this, he fell asleep. Now Saul was consenting to his death. At that time a great persecution arose against the church which was at Jerusalem; and they were all scattered throughout the regions of Judea and Samaria, except the apostles. And devout men carried Stephen to his burial, and made great lamentation over him. As for Saul, he made havoc of the church, entering every house, and dragging off men and women, committing them to prison.

Who is the greatest baseball player that ever lived? Who is the best running back in the NFL? People argue the answers to such questions endlessly. We are always arguing about who is the best. The answer is clear, however, when we ask the identity of the greatest theologian who has ever lived—the Apostle Paul. He was also the greatest missionary and evangelist and pastor. What God wrought in and through the life of that man whom He gifted so graciously, and who performed so valiantly and gallantly on behalf of the gospel, staggers the imagination.

Much of Acts is a profile of this man, Paul—of his life, his ministry, his suffering, and his faithfulness to his Master. When we first meet him here in

Acts, however, we do not meet the greatest pastor, the greatest missionary, the greatest evangelist, or the greatest man. We meet the early church's public enemy number one. We meet a man filled with hostility and hatred toward Christ and Christ's church, a man whose consuming passion was to eradicate Christianity from the face of the earth.

Paul's Early Life

Paul was born, according to tradition, in the same year that Jesus was born. He was born in Asia Minor, in the city of Tarsus; hence he was called Saul of Tarsus, Paul being the name he used in Gentile circles. His father was a Roman citizen and a well-respected merchant. The fact that he was a Roman citizen indicates that he likely had done something significant. Because Saul's father was a Roman citizen, Saul was born a free man, and he inherited that citizenship from his father. Tarsus was at the extreme southeastern tip of Asia Minor, close to Antioch, just a little bit north of Jerusalem. Tarsus was on the trade routes, where all merchandise moved from Europe and Asia south through the Middle East, down into Africa, and back. In antiquity Tarsus was one of the wealthiest cities of that region. Tarsus had the largest university in the world at that time, bigger than the universities in Athens and Alexandria. Tarsus was a cosmopolitan city, a city in which merchants, scholars, intellectuals, and travelers from all over the world mingled.

The young Saul grew up in that environment. Initially he followed a commonplace tradition of the time, which was learning a trade through apprenticeship. One of the most lucrative trades in that day and region was tentmaking. As a young lad, Saul learned the trade of making tents, which served him well throughout his life.

At the age of thirteen, because of the prowess and brilliance that he had already displayed, he was sent away from Tarsus to Jerusalem to go to seminary, as it were, to study under the tutorship of the leading theologian in the world of that time, Gamaliel. (We were introduced to Gamaliel in Acts 5.) Saul studied under Gamaliel for seven years and received the equivalent of two PhDs in theology. It has been said that by the age of twenty-one Saul of Tarsus was the most educated Jew in Palestine. He had mastered the Old Testament and all the rabbinic interpretations of it, and his star had risen in meteoric fashion.

Consenting

Paul was well known in and around the academic circles of Jerusalem by the time of the episode before us now, where we find him present at the stoning of Stephen: **They cast him out of the city and stoned him. And the witnesses**

laid down their clothes at the feet of a young man named Saul (v. 58). This is the first thing for which Paul is known in biblical history. The Bible does not tell us why the witnesses laid their clothes at the feet of Saul, but it is not hard to guess. Not only was his scholarship known to everyone in the crowd, but his profound hostility to Christianity was also well known. No one present would have doubted that Saul, at the very least, would acquiesce to the act. Two verses later Luke tells us, **Now Saul was consenting to his death** (8:1).

One thing that frightens me about the judgment recorded in the book of Revelation is that the first group that will be thrown into the lake of fire will be the cowards. A coward is a person who, when evil is being done, does and says nothing to stop it. A coward is someone who says, "I'm not going to participate in the evil myself, but what other people want to do is their own business." How many times in our lives have we seen evil taking place right in front of us, but we did not say a word or take a stand? The philosophy of relativism has so infected our culture that some Christians say, "I believe in the resurrection of Christ, but if someone else does not, well, to each his own. I'm not going to get embroiled in that controversy." We come to the place where we are willing to say what we believe, but we will not raise our voices against the antithesis of the truth of Christianity. If there is anything that characterizes the spirit of our age, it is that, and it is rooted and grounded in cowardly hearts.

Paul knew that the execution of Stephen was unjust. Paul knew that the execution was against the Law of Moses, of which he was an expert. Yet he let it happen. That is our introduction to this man. He almost certainly at this time in his life thought that he was doing the right thing, just as many people today believe that women ought to have the right to kill their own babies.

Years ago while I was a camp counselor, a boy nicknamed Rock disappeared. We had no idea where he was. It seemed that he had simply vanished, and we were terrified. I was sent up into the mountain by myself to look for him, and as I came through a thick grove of trees, I saw Rock sitting with his head in his hands. I was enormously relieved. "Rock, what are you doing here?" I asked.

"I'm just sitting here," he said. "I don't want to be at the camp anymore."

"But you know you're not allowed to leave the campgrounds like this without telling anybody where you're going. What were you thinking?"

He looked at me with all the seriousness he could muster and said, "A famous man once said, 'Be sure you're right. Then go ahead.'"

"Who said that?" I asked.

"Davy Crockett."

I do not know whether Davy Crockett really said that, but I have never forgotten it. It has come into my mind many times when I have been halted between two opinions. Be sure you are right before you make your move. I learned something that day from a little boy.

Paul was sure he was right, but he could not have been more wrong than to participate in the murder of a saint. Later on, Paul referred to himself as the chief of sinners (1 Tim. 1:15). He wasn't being dramatic or humble; he really believed it, because if anyone should have known better on that day in Jerusalem, it was Saul of Tarsus.

Luke goes on to tell us that not only did Saul consent to the murder of Stephen, but he wreaked havoc on the early church. **As for Saul, he made havoc of the church, entering every house, and dragging off men and women, committing them to prison** (v. 3). Even though Paul knew after his conversion what it meant to have all his sin forgiven by the blood of Christ, I believe when he put his head on the pillow at night and closed his eyes, he could see Stephen on his knees, bleeding from every part of his body, looking up into heaven with his face like an angel, saying, "Look! I see the heavens opened and the Son of Man standing at the right hand of God!" (7:56). Maybe when he prayed, "Lord, do not charge them with this sin," he was looking right at Saul.

After Saul met the risen Christ, and Christ turned his life upside down and blinded him by the radiance of His glory, this man, who had wreaked havoc against the body of Christ, became the greatest champion that the church of Jesus Christ has ever known. As we study the rest of the book of Acts—the activities of the Apostles, especially Paul—let us never forget his starting place, the kind of a man he was before the Lord of glory touched his soul and transformed him to the greatest Christian the church has ever known.

20

THE GOSPEL TO SAMARIA

Acts 8:4–24

Therefore those who were scattered went everywhere preaching the word. Then Philip went down to the city of Samaria and preached Christ to them. And the multitudes with one accord heeded the things spoken by Philip, hearing and seeing the miracles which he did. For unclean spirits, crying with a loud voice, came out of many who were possessed; and many who were paralyzed and lame were healed. And there was great joy in that city. But there was a certain man called Simon, who previously practiced sorcery in the city and astonished the people of Samaria, claiming that he was someone great, to whom they all gave heed, from the least to the greatest, saying, "This man is the great power of God." And they heeded him because he had astonished them with his sorceries for a long time. But when they believed Philip as he preached the things concerning the kingdom of God and the name of Jesus Christ, both men and women were baptized. Then Simon himself also believed; and when he was baptized he continued with Philip, and was amazed, seeing the miracles and signs which were done. Now when the apostles who were at Jerusalem heard that Samaria had received the word of God, they sent Peter and John to them, who, when they had come down, prayed for them that they might receive the Holy Spirit. For as yet He had fallen upon none of them. They had only been baptized in the name of the Lord Jesus. Then they laid hands on them, and they received the Holy Spirit. And when Simon saw that through the laying on of the apostles' hands the Holy Spirit was given, he offered them money, saying, "Give me this power also, that anyone on whom I lay hands may receive the Holy Spirit. But Peter said to him, "Your money perish with you, because you thought that the gift of God could be purchased with money! You have neither part nor portion in this matter, for your heart is not right in the sight of God. Repent therefore of this your wickedness, and pray God if perhaps the thought of your heart may be forgiven you. For I see that you are poisoned by bitterness and bound by iniquity." Then Simon answered and said, "Pray to the Lord for me, that none of the things which you have spoken may come upon me."

The events in Acts 8:4–25 took place during the outbreak of a great persecution in Jerusalem, and because of this outbreak, the whole church was scattered abroad. Christians all fled from the city except for the Apostles. We do not know why the Apostles stayed in Jerusalem, but we know that they did while the rest of the people of God went to the various regions outside Jerusalem.

Therefore those who were scattered went everywhere preaching the word (v. 4). The early church spread the faith not through professional clergy but through the laity. All the people took the gospel to the outer regions of the Empire. **Then Philip went down to the city of Samaria and preached Christ to them** (v. 5). Whether Philip went to the capital city Samaria itself or to another city is unclear from the context here, but in any case, he manifested great power and wonders, performing miracles and preaching the kingdom of God in a town that was under satanic oppression. Multitudes of people were oppressed and even possessed by Satan.

Of all the miracles recorded in the Old Testament, whether performed by Moses or Elijah or someone else, there is no miracle in which demons were exorcised. Jesus came and did that, and when He did, He noted its significance: "If I cast out demons with the finger of God, surely the kingdom of God has come upon you" (Luke 11:20). This was the premium sign of the breakthrough of the kingdom of God, and now that sign had come to Samaria through the ministry of Philip where people were being released from bondage to Satan and healed of various diseases.

Simon the Sorcerer

We are told by Luke that the city was filled with joy, but then comes an ominous note: **But there was a certain man called Simon, who previously practiced sorcery in the city and astonished the people of Samaria, claiming that he was someone great, to whom they all gave heed, from the least to the greatest, saying, "This man is the great power of God"** (vv. 9–10). Simon, identified as a magician, had the people in the palm of his hand. He was so clever and accomplished in his magical tricks that they were scared of him.

We read of the magi from antiquity, those we call "wise men," who came to adore the Christ child. We do not know whether they were astronomers or astrologers, but we do know that in the ancient world, science and magic were often put together and confused. Those who were involved in the occult and in the trickery of magic often used some of their esoteric knowledge of science in tandem with their tricks to make it seem like they had real power.

Years ago while playing golf, my friend Wally Armstrong and I decided to play a trick on some other golfers. Just before I prepared to take my swing, I reached in my bag and took out two long kitchen matches. After I teed up the ball, I took the two matches and placed them in the ground with the match heads right behind the ball. Wally said to those watching, "Watch this! When R.C. hits a drive, the ball just explodes off the tee."

When I swung the golf club, I hit the matches just right, and they went off, making a loud noise and launching the ball like a rocket. The onlookers saw that and asked in amazement, "How is it possible?" That is the way magicians work—with tricks and sleight of hand. Simon Magus was a magician. He was a phony. He had no supernatural power, and he knew it. Then he saw the real thing, the miracles performed by Philip.

Word got back to Jerusalem that the gospel had come to Samaria and that Samaritans had received it, so Peter and John were sent there to confirm this. When they arrived, they laid their hands on the believing Samaritans, bringing the Pentecostal experience, which had been restricted to the Jews, to the Samaritans, so that when the Apostles laid their hands on the Samaritan believers, the power of the Holy Spirit was made visible.

Not for Sale

Among those who claimed to have faith was Simon Magus, and after he was baptized, he attached himself to Philip and began to follow him wherever he went. When Simon witnessed Peter and John praying over the new converts for the receiving of the Holy Spirit, Simon approached them and said, **"Give me this power also, that anyone on whom I lay hands may receive the Holy Spirit"** (v. 19).

Peter looked at Simon Magus and said, **"Your money perish with you, because you thought that the gift of God could be purchased with money!"** (v. 20). We find here a biblical euphemism. What Peter said was this: "You and your money go to hell." He pronounced the worst judgment upon this sorcerer and consigned him with his request to the deepest regions of hell itself. Can you imagine anybody thinking that he could buy the favor of God? Yet there are many in churches today who believe, "If I just give enough money, God will be gracious to me." But the grace of God is not for sale. When we give, we are to give generously from our hearts, not because we expect some kind of power or salvation in return. The grace of God cannot be earned or merited or begged or borrowed or stolen. It certainly cannot be bought. If you think that the grace of God is for sale, then you insult Him as deeply as Simon Magus did.

Peter warned Simon, **"You have neither part nor portion in this matter, for your heart is not right in the sight of God. Repent therefore of this your wickedness, and pray God if perhaps the thought of your heart may be forgiven you. For I see that you are poisoned by bitterness and bound by iniquity"** (vv. 21–23). Peter told Simon that the gall of venom was in his soul and that he was in bondage to sin.

Some argue that the statement Luke makes in verse 13 indicates a genuine conversion of Simon that was quickly followed by a serious and radical fall into sin. I do not think that is correct, because true faith is the result of the regenerative power of the Holy Spirit, and when the Holy Spirit regenerates people, they are set free, no longer slaves to sin. There is a kind of faith that is merely cognitive, which is likely what happened to Simon. Simon could not deny the reality of what he had seen with his own eyes, but he did not have saving faith. His trust was not in Christ, and he was still looking to continue his career as a successful sorcerer.

Peter told Simon that God could see the poison in his heart and his slavery to sin. Then Simon Magus said, **"Pray to the Lord for me, that none of the things which you have spoken may come upon me"** (v. 24). Notice that he does not say, "Pray to the Lord for me, that I may be converted and have true faith and be redeemed." Simon was concerned with escaping punishment, which is also not saving faith.

There is a distinction in repentance between contrition and attrition. Contrition is true repentance that comes from a heart broken for having offended God. Attrition occurs when one repents only because there is a sword at one's neck, which is the kind of repentance we find in the Old Testament with Esau. He went with tears, but it was of no avail. No one can repent just to get a ticket out of hell. A true act of contrition, true repentance, does give you a ticket out of hell, but if what motivates you is simply the escape of punishment, that is not saving faith.

I think we can conclude that even though God brought His power and the glorious gospel to the Samaritans, turned the city upside down, and brought great joy where there had been only fear and terror, the person who was most responsible for terrorizing that city walked away with a hard heart. I pray that that may never be the lot of those who gather and profess faith in our own time.

21

THE ETHIOPIAN EUNUCH

Acts 8:25–40

So when they had testified and preached the word of the Lord, they returned to Jerusalem, preaching the gospel in many villages of the Samaritans. Now an angel of the Lord spoke to Philip, saying, "Arise and go toward the south along the road which goes down from Jerusalem to Gaza." This is desert. So he arose and went. And behold, a man of Ethiopia, a eunuch of great authority under Candace the queen of the Ethiopians, who had charge of all her treasury, and had come to Jerusalem to worship, was returning. And sitting in his chariot, he was reading Isaiah the prophet. Then the Spirit said to Philip, "Go near and overtake this chariot." So Philip ran to him, and heard him reading the prophet Isaiah, and said, "Do you understand what you are reading?" And he said, "How can I, unless someone guides me?" And he asked Philip to come up and sit with him. The place in the Scripture which he read was this:

> "He was led as a sheep to the slaughter;
> And as a lamb before its shearer is silent,
> So He opened not His mouth.
> In His humiliation His justice was taken away,
> And who will declare His generation?
> For His life is taken from the earth."

So the eunuch answered Philip and said, "I ask you, of whom does the prophet say this, of himself or of some other man?" Then Philip opened his mouth, and beginning at this Scripture, preached Jesus to him. Now as they went down the road, they came to some water. And the eunuch said, "See, here is water. What hinders me from being baptized?" Then Philip said, "If you believe with all your heart, you may." And he answered and said, "I believe that Jesus Christ is the Son of God." So he commanded the chariot to stand still. And both Philip and the eunuch went down into the water, and he baptized him. Now when they came up out of the water, the Spirit of the Lord caught Philip away, so that the eunuch saw him no more; and he went on his way rejoicing. But Philip was found at Azotus. And passing through, he preached in all the cities till he came to Caesarea.

In our last study we looked at the beginning of the ministry of Philip in Samaria where, we were told, the whole town, after hearing the gospel and seeing signs and wonders, was given over to joy. The oppression that they had suffered under Simon Magus and the occult powers had been defeated. We also saw the treachery of Simon Magus when he sought to purchase from Peter the gift and the power of the Holy Spirit. Luke now continues the narrative of Philip's missionary journey. We think so much about the missionary journeys of Paul that we sometimes forget that the missionary journeys of the early church began before Paul, some of which we see specifically here in the person of Philip.

So when they had testified and preached the word of the Lord, they returned to Jerusalem, preaching the gospel in many villages of the Samaritans (v. 25). If you look at a map of ancient Palestine, you will find Galilee in the north, Judea in the south, and the region of Samaria sandwiched in between them. Philip had been ministering north of Jerusalem in Samaria. Then the angel of the Lord came to him similarly to the way in which God called Elijah to his desert ministry. The angel said to Philip, **"Arise and go toward the south along the road which goes down from Jerusalem to Gaza"** (v. 26). The city of Gaza, one of five important Philistine cities, had been destroyed by Alexander the Great. As a result, the road that went originally from Jerusalem to Gaza was by this time in almost complete disuse because a new road in that direction had been built. Nobody went on the old Gaza road anymore, so it was almost as if God were directing Philip into the middle of the desert for no apparent reason. But Philip obeyed the commandment of the Lord and went down from Samaria past Jerusalem and made his way along the road.

Philip and the Eunuch

And behold, a man of Ethiopia, a eunuch of great authority under Candace the queen of the Ethiopians, who had charge of all her treasury, and had come to Jerusalem to worship, was returning (vv. 27–28). Who was the Ethiopian eunuch? In antiquity a eunuch was someone who had been emasculated surgically. The practice was not uncommon then because such men were used to stand guard over a king's harem. The reason for their emasculation was obvious: a king could trust a man who was unable to be sexually tempted. Some eunuchs rose to elevated positions of authority. They were household stewards for the royal house, and chamberlains, treasurers in the community. The Ethiopian eunuch was a man of great authority under Candace the queen of Ethiopia.

In ancient Ethiopia, kings did not take care of the royal business of the nation. Ethiopians believed that the kings were descendants of the gods, and being divinely human creatures they were too holy to be charged with taking care of the business of the empire. The king reigned, but he did not rule. Therefore, the business of the empire was put into the hands of the queen mother, and every queen mother for many generations was given the title or the name Candace.

The Ethiopian eunuch had great authority under Candace the queen of the Ethiopians; he had charge of all her treasury. The eunuch had come to Jerusalem to worship, which indicates that he might have been a Jew in the dispersion, but it is more likely that he was a Gentile who, somewhere along the line, had embraced the teachings of Judaism and had made the long journey from Ethiopia to Jerusalem for some special occasion from which he was now returning.

And sitting in his chariot, he was reading Isaiah the prophet (v. 28). The man was riding in a chariot, something like a covered wagon or a stagecoach. The eunuch would have been accompanied by an entourage and thus not driving the chariot himself; a subordinate would have been holding the reigns. The eunuch was seated in the chariot reading, and we see from the passage that he was reading aloud. That may seem unusual to us, but it is normally the way people learn to read. It takes a certain sophistication to be able to read silently. Reading aloud was normal in those days because the manuscripts they had were very difficult to follow. Space was conserved by jamming words together.

Then the Spirit said to Philip, "Go near and overtake this chariot" (v. 29). We do not know how fast the chariot was going, but we are told that Philip had to run to catch up with it. So there was the eunuch, sitting in his chariot reading a text from the Old Testament, and upon looking up he saw a man running alongside of him. As Philip approached the eunuch, he shouted, **"Do you understand what you are reading?"** (v. 30). The eunuch replied,

"**How can I, unless someone guides me?" And he asked Philip to come up and sit with him** (v. 31).

Beginning with Isaiah

The place in the Scripture which he read was this: "He was led as a sheep to the slaughter; and as a lamb before its shearer is silent, so He opened not His mouth. In His humiliation His justice was taken away, and who will declare His generation? For His life is taken from the earth" (vv. 32–33). The text the eunuch was reading begins with these words:

> Who has believed our report?
> And to whom has the arm of the LORD been revealed?
> For He shall grow up before Him as a tender plant,
> And as a root out of dry ground.
> He has no form or comeliness;
> And when we see Him,
> There is no beauty that we should desire Him.
> He is despised and rejected by men,
> A Man of sorrows and acquainted with grief.
> And we hid, as it were, our faces from Him;
> He was despised, and we did not esteem Him.
> Surely He has borne our griefs
> And carried our sorrows;
> Yet we esteemed Him stricken.
> Smitten by God, and afflicted.
> But He was wounded for our transgressions,
> He was bruised for our iniquities;
> The chastisement for our peace was upon Him.
> And by His stripes we are healed.
> All we like sheep have gone astray:
> We have turned, every one, to his own way:
> And the LORD has laid on Him the iniquity of us all. (Isa. 53:1–6)

This reads like an eyewitness description of the passion of Jesus, but these words were written almost eight hundred years before the cross. In that interval of eight hundred years, no one came along to fulfill the prophecy of the suffering servant of the Lord who would bear the sins of God's people. Yet here, eight hundred years later, was an Ethiopian reading this text, and he said to Philip, **"I ask you, of whom does the prophet say this, of himself or of some other man?" Then**

Philip opened his mouth, and beginning at this Scripture, preached Jesus to him (vv. 34–35). Why didn't Philip just turn to Matthew or Mark or Luke or John or Acts or to one of the Epistles? He could not, because those books hadn't been written yet. Nevertheless, when the gospel went to Ethiopia through the evangelist Philip, it went through the preaching of the Word of God, because we are told that faith comes by hearing and hearing from the Word of God, and Philip preached Christ, not from the New Testament but from the Old Testament. I am sure he covered not just the few verses from Isaiah 53 mentioned here, but the whole chapter of Isaiah 53, and then brought him up to date with the work of Christ in His atonement, His resurrection, and His ascension.

Baptized

As the Ethiopian eunuch was listening to Philip and absorbing what he was hearing, the chariot was still moving along the road. They came upon water at the edge of the road, probably a small oasis that they did not expect to find in this vicinity, and when they saw the water, the eunuch said, **"See, here is water. What hinders me from being baptized?"** (v. 36). Philip had surely talked about the Great Commission—the call to go into all the world preaching and teaching Christ and baptizing all nations in the name of the Father, the Son, and the Holy Spirit—and about the fact that baptism was the sign of the new covenant. **Then Philip said, "If you believe with all your heart, you may,"** and the eunuch replied, **"I believe that Jesus Christ is the Son of God"** (v. 37).

In the early church when the gospel was preached to foreigners, people who were coming for the first time to the covenant community as adults, before they could receive the sign of that new covenant, had to make a profession of faith. That is still true in the church today. In the early church, when Gentiles were converted they made a profession of faith, then they were baptized, and after that they were welcomed into the fellowship of the church and immersed in what was called the *Didache*, the teaching of the Apostles and the disciples. They did not have to know the Old Testament; they had only to embrace Jesus, be baptized, and come into the church, and then they were taught all the Old Testament.

New Testament scholar Oscar Cullman discovered in the early church's liturgy something called a "hindrance formula." It goes back to Jesus' rebuke of the disciples with respect to little ones. When little children were trying to crowd around Jesus and get His attention, the disciples shooed them away. Jesus rebuked His disciples and said, "Let the little children come to Me, and do not forbid them; for of such is the kingdom of heaven" (Matt. 19:14). Cullman points out that in the early church no one had to jump through doctrinal hoops in order to be brought into the fellowship. What was required for membership was minimal. If there was no clear hindrance or barrier to people's joining the church, and if they made a profession of faith in Christ, they were given baptism and welcomed into the community, even as Gentiles, and then received their more full instruction. So when Philip told the eunuch, "If you believe with all your heart, you may," and the eunuch replied, "I believe that Jesus Christ is the Son of God," Philip and the eunuch got out of the chariot and went over to the water, and Philip baptized the eunuch.

We must be careful how many inferences we draw from that. There is not one word in this text about the mode of baptism. They may have walked down to water, where Philip took a handful of it and poured it over the eunuch's head. We have baptism depicted that way in paintings of the early church. That was one way of baptism; others reference immersion. We do not know whether the eunuch was sprinkled, sprayed, or dunked. All we know is that he was baptized in and with water.

Philip's Journey

Now when they came up out of the water, the Spirit of the Lord caught Philip away, so that the eunuch saw him no more; and he went on his way rejoicing (v. 39). John Guest, an evangelist from England, told me of his conversion in Liverpool when he was a young man. He had gone to a meeting and heard the gospel for the first time and was converted. On his way home that evening, he ran through the streets of Liverpool jumping over every fire hydrant and kicking his heels together. He said it was the happiest day of his life because it was the day that he met Christ. The eunuch made that arduous trek all the way to Jerusalem to go through the rituals of the Old Testament, and on the way home he discovered Christ. The evangelist who explained Christ to him was taken away, but the joy of Christ stayed with him all the way home to his nation.

But Philip was found at Azotus, which was a name given to Old Testament Ashdod, **and passing through, he preached in all the cities till he came to Caesarea** (v. 40). Philip had made a U-turn. He had gone north to Samaria; then he was called by God to go back south toward Jerusalem, down toward Gaza, and then back up to the cities of the plain, the five cities of the Philistines. Finally he headed north, back to the city of Caesarea, which had been built by Herod and given its name in honor of Caesar Augustus. Caesarea was the headquarters of the Roman procurator. (Pontius Pilate did not live in Jerusalem; he lived in Caesarea and came on special occasions to Jerusalem.) So the gospel went first north, then back south, and then back up the plain again north to Caesarea.

At this point we leave the study of the missionary journeys of Philip, and we hear no more about him in Acts until his ministry is picked up many years later. We are being prepared for the introduction of the supreme missionary of the New Testament church, the Apostle Paul.

22

PAUL'S CONVERSION

Acts 9:1–9

Then Saul, still breathing threats and murder against the disciples of the Lord, went to the high priest and asked letters from him to the synagogues of Damascus, so that if he found any who were of the Way, whether men or women, he might bring them bound to Jerusalem. As he journeyed he came near Damascus, and suddenly a light shone around him from heaven. Then he fell to the ground, and heard a voice saying to him, "Saul, Saul, why are you persecuting Me?" And he said, "Who are You, Lord?" Then the Lord said, "I am Jesus, whom you are persecuting. It is hard for you to kick against the goads." So he, trembling and astonished, said, "Lord, what do You want me to do?" Then the Lord said to him, "Arise and go into the city, and you will be told what you must do." And the men who journeyed with him stood speechless, hearing a voice but seeing no one. Then Saul arose from the ground, and when his eyes were opened he saw no one. But they led him by the hand and brought him into Damascus. And he was three days without sight, and neither ate nor drank.

When we looked at the martyrdom of Stephen, Saul of Tarsus was briefly introduced as one who gave consent to that murderous act and who stood by and held the garments of those who murdered Stephen. Afterward, briefly, Saul passes from sight as Luke fills us in on the narratives of the ministry of Philip among the Samaritans and to the Ethiopian eunuch. Here Luke returns to his narrative of Saul of Tarsus.

Saul the Terrorist

Then Saul, still breathing threats and murder against the disciples of the Lord . . . (v. 1). Paul, or Saul, is described in some translations as "one breathing out fire," thereby providing an image of a dragon that seeks whom he may devour. The Greek word translated "breathing" does not refer to breathing out, but to breathing in. Breathing in threats of murder and destruction may sound strange, but the idea is that Saul was so passionately determined to carry on his persecution against the nascent Christian community that he was like a wild beast that snorts before it attacks. Bulls paw the earth and snort before charging in the bullring, and in order to snort, they first have to inhale. That is the image Luke gives to describe the intensity of Saul's fierce hostility as he made his way toward Damascus.

Before Saul left, he went to the high priest seeking authorization to carry forth the persecution that he had initiated in Jerusalem against those who were in the northern regions of Damascus, which is one of the oldest cities in the history of the world. Damascus was known even to Abraham. There was a large settlement of Jews in Damascus. During the reign of Nero, Nero killed ten thousand Jews assembled there. So Saul, suspecting that some of the Jews who lived in Damascus had already been seduced by the proclamation of the Christians, got the necessary papers to go to each synagogue in that area with legal authority from the theocratic leader of Israel, the high priest, to place them under arrest and then bring them back to Jerusalem for further punishment, perhaps even execution.

Saul's conversion occurred while he was on this journey, which Luke is about to describe. This is only one of several accounts of the conversion of Saul that we find in the book of Acts, and there is a reason for that. One of the most serious questions that the early church faced was the question of the legitimacy of the apostleship of Paul, who lacked the two primary criteria for apostleship that the original Twelve had: they had been eyewitnesses of the resurrection and had received a direct and immediate call by Jesus. The criteria necessary for becoming an Apostle line up with biblical history. Old Testament prophets were called directly by God. That is why prophets such as Jeremiah, Amos, and Isaiah were careful to give the circumstances of their call.

Since an Apostle had to have been called directly by Christ, and since Paul had not been an eyewitness of the resurrection, this occurrence on the road to Damascus became supremely important for validating his authority in the early church. Given his recent history of persecuting the church, the first Christians were not likely to trust his call to a position of church leadership. His reputation had preceded him, so his coming would have seemed to the fledgling church much as it would seem to us if Osama Bin Laden were to come to America claiming to be a convert to U.S. patriotism.

The story of Saul's conversion provides the necessary credential—he was called directly and immediately by Christ, and that call is repeated later in the book of Acts. Many say that Luke wrote Acts not simply to tell us of the marvelous activity of the Holy Spirit but also to provide an *apologia*, an apology, for the credentials of Saul of Tarsus, who after his conversion was called Paul.

Encounter with the Ascended Lord

As he journeyed he came near Damascus, and suddenly a light shone around him from heaven (v. 3). Saul had almost reached Damascus. He was on the Transjordan road, which is the desert road. Based on some of the other records in Acts, we know it was about noontime, when the sun shines brightest, that a light appeared from heaven. It was so blazing that it virtually obscured the light of the sun. It is hard for us to imagine how anything could be brighter than the sun itself. The Greek word used here for "shone" is the same word used in the Greek language to describe the light that comes with a bolt of lightning.

Central Florida, where I live, is the lightning capital of the world. More lightning bolts strike Central Florida each year than the whole rest of the U.S. combined, so we know what lightning is like. If you have ever been outdoors on a dark night and witnessed the flash of a lightning bolt, you know it lasts only seconds. What Saul experienced endured for several moments. It was clearly of supernatural origin, and Saul was thrown to the ground. Immediately after, he heard these words in Hebrew: **"Saul, Saul, why are you persecuting Me?"** (v. 4).

There are about fifteen times in all of Scripture where someone's name is stated with repetition. As Abraham stood on Mount Moriah with knife upraised to sacrifice his son Isaac, God called to him, "Abraham, Abraham! . . . Do not lay your hand on the lad, or do anything to him; for now I know that you fear God, since you have not withheld your son, your only son, from Me" (Gen. 22:11–12). The same sort of call was issued to Moses in the Midianite wilderness. Out of the burning bush God spoke to him, saying, "Moses, Moses!. . . Do not draw near this place. Take your sandals off your feet, for the place where you stand is holy ground" (Ex. 3:4–5). The same thing happened when God called Samuel while he was under the tutelage of Eli (1 Sam. 3:10). We see it in David's lament at the news of the death of his son, the rebel Absalom. David beat his breast and cried out, "O my son Absalom—my son, my son Absalom" (2 Sam. 18:33). When Elisha saw his tutor, Elijah, being carried into heaven, he cried out, "My father, my father," to the chariots of God (2 Kings 2:12). Jesus spoke tenderly to Martha when He rebuked her: "Martha, Martha" (Luke 10:41). When Jesus wept over Jerusalem He said, "O Jerusalem, Jerusalem . . . how often I wanted to gather your children together, as a hen gathers her chicks under her wings, but you were not willing!" (Matt. 23:37). On the cross our Lord cried, *"Eloi, Eloi"*—"My God, My God, why have You forsaken Me?" (Mark 15:34).

All these instances indicate an intensely personal form of address, underscoring again the warning that Jesus gave to His hearers when He reached the climax of the Sermon on the Mount. He said many would come on the last day saying to Him, "'Lord, Lord, have we not prophesied in Your name, cast out demons in Your name, and done many wonders in Your name?' And then I will declare to them, 'I never knew you; depart from Me, you who practice lawlessness!'" (Matt. 7:22–23). He was indicating that people will claim not only to know Him by name but also, by the repetition "Lord, Lord," to know Him personally and intimately. It is amazing that when Christ decided to pour out this personal and intimate love, He chose not Pilate or Caiaphas, but Saul of Tarsus, and He addressed him in these terms of personal intimacy.

Saul heard his name called from heaven with the question, "Saul, Saul, why are you persecuting Me?" Jesus had already ascended to heaven; His persecution had been completed, but the fact that He claimed persecution by Saul shows that He so identifies with His people that any believer who is persecuted for Christ's sake is identified with Jesus Himself. Jesus was saying, "If you persecute My people, you persecute Me." Everywhere in the world, from the early church through today, attacks against the people of God are in fact attacks against Jesus.

Saul heard the words, "Why are you persecuting Me?" and he knew that whoever was addressing him out of this blinding light was not some passerby from Damascus. He knew that he was in touch with a supernatural someone, but he was not sure who. So he asked. **"Who are You, Lord?"** (v. 5). Here Saul did not use the Greek term *kyrios* in the lower sense of simple polite address, but in the supreme, imperial sense. He knew that he was being addressed by the Sovereign One of heaven.

The answer came to him, **"I am Jesus, whom you are persecuting. It is hard for you to kick against the goads"** (v. 5). That obscure reference to goads may not be meaningful to us, but in antiquity much of produce was hauled on oxcarts, and sometimes oxen, just like mules, were very stubborn, so the drivers had to whip them a bit to get them moving. Sometimes the touch of the whip would make the oxen all the more stubborn, and they would kick against the oxcart, which could shatter it. To prevent that, the drivers mounted goads or spikes in the front of the oxcart, and when the oxen kicked against the goad, the discomfort from doing so would get them moving. Sometimes when an ox kicked against the goad, the goad would pierce its foot and cause it more pain, so it would get even angrier and kick the goad again. So Jesus was saying, "Saul, you stupid ox! You are no different from oxen that kick against the ox goad as you carry on your hostility toward Me." Resisting the lordship of Christ is not only sinful, but it is stupid, because God has raised Him from the grave, placed Him at His right hand, and given Him all authority in heaven and on earth and has called every person to bow the knee before Him. To resist Him is foolish.

A Dramatic Change

So he, trembling and astonished, said, "Lord, what do You want me to do?" (v. 6). Is there any other possible response when we are converted to Christ? Can you remember back to the days of your conversion? The first time you were on your knees before Christ, what did you say? Like Isaiah, we are to say, "Here am I! Send me" (Isa. 6:8). Like Paul, we are to say, "Lord, what do You want me to do?" Upon conversion, our agenda changes dramatically, and that is what happened to Saul.

Then the Lord said to him, "Arise and go into the city, and you will be told what you must do." And the men who journeyed with him stood speechless, hearing a voice but seeing no one. Then Saul arose from the ground, and when his eyes were opened he saw no one. But they led him by the hand and brought him into Damascus (vv. 6–8). I cannot help but wonder whether the Christian community had their spies and whether the word had already spread throughout Damascus. "That fire-breathing Saul is on his way! He's just a little bit outside the city!" Perhaps a sense of terror and fear had gripped the Christians of Damascus until they saw him being led by the hand, blind, into the city.

And he was three days without sight, and neither ate nor drank (v. 9). Three days in darkness, hunger, and thirst. Three days for Saul of Tarsus to contemplate what had happened to him on the road to Damascus. Saul's life was turned upside down in one moment on the road to Damascus, and because his life was turned upside down by the power of the Holy Spirit, the world was turned upside down, and we have been turned upside down through the testimony that God put on his lips and pen that feeds the church even to this day.

23

THE STREET CALLED STRAIGHT

Acts 9:10–19

Now there was a certain disciple at Damascus named Ananias; and to him the Lord said in a vision, "Ananias." And he said, "Here I am, Lord." So the Lord said to him, "Arise and go to the street called Straight, and inquire at the house of Judas for one called Saul of Tarsus, for behold, he is praying. And in a vision he has seen a man named Ananias coming in and putting his hand on him, so that he might receive his sight." Then Ananias answered, "Lord, I have heard from many about this man, how much harm he has done to Your saints in Jerusalem. And here he has authority from the chief priests to bind all who call on Your name." But the Lord said to him, "Go, for he is a chosen vessel of Mine to bear My name before Gentiles, kings, and the children of Israel. For I will show him how many things he must suffer for My name's sake." And Ananias went his way and entered the house; and laying his hands on him he said, "Brother Saul, the Lord Jesus, who appeared to you on the road as you came, has sent me that you may receive your sight and be filled with the Holy Spirit." Immediately there fell from his eyes something like scales, and he received his sight at once; and he arose and was baptized. So when he had received food, he was strengthened. Then Saul spent some days with the disciples at Damascus.

In our last study we looked at the remarkable circumstances of the conversion of Saul of Tarsus. On his way to Damascus, he was confronted with a light from heaven, brighter than the noonday sun, and he fell to the ground and heard a voice speaking to him, saying, "Saul, Saul, why are you persecuting Me?"

131

(9:4). Saul responded, "Who are You, Lord?" and Jesus said to him, "I am Jesus, whom you are persecuting" (v. 5).

At that moment, Saul, who from this time forth is called Paul, said to Jesus, "Lord, what do You want me to do?" (v. 6). Just minutes before his conversion, all that Paul could think of was what he could do *to* Christ, but immediately after, all he could think of is what he could do *for* Christ, which reveals the essence of his radical conversion. He was stricken blind and led by the hand into the city, where he remained for three days.

Ananias

Now there was a certain disciple at Damascus named Ananias; and to him the Lord said in a vision, "Ananias." And he said, "Here I am, Lord" (v. 10). Ananias placed himself at the Lord's disposal. **So the Lord said to him, "Arise and go to the street called Straight, and inquire at the house of Judas for one called Saul of Tarsus, for behold, he is praying. And in a vision he has seen a man named Ananias coming in and putting his hand on him, so that he might receive his sight"** (vv. 11–12). The street called Straight still exists; at one end of the street is the traditional place where Ananias lived and had this encounter with Saul.

Jesus was very specific in His instructions. He told Ananias exactly what to do and where to do it and with whom. After hearing the instructions Ananias, who just moments before had responded, "Here I am, Lord," said, **"Lord, I have heard from many about this man, how much harm he has done to Your saints in Jerusalem. And here he has authority from the chief priests to bind all who call on Your name"** (vv. 13–14).

Ananias had the unspeakable arrogance to correct the Lord Jesus Christ about His plan. Can anything be more ridiculous than a mortal suggesting to the Almighty a better way of doing things? We would think Ananias the biggest fool in history, except that we have done the same thing repeatedly. When we do not like how God is dealing with us or with our circumstances, we take it upon ourselves to set Him straight and suggest a more excellent way. Ananias is not the only biblical example of such reluctance. We also see it with Moses and Jeremiah. Such hesitation is typical; it comes from the weakness of the flesh. So here Ananias, in that very weakness, told Jesus about the horrible reputation that Saul had, as if Jesus did not know it.

One other thing to note about Ananias's response is that this is the first time in the New Testament that believers are called saints. They were so called not because they had performed miracles but because they are "holy ones," those whom Christ has called to Himself, has sanctified by setting them apart.

While not yet perfected, believers are ministered to by the Holy Spirit. In that sense, any believer in Jesus Christ, anyone indwelt by the Holy Spirit, is a saint. The meaning of the term *saint* develops throughout the New Testament. Paul addressed his first letter to the Corinthians, "To the church of God which is at Corinth, to those who are sanctified in Christ Jesus, called to be saints" (1 Cor. 1:2), and then he scolded them for more than fifteen chapters for their poor performance in the Christian life. Nevertheless, they were still called saints, not because they had halos over their heads, but because they had been set apart as the body of Christ.

Let us get to the heart of the message in Acts 9:10–19, where we see the response of Jesus to Ananias's suggestion. **But the Lord said to him, "Go"** (v. 15). I once heard a preacher say, "Everybody loves to hear Jesus when He says, 'Come to Me, all you who are burdened and heavy laden and I will give you rest. But once we get there, He says, 'Now go . . . ,' and that is where the Christian life becomes difficult." Jesus listened to the argument that Ananias gave Him but cut him off and said, "Go. Do what I tell you to do." Why is Ananias to go to Saul? **"He is a chosen vessel of Mine to bear My name before Gentiles, kings, and the children of Israel"** (v. 15).

A Chosen Vessel

A fundamental principle of the law of economics is this: the single most important cause of increasing productivity is better tools. Only 3 percent of Americans today are farmers, yet they feed not only all of America but much of the world. Why is it that the American farmer can produce so much more food than farmers from other countries? It is not because the American has a higher IQ or a better physique or more information about agriculture. It is because the American farmer has better tools. The American farmer has a John Deere tractor, whereas farmers in other countries have a plow that is pulled behind a mule. A farmer working with a tractor and all the harvesting equipment we have in America today can vastly outproduce a farmer working alone with primitive tools.

Karl Marx understood this, and he said that productivity increases when better tools are invented. He also understood the principle that whoever controls the tools controls the game. I learned that when I was a youth playing baseball on the sandlots of Pittsburgh. Before we had organized sports, we used to meet together at the ballpark. We arrived with all the necessary equipment—balls, bats, gloves—and we'd pick teams and play ball. We had no umpires, so whoever witnessed a play from the best angle would make the call. When there was a close play at first base, the first baseman would say, "You're out!" while the runner would claim he was safe. The argument would continue until the runner would say, "It's my bat, so I say that I'm safe." In other words, if the game was going to continue, it would have to go the way the one with the tools said. That is why Marx wanted the state to own the tools, so that it could control the means of production.

It is by the improvement of tools that production increases, and the greater the productivity, the greater the basic level of living for the people. The more shirts produced, the lower the cost per unit. The lower the cost per unit, the more people can afford them. The same principle applies to food. Increased production means lower prices; lower prices means wider distribution. This is elementary, but we tend to forget it from time to time. The key is getting the tool, the instrument, that will increase productivity and then using it to its optimal value and production.

The reason I segued into economics is that the principle we looked at is found in the language Jesus used to explain to Ananias what He was doing in calling the Apostle Paul. The term *vessel* means "instrument, implement, or tool." Jesus had chosen Saul as His instrument to help cultivate the kingdom that He had planted. Saul hadn't chosen Christ, but Christ had chosen him for His purposes—to bear His name. Saul had come bearing papers of authority from the high priest to wipe Christ's name off the face of the earth, but Christ had stopped him. He gave Saul a new burden, to bear His name before Gentiles, kings, and the children of Israel.

The Call

"For I will show him how many things he must suffer for My name's sake" (v. 16). Unspeakable suffering lay ahead for Paul. When he signed up for Christ's mission, he had no idea the suffering that was to come. He would learn gradually, through the remainder of his life, the sufferings he would endure as Christ's instrument. We are not all called to be messengers to kings or to people worldwide, or to have the burden that the Apostle Paul had, but every Christian is an elect instrument of Christ to bear His name to the nations. We are His instruments, to a lesser degree than the Apostle Paul but in no less reality, and the task is still there for us—the task of evangelism—to carry the name of Jesus. There is no higher calling.

People complain to my secretary, Maureen, that it is harder to get hold of me than to get hold of the president of the United States. That is because I have a higher calling than the president, and, as far as I'm concerned, if I stopped doing what I am doing and became the president, it would be a demotion, because there is no higher calling than that of bearing the name of Jesus to the nations.

And Ananias went his way and entered the house; and laying his hands on him he said, "Brother Saul, the Lord Jesus, who appeared to you on the road as you came, has sent me that you may receive your sight and be filled with the Holy Spirit" (v. 17). Why did Jesus send Ananias? Ananias wasn't an Apostle. Why didn't He send John or Peter or Philip? He didn't send one of the Apostles because for this task the Lord was pleased to use as His chosen vessel a heretofore unknown Christian in Damascus named Ananias.

Immediately there fell from his eyes something like scales, and he received his sight at once; and he arose and was baptized (v. 18). The Greek word translated "scales" here is the same word used for fish scales or for shells that are on eggs or for the rinds that are on fruit. Something physical literally fell from the eyes of Paul, some sort of flakes that had concealed the light from his eyes and had kept him blind for three days. **So when he had received food, he was strengthened. Then Saul spent some days with the disciples at Damascus** (v. 19).

When Paul wrote to the Galatians, he made a big point of saying that he did not receive his authority from any human being; his apostolic authority had come immediately and directly from Christ alone. Yet we find elsewhere in the book of Acts times when Paul met with the other disciples and Apostles in Jerusalem. We see that here, where Christ used Ananias to give Paul back his sight and give him the gift of the Holy Spirit. However, even as these things were taking place, Ananias was a tool in the hand of Jesus, ministering to the one whom Jesus had selected to be an Apostle. Ananias was not working on his own authority but on the authority of Christ, so Paul was not deceiving anyone or distorting the truth when he said that he received his authority from none other than Christ. Everyone else involved in the drama was merely confirming and corroborating what Christ did for Paul on the road to Damascus.

We are called to be chosen vessels, instruments, tools to change the world by carrying the name of Jesus wherever we can.

24

A BASKET CASE

Acts 9:20–31

Immediately he preached the Christ in the synagogues, that He is the Son of God. Then all who heard were amazed, and said, "Is this not he who destroyed those who called on this name in Jerusalem, and has come here for that purpose, so that he might bring them bound to the chief priests?" But Saul increased all the more in strength, and confounded the Jews who dwelt in Damascus, proving that this Jesus is the Christ. Now after many days were past, the Jews plotted to kill him. But their plot became known to Saul. And they watched the gates day and night, to kill him. Then the disciples took him by night and let him down through the wall in a large basket. And when Saul had come to Jerusalem, he tried to join the disciples; but they were all afraid of him, and did not believe that he was a disciple. But Barnabas took him and brought him to the apostles. And he declared to them how he had seen the Lord on the road, and that He had spoken to him, and how he had preached boldly at Damascus in the name of Jesus. So he was with them at Jerusalem, coming in and going out. And he spoke boldly in the name of the Lord Jesus and disputed against the Hellenists, but they attempted to kill him. When the brethren found out, they brought him down to Caesarea and sent him out to Tarsus. Then the churches throughout all Judea, Galilee, and Samaria had peace and were edified. And walking in the fear of the Lord and in the comfort of the Holy Spirit, they were multiplied.

S aul had left Jerusalem on a mission to root out Christians in Damascus, and he got orders from the high priest that authorized him to drag them from their homes and bring them back. So with an entourage he left the city breathing out threats, but he was interrupted on the route to Damascus by the intrusion into his life of the risen Christ. In that episode the Apostle Paul was converted. He entered into Damascus, being led by the hand because God had struck him blind. Then he was taken to the street called Straight where Ananias laid hands on him, the Holy Spirit anointed him, and scales fell from his eyes, and he was able to see.

Then we read that this one who came blind into the city of Damascus, being led by the hand, became so powerful in such a short period of time that he had to leave the city because there was a conspiracy there to kill him. He left by way of a window in the wall of the city, secreted out and lowered down in a woven basket, like so much dirty laundry. There had been a radical shift in the circumstances of the Apostle from the time he first left Jerusalem in power: he was led in humility into Damascus, and then he had to flee from the city in weakness in a basket so that his life would be spared.

In between his entrance into Damascus and his departure by the basket, he had a mighty ministry, and I want to spend some time looking specifically at the first statement that Luke tells us about this interim period of the apostolic ministry in Damascus.

Son of God

Immediately he preached the Christ in the synagogues, that He is the Son of God (v. 20). From the moment Paul began preaching in the synagogues in Damascus, his message was about Jesus as the Christ, and he declared to the Jewish people that Jesus was the Son of God. It is important to notice this because it is the only time in the book of Acts that the title "Son of God" is used for Jesus. We see two titles for Jesus juxtaposed in the New Testament: "Son of Man" and "Son of God." It is tempting to think that the term "Son of Man" refers to Jesus' human nature and that the title "Son of God" refers to His divine nature, but if we draw that conclusion we will be making a serious error. It is true that when Jesus is called the "Son of Man," it has something to do with His human nature, but the chief significance of that title is that it refers to an Old Testament personage, a heavenly being who dwelt in the presence of the Ancient of Days and was sent from heaven to descend to the earth for a mission. In a sense, therefore, the title "Son of Man" describes more of Jesus' divine nature than it does His human nature. Likewise, when we come to the title "Son of God," we assume that its primary reference is to His deity, but again we would trip over ourselves if we drew that inference without great care.

I want to focus on that here because Paul, from the beginning of his ministry, preached in the synagogues that Jesus is the Son of God. What did he mean? In the Old Testament, that title "son of God" is used in several ways. First, the angels of heaven are called the sons of God; the sons of God, in that sense, are still creatures. They are not divine beings. Second, Israel itself, as a nation, is called the son of God. In God's redeeming the people of Israel, He adopted them into His family and called the whole corporate nation His son. Third, kings in the Old Testament were called the sons of God. Fourth, as the concept of the messiah developed over time, the messiah also became known as the Son of God. In the New Testament, God spoke audibly from the clouds and announced to those present, "This is My beloved Son, in whom I am well pleased" (Matt. 17:5). Later God again spoke from heaven audibly, saying basically the same message: "This is My beloved Son. Hear Him" (Mark 9:7).

What are we to make of this? In the New Testament, the idea of sonship is inseparably related to obedience. This truth lay at the root of the controversies Jesus had with the Pharisees over their relationship with Abraham. The Pharisees said, "Abraham is our father," and Jesus said, "If you were Abraham's children, you would do the works of Abraham. But now you seek to kill Me, a Man who has told you the truth which I heard from God. Abraham did not do this . . . before Abraham was, I AM . . . You are of your father the devil" (John 8:39–40, 58, 44). There is quite a contrast between being called "children of Abraham" and "children of Satan." Why did Jesus say that His opponents were children of the Devil? He answers that question for us: "You are of your father the devil, and the desires of your father you want to do" (John 8:44).

The same idea is used to describe sonship with respect to Jesus. Jesus is uniquely the Son of God in the sense that He, of all people in history, was completely and absolutely obedient to the Father. In His humanity, He was the Son of God. In His humanity, because of His sinlessness and perfect obedience, He warranted the title "Son of God." We could stop there and say that the term "Son of God" has nothing to say about Jesus' divine nature and that it simply refers to His human nature in His perfect obedience. That is wrong because the New Testament goes beyond that to the transcendent aspect of Christ's unique relationship to the Father.

In John's Gospel Jesus is described as the *monogenes*, the only begotten of the Father. The term "only begotten" does not mean "first begotten"; the prefix *mono*-means "only," rendering the "only begotten one." It is the language of *begottenness* that provoked one of the most serious controversies in all of church history, which led to the fourth-century Council of Nicaea, out of which came the Nicene Creed. In the fourth century a dispute arose when Arius denied the deity of Jesus. Arius said that Jesus was a human being who, while uniquely adopted by the Father for His mission, was not divine. Arius said that Jesus was not eternal; He was not of the same substance or essence as God; He was merely a creature. However, we know that Jesus was divine because the Bible says He was begotten, and the Greek verb "to beget," *ginomai*, means "to be," "to become," or "to happen." It refers to those incidents and events that indicate the beginning of something in time and space. Arius argued from the text that Jesus was begotten, which means that He had a beginning, and if He had a beginning, He is not eternal; and if He is not eternal, He is not God. So, Arius concluded, we ought not to attribute deity to Christ. That was what the Council at Nicaea was all about. The Nicene Creed declared that Christ was *homoousios*—of the same substance as the Father and therefore co-substantial and co-eternal with the Father. The creed uses the language of begottenness: "Christ was begotten, not made."

The church acknowledges that the Bible speaks of the begottenness of Jesus, but the begottenness here refers to an eternal relationship, an eternal begottenness set apart from any other kind of begottenness by the term *monogenes*. Christ is the only one ever uniquely begotten eternally of the Father; He is very God of very God. There never was a time when the Son was not. God was, is, and always will be triune. That was the radical message immediately proclaimed by the Apostle Paul. He had seen Jesus as an enemy to the purity of the Jewish monotheistic religion, but upon his conversion he realized that the Messiah of Israel was nothing less than God incarnate.

When Paul preached in the synagogues that Jesus was the Son of God, he was using that title in the fullest measure. Of course, when he made that declaration, his hearers were astonished. Because of his about-face they said, **"Is this not he who destroyed those who called on this name in Jerusalem, and has come here for that purpose, so that he might bring them bound to the chief priests?"** (v. 21). The answer to that question was yes. Paul was the one who had come to bind the followers of Jesus and drag them back to Jerusalem, and he hadn't come as a one-man vigilante against Christians; he had come with the full authorization of the high priest.

However, something happened between the beginning of that mission and his arrival in Damascus: he met *the* High Priest. He met the eternal High Priest, who will never retire or abdicate His office by dying as all the lines of high priests in Israel had, one after another. Their term was limited, but *the* High Priest changed the orders, gave a new commission, overruled the high priest in Jerusalem, and gave Paul a whole new mission, which he began to carry out immediately.

At first he was greeted by amazement. **But Saul increased all the more in strength, and confounded the Jews who dwelt in Damascus, proving that this Jesus is the Christ** (v. 22). This continued for a few days until the astonishment of the local Jewish community turned to rage, and they plotted to kill him; but Paul heard of the plot, and he escaped through the wall in a basket. In those days, homes were often built right into the city walls.

When Saul had come to Jerusalem, he tried to join the disciples; but they were all afraid of him, and did not believe that he was a disciple. But Barnabas took him and brought him to the apostles. And he declared to them how he had seen the Lord on the road, and that He had spoken to him, and how he had preached boldly at Damascus in the name of Jesus (vv. 26–27). Again we are told that Paul spoke boldly in the name of the Lord Jesus in Jerusalem, disputing with the Greek-speaking Jews, the Hellenists, and then they tried to kill him. When the disciples found out about this, they brought him down to Caesarea and sent him out to Tarsus.

Worship

Luke inserts a brief interlude: **Then the churches throughout all Judea, Galilee, and Samaria had peace and were edified. And walking in the fear of the Lord and in the comfort of the Holy Spirit, they were multiplied** (v. 31). Before we heard of the conversion of Paul, we heard something of Peter's ministry in Jerusalem, and then in this brief interval we are introduced to Paul and find out about his conversion, his brief ministry in Damascus, and his return to Caesarea until he was sent back to Tarsus. After this the text returns to the ministry of Peter in Jerusalem before it recounts Paul's missionary journeys. Paul's ministry began in Damascus, and it began by declaring that Christ was the Messiah. It began by proclaiming Jesus in His fullness, in His perfect humanity, and in His perfect deity as the Son of the living God.

What Paul declared there in Damascus is the same thing that Peter declared when Jesus asked, "Who do you say that I am?" and Simon said, "You are the Christ, the Son of the living God" (Matt. 16:15–16). God hates religion because religion is something that humans invent, and religious behavior is something we conjure up. Christianity is about devotion to our creed, not because it has been written down but because of the substance of the truth contained therein. We are to be people who are persuaded that Jesus is the Christ—that God's Son, His only begotten Son, came into this world for us and for our salvation, which is why we gather together to give the sacrifice of praise and to give honor, worship, and adoration to Him.

How shall we then worship? The big question today is the "who" question.

Whom do we worship? *Who* we worship defines *how* we worship. I almost cry when I drive past churches and see advertisements for worship services that say, "9:30 service, traditional; 11:00 service, contemporary," or "Our worship is blended. We are an ecclesiastical cafeteria. If you want one style, come at 9:30; if you want another style, come at 11:00." That is the language of the contemporary church. The church-growth movement is always and everywhere asking, "What do the people want?" The issue is what does God want? Who is it that we are here for? We are not here to please unbelievers. Surely we are to evangelize them, but corporate worship on Sunday morning is for the body of Christ, for believers to be brought before their living God and approach Him as holy. So the "how" question must always be answered by the "who" question.

That should be true in every aspect of our lives; how we live our Christian lives should be determined by who we understand God to be and by who Jesus is. We have to deal with the Son of God, and though we are called to enter boldly into His presence, He never stops being holy, and that should be manifested in how we worship Him. I believe that how people worship God speaks louder about their understanding of who He is than any creed or theology ever written.

25

THE RAISING OF DORCAS

Acts 9:32–43

Now it came to pass, as Peter went through all parts of the country, that he also came down to the saints who dwelt in Lydda. There he found a certain man named Aeneas, who had been bedridden eight years and was paralyzed. And Peter said to him, "Aeneas, Jesus the Christ heals you. Arise and make your bed." Then he arose immediately. So all who dwelt at Lydda and Sharon saw him and turned to the Lord. At Joppa there was a certain disciple named Tabitha, which is translated Dorcas. This woman was full of good works and charitable deeds which she did. But it happened in those days that she became sick and died. When they had washed her, they laid her in an upper room. And since Lydda was near Joppa, and the disciples had heard that Peter was there, they sent two men to him, imploring him not to delay in coming to them. Then Peter arose and went with them. When he had come, they brought him to the upper room. And all the widows stood by him weeping, showing the tunics and garments which Dorcas had made while she was with them. But Peter put them all out, and knelt down and prayed. And turning to the body he said, "Tabitha, arise." And she opened her eyes, and when she saw Peter she sat up. Then he gave her his hand and lifted her up; and when he had called the saints and widows, he presented her alive. And it became known throughout all Joppa, and many believed on the Lord. So it was that he stayed many days in Joppa with Simon, a tanner.

I t is obvious from the book of Acts and from extrabiblical writings that the first-century church was based initially in Jerusalem. Peter apparently became the chief of the Apostles, and his principle mission was to the Jews. When Saul was converted and became the Apostle Paul, his chief mission, given to him by Christ, was to be the Apostle to the Gentiles. Paul did not ignore the Jews, but he went to the Gentile world on his missionary journeys, as Acts records for us, taking the gospel to the Gentile nations.

In the meantime, back in Palestine, **it came to pass, as Peter went through all parts of the country, that he also came down to the saints who dwelt in Lydda** (v. 32). Peter went on a mission that took him all over Israel—not outside the country but into Judea, Samaria, and Galilee, and so on—following the orders of the Great Commission given to him by Jesus. The record before us in this study finds Peter north of Jerusalem and making his way back south. We are told that while on this journey, he came down to the saints who dwelt in Lydda. Lydda is the New Testament name for the Old Testament village of Lod. Lydda is between Jerusalem and Joppa, which was on the seacoast of the Mediterranean, some miles south of Caesarea. Lydda, just a bit north of Jerusalem, is only about five miles from what was once the town of Emmaus. During the Crusades, Richard the Lionheart visited the Holy Land and spent quite a bit of time in the village of Lydda, and there he built a church in honor of Saint George. The ruins of that church remain even today. This is the site where Peter came and found a man whose name was Aeneas.

"Arise and Make Your Bed"

There he found a certain man named Aeneas, who had been bedridden eight years and was paralyzed. And Peter said to him, "Aeneas, Jesus the Christ heals you. Arise and make your bed" (vv. 33–34). This could just as easily be translated as "Jesus the Christ is at this very moment healing you." Peter took no credit for any of the power being manifested in the healing; he healed in the name of Jesus. Peter said two things here. First, he told the man to stand because Jesus was making him whole. Second, he told the man to make his bed. Why do we make our beds when we get up in the morning? It seems like a waste of energy and time, but for reasons of decorum and utility we do so, and also because from the time we wake up in the morning until we rest our heads on the pillow again at night, we do not need our beds. In the eight-year period that the man had been bedridden, there were surely times when friends or physicians came to turn him over to get rid of bed sores or to wash him, and in the process they would have made the bed, but Peter told him to make the bed because he would not be needing it as a permanent dwelling place.

Every Christian is in the process of sanctification. No two of us begin our Christian walk at the same point; each of us starts out carrying unique baggage. It may take ten years for one to get rid of something that another was rid of in the first three months. No two Christians grow at the same pace. We are to be a fellowship of patient people practicing a love that covers a multitude of sins, because we are altogether growing up into the fullness of Christ into conformity to the image of Christ. He has already saved us from our sins, but He is of sin the double cure. Not only does He remove our guilt and take it upon Himself, but He works with and in us to change us, to bring us from spiritual infancy to maturity, to wholeness. None of us are totally whole. We all have deficiencies in our character, in our obedience, in our physical bodies, and in every other way. We look forward to heaven when we will cross through the veil to the day of our glorification, when we will receive our final wholeness, where sin and all its effects will be removed from us forever. We will live forever free of the ravages of sin.

A taste of that was given to the man who had been paralyzed. Every Christian has points of spiritual paralysis. We may be able to walk unaided. We may even be able to make our own beds. But there are certain things that grip us with fear and paralyze us from being all that God has created us to be, and that is the point at which we are not whole people. Yet Peter did not hang up a shingle and say, "Come to me and I will make you whole." No, he said, "Jesus the Christ is making you whole." Whatever condition you are in today, if you put your faith in Jesus Christ, He is making you whole so that you can make your bed and walk. **So all who dwelt at Lydda and Sharon saw him and turned to the Lord** (v. 35).

Dorcas

At Joppa there was a certain disciple named Tabitha, which is translated Dorcas. This woman was full of good works and charitable deeds which she did (v. 36). The name Joppa means "beautiful." It wasn't a great commercial seaport, but it was the only one they had, and from a distance, at least, it looked pretty, so they called it beautiful.

Dorcas, or Tabitha, means "gazelle" or "antelope." We are told that Tabitha was full of good works and charitable deeds. She was overflowing with good works of charity. Here was a woman giving herself to helping people in need, and we can glean from this text that those she most helped were widows. This calls to mind the instruction of James, who wrote that the essence of true religion is to care for orphans and widows (James 1:27). Jesus has a special sense of compassion for those who have lost their mates. There was ministry in the very beginning of the church for orphans and widows, and Dorcas is an example of that.

But it happened in those days that she became sick and died. When they had washed her, they laid her in an upper room (v. 37). In those days, funeral services were held at home. People were laid out for a brief time, and friends and relatives would come to pay their last respects. **And since Lydda was near Joppa** [about ten miles away], **and the disciples had heard that Peter was there, they sent two men to him, imploring him not to delay in coming to them** (v. 38). This seems parallel to the situation of the death of Lazarus (John 11).

Then Peter arose and went with them. When he had come, they brought him to the upper room. And all the widows stood by him weeping, showing the tunics and garments which Dorcas had made while she was with them (v. 39). When Peter entered the upper room, he saw this large crowd of widows displaying the gifts that Dorcas had made for them, the clothing that she had lovingly stitched and sewed and prepared. He saw the fruit of the ministry of this woman.

But Peter put them all out, and knelt down and prayed (v. 40). The weeping women left the room, and this time Peter didn't just speak to the corpse as he had spoken to the paralytic; here he knelt down and prayed. He got on his knees right next to the bed where the corpse of Dorcas lay, and he said, **"Tabitha, arise"** (v. 40). He dismissed the women because he did not want any witnesses. For an Apostle to come to a paralyzed man on his bed and say, "Get up and walk," takes great faith. Yet consider how much faith was necessary to kneel next to a corpse and command it to arise. What if she hadn't responded? As soon as he said, "Tabitha, arise," she did not arise, but she opened her eyes—eyes that just a moment before had been closed in death.

The first thing she saw was the face of Peter, and when she saw him, she sat up. **Then he gave her his hand and lifted her up; and when he had called the saints and widows, he presented her alive** (v. 41). The English translation of this sentence is a bit awkward. It doesn't quite get at what the text actually says. It is not as though she opened her eyes and sat up, but that was as far as she could go. It is not as if she were only half alive until Peter picked her up and helped her out of bed. Peter's giving her his hand was more like a gesture of chivalry, as if to say, "Madam, worker of many good deeds, one who has given alms, has made garments for all your friends who are outside weeping, take my hand and let me escort you to them." So he did. He led her from the room, called the saints and the widows, and presented her alive. This was only a foretaste of heaven, for Dorcas would die again. It was a downpayment of the apostolic truth that everyone who is in Christ will be presented to the Bridegroom alive to live forever with no more tears and no more sin and no more death. This taste of heaven that Peter manifested to the people in this town spread abroad throughout the whole region, and multitudes were converted.

So it was that he stayed many days in Joppa with Simon, a tanner (v. 43). The fact that Luke mentions where Peter resided the rest of his time at Joppa, with Simon the tanner, holds significance for what happens next in the drama of the outworking of the early church and its inclusion among Jews and Gentiles, which is the focus of our next lesson. The point of transition, the bridge between this miracle and what happens next in Cornelius's household, is hinted at by the fact that Peter stayed in the home of a man whose occupation among the Jews was considered unclean. Tanners had to deal with the carcasses of dead animals, a practice prohibited to Jews. So, as Jesus before him, Peter went to places and to people that nobody else wanted to touch.

26

PETER'S VISION

Acts 10:1–16

There was a certain man in Caesarea called Cornelius, a centurion of what was called the Italian Regiment, a devout man and one who feared God with all his household, who gave alms generously to the people, and prayed to God always. About the ninth hour of the day he saw clearly in a vision an angel of God coming in and saying to him, "Cornelius!" And when he observed him, he was afraid, and said, "What is it, lord?" So he said to him, "Your prayers and your alms have come up for a memorial before God. Now send men to Joppa, and send for Simon whose surname is Peter. He is lodging with Simon, a tanner, whose house is by the sea. He will tell you what you must do." And when the angel who spoke to him had departed, Cornelius called two of his household servants and a devout soldier from among those who waited on him continually. So when he had explained all these things to them, he sent them to Joppa. The next day, as they went on their journey and drew near the city, Peter went up on the housetop to pray, about the sixth hour. Then he became very hungry and wanted to eat; but while they made ready, he fell into a trance and saw heaven opened and an object like a great sheet bound at the four corners, descending to him and let down to the earth. In it were all kinds of four-footed animals of the earth, wild beasts, creeping things, and birds of the air. And a voice came to him, "Rise, Peter; kill and eat." But Peter said, "Not so, Lord! For I have never eaten anything common or unclean." And a voice spoke to him again the second time, "What God has cleansed you must not call common." This was done three times. And the object was taken up into heaven again.

Acts 10 is one of the most important chapters of the entire book of Acts, if not the most important chapter. Actually, it is one of the most important chapters in the entire New Testament because it brings to our attention an extremely important moment in redemptive history, a time of transition from the old way of doing things to a whole new epoch of God's redemptive activity. To the Colossians Paul wrote,

> I now rejoice in my sufferings for you, and fill up in my flesh what is lacking in the afflictions of Christ, for the sake of His body, which is the church, of which I became a minister according to the stewardship from God which was given to me for you, to fulfill the word of God, the mystery which has been hidden from ages and from generations, but now has been revealed to His saints. To them God willed to make known what are the riches of the glory of this mystery among the Gentiles: which is Christ in you, the hope of glory. (Col. 1:24–27)

Paul had been afflicted on every side, yet he was able to rejoice in his sufferings because other believers benefited from them. Through his apostolic ministry, Paul filled up that which was left unfinished in the sufferings of Christ. In his letter to the Colossians he reveals a mystery, a *mysterion*, that had been hidden for ages. In the New Testament sense, a mystery is something that God has held back but at a certain time reveals openly. This particular mystery is that the Gentiles, through the ministry of Christ, have become part of the church. Up until this time, Gentiles were considered outside the scope of the covenant God had made with Abraham and Moses and were therefore without hope. When Christ inaugurated the new covenant, the barrier between Jew and Gentile was broken and hope was extended to Gentiles. Most of us in the church today are from a Gentile background, but we are included because of what took place in Cornelius's household at Caesarea.

Acts 9 ends with a postscript, a seemingly offhand comment of Luke's, that Peter remained for a while in Joppa, where he stayed at the home of Simon the tanner. This fact about Simon provides us with a clue as to what comes next. Tanners' work necessitated touching the carcasses of dead animals, which was taboo to pious Jews. So, in all probability, this Simon with whom Peter stayed in Joppa was a Gentile and therefore unclean. Additionally, it was one thing for a Jew to welcome a Gentile into his home, but it was quite another to go into the home of a Gentile. Entering the home of a Gentile rendered a Jew unclean.

Cornelius

There was a certain man in Caesarea called Cornelius (v. 1). Cornelius was a centurion. Most centurions were captains over a hundred men in the Roman army, but sometimes the term *centurion* was used for someone of a higher office in the military. That seems to be the case with Cornelius, because he was of the elite guard of the Italian Regiment. Cornelius is described as **a devout man and one who feared God** (v. 2).

By way of review, the book of Acts follows the Great Commission, where Jesus gave His disciples the responsibility of preaching the gospel first in Jerusalem, then in Judea, then Samaria, and then to the uttermost parts of the earth. Acts follows that progress of the church, opening in Jerusalem, expanding into Judea and out to Samaria, and then to the uttermost parts of the earth. Also, the book of Acts deals with four distinct groups of people: Jews, Samaritans, Gentiles, and God fearers. The God fearers were those Gentiles, usually Greek-speaking Gentiles, who had converted to Judaism in every respect except one—they did not subject themselves to circumcision. They were called God fearers because, even though they were Gentiles, they did not believe in the gods and goddesses of Rome, or in the pantheon of Greek deities, or in any of the Oriental religions of the day. Rather, they believed in the Most High God and were faithful followers of Yahweh, the God of Israel.

Luke describes Cornelius as one of those God fearers. He, along with his household, feared God. Cornelius gave alms generously and prayed to God always. One day at about three o'clock in the afternoon, Cornelius had a vision in which an angel of God came and said to him, **"Cornelius!"** (v. 3). When Cornelius saw this angel and heard the voice addressing him, he was terrified, as anybody would be, and he answered, **"What is it, lord?"** (v. 4). His response calls to mind Paul's response on the road to Damascus when Christ had appeared to him and said, "Saul, Saul, why are you persecuting Me?" Saul had cried out, "Who are You, Lord?" In like manner, Cornelius knew it was the Lord speaking to him, but he did not know why.

The angel said to him, **"Your prayers and your alms have come up for a memorial before God"** (v. 4). Jews who had access to the inner court of the temple brought in their sacrifices, and smoke from the burnt offering, as well as incense from the altar of incense, which is the altar of prayer, wafted into the air. The smoke lifted heavenward, symbolizing a sweet aroma to God. The angel was saying to Cornelius, "Even though you are not a Jew, your prayers and sacrifices have been sweet to God, and God is recognizing you." Then the angel told Cornelius what to do: **"Now send men to Joppa, and send for Simon whose surname is Peter. He is lodging with Simon, a tanner, whose house** is by the sea. He will tell you what you must do." And when the angel who spoke to him had departed, Cornelius called two of his household servants and a devout soldier from among those who waited on him continually. So when he had explained all these things to them, he sent them to Joppa (vv. 5–8). God gave specific directions, not only what city to go to, but what house to go to and where it was—by the sea.

What God Has Cleansed

The next day they went on their way to Joppa. In the meantime, Peter went up on Simon's housetop to pray at about the sixth hour, which is noon. Then he became very hungry and wanted to eat, so the servants began to prepare a meal for Peter. While they were making it, Peter fell into a trance, and in this trance he saw heaven opened and an object like a great sheet. That descriptive term, "the great sheet," is also the same term used for a huge sail on a ship. **In it were all kinds of four-footed animals of the earth, wild beasts, creeping things, and birds of the air. And a voice came to him, "Rise, Peter; kill and eat"** (vv. 12–13).

In response to what Peter saw in the trance he said, **"Not so, Lord!"** (v. 14). What could be more insane than saying no to Almighty God? This is part of the reason that Peter gained a reputation for impetuosity on occasion. Peter explained the reason for his negative response: **"I have never eaten anything common or unclean"** (v. 14). Peter had been a Jew from birth and had never broken Jewish dietary laws. God listened to Peter's protest and said, **"What God has cleansed you must not call common"** (v. 15).

In that moment, centuries of dietary laws and legal requirements that God had sent to His people through Moses were instantly repealed. Keeping those laws had been vital to the Old Testament Jew. That was why Shadrach, Meshach, and Abednego went into the fiery furnace and why Daniel wound up in a lions' den. Those men, held captive in Babylon, were keeping kosher. They refused to bow down and worship the king or to eat the king's food because they wanted to be faithful to the law of God. They put their lives on the line for it. Now, all of a sudden, God changed the rules.

That may seem to indicate something whimsical or capricious about the character of God, but we have to understand that when God legislated to His people in the Old Testament, He did so in two different ways. On the one hand, He gave laws that came out of His character, which, if ever repealed, would do violence to His sanctity and holiness. Therefore, God would never repeal the moral law, the Ten Commandments, because to do so, He would be denying His character. So God will never permit His people to craft idols or to take His name in vain. Oh, that people would treat the name of God with such reverence and respect that they would never think of using it in a flippant manner. Those laws that are based on God's character are without repeal. They remain forever.

Yet there are other rules that God set down for historical purposes. He created a nation, a tiny nation, of Jews, but not because they were better than anybody else. He called Abraham out of paganism, and Abraham had done nothing to deserve that. Yet God told Abraham that through him many nations would be blessed (Genesis 17). He did not choose them and then give them special diets so that they could enjoy the best position before God forever. They were called for a purpose—to be a holy priesthood to the world. After a while, however, they began to think that ethnic separation—being Jewish—was what mattered for salvation. So to maintain their Jewish purity and identity, the dietary laws were added to the covenant until the coming of Christ, who tore down the wall of separation and began to build His church, not just with Jews but with Samaritans, Gentiles, and God fearers.

Peter's vision was not about food or animals; it was about people. Through the remainder of Acts 10 Luke will show why God repealed the dietary laws. It was to show that the unclean were being gathered together and made clean by Christ. We all start this life unclean, and in some respects we are still unclean, but if we have confessed Christ and put our hope and trust in Him alone for salvation, then He is in us and we are in Him. If that relationship exists in your life right now, do not let anybody call you unclean, because God has declared you clean. That is what justification is all about.

God has removed your impurities from His sight and given you access into His presence. He knows the sin that remains in you, but if you have put yourself at the feet of Christ, He has embraced you and adopted you into His family. Others may call you unclean, but remember that God said to Peter, "What God has cleansed you must not call common." That is the mystery Luke is speaking of, that we, who by nature are unclean, have been declared clean by God. When God declares us clean, we are clean in His sight.

27

CORNELIUS'S HOUSEHOLD

Acts 10:17–43

Now while Peter wondered within himself what this vision which he had seen meant, behold, the men who had been sent from Cornelius had made inquiry for Simon's house, and stood before the gate. And they called and asked whether Simon, whose surname was Peter, was lodging there. While Peter thought about the vision, the Spirit said to him, "Behold, three men are seeking you. Arise therefore, go down and go with them, doubting nothing; for I have sent them." Then Peter went down to the men who had been sent to him from Cornelius, and said, "Yes, I am he whom you seek. For what reason have you come?" And they said, "Cornelius the centurion, a just man, one who fears God and has a good reputation among all the nation of the Jews, was divinely instructed by a holy angel to summon you to his house, and to hear words from you." Then he invited them in and lodged them. On the next day Peter went away with them, and some brethren from Joppa accompanied him. And the following day they entered Caesarea. Now Cornelius was waiting for them, and had called together his relatives and close friends. As Peter was coming in, Cornelius met him and fell down at his feet and worshiped him. But Peter lifted him up, saying, "Stand up; I myself am also a man." And as he talked with him, he went in and found many who had come together. Then he said to them, "You know how unlawful it is for a Jewish man to keep company with or go to one of another nation. But God has shown me that I should not call any man common or unclean. Therefore I came without objection as soon as I was sent for. I ask, then, for what reason have you sent for me?" So Cornelius said, "Four days ago I was fasting until this hour; and at the ninth hour I prayed in my house, and behold, a man stood before me in bright clothing, and said, 'Cornelius, your prayer has been heard, and your alms are remembered in the sight of God. Send therefore to Joppa and call Simon here, whose surname is Peter. He is lodging in the house of Simon, a tanner, by the sea. When he comes, he will speak to you.' So I sent to you immediately, and you have done well to come. Now therefore, we are all present before God, to hear all the things commanded you by God." Then Peter opened his mouth and said: "In truth I perceive that God shows no partiality. But in every nation whoever fears Him and works righteousness is accepted by Him. The word which God sent to the children of Israel, preaching peace through Jesus Christ—He is Lord of all —that word you know, which was proclaimed throughout all Judea, and began from Galilee after the baptism which John preached: how God anointed Jesus of Nazareth with the Holy Spirit and with power, who went about doing good and healing all who were oppressed by the devil, for God was with Him. And we are witnesses of all things which He did both in the land of the Jews and in Jerusalem, whom they killed by hanging on a tree. Him God raised up on the third day, and showed Him openly, not to all the people, but to witnesses chosen before by God, even to us who ate and drank with Him after He arose from the dead. And He commanded us to preach to the people, and to testify that it is He who was ordained by God to be Judge of the living and the dead. To Him all the prophets witness that, through His name, whoever believes in Him will receive remission of sins."

We will not cover in detail every verse of this study on Acts 10:17–43 because Luke repeats much of what we have already considered. God had directed Cornelius to send some of his comrades to request a visit from Peter. At the same time, God had prepared for this meeting by sending a vision to Peter of a sheet filled with all kinds of animals, both clean and unclean.

Icons and Images

After this, Peter left Joppa and went to Caesarea to meet with Cornelius. **As Peter was coming in, Cornelius met him and fell down at his feet and worshiped him** (v. 25). I think we all have a proclivity for giving certain attention and adulation to those who have meant a lot to us in our spiritual journey. I have pictures of Jonathan Edwards and Martin Luther in both my offices and my home. However, as much as I love Edwards, Luther, Calvin, and others, not once in my life have I ever prayed to them, nor ever have I gotten down on my knees and made an act of devotion before them, nor have I ever asked them to intercede with God on my behalf.

One of the crises of the sixteenth-century Protestant Reformation concerned the use of icons and images in the church. The Reformers were opposed to the use of images because of the practice in the medieval church of giving veneration to the saints, in general, and to the Virgin Mary, in particular. The Church of Rome was very careful to distinguish between worship of the saints and veneration of them. The distinction they made was between *dulia*, which means "service," and *latria*, which means "worship." They encouraged *ida dulia*, the service of idols, but discouraged *ida latria* or idolatry, the worship of these images. The Virgin Mother especially was to receive not only *dulia* but *hyperdulia*, which was an elevated and extreme form of service.

In objection Calvin said that this was a distinction without a difference. He said that when people bow before the images of human beings and ask them to intercede for them in heaven, they have crossed the line from service to worship. That is because in the process they must attribute to these human characters powers and authority reserved for Christ alone, whom the New Testament makes clear is the only mediator between God and man. Throughout Scripture the typical reaction of those who have a vision of angels is to fall on their face in worship. We would be inclined to want to do that ourselves. So it is understandable that when Cornelius saw a great personage such as Peter, particularly after Peter's reputation had grown exponentially after raising Dorcas from the dead, he fell down and worshiped him.

However, every time this sort of thing happens in Scripture, whether it be bowing to an angel, an Apostle, or a prophet, the response is the same. Here Peter said, **"Stand up; I myself am also a man"** (v. 26). Paul had to do the same thing, as did angels. The only person we see anywhere in Scripture who accepted the worship of people is our Lord Himself because He is God incarnate. That is why we have to be careful that in our appreciation for those who have gone before us—and we are to give respect and honor to those who have been faithful in the past—we need to guard ourselves carefully that we never cross that line to veneration and detract anything from the glory of God, about which God says, He will not give to another (Isa. 48:11). So the first thing to note here in this encounter between Peter and Cornelius is the original greeting.

The Kerygma

They talked together for a while, and then Cornelius recounted to those who had gathered all that had happened. **Then Peter opened his mouth and said: "In truth I perceive that God shows no partiality. But in every nation whoever fears Him and works righteousness is accepted by Him"** (vv. 34–35). Luke tells us that Peter opened his mouth, which meant that he was about to preach, to share the gospel.

The Greek word for "good news" is *euangelion*, which is translated "gospel."

We hear people all the time saying, "I'm committed to sharing the gospel," yet if we look at the content of what it is they share, it is not gospel at all. I may share with my neighbor that Jesus changed my life; that is a wonderful testimony, but it is not the gospel. I can say to my friends, "I've got good news for you: God loves you." That is good news, but it is not the gospel. In New Testament categories, the gospel is understood in terms of a definite content, and that content is not about me, and it is really not about you. The content focuses attention on the person and work of Jesus—who He is and what He has done—and added on is how we can receive the benefits of His ministry by faith.

I said earlier in our study of Acts that on several occasions we find examples of apostolic preaching. We get examples of what the scholars call the *kerygma*, which is just a fancy word for the proclamation of the early church. The gospel, needed by a watching, dying pagan world, is this *kerygma* that we find encapsulated in the book of Acts in sermon after sermon. We see it again here in Acts 10 when Peter visited Cornelius, and he opened his mouth and preached the gospel. What Peter preached is the life and ministry of Jesus. I think it is good for us to give our testimony, but we must not confuse our testimony with evangelism. Our testimony is pre-evangelism. It may be of interest to our friends, but, again, our life is not the gospel; Christ's life is the gospel. The power of God unto salvation is the gospel of Jesus Christ, which is given here in summary form.

"The word which God sent to the children of Israel, preaching peace through Jesus Christ—He is Lord of all—that word you know, which was proclaimed throughout all Judea, and began from Galilee after the baptism which John preached" (vv. 36–37). It is not by accident that Mark's Gospel begins with John the Baptist and how the baptism of Jesus marks the beginning of His public ministry. John saw Jesus approaching the Jordan, and he sang the *Agnus Dei*, "Behold! The Lamb of God who takes away the sin of the world" (John 1:29). Immediately Peter pointed out that Jesus is the One promised by the prophet Isaiah—the Anointed One, the *Christos*, the Messiah, the One upon whom God placed His Holy Spirit and empowered to go about preaching and teaching and delivering people from the power of Satan, healing them, and even raising them from the dead (Isaiah 61). He is the Anointed One of God, an essential truth of the gospel.

When the Apostles went out to preach the gospel, they started with Jesus, as we see here. **"God anointed Jesus of Nazareth with the Holy Spirit and with power, who went about doing good and healing all who were oppressed by the devil, for God was with Him. And we are witnesses of all things which He did both in the land of the Jews and in Jerusalem, whom they killed by hanging on a tree"** (vv. 38–39). Peter went straight to the death of Christ, focusing on the cross, the atonement. A message that does not include the cross is not evangelism; it is not the gospel. **"Him God raised up on the third day, and showed Him openly"** (v. 40). We can tell people wonderful things about God and about how He can change their life, and even about Jesus, but if the affirmation of the resurrection of Christ is absent from that testimony, it may be good news, but it is not the biblical gospel, because the cross of Christ and His resurrection are essential elements of the gospel. Peter called attention to the resurrection here.

The doctrine of the resurrection of Jesus is not an esoteric element of a secret mystery religion. The manifestation of the resurrected Christ is public. It is open. It is not open to everybody, but it is shown to those whom God chose from the foundation of the world to manifest His resurrected Son. Peter was one of them, which is why he will say later, "We did not follow cunningly devised fables when we made known to you the power and coming of our Lord Jesus Christ, but were eyewitnesses of His majesty" (2 Pet. 1:16). This is not a philosophy of life conjured up by Peter. This is not a brilliant idea that somebody received in the first century. Peter was declaring what he had seen. He had been there. He and the other Apostles had seen and heard Jesus. They had broken bread and drunk wine with Him.

Jesus Is Lord

"And He commanded us to preach to the people, and to testify that it is He who was ordained by God to be Judge of the living and the dead. To Him all the prophets witness that, through His name, whoever believes in Him will receive remission of sins" (vv. 42–43). We think that the gospel is to preach Jesus as the Savior of all, and that is part of it, but Peter said that after Jesus was risen, He had commanded them to preach that Jesus is the judge of everybody. This runs counter to contemporary evangelical lingo. Today people say, "I gave Jesus permission to be the Lord of my life," but that is arrogant patronage. We do not give Jesus permission to be the Lord of our life—He *is* the Lord of our life. He is the One who gives permission, not we. We are a narcissistic culture such as the world has never seen before. We think that salvation is all bound up in what we do and what we allow. Today we do not tell people what Christianity is really about: Jesus is our judge, not just after we die but right now. How popular is that gospel? That doesn't sound like good news because it isn't. It is bad news unless He is also our advocate, our defense attorney, our redeemer—unless we put our trust only in Him for our salvation. Then the Judge becomes our friend and advocate. Then the Judge gives remission of sin; that is, He removes from the record all charges against us. But until or unless we put our trust in Christ alone, He is our judge, and our sins are written large in front of Him. If we do not submit to Him, the gavel will come down, and there will be no mercy. We will stand on the basis of our righteousness, or lack thereof, before that Judge.

That is what Peter was moved by the Holy Spirit to explain to Cornelius. What happens when Cornelius heard the gospel is fantastic, but we have to wait until our next study for that. In the meantime, we must remember the mandate to preach the gospel.

28

THE HOLY SPIRIT
TO THE GENTILES

Acts 10:44–11:18

While Peter was still speaking these words, the Holy Spirit fell upon all those who heard the word. And those of the circumcision who believed were astonished, as many as came with Peter, because the gift of the Holy Spirit had been poured out on the Gentiles also. For they heard them speak with tongues and magnify God. Then Peter answered, "Can anyone forbid water, that these should not be baptized who have received the Holy Spirit just as we have?" And he commanded them to be baptized in the name of the Lord. Then they asked him to stay a few days. Now the apostles and brethren who were in Judea heard that the Gentiles had also received the word of God. And when Peter came up to Jerusalem, those of the circumcision contended with him, saying, "You went in to uncircumcised men and ate with them!" But Peter explained it to them in order from the beginning, saying: "I was in the city of Joppa praying; and in a trance I saw a vision, an object descending like a great sheet, let down from heaven by four corners; and it came to me. When I observed it intently and considered, I saw four-footed animals of the earth, wild beasts, creeping things, and birds of the air. And I heard a voice saying to me, 'Rise, Peter; kill and eat.' But I said, 'Not so, Lord! For nothing common or unclean has at any time entered my mouth.' But the voice answered me again from heaven, 'What God has cleansed you must not call common.' Now this was done three times, and all were drawn up again into heaven. At that very moment, three men stood before the house where I was, having been sent to me from Caesarea. Then the Spirit told me to go with them, doubting nothing. Moreover these six brethren accompanied me, and we entered the man's house. And he told us how he had seen an angel standing in his house, who said to him, 'Send men to Joppa, and call for Simon whose surname is Peter, who will tell you words by which you and all your household will be saved.' And as I began to speak, the Holy Spirit fell upon them, as upon us at the beginning. Then I remembered the word of the Lord, how He said, 'John indeed baptized with water, but you shall be baptized with the Holy Spirit.' If therefore God gave them the same gift as He gave us when we believed on the Lord Jesus Christ, who was I that I could withstand God?" When they heard these things they became silent; and they glorified God, saying, "Then God has also granted to the Gentiles repentance to life."

We have already spent considerable time in Acts 10 with the episode of Peter's visit to Cornelius's household, the abrogation of the dietary laws of the Old Testament, and Peter's preaching of the gospel to Cornelius and his family. In this section of Acts, Luke gives us the same story again. Why would the Spirit of God, who is the Spirit of truth, be so repetitive in this section of Acts? The only answer I can give is that learning comes through repetition. Obviously, whatever we are to learn is of importance to our life, which underscores the fact that this is one of the most important chapters in the New Testament. I want to stress its importance also because I believe it is one of the most misunderstood and confused portions of Scripture in our day.

The Holy Spirit Poured Out

While Peter was still speaking these words, the Holy Spirit fell upon all those who heard the word. And those of the circumcision who believed were astonished, as many as came with Peter, because the gift of the Holy Spirit had been poured out on the Gentiles also. For they heard them speak with tongues and magnify God (vv. 44–46). While Peter was still preaching, the Spirit of God was suddenly poured out on the Gentiles. Those who were Jews recognized this outpouring because the same manifestation that had occurred in Jerusalem on the day of Pentecost occurs here—the Gentile converts began speaking in tongues.

There is something important to note here that also happened in Jerusalem in the original Pentecost—the Holy Spirit fell on all the Gentile believers. On the day of Pentecost, when the Jewish believers were assembled, the Holy Spirit was poured out on all the Jewish believers. It wasn't as though some received it while others missed out. In like manner, when the Spirit was poured out on the Gentiles here, every single one of them received this gift, the outpouring of the Holy Spirit.

When I became a Christian in 1957, my conversion was obviously the most significant watershed moment of my life. It conditioned everything that followed. My life was turned upside down because, instantly, by the power of the Holy Spirit, I was changed from a child of darkness to a child of light. Before my regeneration, I had no interest in the things of God. Suddenly I became in love with the things of God. Christ had been just a religious name or a swear word that frequented my lips, but upon my conversion He became to me the sweetest thing in the world. My life changed dramatically from that day onward. However, my sin didn't stop. My life changed in dramatic ways, but there were still patterns of sin that I brought with me into the Christian life that I struggled with every day. At times I wondered whether I was really a Christian. How could a Christian think and say and do the things I continued to struggle with? Sometimes I had to hang onto the cross by my fingernails. In the providence of God I was given the opportunity to room with an upperclassman who seemed to be the godliest student in the college. I never heard him use a foul word or get angry; I never saw him fail to do his chores or exhibit laziness. Everything I was struggling with, he had completely under control. I couldn't stand it after a while, so I finally said to him, "Larry, what's the secret?"

Larry answered, "The secret is the second blessing." Until our discussion, I had no idea what that was. He explained that he was a member of a Holiness Church, and he believed that after one is regenerated, the Holy Spirit comes and does a second work that gives Christians instant victory over sin.

I wanted that, and I said, "This is what I've been looking for. How can I get it?"

He said, "That's easy. I'll call the pastor and make an appointment, and he'll give the laying on of hands, and you'll receive this second blessing of sanctification."

So he set up the appointment, and I met with the minister, and he told me to kneel. He put his hands on my head, and he prayed for me to receive the blessing, the baptism of the Holy Spirit, which was supposedly lacking in my life. He prayed, and I prayed along with him, but the next day I was still struggling with the sins that I'd been struggling with the day before.

At the time I did not know anything about theology or ecclesiology. I'd never heard of Pentecostalism or Holiness Churches that had this view of the second work of grace. As I studied and began to learn, I discovered that historic Pentecostalism believed that the baptism of the Holy Spirit, a second work of grace, is given to those who seek it for sanctification unto perfection. They taught and still do teach the idea of a victorious Christian life. They say that some Christians have it and some do not, but even those who do not have it can get it if they earnestly seek it.

The Charismatic Movement

That was the basic thrust of Pentecostalism at the beginning of the twentieth century. Then a very important event took place in Los Angeles at the Azusa Street Mission. There was an outbreak of speaking in tongues, and those in attendance believed that this was a new visitation of God's *charismata*, His charismatic gifts, ushering in the latter rain of the outpouring of the Holy Spirit. For the most part, the charismatic movement of the first half of the twentieth century was confined to Pentecostal churches, but in the middle of the century, it began to be manifested in the mainline churches. Speaking in tongues broke out at the University of Notre Dame in the Roman Catholic community and at Duquesne University in Pittsburgh. It broke out in Lutheran, Methodist, Presbyterian, and Episcopalian churches. When evaluating the second half of the twentieth century, church historians will say that the most significant movement was the so-called charismatic movement.

Several things happened because of the charismatic movement. Pentecostal theology stopped being monolithic and singular because it was tweaked within each denomination that practiced it. The Presbyterians gave it a bit of Calvinism, the Lutherans gave it Lutheranism, and the Methodists gave it some Arminianism. There was no longer a simple, standard, unified doctrine of the baptism of the Holy Spirit. If there is such a thing as a prevailing neo-Pentecostal theology in our day, the majority within the movement holds certain premises. First, not all Christians have the baptism of the Holy Spirit. Second, the indispensable sign for having received this baptism is speaking in tongues, which is called *glossolalia*.

When the theology of neo-Pentecostal, charismatic thinking is articulated, the primary basis for their conclusions are inferences drawn from the narratives of the book of Acts, where they see, for example, even in Jerusalem on the day of Pentecost, that there were genuine believers gathered who had not yet received the Holy Spirit. Neo-Pentecostals see a time gap between coming to faith and receiving the gift of the Holy Spirit. They see this in the events at Pentecost and again in the incident at Cornelius's household. Cornelius was already a believer but only later did the Holy Spirit fall. Neo-Pentecostals believe that the Holy Spirit comes to someone upon his or her conversion, but the baptism of the Spirit comes later as a second work of grace. In neo-Pentecostal theology the point of the baptism of the Holy Spirit is not to make one perfect but to empower one for ministry as a more effective witness for Jesus Christ. So there are the haves and the have-nots, which is 180 degrees different from the conclusions the Apostles drew.

The Bible never says there are two kinds of Christians, it says just the opposite. All the believers in Jerusalem received the Spirit, and all the believers at the household of Cornelius received the Spirit. The inference drawn by the Apostles from the narrative history is that God pours out His Spirit, as the Old Testament prophesied, upon all believers, something also taught by the Apostle Paul when he wrote to the Corinthians, "For by one Spirit we were all baptized into one body" (1 Cor. 12:13). There is absolutely no biblical warrant for teaching a so-called baptism of the Holy Spirit that only some Christians receive. Every time the Spirit is poured out in this manner in Scripture, all who were present received it.

Among true Christians there is no such thing as haves and have-nots. Anyone who is a Christian is born of the Spirit, indwelt by the Spirit, and has been baptized by the Spirit and empowered by God for ministry. The baptism of the Holy Spirit is not the same thing as regeneration; regeneration is not the same thing as the indwelling of the Holy Spirit. We can make distinctions about the work of the Holy Spirit, but the point is that all gifts of the Spirit are given at conversion.

That does not mean that there aren't haves and have-nots in the church. There are people in churches who have the Spirit and people who do not. The ones who do not are the unconverted. It is very possible to attend church for years and to profess faith in Christ and yet be unregenerate and without the Holy Spirit. However, if you are a Christian, then you have the Holy Spirit in His full redemptive work. There is no second blessing that is going to fix all the problems you will have in the lifelong pursuit of godliness. Sanctification is not instantaneous; it takes the whole of our lifetime.

"Can anyone forbid water, that these should not be baptized who have received the Holy Spirit just as we have?" And he commanded them to be baptized in the name of the Lord. Then they asked him to stay a few days (vv. 47–48). Peter gave the same inference here that he did when he spoke to the delegation from Jerusalem—the Gentiles are included in the body of Christ. They received the covenant sign of water baptism because that which the water baptism signifies in part is the baptism of the Spirit. If they have received the baptism of the Spirit, then certainly they are eligible for full membership in the church, so they have to be baptized in water.

The Work of the Holy Spirit

Why then today are there multitudes who want to divide the work of the Spirit between the haves and the have-nots and who are still looking for some secret remedy for overcoming besetting sin? The basic testimony is this: "I was a Christian for years, but my prayer life was weak. I didn't live as if I had the power of the Holy Spirit. Then I went to a meeting, and somebody laid hands on me, and I began to speak in tongues, and my life was changed. Now, my prayer life is rich. I love to pray. It's not a mere duty. I've experienced a whole new excitement about my Christian life." I do not argue with people's experiences. If they come and tell me that since they started speaking in tongues they have had great growth in their spiritual life, I say, "Praise the Lord." It is not their experience I challenge but their understanding of their experience, which I do challenge on the basis of the Word.

We get into trouble when experience becomes the law of the Christian life. "It happened to me in a certain way; therefore, that's the way it has to happen to everybody."

We do that not only with the baptism of the Holy Spirit but also with conversion. I can tell you the day and hour that I became a Christian, but many never had such a life-transforming experience. One night Billy Graham went to hear an evangelist after playing baseball, and he was converted and became the evangelist Billy Graham. Conversely, Ruth Graham, who was born and raised in a Calvinistic household, could not say within five years of when she was converted. Sometimes people who had a sudden conversion are suspicious of people who did not have a sudden conversion. Others who become aware of their faith gradually begin to suspect those who think that they can name the day and the hour. The issue is not how someone becomes a Christian or when someone becomes a Christian, but whether someone *does* become a Christian.

We also must understand that no two of us come into the Christian life at the same point in development. We all bring different baggage into our Christian life. Sins that you may struggle with concern things I put away the first week I was a Christian, whereas things that never bothered you took me forty years to get over. The point of this text is that God's Holy Spirit is poured out on each one of us, and if we are in Christ, we have His Spirit. However, there is no magic bullet that is going to get us out of our weakness instantly. There is no substitute for making diligent use of the means of grace, of diligently pursuing the truth of God through the Word of God, because the Spirit of God works with the Word and through the Word and never against the Word.

I wish I had a dollar for every person who has ever told me that the Spirit led them to do something that the Word of God forbids. "The Spirit led me." "I felt His leading." That is gnosticism with a vengeance. I ask them, "What about what the Bible says?" They answer, "Well, I prayed about it, and the Spirit gave me peace." No, He did not. God the Holy Spirit is holy; He is the Spirit of truth, and you must never blame Him for the peace you feel for your sin. The Holy Spirit convicts you of sin; He does not cause you to surrender to your sin. That is the danger. We want it the easy way, the quick way, but there is no easy way. The power is there; it is already in us. We are to live as Christians without having to speak in tongues to be able to verify that the Spirit is with us.

Back in the 1960s I went into the charismatic movement headfirst. Through the speaking and interpretation of tongues, I heard dozens of concrete prophecies of specific events that were supposed to take place at specific times. If I heard fifty of them, the results were zero for fifty, which creates a crisis of faith with people who are caught up in this. Christianity is not magic, and God has not given us the power to bend spoons or to visualize world peace. That is New Age. It is gnosticism tearing the church away from the will of God.

When I was involved in this movement, I had groups of students with me that were also involved in it, and we would meet together in my house every night. We would usually start praying at seven o'clock, and we prayed at least till midnight. More than once we prayed until the next morning. When you want people who will pray for you, ask your charismatic friends because they do love to pray; they believe in the power of God. That is great. The downside is that soon thereafter, the experience becomes the authority rather than the Word. All the promises, predictions, and prophecies I uttered during those nights did not come to pass. I finally realized that if I wanted to know what the Spirit is saying and where He is leading, I would have to go to the Spirit's book. Like Ulysses tying himself to the mast, I tied myself to the Word. It is that I can trust, not my inner hunches.

We are called to test the spirits to see if they are of God. The litmus test for the leading of the Holy Spirit, who does indeed lead us at times, is the Word of God. The Holy Spirit is alive and powerful, and if you are in Christ and Christ is in you, then God the Holy Spirit is in your heart and soul, and you have received the promise that the Old Testament gave. My problem with Pentecostalism is that it has too low a view of Pentecost. It does not understand that the Old Testament promise for Pentecost is that the charismatic outpouring of God would not be given just to some but to all who were in the covenant by faith. If you have Jesus, you have the Holy Spirit.

Maybe you have been an infant in your spiritual growth. Maybe you have grieved the Holy Spirit. Nevertheless, all the power that you will ever need to be a witness to this world, you received at your conversion. That is the point that Peter was making to the people. At the end of it, he said, **"If therefore God gave them the same gift as He gave us when we believed on the Lord Jesus Christ, who was I that I could withstand God?" When they heard these things they became silent; and they glorified God, saying, "Then God has also granted to the Gentiles repentance to life"** (11:17–18). That is the significance of this Gentile Pentecost, that we are all brought in to the body of Christ.

29

THE TEAM OF BARNABAS AND SAUL

Acts 11:19–30

Now those who were scattered after the persecution that arose over Stephen traveled as far as Phoenicia, Cyprus, and Antioch, preaching the word to no one but the Jews only. But some of them were men from Cyprus and Cyrene, who, when they had come to Antioch, spoke to the Hellenists, preaching the Lord Jesus. And the hand of the Lord was with them, and a great number believed and turned to the Lord. Then news of these things came to the ears of the church in Jerusalem, and they sent out Barnabas to go as far as Antioch. When he came and had seen the grace of God, he was glad, and encouraged them all that with purpose of heart they should continue with the Lord. For he was a good man, full of the Holy Spirit and of faith. And a great many people were added to the Lord. Then Barnabas departed for Tarsus to seek Saul. And when he had found him, he brought him to Antioch. So it was that for a whole year they assembled with the church and taught a great many people. And the disciples were first called Christians in Antioch. And in these days prophets came from Jerusalem to Antioch. Then one of them, named Agabus, stood up and showed by the Spirit that there was going to be a great famine throughout all the world, which also happened in the days of Claudius Caesar. Then the disciples, each according to his ability, determined to send relief to the brethren dwelling in Judea. This they also did, and sent it to the elders by the hands of Barnabas and Saul.

T he brief text before us is something of a transition, a bridge that reaches back to the stoning of Stephen, spans the outreach of Philip and the missionary activity of Peter throughout Palestine, and takes us to the great missionary experience of the Apostle Paul. Luke is laying a foundation for the work of Paul, which takes up the majority of Acts. Here we see how Barnabas and Saul connected and how they were prepared to advance the gospel into the Gentile world. When I was in college and took a course on the book of Acts, we had to memorize Paul's missionary journeys. We were required to keep the geography in our minds of all the places Paul traveled, and I found the focus on those details utterly distracting. It is much more important to focus on certain aspects of Paul's journeys as we trace his footsteps.

Expansion

Now those who were scattered after the persecution that arose over Stephen traveled as far as Phoenicia, Cyprus, and Antioch (v. 19). Palestine is a land bridge between Asia, Europe, and Africa, and it borders the Mediterranean Sea on its western side. We have been studying events that took place in Joppa and Caesarea, cities that were on the Mediterranean Sea in Palestine. The expansion goes up the coast of the western side of Palestine, along the Mediterranean, up above Israel, past Phoenicia, then above there to the island of Cyprus, which is in the extreme eastern end of the Mediterranean Sea, and then above Cyprus to Antioch. Luke is telling us about the expansion of the Gentile community to Asia Minor, to Antioch, which became the home base, the metropolitan center, for the expansion of the gospel to the Gentile world.

Jerusalem was the Jewish base, but further expansion into the world was headquartered from this time forward in the town of Antioch. We do not know as much about Antioch as we do about other ancient cities and towns, but we do know that in 300 B.C. Antioch, which was about 18 miles inward along the Orontes River from the Mediterranean, was built by a man named Seleucus Nicator. Seleucus was the son of Antiochus.

In the fourth century B.C., Alexander the Great conquered an astonishing amount of territory in his efforts to Hellenize the ancient world. All the more astonishing is the fact that Alexander did all this while in his early twenties (he died at about age twenty-six). When Alexander the Great died, his empire was divided among four generals, and it was then consolidated into two distinct dynasties, the Seleucid Dynasty and the Ptolemaic Dynasty. The Ptolemaic section had a tremendous impact on Palestine and also on Egypt and Alexandria, but the Seleucids, who controlled Syria and that portion of Alexander's conquests, also became very important to Jewish history in the Intertestamental period. Daniel prophesied the desecration of the temple with the abomination of desolation, which the Jews saw in the radical defilement of the temple by one of the Seleucids, Antiochus Epiphanes.

The little town of Antioch was built by the son of Antiochus, Seleucus Nicator, who named the town in honor of his father. Antioch prospered tremendously in a short period of time because of the caravan routes that facilitated its becoming a commercial center. Not only did it become a commercial center, but it also became a religious center for pagan religions that practiced temple prostitution. It was a city of moral laxity; it was also very sophisticated. Antioch was much like modern New York City.

In 64 B.C. the Roman general Pompey conquered the city of Antioch and involved it in Roman enterprise. As a result, from that time on up to the time of Christ and the Apostles, Antioch was the third largest city in the ancient world. Rome was the largest, and Alexandria was second. We tend to overlook the significance of the size of Antioch. Because of its size, the city was pivotal for the first-century expansion of Christendom. It also became the intellectual center for the development of Christian theology during the first three hundred years of church history. In the third century, some great things were done in Antioch to combat heresy. Unfortunately, in the fourth century heresy arose there that caused the necessity of the Council of Nicaea. Overall, Antioch was of critical importance as a staging area and as the actual metropolitan headquarters for the Gentile expansion of the Christian church, and it is introduced here in Acts.

Those who were scattered preached the Word only to the Jews, so when they came to Antioch, they went only to the synagogues. **Some of them were men from Cyprus and Cyrene, who, when they had come to Antioch, spoke to the Hellenists, preaching the Lord Jesus** (v. 20). The emphasis here is on Jesus as Lord rather than on the Lord as Christ. Why would that be? In the Gentile environs there was no expectation for the coming of a messiah; they were looking for and open to the expression of one who would manifest lordship by saving them from calamity and by offering them life after death. It took a while for them to gain an understanding of the meaning of the title "Christ." The title "Christ" sounded foreign to them because they had no Old Testament background, but they did understand the meaning of the term "Lord."

And the hand of the Lord was with them, and a great number believed and turned to the Lord (v. 21). Here we see a pattern that occurs frequently in the book of Acts. When the Holy Spirit has His hand upon the church, there are astonishing levels of church growth. That is why we are sometimes so easily impressed by numbers when evaluating how our churches are doing. We tend to think that a church's membership is the quantitative measurement of how much God is blessing it. We have to be careful about that. The largest recorded worship service in the Bible occurred at the base of a mountain in a dance of idolatry and blasphemy around a golden calf (Exodus 32). The church of Aaron at that point was a megachurch, doing everything that God despised. We could say that the hand of the Devil was upon them rather than the hand of the Lord, because God was infuriated by what His people were doing. Their activity caused church growth, but it was the wrong kind. If the hand of the Lord is on a Christian work, we have every right to expect it to grow and be effective; when the Lord's hand is there, growth follows. However, we have to be careful because such growth does not *prove* that the hand of the Lord is there. We cannot have the hand of the Lord and not have growth, but we can have growth without the hand of the Lord.

Barnabas the Encourager

Then news of these things came to the ears of the church in Jerusalem, and they sent out Barnabas to go as far as Antioch. When he came and had seen the grace of God, he was glad, and encouraged them all that with purpose of heart they should continue with the Lord (vv. 22–23). The Westminster Shorter Catechism asks, "What is required in the tenth commandment?" and the answer given is this: "The tenth commandment requires full contentment with our own condition, with a charitable frame of spirit toward our neighbor, and all that is his." The catechism then asks what is forbidden in the tenth commandment: "The tenth commandment forbids all discontentment with our own estate, envying or grieving at the good of our neighbor, and all inordinate emotions and affections to anything that is his." At the heart of so much social unrest, hatred, and warfare is the sin of envy. What makes envy or jealousy such a grievous sin is not simply the violence that it produces in people and the way in which we injure each other but the fact that it is a dreadful sin against God. When we are jealous of what somebody else has or does, that feeling in our soul reflects dissatisfaction with the benefits and blessings that God has bestowed upon us. We are saying in our souls, "God, it's not fair. Why should he get that job? Why does she get to have more money than I have? Why do they have a bigger house than I have?" We are saying, "God, you have not treated me the way you ought to have treated me," when, in fact, everything we do have comes from His hand. I call attention to our propensity for envy and jealousy because when we read this brief little statement about the character of Barnabas, we see a man who is the antithesis of an envious or jealous person.

When a minister hears about a church experiencing greater growth than his own, he might be tempted to criticize, to look for faults in that bigger church. His criticism in that case comes not from a genuine desire to edify and establish but from jealousy and envy. Almost all so-called constructive criticism is destructive criticism. There is such a thing as constructive criticism, but it is always bathed in a spirit of encouragement. That is what I love about Barnabas.

Barnabas saw all God was doing among the Gentiles in Antioch, and he was glad. Just as the Scriptures tell us, that if somebody among us receives an honor, rather than moping and groaning, thinking we should have been the ones to receive the honor, we are to rejoice in our brother's or sister's good fortune. We are to weep with those who weep and rejoice with those who rejoice (Rom. 12:15). That is what Barnabas did, and it is why his name means "son of encouragement." **For he was a good man, full of the Holy Spirit and of faith. And a great many people were added to the Lord** (v. 24).

Then Barnabas departed for Tarsus to seek Saul (v. 25). This also speaks volumes about Barnabas because Barnabas was not an Apostle. When the pulpit of a senior minister is vacated, associate ministers are rarely eager to work with someone new who is automatically higher in the church pecking order. Yet Barnabas saw this wonderful work of God going on and wanted to see it prosper, so he sought out Saul, whom he knew was more gifted for the work than he. That is what William Farel did when he visited John Calvin and appealed to him to come to Geneva. Farel stepped aside because he recognized that Calvin had greater gifts and could therefore take the church into greater depths.

That is what Barnabas did here. The verb "to seek" used here indicates that he was going on a difficult search; nobody knew for sure where Saul was. He had dropped out of sight, and surely his parents had disinherited him for leaving orthodox Judaism and embracing this new sect of Christianity. The last Barnabas had heard about Saul was that he was somewhere in and around Tarsus, but he had no address. So Barnabas departed for Tarsus to seek Saul, and when he had found him, he brought him to Antioch.

So it was that for a whole year they assembled with the church and taught a great many people. And the disciples were first called Christians in Antioch (v. 26). Up until this time, the early Christian community had been called the people of the Way. They were not known as Christians until this moment in church history. The term *Christian* was derogatory, a term of derision, but those in the church welcomed it because they were taking their stand in the name of Christ; they were pleased to bear this label of derision.

In these days prophets came from Jerusalem to Antioch (v. 27). The prophets mentioned here were not on the same level as prophets of the Old Testament, but the Apostles were. The New Testament prophets were subordinate to the Apostles.

Mercy Ministry

Then one of them, named Agabus, stood up and showed by the Spirit that there was going to be a great famine throughout all the world, which also happened in the days of Claudius Caesar. Then the disciples, each according to his ability, determined to send relief to the brethren dwelling in Judea. This they also did, and sent it to the elders by the hands of Barnabas and Saul (vv. 28–30). Here we see the tremendous sensitivity of the Christians gathered in Antioch. When they heard the prophetic announcement of this dreadful global famine, which had already hit Jerusalem, they came together and they gave what they could to help those who were hungry and in need. The first Christian church had a full commitment to mercy ministry.

One of the great tragedies of nineteenth-century liberal theology was its attempt to repudiate all supernatural aspects of the gospel, denying the virgin birth, the resurrection of Christ, and the cross as an atoning work, and trying to reduce Christianity to simply a humanitarian concern of social issues. Walter Rauschenbusch's so-called social gospel declared that the real gospel is not Jesus' atonement for sinners but rather the sharing of our goods with our neighbor. We do have to be concerned with those who have no home, clothes, or food, but liberal theologians tried to make the alleviation of those concerns the real mission of the church. As a result, there was a split between those who wanted to maintain the central importance of the gospel of Christ and those who wanted to redefine Christianity simply in terms of social action.

A commitment to the real gospel of salvation carries along with it a commitment to the material welfare and well-being of people. True religion involves not just praying and receiving Christ, but it also involves feeding the hungry, clothing the naked, visiting the prisoners, and helping bring relief in times of calamity, such as the famine we read about in Acts. The Christians sent a collection back to Jerusalem, interrupting the work of Paul and Barnabas, so that they could deliver the collection to the elders of the church in Jerusalem.

That is what it means to be a Christian. It means to encourage. It means to reach out to the lost, and it means to give to relieve the pain and suffering of our brothers and sisters—locally, nationally, and internationally. That is how the connection was made between Antioch and Jerusalem, and it formed the foundation for the great missionary outreach of Paul and Barnabas.

30

PETER IN PRISON

Acts 12:1–19

Now about that time Herod the king stretched out his hand to harass some from the church. Then he killed James the brother of John with the sword. And because he saw that it pleased the Jews, he proceeded further to seize Peter also. Now it was during the Days of Unleavened Bread. So when he had arrested him, he put him in prison, and delivered him to four squads of soldiers to keep him, intending to bring him before the people after Passover. Peter was therefore kept in prison, but constant prayer was offered to God for him by the church. And when Herod was about to bring him out, that night Peter was sleeping, bound with two chains between two soldiers; and the guards before the door were keeping the prison. Now behold, an angel of the Lord stood by him, and a light shone in the prison; and he struck Peter on the side and raised him up, saying, "Arise quickly!" And his chains fell off his hands. Then the angel said to him, "Gird yourself and tie on your sandals"; and so he did. And he said to him, "Put on your garment and follow me." So he went out and followed him, and did not know that what was done by the angel was real, but thought he was seeing a vision. When they were past the first and the second guard posts, they came to the iron gate that leads to the city, which opened to them of its own accord; and they went out and went down one street, and immediately the angel departed from him. And when Peter had come to himself, he said, "Now I know for certain that the Lord has sent His angel, and has delivered me from the hand of Herod and from all the expectation of the Jewish people." So, when he had considered this, he came to the house of Mary, the mother of John whose surname was Mark, where many were gathered together praying. And as Peter knocked at the door of the gate, a girl named Rhoda came to answer. When she recognized Peter's voice, because of her gladness she did not open the gate, but ran in and announced that Peter stood before the gate. But they said to her, "You are beside yourself!" Yet she kept insisting that it was so. So they said, "It is his angel." Now Peter continued knocking; and when they opened the door and saw him, they were astonished. But motioning to them with his hand to keep silent, he declared to them how the Lord had brought him out of the prison. And he said, "Go, tell these things to James and to the brethren." And he departed and went to another place. Then, as soon as it was day, there was no small stir among the soldiers about what had become of Peter. But when Herod had searched for him and not found him, he examined the guards and commanded that they should be put to death. And he went down from Judea to Caesarea, and stayed there.

Meanwhile, back in Jerusalem . . . That is an apt way to begin this lesson. Luke has just finished recounting what happened with Paul and Barnabas in Antioch. While they were there, a band of prophets came along and predicted a severe worldwide famine, which had already hit Jerusalem. The people in Antioch who were under the tutelage of Barnabas and Saul took up an offering to help the saints who were suffering from the famine in Jerusalem. Saul and Barnabas were commissioned to return to Jerusalem with the gift.

Herod Agrippa

Acts 12 picks up back in Jerusalem where we find a new dimension of persecution breaking out against the Christian leaders, the Apostles. **Now about that time Herod the king stretched out his hand to harass some from the church** (v. 1). This king was not the Herod who slaughtered the infants at the time of the birth of Jesus, Herod the Great. In fact, it is the grandson of Herod the Great, the first Herod Agrippa. When Herod the Great died, his dominion was separated into four parts, each with its own ruler called a tetrarch, which means "ruler of a fourth." We find tetrarchs, such as Philip, mentioned in the New Testament. Each tetrarch was an immediate descendant of Herod the Great.

However, by the time we get to Acts 12 we see that a different set of authorities has been established. In the year 7 B.C. the father of Agrippa, Aristobulus, who was the son of Herod the Great, was killed. His family was fearful that more vengeance would be wrought against the grandson of Herod, so to keep the four-year-old Agrippa safe, his family sent him off to Rome. There he was raised in the confines of the royal household, very close to Gaius, the grandnephew of the reigning Caesar Tiberius, and to his contemporary Claudius. He was raised almost as a family member of the Caesars. When Tiberius died, Gaius ascended to emperor of Rome, and in A.D. 37 Gaius appointed his old friend king over Israel.

No longer was it divided into four parts; initially all four parts were given into the hands of Agrippa. A couple of years later, Gaius died, and he was replaced by Claudius. Under the reign of Claudius, the rest of the nation, including Jerusalem and Judea, which traditionally had been ruled by a Roman prefect such as Pontius Pilate, was given back into the hands of a king from the Hasmonean dynasty. King Agrippa, therefore, got control of the whole country. He was king, but he was merely a puppet king.

When Herod came to Jerusalem, he was immediately aware of the sect of Jewish Christians who were upsetting the rest of the Jews in Jerusalem, and he set out to put that right. The first thing he did in his harassment campaign was to arrest James and have him beheaded by the sword. James is identified in the text as the brother of John. Back in the Gospels when Jesus called His disciples, He called the sons of Zebedee, James and John, as well as calling Peter and Andrew. However, the inner circle of disciples throughout the earthly ministry of our Lord consisted of three people—Peter, James, and John. This was the James singled out by Herod for execution.

A tradition from early sources of church history tells us that when James was beheaded, his guard was so impressed by his faith and his testimony to Jesus that the guard professed faith in Christ and was summarily executed along with James. James was not the first Christian martyr; that was Stephen. But Stephen was not an Apostle; James was the first of the Apostles to be martyred. According to church history, eleven out of the twelve Apostles were martyred. Only one lived to a ripe old age and died as an old man by natural causes, and that was James's brother, John. So of the two sons of Zebedee, one was the first Apostle to die and the other was the last.

Peter under Lock and Key

And because he saw that it pleased the Jews, he proceeded further to seize Peter also. Now it was during the Days of Unleavened Bread (v. 3). After Herod had James killed, he kept an eye on the population to see how it was reacting. Were the people going to get excited like they did when Jesus was killed? In this case, the populace approved of the persecution, so he decided to go after the big one, the fisherman Simon Peter. He subjected Peter to arrest and threw him into prison. Since this was done during the celebration of the Passover, and Jewish tradition did not approve of an execution during the Pascal feast, Herod had to wait until the feast was completely over before he could execute Peter, which is why he locked up Peter in prison.

We are told that Herod sent four squads of soldiers to guard him until his execution could be carried out. There were four squads because each was broken up into four watches. That meant there were four teams of four—sixteen Roman soldiers—guarding Peter in prison. Two soldiers were inside his cell with him. Peter had one leg chained to each guard, while two other guards stood watch at the outer gates. This was a high-security imprisonment, a part of the narrative we do not want to miss.

Peter was therefore kept in prison, but constant prayer was offered to God for him by the church (v. 5). We are besieged today by what is called the "health and wealth gospel," where preachers promise people that God always wills healing and never wills suffering, and all you have to do to escape from any malady is to "name it and claim it." If blind people want to be healed, they need only claim sight, have faith, and ask others to pray. If afterward they do not receive sight, the problem is attributed to their lack of faith. Health and wealth teachers say that we have to learn the art of praying in such a way that God will answer our prayers. When we sing, "What a friend we have in Jesus," we are expressing gratitude that whatever burden or care is upon our souls, we can go to Christ because He is our intercessor. Yet the health and wealth gospel puts forth several ways in which to have an effective prayer life, ways to get God to hear us and get Him to answer our prayers. But God is not deaf. I can say with absolute certainty that God Almighty hears every prayer we pray. We do not have to speak any louder to get His attention. He hears our prayers.

"Why," some ask, "do some of my prayers go unanswered?" But that is a false question. God always answers our prayers. Sometimes, however, the answer is no. We tend to insult God's intelligence when He doesn't answer our prayers the way we ask Him to by failing to consider the no as an answer. Did Jesus walk away from His agony in Gethsemane after crying to the Father, "Let this cup pass from me"? We know He did not. God answered His prayer by not removing the cup, so Jesus prayed again, but for the strength and courage to do what God had commanded Him to do. So let us not confuse prayer with magic or consider God as a cosmic bellhop who is there to do our bidding. That is not how prayer works.

Do we not think that when James was arrested, those first-century Christians didn't get on their knees right away and pray for his rescue? Of course they did. However, in God's providence He was pleased to allow James to be martyred, and the answer He gave to those prayers was the exact opposite of the answer He gave to those who were praying for Peter. When James was executed, the people did not despair of prayer. They had prayed for James, and they were devastated when James was executed. Then it got worse—Peter stood next in line for execution—but the Christians did not abandon prayer. They prayed all the more earnestly.

Miraculous Release

And when Herod was about to bring him out, that night Peter was sleeping, bound with two chains between two soldiers; and the guards before the door were keeping the prison. Now behold, an angel of the Lord stood by him, and a light shone in the prison; and he struck Peter on the side and raised him up, saying, "Arise quickly!" And his chains fell off his hands (vv. 6–7). Charles Wesley described his conversion as that of coming out of a dark dungeon. The Spirit of God came upon him, his chains fell off, and he stood up and followed after Christ. From his description, it seems that he had this text in mind.

Then the angel said to him, "Gird yourself and tie on your sandals"; and so he did. And he said to him, "Put on your garment and follow me" (v. 8). In those days men wore what today we call dresses. The garments were long, down to the ankles. When men went into battle or sport, they hiked up the garment in order to run, and they tightened a belt around the garment to hold it in place. This "girding of their loins" would free their knees so that they could pump their legs and run fast. That is what the angel was instructing Peter to do.

Peter, who thought he was seeing a vision in a dream, did what he was told. Peter went out and followed the angel. He did not know that what was done by the angel was real, but he thought he was seeing a vision. **When they were past the first and the second guard posts, they came to the iron gate that leads to the city, which opened to them of its own accord; and they went out and went down one street, and immediately the angel departed from him** (v. 10). This description suggests that Peter was being held captive in the Fortress of Antonia. The angel led Peter past the first two guard posts, and then they approached the Iron Gate, the primary passage in and out of the city, which just swung open before them. In today's world of automatic electronically operated doors, the opening of the Iron Gate seems a small feat but imagine how amazing this was to Peter.

And when Peter had come to himself, he said, "Now I know for certain that the Lord has sent His angel, and has delivered me from the hand of Herod and from all the expectation of the Jewish people." So, when he had considered this, he came to the house of Mary, the mother of John whose surname was Mark, where many were gathered together praying (vv. 11–12). Here we are introduced to John Mark. He went with Paul on a missionary journey, a partnership that did not work out. Paul fired him, and John Mark was devastated. Later on, however, he came back and became Peter's aide, and he also wrote the Gospel of Mark. He had a higher vocation than his missionary apprenticeship with Paul.

At Mary's House

As the story before us continues, Peter went to the home of Mary, the mother of John Mark. It was apparently a splendid edifice. By this time the church in Jerusalem had become so large that no public building in the city could have accommodated the multitude when they gathered for worship. They met in the homes of wealthy believers, who had the largest houses. Probably the most splendid was Mary's home, which is where Peter went. He made his way there quickly and quietly. He knew that as soon as his escape from the prison was discovered, Mary's house was the first place Herod and others would search for him.

When Peter arrived at Mary's house, he knocked at the door and waited for someone to open it. No one came right away because those inside were engaged in prayer and did not hear Peter knocking. Finally, a servant girl named Rhoda opened the door and heard Peter's voice. She did not know what to think about what she was seeing, but she recognized Peter's voice, just as Mary Magdalene had recognized the voice of Jesus in the garden. Rhoda was so excited that she forgot to open the door: **When she recognized Peter's voice, because of her gladness she did not open the gate, but ran in and announced that Peter stood before the gate** (v. 14). Those inside responded, **"You are beside yourself!"** (v. 15). That was a euphemism. They thought Rhoda was out of her mind. Despite the fact that they had been praying for Peter's release, they did not believe Peter could possibly be the one standing at the door. We see that we are not the first generation to be that weak in recognizing God's answers to our prayers.

Rhoda was insistent that she had heard the voice of Peter, so the people decided that Rhoda had come in contact with Peter's angel. Many believe that each person has a guardian angel. In the Old Testament, Elisha had an entire army of angels guarding him. Whatever the specifics of what these people believed, they finally went to the door to see for themselves. **When they opened the door and saw him, they were astonished** (v. 16).

Every time I sing "Amazing Grace," I think of two things. First, we should never be amazed by grace because God is so gracious that when He pours his grace upon us, it should not come as a surprise. Second, conversely, there is a certain sense in which we ought always to be amazed by grace so that we never presume upon God. The astonishment here was born not of faith but of unbelief.

They could not believe that God had provided the very thing that they had asked for. Are we any different?

But motioning to them with his hand to keep silent, he declared to them how the Lord had brought him out of the prison. And he said, "Go, tell these things to James and to the brethren." And he departed and went to another place (v. 17). Did Peter not know that they had just killed James, and if he did know, was he asking the people to try to communicate with the departed soul of James? No, indeed. Peter was talking about a different James—not James the brother of John, but James the Just, who, by the time we get to Acts 15, has become the presiding leader of the church in Jerusalem. James the Just, the fraternal brother of Jesus Himself, wrote the book of James. Peter told the people to go tell James and the rest of the Apostles that God had delivered him from prison, and then he departed and went to another place.

Then, as soon as it was day, there was no small stir among the soldiers about what had become of Peter. But when Herod had searched for him and not found him, he examined the guards and commanded that they should be put to death (vv. 18–19). This command was no arbitrary act on the part of Herod Agrippa. He was implementing the Justinian Code, which applied to all prison guards. According to this code, if a prisoner escaped, that prisoner's sentence—beating, scourging, crucifixion, or beheading—became that of the guards from under whose watch the prisoner had escaped. (We will see the Justinian Code come into play again later in Acts 16.)

As a footnote we are told that Peter went down from Judea to Caesarea and stayed there. In our next study we will look at another footnote, which tells us of the fate of Herod Agrippa, who killed James, harassed the church, and tried to execute the Apostle Peter. But he failed in his endeavor as the people of God were on their knees before the Lord of glory, who sent the angel to rescue His saint.

31

DEATH OF HEROD

Acts 12:20–13:3

Now Herod had been very angry with the people of Tyre and Sidon; but they came to him with one accord, and having made Blastus the king's personal aide their friend, they asked for peace, because their country was supplied with food by the king's country. So on a set day Herod, arrayed in royal apparel, sat on his throne and gave an oration to them. And the people kept shouting, "The voice of a god and not of a man!" Then immediately an angel of the Lord struck him, because he did not give glory to God. And he was eaten by worms and died. But the word of God grew and multiplied. And Barnabas and Saul returned from Jerusalem when they had fulfilled their ministry, and they also took with them John whose surname was Mark. Now in the church that was at Antioch there were certain prophets and teachers: Barnabas, Simeon who was called Niger, Lucius of Cyrene, Manaen who had been brought up with Herod the tetrarch, and Saul. As they ministered to the Lord and fasted, the Holy Spirit said, "Now separate to Me Barnabas and Saul for the work to which I have called them." Then, having fasted and prayed, and laid hands on them, they sent them away.

This section of Acts departs from the story of Peter's rescue from prison and takes up the subsequent events that took place in the life of Herod Agrippa, the one who had executed James and cast Peter into prison.

Pomp and Circumstance

Herod had been very angry with the people of Tyre and Sidon (v. 20). Tyre and Sidon were the two principal cities of Phoenicia, and the Phoenicians had for centuries dominated the Mediterranean world with their highly developed sea trade. They had developed a sophisticated seacoast and built a nation on thriving commerce. In their commercial enterprises they had engaged in international business relationships with Israel that went back one thousand years before the time of the early church. When King Solomon was engaged in building the temple, he did business with Hiram of Tyre in order to secure some of the necessary provisions and materials for the structure, which illustrates the reciprocal business relationship between Phoenicia and Israel.

At the time of the narrative before us, something had arisen (the text doesn't tell us what) that put the centuries-old trade agreement in jeopardy. Apparently, the Phoenicians had done something to provoke the anger of Agrippa, which led Agrippa to move from Jerusalem up to Caesarea, his headquarters, the city built in honor of the emperor Tiberius. Agrippa went there to play out his animosity toward the Phoenicians. The Phoenicians depended on the import of grain from Israel; their basic supply of food depended upon this trade relationship with the Jewish people. I add parenthetically that it has been proven repeatedly throughout history that when goods and services cross borders, soldiers rarely do. It is often when international trade is disrupted for one reason or another that warfare is provoked, which was about to happen here.

The wrath of Agrippa had been kindled against the Phoenicians, but the Phoenicians were very much concerned to settle the controversy. **They came to him with one accord, and having made Blastus the king's personal aide their friend, they asked for peace** (v. 20). The delegation from Tyre and Sidon sought out their friend Blastus, who was high up in the cabinet of King Agrippa.

So on a set day Herod, arrayed in royal apparel, sat on his throne and gave an oration to them. And the people kept shouting, "The voice of a god and not of a man!" Then immediately an angel of the Lord struck him, because he did not give glory to God. And he was eaten by worms and died" (vv. 21–23). The Jewish historian Josephus sheds light on what was happening here. Apart from sacred Scripture, the work of Josephus provides us with the most important historical record of many events that occurred at that time. He wrote a work called *On the Antiquities of the Jews*. It is a fascinating and interesting work, particularly where it describes the invasion of Palestine by the Romans and the destruction of Jerusalem in A.D. 70. It is here that Josephus gives an extensive description of the death of Agrippa. As a Jewish historian, Josephus was concerned about what happened to the various Jewish monarchs.

Josephus's record of the death of Agrippa follows Luke's step by step; at every point they agree. Josephus's work is more detailed, whereas Luke's gives a brief and terse account of what happened. We are told by Josephus that on this occasion (probably August 1 in the year A.D. 45) Herod, in order to entertain the envoys that had come from Tyre and Sidon, as well as his own people, put on a series of shows at the amphitheater celebrating the founding of the city of Caesarea. The amphitheater was the site of many open-air dramas and other productions. The ruins of that amphitheater remain to this day.

We are told by Luke that Herod made a dramatic appearance, royally garbed, early in the morning, when the sun shone brightly on the stage. Josephus tells us that King Agrippa wore a special costume, as it were, for this event. In place of his regular royal garments, he wore a royal robe woven from pure silver. With the sun shining on this garment, Josephus said it gleamed as the light beams bounced off the silver threads. It was so magnificent that it manifested not only a sense of royalty, but, to the many onlookers, the very manifestation of deity.

Luke tells us that on that day, arrayed in the special apparel, Herod sat on his throne and gave an oration. The people shouted. They went wild, crying, "The voice of a god and not of a man!" This is similar to what happened to Peter, when the crowd, in awe of what he had done, fell on the ground and worshiped him. Peter rebuked them, as Paul will do later. Throughout Scripture we see that whenever a godly person is mistaken for deity, he immediately rebukes those trying to worship him. That was not the response of Agrippa. When the crowd started screaming, "The voice of a god and not of a man!" Herod basked in that glory.

However, in the midst of the crowd's acclamation, Herod suddenly doubled over in pain. So excruciating was the pain, we are told by Josephus, that Herod had to be carried out of the amphitheater, and he remained in intense pain for five days before he succumbed to the fatal illness, which, according to Luke, was inflicted upon him by the angel of the Lord because Agrippa was taking for himself glory that belonged to God. In Josephus's account, we are told that an owl had appeared in the auditorium, which provoked terror in the bones of Agrippa. Many years earlier he had been in trouble with Tiberius Caesar and, while Agrippa was imprisoned in chains, an owl had appeared and perched right above his head. Another prisoner, who was filled with the knowledge of ancient magic, told Agrippa that the owl was a messenger or angel, which is the translation of the Greek word *angelos*. The prisoner told Agrippa that the owl was an omen of good fortune, indicating his imminent rescue from the prison. However, another fellow inmate told him that if that owl ever appeared to Agrippa again, it would mean he had only five days to live.

Here was a man—the most powerful ruler in Palestine—who seemed omnipotent. Yet, in the midst of his most glorious moment of fame and triumph, arrayed in garments of silver, he was afflicted instantly by God. He doubled over in pain, and five days later he was dead. Although Luke was a physician, he does not supply details of the illness, nor does Josephus, but people who have examined both writings have made some assumptions about it. The most common assumption is that Agrippa's appendix burst and peritonitis set in. Others say that his symptoms reflect the impact of arsenic poisoning, which was not uncommon in the courts of the ancient world. Whatever the means of his demise, it was obviously a dreadful way to go, and it suggests a judgment of God upon this king, who dared to assault the infant church of Christ and to kill even the Apostle James.

Notice also the irony of the next verse: **But the word of God grew and multiplied** (v. 24). The king died and was eaten by worms, but the Word of God did not die. The Word of God prospered. The Word of God continued to grow and multiply.

Manaen

Then the story shifts back to the Apostles: **And Barnabas and Saul returned from Jerusalem when they had fulfilled their ministry**—that of taking the collection there—**and they also took with them John whose surname was Mark** (v. 25). We get a brief list here of the leaders of the early church: **Now in the church that was at Antioch there were certain prophets and teachers: Barnabas, Simeon who was called Niger, Lucius of Cyrene, Manaen who had been brought up with Herod the tetrarch, and Saul** (13:1). We read of Barnabas, whom we have already heard about, and of Simeon, who was called Niger. The Latin term *niger* means "black," and that suggests that Simeon may have been a resident of one of the Ethiopian nations. It may also be a reference, as some commentators believe, to Simon of Cyrene, the man compelled to carry the cross piece for our Lord at the time of His crucifixion. We also read of Lucius of Cyrene, who has sometimes been identified with another Lucius that Paul mentions in Romans or even as Luke himself.

The one I am most interested in here is Manaen, who had been brought up with Herod the tetrarch, and Saul. Other translations say that Manaen was the half-brother of the tetrarch Herod Antipas. In our last study I pointed out that upon the death of Herod the Great, his kingdom was divided among his sons, and each became a ruler over a fourth, which is why they were called tetrarchs. The youngest son of Herod the Great was Herod Antipas, who had had John the Baptist beheaded. Herod Antipas was the tetrarch involved with the judgment and trial of Jesus at the time of His crucifixion. He had a long reign over a portion of the Jewish people and played a significant role in the events of the first-century church. Manaen was his half-brother and had grown up in the household of Herod the Great, exposed to great luxury.

Manaen's history calls to mind the early years of Moses, who was adopted into the household of Pharaoh and educated in the finest universities of the Egyptians, only to be sent into exile. He was later rescued by God and became the leader of the Jewish nation at the exodus. Manaen, a leading representative of the Christian gospel in Antioch, grew up with the man who killed John the Baptist and who conspired with the Romans to have Jesus executed. Behind all this was God, of course, who will take from the same family, as Jacob rather than an Esau, a Manaen rather than an Antipas. One will be taken; one will be left. One receives justice; one receives mercy. This serves as a microcosm for all of us. God in His kindness rescued this man Manaen from the rank paganism of the household in which he was reared.

Set Apart

These men, we are told, ministered to the Lord and fasted, and the Holy Spirit said, **"Now separate to Me Barnabas and Saul for the work to which I have called them." Then, having fasted and prayed, and laid hands on them, they sent them away** (vv. 2–3). The laying on of hands, still practiced in the church today, is a symbol; there is no actual power in those hands that conveys anything from one to another. The laying on of hands represents the blessing of God, the anointing of God's power. The rite dates back to the earliest times in the Christian community. In the first-century church, at the conclusion of a worship service a minister would move through the room and physically lay his hand upon all individuals, praying for them and asking God's blessing upon them. When the groups grew in size, making the practice impossible, the minister would simply raise his hands above the congregation, conveying the blessing symbolically.

The reason for the laying on of hands here in Acts is that Paul and Barnabas were about to begin the first missionary journey, nine years after Paul had been converted on the road to Damascus. The church laid its hands upon him as a sign of consecration, symbolizing the real touch that they needed—the touch of God in separating Paul and Barnabas and John Mark for the task God had given them.

32

PAUL AT CYPRUS

Acts 13:4–12

⟨✦⟩

So, being sent out by the Holy Spirit, they went down to Seleucia, and from there they sailed to Cyprus. And when they arrived in Salamis, they preached the word of God in the synagogues of the Jews. They also had John as their assistant. Now when they had gone through the island to Paphos, they found a certain sorcerer, a false prophet, a Jew whose name was Bar Jesus, who was with the proconsul, Sergius Paulus, an intelligent man. This man called for Barnabas and Saul and sought to hear the word of God. But Elymas the sorcerer (for so his name is translated) withstood them, seeking to turn the proconsul away from the faith. Then Saul, who also is called Paul, filled with the Holy Spirit, looked intently at him and said, "O full of all deceit and all fraud, you son of the devil, you enemy of all righteousness, will you not cease perverting the straight ways of the Lord? And now, indeed, the hand of the Lord is upon you, and you shall be blind, not seeing the sun for a time." And immediately a dark mist fell on him, and he went around seeking someone to lead him by the hand. Then the proconsul believed, when he saw what had been done, being astonished at the teaching of the Lord.

So, being sent out by the Holy Spirit, they went down to Seleucia, and from there they sailed to Cyprus (v. 4). We can commission people, but we have no power. We can license, ordain, and send people on sacred tasks, but unless the Holy Spirit anoints them, their labors will be in vain.

In this brief text we find the onset of the most significant missionary undertaking in the entire history of the church, indeed in the entire history of the world. It begins with some geographical details. They had been at Antioch on the Orontes River, and from there they went first to Seleucia, the harbor that served that part of Syria, and they boarded a ship. We are told, even by geographers today, that on a clear day, if you stand on the coast of Syria in what was once Seleucia and look out into the Mediterranean—130 miles in the distance on a clear day—you can still see the shape and outline of that large island of Cyprus. That was in the vision of Paul and Barnabas as they set sail.

If fair winds availed, the journey across the water could have been accomplished in just a few hours. They landed in Salamis, which was the easternmost port of Cyprus. **And when they arrived in Salamis, they preached the word of God in the synagogues of the Jews. They also had John as their assistant** (v. 5). They immediately began to preach to the Jews in the synagogue, which was their most fertile fishing place, as it were, for converts to Christianity. Paul reminds us later, in his letter to the Romans, that his commission was to give the gospel to the Jew first and then to the Gentile.

Bar-Jesus and Sergius Paulus

We do not know how long they stayed in Salamis, but then they went to Paphos on the other end of the island, some 90 miles west of Salamis, and there they had an encounter with a false prophet. **They found a certain sorcerer, a false prophet, a Jew whose name was Bar-Jesus, who was with the proconsul, Sergius Paulus, an intelligent man. This man called for Barnabas and Saul and sought to hear the word of God** (vv. 6–7). Sergius Paulus was obviously from the west. He was of Roman orientation, and even in antiquity those in the west were fascinated by the mysterious arts and practices that came out of the east, which was given to a practice of the occult. We expect participation in the occult from mystery religions of the east, but this man, known as Bar-Jesus, is identified as a Jew. Jews who cast fortunes—soothsayers and fortune-tellers— came under the wrath of God. In the Old Testament the practice of this kind of sorcery was an abomination to God and, according to the Law of Moses, subject to the death penalty. But this man, Bar-Jesus, had no scruples whatsoever about making his living by offering future predictions for leaders looking for investments and for military generals wondering about the outcome of battles. Bar-Jesus had associated himself with the ruler of Cyprus, the proconsul Sergius Paulus. How ironic that the sorcerer's name was Bar-Jesus or *Bar-Jeshua*, which means "son of Jesus." Bar-Jesus was in attendance when Paul and Barnabas were invited by the proconsul to tell them the Word of God that they had been proclaiming there in Cyprus.

For many years some claimed that Luke had made a historical error in identifying Sergius Paulus as a proconsul. It was well known that Caesar Augustus had divided his dominion in the Roman Empire into two groups. One group contained the provinces that had been conquered by the Roman legions. Those in this group were still hostile, so military personnel were stationed in the provinces to keep the peace. Those provinces came under the direct dominion of Caesar Augustus, who directed the affairs of the military outposts. The other group contained provinces that indicated no significant threat of uprising, and over them were stationed the *Senatus Populus Que Romanus* (SPQR), the Senate and People of Rome. Augustus gave these provinces into the hands of the senate, and the senate then commissioned rulers who were given the title of proconsul. The debate about Luke's historical accuracy comes into play here. Critics say that under the reign of Caesar Augustus, Cyprus was ruled by Caesar, not by the senate, and therefore Luke erred in giving Sergius Paulus the title of proconsul.

A great thing about archaeology is that every time a shovel of dirt is moved in the Holy Land, some debated detail of history is confirmed and corroborated by external evidence. In our day, a stela has been uncovered that had been set up during the reign of Claudius, who reigned at the time of this trip. This indicates that early in the reign of Claudius, the island of Cyprus was shifted from the dominion of Caesar to the dominion of the Senate and that the local ruler at that time was given the title "proconsul." Once again we see Luke vindicated, and we understand why he has earned the reputation as the most accurate historian in all of antiquity. Details such as this can be falsified or verified by external forces.

Speaking Truth

Our primary concern here, however, is what happened in the meeting between Paul and Barnabas and Sergius Paulus. As Paul was trying to give the word of God to the proconsul, he was interrupted by this false prophet who was doing everything he could to impede the presentation of the gospel and prevent the proconsul from having a favorable response to it. Some of you likely remember how, when you were first converted, some people in your life did all they could to dissuade you. Upon my own conversion I went home to see my pastor. Of all the people in the world, I thought he would be the one most thrilled to hear of it. When I told him the story, he looked at me in disdain and said, "If you believe in the resurrection of Christ, you're a damn fool." I felt as though a stake had been driven through my heart. We know that Bar-Jesus was a false prophet because he fought against the truth of God.

Paul could have taken aside Bar-Jesus in an attempt to speak privately with him and to avoid a confrontation in front of the proconsul. He also could have charmed the false prophet by being gentle in his refutation. But Paul chose another manner altogether. **Then Saul, who also is called Paul, filled with the Holy Spirit, looked intently at him and said, "O full of all deceit and all fraud, you son of the devil, you enemy of all righteousness, will you not cease perverting the straight ways of the Lord?** (vv. 9–10). Obviously the Apostle had not taken time to read Dale Carnegie's book *How to Win Friends and Influence People*. He lashed into this man and gave him what for, and we are told that he spoke in this manner while filled with the Holy Spirit.

If you are familiar with the life of Paul, you know that he manifested a pastor's heart. In his letters he admonished believers to be gentle, patient, long-suffering, kind, and merciful, and not combative, belligerent, or bellicose in their relationships. In that sense he mirrored Jesus. Jesus was tender with the downtrodden and the weak, yet when those in positions of power stood up to resist the truth of God, Jesus called them children of hell, just as Paul now calls this false prophet a "son of the devil." We are not accustomed to that in our Christian practice.

Some time ago Max McLean recorded a recitation of the most famous sermon in America, "Sinners in the Hands of an Angry God," preached by Jonathan Edwards in Enfield, Connecticut, in 1741. Max received angry, nasty letters from people who did not like it. Ligonier broadcast that recording and also received angry letters. People wrote, "I don't want to hear this kind of preaching because my God is a God of love, and this sermon is about hell." At the time I told my wife, Vesta, "It scares me that there are people in the church today who are hostile to that sermon because the message in it is the application of one biblical principle after another taken from Deuteronomy, 'Their foot shall slip in due time' (Deut. 32:35).

The Great Awakening swept through New England and moved into Northampton, where Edwards was the pastor, and then George Whitefield came from England and itinerated through the area, whereby the Great Awakening spread almost to every village in Connecticut except one—Enfield. All the villages around Enfield were caught up in the revival and people were coming to Christ, but the people of Enfield were stiff-necked, hardened in their hearts, so some leaders of Enfield prevailed upon Edwards to travel to Connecticut and preach there. He came one morning to preach that sermon, and halfway through, there was an outcry from the congregation, not an outcry of anger but of grief and mourning as people were slain in their consciences and pricked by the truth of the Word of God. They were crying out for relief from their guilt. Edwards stopped and had elders minister to those people, and then the sermon resumed, and it kept on going. An eyewitness recounted that Edwards wasn't ranting and raving. He merely fixed his gaze on the bell rope in the back of the church and in a gracious tone continued preaching and warning the people. He asked them to consider whether they realized that some of them within the next twelve months would be in hell. Some of them, he said, might be there before the sun rose the next day.

We don't know the extent of our days. We do not know how long God will be patient with us. He is long-suffering, desiring to give us an opportunity to take advantage of the grace given in Christ; but what happens, according to the Scriptures, is that the longer God delays, the more arrogant we become. The bolder we are in our defiance against Him, the more we get rid of any notion of judgment, saying, "Our God is a God of love." However, a god who loves and never punishes sin would not be very loving. We have it straight from the lips of Jesus that every human being will stand before Almighty God and be held accountable for every thought, deed, and idle word. I cannot see the hearts of those reading this book, but the odds indicate that some of you will at some future point be in hell. Once in hell they will say, "I heard about Christ, but I was like Bar-Jesus. I never stopped fighting it. I never ceased rejecting it until the day I died, and now alas, it's too late."

I thank God that the Apostle Paul loved Bar-Jesus enough to call him a fraud. Paul put the gospel out right in front of him and exposed him. He was a deceiver who sought by his vocation to undermine the preaching of the truth. Paul spent so much of his time in jail and being beaten and was finally executed because he loved the lost and cared about their eternal destiny. Oh, that we would be awakened to that kind of passion that marked the very beginning of the missionary enterprise of the Apostle Paul.

And now, indeed, the hand of the Lord is upon you, and you shall be blind, not seeing the sun for a time." And immediately a dark mist fell on him, and he went around seeking someone to lead him by the hand (v. 11). For a time Bar-Jesus was stricken with blindness. This false prophet, who supposedly could tell everybody else what was coming next, was groping around for somebody to hold his hand, to lead him in the dark mist that God had put upon him.

As for Sergius Paulus, he was astonished. **Then the proconsul believed, when he saw what had been done, being astonished at the teaching of the Lord** (v. 12). There is a footnote here. Sergius Paulus didn't believe simply because he was an eyewitness of the judgment that befell the false prophet; rather, he was astonished, we are told, at the teaching of the Lord. It was the word of God. It was the truth that was proclaimed by Paul and Barnabas and John Mark that overwhelmed Sergius Paulus. God gave that man ears to hear and eyes to see, so that when he died, he did not end up in hell.

Every now and then we have to look in a mirror. We have to cut away the facade and ask, "Where's my heart? Am I really trusting in Christ alone for my salvation, or am I resting on my performance—how often I go to church, how many good deeds I've done, how much money I've given away? Have I fled to the cross as my only hope in life and death?" If we flee to Jesus, He alone is the gateway to heaven and everlasting life. Every moment that we resist the full commitment of our hearts to Him, the same Apostle who spoke to this false prophet says that we are heaping up wrath. So I say, flee to Jesus if for no other reason than to save your own soul.

33

PAUL'S SERMON AT ANTIOCH

Acts 13:13–26

Now when Paul and his party set sail from Paphos, they came to Perga in Pamphylia; and John, departing from them, returned to Jerusalem. But when they departed from Perga, they came to Antioch in Pisidia, and went into the synagogue on the Sabbath day and sat down. And after the reading of the Law and the Prophets, the rulers of the synagogue sent to them, saying, "Men and brethren, if you have any word of exhortation for the people, say on." Then Paul stood up, and motioning with his hand said, "Men of Israel, and you who fear God, listen: The God of this people Israel chose our fathers, and exalted the people when they dwelt as strangers in the land of Egypt, and with an uplifted arm He brought them out of it. Now for a time of about forty years He put up with their ways in the wilderness. And when He had destroyed seven nations in the land of Canaan, He distributed their land to them by allotment. After that He gave them judges for about four hundred and fifty years, until Samuel the prophet. And afterward they asked for a king; so God gave them Saul the son of Kish, a man of the tribe of Benjamin, for forty years. And when He had removed him, He raised up for them David as king, to whom also He gave testimony and said, 'I have found David the son of Jesse, a man after My own heart, who will do all My will.' From this man's seed, according to the promise, God raised up for Israel a Savior—Jesus—after John had first preached, before His coming, the baptism of repentance to all the people of Israel. And as John was finishing his course, he said, 'Who do you think I am? I am not He. But behold, there comes One after me, the sandals of whose feet I am not worthy to loose.' Men and brethren, sons of the family of Abraham, and those among you who fear God, to you the word of this salvation has been sent.

The text before us now contains the first recorded sermon of the Apostle Paul. We have an opportunity to eavesdrop on the testimony that Paul brought to the people at Pisidia and Antioch. Before that, we have a transition that gets Paul and Barnabas from Cyprus to Asia Minor, to the area that is modern-day Turkey. **Now when Paul and his party set sail from Paphos, they came to Perga in Pamphylia; and John, departing from them, returned to Jerusalem** (v. 13).

In this little transition some very significant things take place. Paphos, on the coast of Cyprus from which they were leaving, was noted in that day for its temple to Venus, the goddess of love. The way in which Venus was worshiped involved temple prostitution. They sailed from there to Perga in Asia Minor, and in Perga was a temple established to the goddess Diana. It was not as extensive or as famous as the one in Ephesus, which we will read about later, but the point is that they went from one pagan religious center in Paphos to another in Perga.

We also read that John Mark departed from them and returned to Jerusalem. When these men set out on the missionary journey, Barnabas was leading. Barnabas selected Paul to go along as his associate, and he also involved his nephew John Mark as part of the team. Their first stop was Cyprus, and there was a good response to the ministry there. From there they planned to go across the ocean up into Asia Minor and continue the missionary endeavor, but John Mark left and went back to Jerusalem.

Luke does not tell us here why John Mark left, but we get a clue a bit later in the book when Paul and Barnabas split up before the second missionary journey. They split because Barnabas wanted to bring John Mark back onto the team, but Paul did not. Paul was obviously upset that John Mark had bailed out of the first missionary journey. We still do not know why John Mark left them. Maybe he was afraid of possible persecution in Asia Minor, the dangerous territory into which they were going.

Most commentators agree that in all probability the reason John Mark resigned his role was that there was a management change. We tend to think of the first-century Christian community as a group of plastic saints, people who never had disagreements among themselves, but they were no different from Christians in every age. When an organization undergoes a management change, people get nervous. The security they have known can be jeopardized by new management, as can the familiarity of routine. Difficulties abound when a subordinate is placed over those to whom he or she used to report. Here in Acts, it is very clear, if we look at the text closely, that from this moment on Paul is the one in charge of the missionary journey, not Barnabas.

We hear no complaint from Barnabas about his loss in status, but obviously there was a complaint from John Mark. John Mark did not appreciate that Paul had been given the leadership position over his Uncle Barnabas. That is somewhat speculative; nevertheless, Paul (as we will see in Acts 15) saw John Mark's departure as an act of desertion from the mission.

At Pisidium Antioch

But when they departed from Perga, they came to Antioch in Pisidia, and went into the synagogue on the Sabbath day and sat down (v. 14). There is no indication that they had established a beachhead of ministry in Perga. This missionary journey began in Antioch, and it seems now that we are coming full circle back to Antioch. But this is a different Antioch. The Antioch to which they came now is called in the New Testament Pisidium Antioch, which is in the interior of Asia Minor. In fact, if we look carefully at a map of that time, we would see that just a little bit north of this Antioch, there was yet another Antioch. The term "Antioch" is used for at least three different cities that we encounter in the New Testament. The reason for that is the widespread power and authority of one of the heirs to the empire left by Alexander the Great. Out of the Seleucid Empire came one known as Antiochus the Great. There were at least three cities named after him, just as we find many places in America named Lincoln or Washington or Jefferson. The Antioch before us now was in Pisidia, which was inland from the coast.

There is other geographical detail that may have significance here. In 2 Corinthians 11 (the most autobiographical chapter in the Bible), Paul wrote a defense of his credentials in protest of some who were challenging his authority in the church with fallacious arguments. About them he wrote, "Are they Hebrews? So am I. Are they Israelites? So am I. Are they the seed of Abraham? So am I. Are they ministers of Christ?—I speak as a fool—I am more: in labors more abundant, in stripes above measure, in prisons more frequently, in deaths often" (vv. 22–23). Then he detailed his personal struggles, which included "journeys often, in perils of waters, in perils of robbers, in perils of my own countrymen, in perils of the Gentiles, in perils in the city, in perils in the wilderness, in perils in the sea, in perils among false brethren" (v. 26). What we know about this part of the world in antiquity is that this stretch of land between Perga and Pisidium Antioch was notoriously troubled by bandits and outlaws who lay in wait for travelers who dared to venture into their territory. The bandits would fall upon the travelers, beat and rob them, and often leave them for dead. Fear of that is another possible reason why John Mark left Paul and Barnabas. This was obviously a very perilous place, and Paul had to transverse it in order to continue his ministry.

They came to Antioch and went into the synagogue on the Sabbath day and sat down. **And after the reading of the Law and the Prophets, the rulers of the synagogue sent to them, saying, "Men and brethren, if you have any word of exhortation for the people, say on"** (v. 15). They read the text of the Law and of the Prophets, which was customary in the synagogue. Paul, probably already known there due to his credentials as a student of Gamaliel, was invited to give an exposition of the text, very much like Jesus had been invited to speak at Capernaum early in His public ministry.

Our Fathers

Then Paul stood up, and motioning with his hand said, "Men of Israel, and you who fear God, listen. The God of this people: Israel chose our fathers" (vv. 16–17). After Jesus' crucifixion, a group traveled from Jerusalem on the road to Emmaus, and as they walked they talked about the catastrophic events that had just taken place on Good Friday. Jesus fell in with them and asked them what they were talking about. He listened to their tales of woe and frustration, and then "beginning at Moses and all the Prophets, He expounded to them in all the Scriptures the things concerning Himself" (Luke 24:27). Afterward the travelers said, "Did not our heart burn within us while He talked with us on the road, and while He opened the Scriptures to us?" (v. 32).

That was exactly the approach Paul used here in Antioch. Paul did not start with Jesus; he started with Abraham. He began with the sovereign election of God of a certain nation: **"The God of this people Israel chose our fathers, and exalted the people when they dwelt as strangers in the land of Egypt, and with an uplifted arm He brought them out of it"** (v. 17). This is the history of sovereign election in the Old Testament. God took a people who were no people and called them His people. Paul gave a historical reconnaissance, a brief overview, of the whole history of redemption. God raised His arm into the face of Pharaoh and delivered His people from bondage in Egypt.

"Now for a time of about forty years He put up with their ways in the wilderness" (v. 18). God put up with their ways; He endured them. An image contained therein is that of a nurse, not one who gives nourishment but one who cares for a helpless infant. God did that, and all the while the people complained and moaned and wished to return to Egypt. **"And when He had destroyed seven nations in the land of Canaan, He distributed their land to them by allotment"** (v. 19). So Paul gave them a quick summary of Numbers and Joshua and then Judges. **"After that He gave them judges for about four hundred and fifty years, until Samuel the prophet"** (v. 20). In between Israel's rule by patriarchs and the monarchy, God gave them judges. The judges were charismatic leaders sovereignly raised up by God. They were not elected officials. They did not reign as kings in dynastic succession. God raised them individually and provided Samson, Gideon, Deborah, and others as need arose. During this loose tribal federation of Jewish people, it was clear who the Sovereign was—God. He was their King.

Paul then reminded them that the people had been dissatisfied with such rule, so they had asked God for a king. They wanted a king like the other nations had. They wanted to be secular like the rest of the world. God warned them that such a king would raise taxes, and send their young men into battle to be killed, and confiscate their property. Nevertheless, the people wanted a king, **"so God gave them Saul the son of Kish, a man of the tribe of Benjamin, for forty years"** (v. 21). This is the first time we are told the length of Saul's reign. The Old Testament does not provide that information, although it squares exactly with Josephus's records.

Paul's history lesson is leading in a specific direction—to David. David ushered in the golden age of Israel. He expanded Israel's boundaries from Dan to Beersheba and established the most prosperous period in all of its history. David became the great king—a warrior king, a shepherd king, and a poet king—and was also a prophet through whom God gave a new covenant. The covenant He made with David was the promise that from his seed would come God's Son, who would also be David's Lord and Savior. Paul was preaching his way through redemptive history to David.

Seed of David

"And when He had removed him, He raised up for them David as king, to whom also He gave testimony and said, 'I have found David the son of Jesse, a man after My own heart, who will do all My will'" (v. 22). David was one of the most bloodthirsty, ruthless, barbaric leaders of all time. He was the chief of sinners of Old Testament leaders. Yet there was something about David that delighted God. He looked beyond David's sin and ruthlessness and saw the heart of David. A man or woman after God's own heart is one who wants to know God more than just superficially. This is someone who wants more than a casual awareness or understanding of God. This is a person who loves to do God's will. Because David is described this way by God in the Old Testament, the people looked to him, despite his sin and failures, as the model of the One who would come, the beloved of the Father, who would reveal the Father's heart.

"From this man's seed, according to the promise, God raised up for Israel a Savior—Jesus—after John had first preached, before His coming, the baptism of repentance to all the people of Israel. And as John was finishing

his course, he said, 'Who do you think I am? I am not He. But behold, there
comes One after me, the sandals of whose feet I am not worthy to loose'"
(vv. 23–25). Several years ago I taught an evening class on the book of Romans.
Together we went through Romans, verse by verse, line upon line, precept upon
precept, and I set forth the doctrine of justification by faith alone. Somewhere
during that time I learned about a program called Evangelism Explosion. Initially
I was reserved about the program. It seemed a bit simplistic in its approach to
evangelism, but as I observed it in action, I saw many come to Christ through it.
It presents the gospel after preparing listeners by means of two questions. After
witnessing firsthand the effectiveness of the program, I put before my Romans
students the two questions: (1) "Are you sure that if you should die today, you
will definitely go to heaven?" and (2) "If you should die today and God should
ask you why you should be allowed into heaven, what would you answer Him?"
I asked my son that question when he was five years old, and he answered,
"Because I'm dead." His answer reflected not his father's theology or the church's
but that of the culture, which claims that all you have to do to go to heaven is
die; everybody goes. When I asked my Romans students, at least 80 percent
gave a "works righteousness" answer. Despite being taught justification by faith
alone week after week, my students were still trusting their own righteousness
to get them to heaven.

Part of the problem is that today we think we can educate people into the
kingdom of God. I had been presenting the theology of Romans verse by verse,
but they had missed the big picture, which is the gospel. Whenever we see Paul
teaching the gospel in his epistles, he always begins with this: Jesus according to
the Scriptures was born as the seed of David. If I asked you to write an outline
of the gospel, would that be your first step? It was Paul's. He started in the Old
Testament, proceeded to David, and from David he went to the latest prophet,
John the Baptist, who announced to Israel that the son of David, the Lamb of
God, had come.

Surely every Jew in the audience that day in Asia Minor had heard of John
the Baptist, because at that time John the Baptist was more famous than Jesus.
That is why Paul had to tell them that by John's own testimony, the One who
came after him was before him and that John was not worthy to loosen His
sandals, a task given to the most menial of slaves. Noblemen never stooped to
untie their own shoes.

In our next study, we will see where the Apostle goes next in his sermon, but
thus far the focus has been on David and his seed.

34

CHRIST AND DAVID

Acts 13:28–39

"And though they found no cause for death in Him, they asked Pilate that He should be put to death. Now when they had fulfilled all that was written concerning Him, they took Him down from the tree and laid Him in a tomb. But God raised Him from the dead. He was seen for many days by those who came up with Him from Galilee to Jerusalem, who are His witnesses to the people. And we declare to you glad tidings—that promise which was made to the fathers. God has fulfilled this for us their children, in that He has raised up Jesus. As it is also written in the second Psalm:

> 'You are My Son,
> Today I have begotten You.'

And that He raised Him from the dead, no more to return to corruption, He has spoken thus:

> 'I will give you the sure mercies of David.'

Therefore He also says in another Psalm:

> 'You will not allow Your Holy One to see corruption.'

"For David, after he had served his own generation by the will of God, fell asleep, was buried with his fathers, and saw corruption; but He whom God raised up saw no corruption.

Therefore let it be known to you, brethren, that through this Man is preached to you the forgiveness of sins; and by Him everyone who believes is justified from all things from which you could not be justified by the law of Moses."

Some time ago I spent a week in New York City. I happened to be there on the most sacred day of the Jewish calendar, the day of Yom Kippur. In fact, a group of Hasidic Jews was celebrating in the hotel where I was staying. I sat and watched a parade of devout Jewish men coming to celebrate Yom Kippur. I felt as if there was lead in my stomach as I watched these people celebrating the Day of Atonement with such intensity, urgency, and sincerity. They were celebrating because they believe that this special day brings them forgiveness for their sins for another year. I wanted to jump up and say, "Men of Israel, you missed Him. Don't you understand that your Messiah has already come and that He made atonement once for all? Don't you see that every time you celebrate this Day of Atonement, you draw another line against your Messiah and Savior as you continue to look for someone else?" I did not say that, but it is exactly what Paul said in Pisidium Antioch when he went into the synagogue. Paul was burdened for his Jewish kinsmen, people that he loved with all his heart. There wasn't an ounce of anti-Semitism in Jesus or in the Apostle Paul. To the contrary, Paul was driven by a love for his kinsmen, which is why he came to plead the case of the One crucified in Jerusalem by the elders who rejected the Messiah. Paul pleads with those in Pisidium Antioch not to make the same mistake that the leaders in Jerusalem had made.

In our last study we looked at the initial part of Paul's first-recorded sermon. He began by reaching back into the pages of the Old Testament to the promises God had made to Abraham, to the deliverance God had brought to the people in the exodus, and to David. Paul sought to establish the foundation for the point of contact between the people of Israel and the gospel of Jesus Christ, and that point of contact was David. He said in essence, "Look to your hero, the great king and warrior prince. Look to your poet laureate, the author of the Psalms." Simply looking at all David wrote in the Psalms should have been sufficient to drive them to Christ, because God had used David's work there to speak of the coming Messiah. The One who would be David's son would at the same time be David's Lord.

"Though they found no cause for death in him, they asked Pilate that He should be put to death. Now when they had fulfilled all that was written concerning Him, they took Him down from the tree and laid Him in a tomb" (v. 28). The leaders in Jerusalem were so adamant in their rejection of the claims of Jesus that they fulfilled the claims of Jesus inadvertently by doing exactly what the Scriptures had predicted thousands of years before that they would do. Paul reminds his hearers that they had delivered Him to judgment and death and afterward they took Him down from the tree and laid Him in a tomb.

Getting the Gospel Right

"But God raised Him from the dead. He was seen for many days by those who came up with Him from Galilee to Jerusalem, who are His witnesses to the people. And we declare to you glad tidings" (vv. 30–32). The Greek verb used here for "glad tidings" comes from the word *euangelion*, which is the noun translated by the word "gospel." Paul is saying, "We are declaring to you now the gospel, the promise that was made to the fathers. God has fulfilled this to their children in that He raised up Jesus."

One of my books recently went out of print, and if my memory serves me right, it went out of print faster than any I have ever written. In terms of the Christian bookselling market, it was a literary bomb, an unqualified disaster. The title of the book was *Getting the Gospel Right*. I wrote that book because I am burdened by the unprecedented ignorance in the Protestant evangelical community today about what the gospel is. Some time ago a survey was taken at a booksellers' convention. The attendees, people involved in Christian publishing, were asked to give their definition of the gospel. When the results were tallied, only one response matched the New Testament concept of the gospel. Ninety-nine out of one hundred professing evangelicals had no clue as to what the gospel is. Some said, "The gospel is that God loves you and has a wonderful plan for your life." That is not the gospel. Others said, "The gospel is that Jesus can change your life if you ask Him into your heart." That is good news, but it is not the gospel. Still others said, "The gospel is that you can have a personal relationship with Jesus." That too is not the gospel. Everyone already has a personal relationship with Jesus. It may be a negative one, but everyone alive today is in a personal relationship with Jesus whether they want to be or not.

The gospel has objective content. There are three ways in which we use the term *gospel*. One is used for a category of literature. The Bible books that give us an overview of the life of Jesus are called the "good news" or "Gospels." There are four canonical Gospels: Matthew, Mark, Luke, and John.

We are given to understand the content of the word *gospel* from the lips of John the Baptist and then from Jesus. On the lips of Jesus the content of the gospel is the gospel of the kingdom. Jesus proclaimed that the breakthrough of the kingdom of God was at hand. God has always been King. God has always been sovereign over all He has created, so there is nothing new about the fact that the Lord God omnipotent reigns. The concept of the kingdom of God as set forth in the Old Testament depicts a kingdom that was to come into this world by virtue of God the Father anointing His King. So when Christ came into the world, He proclaimed that the kingdom had come in the sense that He, the King, had arrived.

After Jesus died and ascended into heaven, we have the apostolic testimony to the gospel. It's not that the Apostles ignored the kingdom concept, but rather a subtle shift came into play. Paul, for example, constantly refers to the gospel as "the gospel of Jesus Christ," who, of course, is the King, but the gospel is actually the good news about Jesus.

We have to understand the difference between our personal testimony and the gospel. When I tell you what Christ has done for me, that is not evangelism. It is not bad—it is a good thing to do—but it is pre-evangelism. It may or may not resonate with the one listening to my story. It is not my story that God invests with power unto salvation; it is the story of Jesus—who He is, what He has done, and how the benefits of what He has done may be appropriated by us. So the gospel that Paul preached is the gospel of the seed of David, the incarnate Jesus Christ, who was put to death on the cross and raised from the dead, who ascended into heaven and will come again at the end of the age. Jesus has won for us our forgiveness and our justification, which is by faith alone. If we remove any of those elements, we remove the gospel of Jesus Christ.

"... That promise which was made to the fathers. God has fulfilled this for us their children, in that He has raised up Jesus. As it is also written in the second Psalm: 'You are My Son, today I have begotten You'" (vv. 32–33). Paul appeals to Psalm 2, which begins, "Why do the nations rage, and the people plot a vain thing? The kings of the earth set themselves, and the rulers take counsel together, against the Lord and against His Anointed" (vv. 1–2). The Lord looks down from heaven at the collective antagonism against His Son and laughs. He holds those rulers in derision, yet he responds to the hostility of a fallen world by pointing them to His Son, the Messiah, saying through David: "You are My Son, today I have begotten You" (v. 7). The term "begotten" was used here in a metaphorical way. I agree with just about every commentator on Acts, that when Paul made this appeal to Psalm 2, he was not talking about a moment when Jesus was begotten. The begottenness of this psalm was fulfilled at the resurrection, where in a sense "begottenness" became a synonym for exaltation.

Throughout the ministry of Jesus, God opened up the heavens from the clouds and spoke audibly. At the very beginning of Jesus' ministry, God said, "This is My beloved Son, in whom I am well pleased" (Matt. 3:17). Later, on the mountain, God said, "This is My beloved Son. Hear Him!" (Mark 9:7). That voice had greatest clarity when God raised His Son from the dead. That is the great difference between David and David's Son. David was a man after God's own heart, but he was not God's beloved Son. He was not God's only begotten.

Death and Resurrection

Paul went to other Old Testament texts: **"And that He raised Him from the dead, no more to return to corruption, He has spoken thus: 'I will give you the sure mercies of David.' Therefore He also says in another Psalm: 'You will not allow Your Holy One to see corruption'"** (vv. 34–35). Paul quoted David again. Here Paul was saying, "See the difference between Jesus and David." The mercies that God promised to His Son are certain. They are the sure promises of God. Paul also cited Psalm 34: "You will not allow Your Holy One to see corruption." Jesus was not the first person in human history to be raised from the dead. There were rare instances in the Old Testament of people being raised from the dead. Jesus during His own ministry raised some from the dead. As astonishing as those occasions were, each person whom Jesus raised from the dead died again later. Though their souls were taken to heaven, their bodies underwent corruption.

In the story of the raising of Lazarus, an unpleasant detail is given. We are told that Jesus had delayed three or four days before coming to the home of Mary and Martha in Bethany, and by then Lazarus had died. As Jesus approached the tomb where Lazarus had been buried, Martha said to him, "Lord, by this time there is a stench, for he has been dead four days" (John 11:39). Martha was speaking of the natural odor that emanates from corpses in the process of decomposition, but Christ's power of resurrection overcame the rottenness that had surrounded the bones of Lazarus. When Jesus died and was laid in a tomb, His body underwent not the slightest bit of physical decomposition. The day He was raised, His skin was as toned and perfect as it had been when they laid Him in the tomb, because God had promised that He would not allow His Holy One to suffer corruption—not just moral corruption, but physical decay.

A television program I saw featured archaeological digs in Egypt. Archaeologists had uncovered the tomb of someone who had lived one thousand years before King Tut. The program showed close-ups of the skeletal remains. A forensics expert explained how details of the deceased's life could be discerned from those remains. I noted as I was watching that those ancient bones had no tissue on them. It was evident that the body of that individual had suffered corruption. No such corruption came to the body of Jesus. **"For David, after he had served his own generation by the will of God, fell asleep, was buried with his fathers, and saw corruption; but He whom God raised up saw no corruption. Therefore**

let it be known to you, brethren, that through this Man is preached to you the forgiveness of sins; and by Him everyone who believes is justified from all things from which you could not be justified by the law of Moses" (vv. 36–39). The reason our bodies die and are subject to decomposition and corruption is that there is an inherent rottenness—sin—that emanates from the core of our being. It is sin that corrupts the whole person. That is the message of Scripture. We look for the resurrection of the body and the life everlasting because it means that sin has been vanquished and forgiven through the atonement that was perfectly offered once and for all by Jesus on the cross. It is because of the cross that there is a resurrection. It is because of the cross that our souls will not rot in the grave. It is because of the cross and the resurrection of Christ that He was appointed the firstborn of all creation, so that all who put their trust in Him will live forever without corruption. Paul attached to this glorious news the truth that "everyone who believes is justified from all things," which the Law of Moses could not accomplish. Paul wrote elsewhere, "By the works of the law no flesh shall be justified" (Gal. 2:16).

I received a letter from a physician who had heard me talking on the radio about justification by faith alone. He wrote, "I know that you are lying when you say the Bible teaches justification by faith alone. You don't really believe that, because it's nowhere to be found in sacred Scripture." I was saddened, and I wanted to say, "The very thing that you think I don't believe is the core belief of my whole faith." If we take away justification by faith alone, we have no hope, either in this world or that to come. That is why justification by faith alone is not an unscientific postscript to the gospel. It is the heart of the gospel. The gospel is who Jesus is, what Jesus did, and how we receive for our own all that He is and has done. Anyone who puts their faith and trust in Him and stops trusting in their own goodness will spend eternity in His blessed presence.

35

ETERNAL APPOINTMENT

Acts 13:40–52

"Beware therefore, lest what has been spoken in the prophets come upon you:

'Behold, you despisers,
Marvel and perish!
For I work a work in your days,
A work which you will by no means believe,
Though one were to declare it to you.'"

So when the Jews went out of the synagogue, the Gentiles begged that these words might be preached to them the next Sabbath. Now when the congregation had broken up, many of the Jews and devout proselytes followed Paul and Barnabas, who, speaking to them, persuaded them to continue in the grace of God. On the next Sabbath almost the whole city came together to hear the word of God. But when the Jews saw the multitudes, they were filled with envy; and contradicting and blaspheming, they opposed the things spoken by Paul. Then Paul and Barnabas grew bold and said, "It was necessary that the word of God should be spoken to you first; but since you reject it, and judge yourselves unworthy of everlasting life, behold, we turn to the Gentiles. For so the Lord has commanded us:

'I have set you as a light to the Gentiles,
That you should be for salvation to the ends of the earth.'"

Now when the Gentiles heard this, they were glad and glorified the word of the Lord. And as many as had been appointed to eternal life believed. And the word of the Lord was being spread throughout all the region. But the Jews stirred up the devout and prominent women and the chief men of the city, raised up persecution against Paul and Barnabas, and expelled them from their region. But they shook off the dust from their feet against them, and came to Iconium. And the disciples were filled with joy and with the Holy Spirit.

The world we live in is radically different from the world of the apostolic church, and it is helpful to keep that in mind as we continue our study of Paul's first-recorded sermon. Imagine for a moment that Paul had available to him all the technology of today, the era Neil Postman has called the Age of Technopoly. When Paul was asked by the rulers of the synagogue to speak to them about the Word of God, Paul might have said something like this: "I'm happy to do that, but before the sermon, would you mind if I bring my drama team to the front of the chancel and remove the Plexiglas pulpit so that, before I preach, we can give a visually pleasing dramatic presentation? Also, I hope you won't mind if I punctuate my sermon with a multimedia presentation, which will appear on the screen in the front of the sanctuary. I also ask that the available press broadcast the message live to Jerusalem via satellite and that they try to be as unobtrusive as possible while doing so. I hope also that you'll be kind to me after I finish this sermon, as the press convenes to analyze my words and give a critique of them as part of their broadcast. Finally, I hope and pray, dear brothers, that as you listen to me expound the Word of God that you focus on the content of the Word rather than counting how many times I frown or scowl or furrow my brow, because substance is more important than style."

That final appeal in our day would fall on deaf ears. In a technopoly such as ours, we do not respond intellectually to the content of words. Rather, we respond to images broadcast before us. Those images are the message, and we try to make them as entertaining as we possibly can, as Postman's first book indicated by its title: *Amusing Ourselves to Death*. Even the nightly news is framed by sound bites that are designed to entertain rather than to inform, and we move in rapid succession from one report to the next without time to digest or analyze content. We react to images, so if we want to communicate, we have to frame our message in terms of entertaining images. That is not how we do things at Saint Andrew's, but we are swimming almost impossibly against the stream.

The Cry of Habakkuk

Had Paul written his sermon before preaching it, his corps of speechwriters would have examined it and said, "Well, Paul, this message is fine up until the last few sentences. Everything is upbeat. Everything is good news. Everything is appealing to the senses of the audience, but then you close with this quotation from the Old Testament. You have compressed it from the word of the prophet Habakkuk, but we really don't think that's going to fly. It's too negative, and we ought to eliminate it from your sermon." Thanks be to God that Paul didn't have speechwriters like that.

At the conclusion of his message at Pisidium Antioch, after his masterful presentation of the gospel, he gave a warning to those assembled: **"Beware therefore, lest what has been spoken in the prophets come upon you"** (v. 40). Then Paul gave the compressed quote from Habakkuk: **"Behold, you despisers, marvel and perish! For I work a work in your days, a work which you will by no means believe, though one were to declare it to you"** (v. 41). Let us look just briefly at a larger portion of that citation. The book of Habakkuk begins with a cry from the prophet. He cannot understand the abundance of suffering coming upon his own people or the threatened invasion of the Chaldeans against the people of God.

> O Lord, how long shall I cry,
> And You will not hear?
> Even cry out to You, "Violence!"
> And You will not save.
> Why do you show me iniquity,
> And cause me to see trouble?
> For plundering and violence are before me;
> There is strife, and contention arises. (Hab. 1:1–3)

And here's the conclusion that Habakkuk came to: "Therefore the law is powerless, and justice never goes forth" (v. 4). Habakkuk was thinking, "How can this be? God is on our side. How can God, who is too holy to even look upon evil, tolerate this calamity that is befalling us right now?"

Habakkuk complained that ethics had disintegrated. Nobody cared about virtue. Nobody cared about what was right. Everything was decided on the basis of violence. God answered Habakkuk:

> Look among the nations and watch—
> Be utterly astounded!

For I will work a work in your days

Which you would not believe, though it were told you.

For indeed I am raising up the Chaldeans,

A bitter and hasty nation

Which marches through the breadth of the earth,

To possess dwelling places that are not theirs.

They are terrible and dreadful;

Their judgment and their dignity proceed from themselves.

Their horses also are swifter than leopards,

And more fierce than evening wolves.

Their chargers charge ahead;

Their cavalry comes from afar;

They fly as the eagle that hastens to eat.

They all come for violence. (Hab. 1:5–9)

When they are finished, Habakkuk said, they are going to leave destruction and catastrophe in their midst, such as one could not possibly imagine.

Forewarned

Centuries later, Paul harkened back to this Old Testament warning from the prophet and told the Jews assembled in the synagogue to beware that the same thing doesn't happen to them that happened to their fathers when the hand of God's judgment fell upon them. He was warning them of things that could come at any time, things that they wouldn't believe, no matter who was to tell them. Jesus also punctuated His sermons with future predictions of this same sort. Jesus said, "The days will come in which not one stone shall be left upon another that shall not be thrown down. . . . And Jerusalem will be trampled by Gentiles until the times of the Gentiles are fulfilled" (Luke 21:6, 24). Nobody in Israel believed that, but in A.D. 70 came the worst holocaust ever to occur up to that point in Jewish history. Thousands upon thousands of Jews were killed under the Roman forces of Titus as the city was leveled and burned and the temple destroyed, not to be rebuilt even to this day. Nobody believed Jesus, nor did they believe Paul.

Jesus told a parable about a wicked man who died and went to hell and then wanted to go back and warn his brothers about the violence and the catastrophe that lay ahead of them (Luke 16:19–31). If we think Jerusalem's fall and the genocide of the Jewish people in World War II were holocausts, let me tell you what a real holocaust is—to come into the hands of the living God and be exposed to His everlasting judgment. When the rich man wanted to go back and warn his brother, in the parable, Jesus said, "If they do not hear Moses and the prophets, neither will they be persuaded though one rise from the dead" (v. 31). That is how stubborn we are, how hard our hearts have become. We have become immunized against the truth of the Word of God. That is why today we get rid of unpleasant aspects from our preaching. We do not want to look at unpleasant images.

I visited Ground Zero in New York City some time ago, and what I saw that day is burned in my mind forever. I wasn't an eyewitness of the events of 9/11. I saw it through modern technology. I saw that plane crash into the second tower and the implosion of those buildings. I saw the horrendous dust cloud that emerged, and I saw people running for their lives down the street. I saw the pictures of people jumping from buildings. The next day I saw on television people filled with resolve not to ever let it happen again. I said to Vesta, "That resolve will be gone within a year, I promise you." And it has gone. We are back to business as usual and to the technopoly that we prefer. We do not heed Paul's warning to be careful and to watch out.

So when the Jews went out of the synagogue, the Gentiles begged that these words might be preached to them the next Sabbath (v. 42). The God-fearing Jews and devout proselytes who were there that day loved the gospel that they heard. They were so intrigued by the preaching of the gospel that some of the rulers asked Paul and Barnabas to return the next week. **On the next Sabbath almost the whole city came together to hear the word of God. But when the Jews saw the multitudes, they were filled with envy; and contradicting and blaspheming, they opposed the things spoken by Paul** (vv. 44–45). Paul got the crowd's attention, but the people were filled with envy and jealousy against God's anointed messenger. Instead of embracing the gospel and being quick to delight in the truth of God, they began spreading lies. They began contradicting what the Apostle had proclaimed to them.

There is nothing new about that. It has been the response of people from the first century down to today. It is scary that people think they can stand in opposition to the truth of God and get away with it. They think, "I've been contradicting God thus far, and no lightning bolts have hit me, so I have no need to fear God." The most terrifying thing in the world is to fall into the hands of the living God if you are in a state of rebellion against Him.

God's Word Glorified

The more the people blasphemed, the bolder Paul and Barnabas became, and they said, **"It was necessary that the word of God should be spoken to you first; but since you reject it, and judge yourselves unworthy of everlasting**

life, behold, we turn to the Gentiles. For so the Lord has commanded us: 'I have set you as a light to the Gentiles, that you should be for salvation to the ends of the earth.'" Now when the Gentiles heard this, they were glad and glorified the word of the Lord (vv. 46–48). The Gentiles did not glorify Paul or Barnabas; they glorified the word of the Lord. They loved the truth of God. They couldn't get enough of it. They were not satisfied to come to the synagogue for one hour a week. They wanted to listen to Paul and Barnabas every day. How excited are you about the Word of God? How many times have you read the Scripture from beginning to end? More than 90 percent of professing believers have never done it. They taste the Word and allow it to tickle their conscience and give some occasional comfort to their soul, but lacking is that delight that draws one deeper into the Word day and night.

That delight is what happens to people when they have been changed by the Holy Spirit. They begin to love the Word of God. They cannot wait to get more of it. They take every opportunity they get to hear and study the Word of God because they glory in the Word of God. People have said to me, "I've tried to read the Bible, but it's boring." It is boring to them because they are dead. If people can come to the pages of a book that reveals the truth from the eternal God and be bored, that says nothing about the book. It says everything about their soul. Those in Pisidium Antioch who were alive to God, whom the Spirit grasped on that occasion, glorified the word of God.

And as many as had been appointed to eternal life believed (v. 48). People have told me, "When I first became a Christian, I believed it was my choice; it was my decision that led to my conversion. I was grateful to God, who had made it possible, but I really believed that the reason why I became a Christian while my neighbor didn't is that I exercised free will. But I've been listening to you, R.C., and I have finally come to the conclusion that it was, in fact, God who chose me. It was God, the Hound of Heaven, who renewed me by the Holy Spirit and created faith in my heart, and then I responded. Now I see that the Bible is very clear about that." They are right about that. It is so plainly there that there is no excuse for ever missing it. Verse 48 is one of those places: "As many as had been appointed to eternal life believed." All who came to faith that day did so by divine appointment. God had decreed from all eternity that they would come and hear the Apostle Paul and be quickened to faith by the Holy Spirit, and everyone that had been so appointed from eternity believed.

Many come to this text and try to skip over it or try to change it to read, "As many as believed, God appointed to eternal life," but the appointment here is the appointment to believe. A classic work on the book of Acts was written in the nineteenth century by H.B. Hackett, a classmate of Oliver Wendell Holmes.

About this verse Hackett said that there is just no other way to read it. Yet commentators create a variety of slants on this text and do funny things with the context and syntax of the Greek to change the clear meaning. You cannot get away from it. That is what Luke wrote, and that is what Luke meant. The only reason anybody was saved out of that ungodly mass of people who were blaspheming and criticizing the preaching of the Word of God was that God intervened in the hearts of His elect and translated them from the kingdom of darkness to the kingdom of light.

The True Church

There is a distinction between the visible church and the invisible church. The visible church is made up of those who profess to be Christians. It is comprised of those who appear on the rolls of a specific church. You can count them; you can see them in church on Sunday morning. We make a distinction between the visible and the invisible church not just because Augustine invented the distinction but because the concept was in the teaching of Jesus. Jesus said that there will always be tares growing along with the wheat. He warned the church to be careful about not weeding out the wheat along with the tares (Matt. 13:24–30). Certainly we do not want the church to be overrun by the tares; according to Jesus there is a place for church discipline, but care must be exercised in the process not to damage the people of God. Jesus also said, "These people draw near to Me with their mouth, and honor Me with their lips, but their heart is far from Me" (Matt. 15:8).

No one can read your heart. If you make a credible profession of faith with your lips, you can join a church and become a member of the visible church. Yet every day people join the visible church who are far from the kingdom of God. They profess Christ with their lips, but their hearts aren't in it, which is why the distinction between the visible and the invisible church exists. Augustine said that the invisible church is the true church made up of the body of the elect, those who have been truly redeemed and transformed by the power of the Holy Spirit. They are invisible to our sight but clearly visible to God, who can read the heart. In Pisidium Antioch the visible church was divided, but the invisible church was in one accord, for all those who had been appointed to eternal life believed, and the word of the Lord was spread throughout the whole region.

But the Jews stirred up the devout and prominent women and the chief men of the city, raised up persecution against Paul and Barnabas, and expelled them from their region. But they shook off the dust from their feet against them, and came to Iconium (vv. 50–51). The Jews did everything they could to oppose the spread of the word. They stirred up the wives of those in high places, the noblemen of the area, to raise persecution against Paul and Barnabas. Finally they kicked out Paul and Barnabas from the region. Paul and Barnabas did what Jesus told them to do—they shook off the dust from their feet. That could mean that they were in a hurry to get to the next town, but that is not the force of the idiom. The idiom means "don't take the dirt with you." There are many today who have heard the gospel many times, and still they do not believe. We need to thank God that he has not yet shaken the dust off His feet. If you are among the unbelievers, you must delay no more—not another day or hour—but submit body and soul to the lordship of Christ, embrace the gospel without compromise, take delight in the Word of God, make the seeking of the kingdom of God the main business of your life, and forget about religion. Religion is for people who hedge their bets. Christianity is for people who are sold out to the truth of God. May it be so with each of us.

36

ZEUS AND HERMES

Acts 14:1–18

Now it happened in Iconium that they went together to the synagogue of the Jews, and so spoke that a great multitude both of the Jews and of the Greeks believed. But the unbelieving Jews stirred up the Gentiles and poisoned their minds against the brethren. Therefore they stayed there a long time, speaking boldly in the Lord, who was bearing witness to the word of His grace, granting signs and wonders to be done by their hands. But the multitude of the city was divided: part sided with the Jews, and part with the Apostles. And when a violent attempt was made by both the Gentiles and Jews, with their rulers, to abuse and stone them, they became aware of it and fled to Lystra and Derbe, cities of Lycaonia, and to the surrounding region. And they were preaching the gospel there. And in Lystra a certain man without strength in his feet was sitting, a cripple from his mother's womb, who had never walked. This man heard Paul speaking. Paul, observing him intently and seeing that he had faith to be healed, said with a loud voice, "Stand up straight on your feet!" And he leaped and walked. Now when the people saw what Paul had done, they raised their voices, saying in the Lycaonian language, "The gods have come down to us in the likeness of men!" And Barnabas they called Zeus, and Paul, Hermes, because he was the chief speaker. Then the priest of Zeus, whose temple was in front of their city, brought oxen and garlands to the gates, intending to sacrifice with the multitudes. But when the apostles Barnabas and Paul heard this, they tore their clothes and ran in among the multitude, crying out and saying, "Men, why are you doing these things? We also are men with the same nature as you, and preach to you that you should turn from these useless things to the living God, who made the heaven, the earth, the

215

sea, and all things that are in them, who in bygone generations allowed all nations to walk in their own ways. Nevertheless He did not leave Himself without witness, in that He did good, gave us rain from heaven and fruitful seasons, filling our hearts with food and gladness." And with these sayings they could scarcely restrain the multitudes from sacrificing to them.

Back in the 1940s and 1950s, fans of the Pittsburgh Steelers had little to cheer about. The Steelers played more than forty years before winning a division championship. Today, the team is known for its great era, the 1970s. During the seventies the Steelers were the mightiest team that ever set forth on a football field. I lived in Pittsburgh during their years of championship drought, and when we spoke of the Steelers, we uttered an SOS. This was not a cry for rescue but of perpetual disappointment—"Same Old Steelers." We can apply that same acronym, SOS, to Acts 14 because it is the "Same Old Story." Everywhere the Apostles went, we see God working mightily, bringing conversions from both Jews and Gentiles. In the midst of bold preaching, divisions occurred, opposition arose, and hostility set in, and the Apostles were barely able on very many occasions to escape with their lives.

This is what happens when people are faithful to the gospel. When people preach the gospel without compromise, inevitably it provokes division because the truth of God divides. We need to understand that, because we live in a time when we abhor anything that could possibly divide us, particularly in the context of the church. As a result, we continually compromise and water down the truth of the Word of God so as to offend no one. Our efforts to keep the peace result in a Rodney King theology—we are all just trying to get along.

The Apostles, however, were convinced of the truth of the resurrection of Christ, and they were willing to turn the world upside down to be faithful to their mission, with the same results as before: **The unbelieving Jews stirred up the Gentiles and poisoned their minds against the brethren. Therefore they stayed there a long time, speaking boldly in the Lord, who was bearing witness to the word of His grace, granting signs and wonders to be done by their hands** (vv. 2–3). I mention in passing that the primary function of miracles in the New Testament was not to prove the existence of God but to authenticate God's true agents of revelation. Nicodemus came to Jesus at night and said, "Rabbi, we know that You are a teacher come from God; for no one can do these signs that You do unless God is with him" (John 3:2). As for the Apostles, the Scriptures tell us that God proved them to be His genuine representatives by working signs and wonders and miracles through their hands. That was the chief purpose of the rash of miracles that we encounter in the New Testament.

In Lystra and Derbe

But the multitude of the city was divided: part sided with the Jews, and part with the apostles. And when a violent attempt was made by both the Gentiles and Jews, with their rulers, to abuse and stone them, they became aware of it and fled to Lystra and Derbe, cities of Lycaonia, and to the surrounding region (vv. 4–6). Luke tells us that the Apostles fled to Lystra and Derbe, which were situated in the province of Lycaonia. This minor detail is of great significance. In the nineteenth century we saw an unprecedented attack by liberal scholarship against the trustworthiness of the biblical record, and at the very front of this assault was an attack against the historical reliability of Luke, who gave us this history of the expansion of the early church. One of the things about which the critics carped was this little clause, "They fled to Lystra and Derbe, cities of Lycaonia, and to the surrounding region." The critics said that Lystra and Derbe, while closely situated, were not in the province of Lycaonia but in different provinces. That, the critics said, is a clear example of a historical error and inaccuracy in Luke's writing.

One of those scholars, distinguished for his historical expertise, was the British Sir William Ramsay. Ramsay decided to embark on a journey that followed the biblical record of Paul's missionary journeys and wherever possible to do archaeological research pertaining to the accuracy of the details supplied by Luke. Ramsay was a skeptic. He agreed with the liberal viewpoint that Luke's book had been filled with error, but everywhere he went, every time he turned over a shovel of dirt, his findings verified the details Luke had included in both his Gospel and in Acts. When Ramsay came in his journey to the places noted in this particular passage, he found the boundary marker between Derbe and Lystra, and indeed the boundary marker had the two cities in different provinces. However, upon further examination he found that at various times in antiquity the boundaries of those provinces changed, and, to his amazement, he discovered that between the years A.D. 37 and A.D. 72 Lystra and Derbe were in the same province—the exact province Luke mentions here in the text. At the end of his tour Ramsay said that he could not find a single error of historical reliability in the book of Acts, and he joined other later scholars who now call Luke the most reliable historian of the ancient world.

A Miracle Misinterpreted

And in Lystra a certain man without strength in his feet was sitting, a cripple from his mother's womb, who had never walked. This man heard Paul speaking (vv. 8–9). Earlier we noted the miraculous healing that Peter and John had effected at the Gate Beautiful with another man who had been born crippled. After being healed, that man had risen up and praised God. Here we have an almost identical episode, but the mediating agent is not Peter; it is Paul. We must keep in mind that one of Luke's concerns in writing Acts was to vindicate Paul's apostleship. There was no question about Peter's apostolic authority, but some challenged Paul's because he had not been converted until after the resurrection.

In verse 3 we were told that they had done many miracles, so we wonder why Luke focused attention on this particular incident. Again, it is possible he did it to show its comparative worth to what Peter had accomplished earlier, but there is another reason—the response of the crowd to this particular miracle. **Paul, observing him intently and seeing that he had faith to be healed, said with a loud voice, "Stand up straight on your feet!" And he leaped and walked** (vv. 9–10). Everyone knows that when you remain in the same position for a long period of time, even if you are not crippled, getting up requires some effort. That did not happen here. When Paul healed this man and said, "Stand up," he leaped up, completely restored with no limp or painful joints. He was completely and totally healed.

Now when the people saw what Paul had done, they raised their voices, saying in the Lycaonian language, "The gods have come down to us in the likeness of men!" And Barnabas they called Zeus, and Paul, Hermes, because he was the chief speaker. Then the priest of Zeus, whose temple was in front of their city, brought oxen and garlands to the gates, intending to sacrifice with the multitudes (vv. 11–13). The Greek text uses Zeus and Hermes, but the Latin text uses Jupiter and Mercury. This leads us to wonder whether the local shrines were started under Greek or Roman influence. Both the Greeks and the Romans were polytheists. They had a pantheon of many gods and goddesses. Each god and each goddess had some particular task in overseeing the well-being of the people. In the case of the Roman god system, Jupiter was the king god. In Greek polytheism, Zeus was the king of the gods. The Greeks and the Romans had the same basic gods and goddesses but with different names—Zeus and Hera, Jupiter and Juno, Hermes and Mercury, Hestia and Vesta, and Athena and Minerva. In this case, the Greek Testament gives us the names of Zeus and Hermes.

Zeus was the king of the gods; Hermes was the messenger of the gods. The science of hermeneutics is based upon the name of Hermes. Hermeneutics is the science that gives us rules for interpreting Scripture. Mercury is displayed in flower shop windows bearing the FTD label. He has wings on his helmet and on his feet because he is the speedy messenger of the gods. In ancient Greek mythology there were mythological episodes where the gods, for one reason or another, came down from Mount Olympus and interacted with human beings. The myths go back to Homer in both the *Iliad* and the *Odyssey*. In the *Odyssey* the Greek name of Ulysses is Odysseus. He was a great warrior trying to get home from Troy after the Trojan War to be reunited with his lovely wife Penelope. All along his perilous journey the gods and goddesses come either to thwart his success or to rescue him. Athena appears to Odysseus and promises to keep him safe along his way. We have such stories all the way back to Homer that talk about the gods and goddesses intervening in people's lives.

Later in history Ovid writes his *Metamorphoses*, a classic work about a change of form of deities and humans. In it he recalls a story in which Jupiter came with his companion Mercury to a particular place disguised as human beings. They were testing the friendliness and hospitality of the local inhabitants. The local inhabitants would not give them the time of day, not realizing that they were rejecting the king of the gods and his messenger. Finally they visit an elderly couple who share their meager supplies with Jupiter and Mercury and show them great kindness and hospitality. The next day Jupiter said, "Let us go up to the top of the mountain," and he took this elderly couple up to the top of the mountain and brought a storm that flooded the entire valley, killing all those who had been unkind and inhospitable to the gods. The gods then took the couple's meager house and turned it into a luxurious mansion with a roof made out of solid gold.

Ovid said that took place in the very valley where Paul and Barnabas are now preaching. So when Paul does the miracle in the midst of the people, they were astounded and said, "Heaven has come down. This must be Jupiter and Mercury, or Zeus and Hermes, and we'd better not treat them like we did the last time, or we're going to be in deep trouble." So instead of rejecting them, they brought them oxen and garlands to celebrate the presence of deities among them. The parade was led by the high priest of the temple of Zeus. Today in Turkey you can see remains of shrines to patron deities of the Greek pantheon.

Soli Deo Gloria

Paul and Barnabas were absolutely beside themselves. **When the apostles Barnabas and Paul heard this, they tore their clothes and ran in among the multitude, crying out and saying, "Men, why are you doing these things? We also are men with the same nature as you, and preach to you that you should turn from these useless things to the living God, who made the heaven, the earth, the sea, and all things that are in them, who in bygone generations allowed all nations to walk in their own ways. Nevertheless He did not leave Himself without witness, in that He did good, gave us rain**

from heaven and fruitful seasons, filling our hearts with food and gladness"
(vv. 14–17). Instead of being flattered by the adulation of the crowd, Paul and
Barnabas were deeply disappointed. Why would people in any age be so silly as
to worship human beings? Why would they be so silly as to create a religion of
multiple deities—one to cover the ocean such as Poseidon or Neptune; one for
hearth and home such as Hestia or Vesta; one for the hunt such as the goddess
Diana; one for wisdom; one for love; one for war; one for peace. They had a
god and goddess for every human occasion. We know that was silly, but what
happened in the later Western church? Instead of gods and goddesses, we have
saints for every occasion.

A tragic accident took place locally a few years ago in which young children
were killed. At the site of the tragedy is a shrine with a sign: "Saint Jude, help
us." Jude is the saint to cover hopeless causes. How many people have Saint
Christopher medals on the dashboards of their cars, praying to that specific saint
who is supposedly responsible for keeping you safe from accidents? We develop a
saint for every occasion, following in the same pattern of ancient people. We are
just not satisfied with the Most High God. We, not just the ancient Greeks and
Romans or the Roman Catholics, have an inclination so deeply rooted in our souls
toward idolatry that it is our nature to exchange the glory of the eternal God for
a lie, serving and worshiping the creature rather than the Creator (Rom. 1:25).

Washington, D.C., contains some beautiful architecture. It is a city of shrines
to our great heroes such as Jefferson and Lincoln. Painted on the ceiling of the
rotunda of the U.S. Capitol is a magnificent scene of a man being lifted up on
the clouds into the company of the gods and goddesses of Olympus. The title
of the painting is "The Apotheosis of George Washington." *Apotheosis* means
deification. Our cultural history does not deify George Washington, but we do
have a tendency to exalt our great men and women to the status that belongs to
God alone. The tendency is so deeply rooted in our souls that we have to be on
guard against it in every circumstance. Only once did the living God become
incarnate. This is no myth but sober history. The Son of God lived on earth
under the law of God, and He was delivered up and crucified.

37

ENTERING THE KINGDOM

Acts 14:19–28

⁓✦⁓

Then Jews from Antioch and Iconium came there; and having persuaded the multitudes, they stoned Paul and dragged him out of the city, supposing him to be dead. However, when the disciples gathered around him, he rose up and went into the city. And the next day he departed with Barnabas to Derbe. And when they had preached the gospel to that city and made many disciples, they returned to Lystra, Iconium, and Antioch, strengthening the souls of the disciples, exhorting them to continue in the faith, and saying, "We must through many tribulations enter the kingdom of God." So when they had appointed elders in every church, and prayed with fasting, they commended them to the Lord in whom they had believed. And after they had passed through Pisidia, they came to Pamphylia. Now when they had preached the word in Perga, they went down to Attalia. From there they sailed to Antioch, where they had been commended to the grace of God for the work which they had completed. Now when they had come and gathered the church together, they reported all that God had done with them, and that He had opened the door of faith to the Gentiles. So they stayed there a long time with the disciples.

We have already seen in our study of the book of Acts that everywhere the Apostles went to proclaim the gospel, God blessed their ministry. Many people were converted and added to the church. We also see that everywhere they went, they encountered a certain level of hostility and opposition against the proclamation of the Word of God. We read now that the opposition became so severe that the Jews rose up in fury against Paul and, after holding a kangaroo court, used the Old Testament means of capital punishment, stoning, in an attempt to execute Paul.

We tend to pass over the fact of that stoning lightly, not considering how brutal it was for Paul to stand exposed before an angry mob as large rocks were hurled at him. Rocks hit him all over his body, tearing his flesh until he was knocked unconscious to the ground. Thinking that he was dead, the people opposed to him grabbed him by the feet and dragged him outside the city. He was not dead, however, and as the disciples gathered around and ministered to him, he was revived and was able to move on to the next city.

How many of us have been stoned and left for dead because of the proclamation of our faith? How many of us have been burned at the stake? How many of us have been used as human torches to illumine the gardens of Nero? How many of us have been sentenced to the Circus Maximus as fodder for roaring lions or for the sport of gladiators? The blood of the martyrs has been the seed of the church. We sing in church about the faith of our fathers, which led them to dungeons, to death, and to all sorts of peril, but we don't live in a place like that. We have freedom of assembly in the United States. Is it because suddenly our country is more open to the proclamation of the gospel, or is it because in a very real sense the church militant has become the church impotent as we seek a safe way to experience our faith?

Deal with the Devil

In a sense, we have made a deal with the Devil. We have agreed to practice our faith, as it were, on a reservation: that is, removed from the public square. We are told that as long as we keep our faith private and personal and do not intrude into the public arena, we will be able to exercise our First Amendment rights in the exercise of religion. If we agree to keep our religion private, then all the financial support we give to the church will remain tax deductible. We are forbidden by law to support in the church any political candidate, based on the axiom of the separation of church and state. Yet there is not a single word about such separation in the Constitution of the United States or in the Declaration of Independence. That phrase found its origin in a private comment by Thomas Jefferson, who meant that no one denomination or religion should be established as the state church. In our day, separation of church and state has come to mean the separation of the state from God. God is to have nothing to do with secular affairs of government. Nothing could be further from the purposes upon which this country was founded. We can argue indefinitely as to whether our founding fathers were Christians or Deists, but one thing is certain—they embraced theism. They believed that the government is to be under God.

A few years ago I was asked to speak at the inaugural prayer breakfast for an incoming governor of Florida. On that occasion I told the governor that he was being ordained as a minister—not as a minister of the church but as a minister of the state. It is God who has ordained the church and the state and their separate divisions of labor. It is not the function of the state to preach the gospel, to do evangelism, or to administer the sacraments; it is not the function of the church to wage war or to have the sword. They are different institutions with different responsibilities, but both have been ordained by God, and both are answerable to God.

The minute a culture or a government claims independence from God, it becomes godless. It is the responsibility of the church to have a prophetic voice in the culture, to call sin "sin" wherever it emerges in government or anywhere else in the public arena. There are many within the church who believe the church has no right to criticize the government. I couldn't disagree more profoundly, in light of the history of sacred Scripture. When King Ahab used his power to confiscate the private property of one of his subjects, Naboth, God sent Elijah the prophet to call that king to repent. Isaiah was commissioned by God to go to the palaces of antiquity and speak to king after king, calling them to repent of their godless practices. John the Baptist was beheaded because he dared to come into the public square and call the king to account for his illicit marriage. He paid for it with his life. Our Lord went into the temple, the place of rulers, and overturned the money changers' tables. He called Herod a fox, and He spoke to cultural and political issues of His day. At the heart of the proclamation of Christ and of John the Baptist was the proclamation of a new kingdom, the kingdom of God, but we are told to be silent in the public arena. The Christian community is perhaps the last disenfranchised minority in our country today.

During a previous presidential election, one of the candidates, John Kerry, appeared at a Baptist church service along with Jesse Jackson and Al Sharpton. The ACLU made an issue of it, which brought into question that particular church's tax-exempt status. In one sense, I applaud those Baptists who had the courage not to make a deal with the IRS, or to let the government tell them whom they can and cannot endorse or what they can and cannot say from the pulpit, because that profoundly undermines the First Amendment of the Constitution of the United States. Tax exemption is the sword held over the church and other nonprofit organizations to keep them from being critical of the government and the government's policies. That is not a good thing, and I hope as Christians we would be willing to risk our tax write-off for the sake of righteousness. If the only reason we give our tithes and offerings to the church is that it gives us a tax write-off, I guarantee you, God is not pleased with our gift. We are to give those gifts, whether or not the government gives us any break in terms of our taxes.

Government and Christian Practice

I believe I am supposed to submit to the civil magistrates even when I disagree with them, so while I will not endorse a candidate, I will try to influence my congregation on how to vote. The Word of God has much to say that is instructive for how we vote. First, we have to understand what a vote is. The word *vote* comes from the Latin *votum*, which means "will." We have an opportunity in our country to express our will by casting our vote in favor of what we want to see happen in the government. In a very real though invisible sense, the ballot is a bullet. Anytime you cast your vote, you are asking that certain policies and laws be enacted, backed, and enforced by the full magnitude of the power of civil government. We are to be careful and thoughtful in the process. The purpose of voting is not what we can get from the government for ourselves. We are to vote for what is right, not for our personal gain.

Today there is no shame in someone's saying, "I'm voting my pocketbook." However, in order for the government to put money in people's pocketbooks, that money first has to be taken from other citizens in order for them to receive it. The government does not produce anything; in other words, the government cannot give to someone what it does not first take away from someone else. When you vote for your own largesse, you are asking the government to use all its force to take from your brother and sister their private property and give it to you.

Several years ago I lodged in Mississippi at a hotel that was hosting a convention of the Mississippi Pork Producers Association. Affixed to walls and bulletin boards all over the hotel were large pie graphs that showed how Mississippi pork producers were using government subsidies in their private business. Far and away the largest segment in the pie depicted monies used to promote and advertise pork as the meat of choice. The pork producers would have little success if they were to ask producers of beef to turn over a portion of their market share, so they ask the government to take money from the profits of the cattlemen and others of us and give it to them. The request is perfectly legal, but it is also immoral and unethical to ask the government for a special subsidy for private enterprise. It is sin, but it is the American way. Washington is filled with lobby groups that do this every day. The lobbyists ask for legislation not for what is right or good for the welfare of the nation but for their vested interests. Voting your vested interests as a Christian is a sin. I plead with you not to join in this activity.

Several years ago, I had dinner with the chairman of the Senate Financing

Committee. During our conversation, I asked the senator why he wasn't attending to various issues that clearly needed to be dealt with at the time. He agreed that the issues I put before him were all important concerns but said he could not address them during an election year. So I said, "Senator, is there anybody in Washington who is thinking about the next generation instead of the next election?"

Alexis de Tocqueville said that there are two things that can destroy America. First, America can be destroyed by the rich and powerful who buy their way into office and use their wealth and power to exploit the poor. Second, America can be destroyed when people discover that they can vote for personal largesse. Either of those will destroy a nation and turn it into the tyranny of the majority. When economics are politicized, when people are encouraged to vote their pocketbooks rather than their conscience, national destruction will follow.

I heard one candidate in a presidential race say again and again that he planned to create a tax relief program for 98 percent of Americans. What about that other 2 percent? Are they to be robbed for the financial gain of the 98 percent? That is not God's way. The Israelite tithe was established on a level playing field. Everybody was required to pay the same percentage; there was no graduated or progressive income tax in Israel. Nobody can play politics with the tithe. Some paid one hundred times more than another, but all paid the same percentage. He would not allow somebody to vote a tax on his neighbor that was not a tax on himself. If you vote for a 98 percent tax reduction, you are simultaneously voting for a 2 percent tax increase on others, an increase that you likely do not have to pay. That is not justice. That is not equitable. It is legalized theft, and we do it every day.

For years in England William Wilberforce lost vote after vote year in and year out when he pled with parliament for the abolition of slavery, but slavery was so connected to the economic welfare of England that his cries of protest went unheeded. He kept arguing and pleading and calling upon Parliament to stop the ungodly activity of man stealing. Finally England's conscience was moved and slavery was abolished. Slavery is the second worst ethical issue ever to divide the United States of America. Even more serious than slavery is the governmental sanction on the wanton destruction of 1.5 million unborn human beings every year in this nation. My book about abortion, *A Rational Look at an Emotional Issue*, went quickly out of print. Ligonier has provided educational materials for churches, but pastors won't use them for fear it will divide their congregation. I say, "So what? Let it divide the congregation. We're talking about the sanctity of life here."

The *Didache*, one the most important extracanonical books of the early church, didn't shrink from calling abortion what it is—murder—and said the church must never be involved in it. Today it has become part of the acceptable fabric of America, and nobody is crying foul. The church is not asking at this point for the state to become the church when we tell the state to stop sanctioning this holocaust. The church is asking the state to be the state, because the primary reason for the existence of the state in the first place is to protect, maintain, and sustain the sanctity of human life. When a state ceases to do that, it has become not only pagan but barbarian.

The primary issues in the presidential elections of today are involvement with the Middle East, terrorism, and the economy. Abortion is way down at the bottom of the list. Personally, I could not sleep if I ever cast a ballot for a candidate who supported abortion on demand. That trumps every other ethical issue of our time. I plead with you as Christians that when you walk into the voting booth, don't leave your Christianity in the parking lot. Let your mind be informed by the Word of God. I have been studying theology all my life, and if I know anything about the character of God, I know that God hates abortion. There are other ways to deal with unwanted pregnancies than the physical destruction of the unborn. So I hope you vote your conscience, not your vested interest or your pocketbook. I hope you will vote for righteousness and justice as your conscience is informed by the Word of God. Until or unless we do that, God will give us leaders after our own hearts, which is a scary thing.

38

THE JUDAIZER THREAT

Acts 15:1–21

And certain men came down from Judea and taught the brethren, "Unless you are circumcised according to the custom of Moses, you cannot be saved." Therefore, when Paul and Barnabas had no small dissension and dispute with them, they determined that Paul and Barnabas and certain others of them should go up to Jerusalem, to the apostles and elders, about this question. So, being sent on their way by the church, they passed through Phoenicia and Samaria, describing the conversion of the Gentiles; and they caused great joy to all the brethren. And when they had come to Jerusalem, they were received by the church and the apostles and the elders; and they reported all things that God had done with them. But some of the sect of the Pharisees who believed rose up, saying, "It is necessary to circumcise them, and to command them to keep the law of Moses." Now the apostles and elders came together to consider this matter. And when there had been much dispute, Peter rose up and said to them: "Men and brethren, you know that a good while ago God chose among us, that by my mouth the Gentiles should hear the word of the gospel and believe. So God, who knows the heart, acknowledged them by giving them the Holy Spirit, just as He did to us, and made no distinction between us and them, purifying their hearts by faith. Now therefore, why do you test God by putting a yoke on the neck of the disciples which neither our fathers nor we were able to bear? But we believe that through the grace of the Lord Jesus Christ we shall be saved in the same manner as they." Then all the multitude kept silent and listened to Barnabas and Paul declaring how many miracles and wonders God had worked through them among the Gentiles. And after they had become silent, James answered, saying, "Men and brethren, listen to me: Simon has declared how God at the first visited the Gentiles to take out of them a people for His name. And with this the words of the prophets agree, just as it is written:

> 'After this I will return
> And will rebuild the tabernacle of David, which has fallen down;
> I will rebuild its ruins,
> And I will set it up;
> So that the rest of mankind may seek the LORD,
> Even all the Gentiles who are called by My name,
> Says the LORD who does all these things.'

"Known to God from eternity are all His works. Therefore I judge that we should not trouble those from among the Gentiles who are turning to God, but that we write to them to abstain from things polluted by idols, from sexual immorality, from things strangled, and from blood. For Moses has had throughout many generations those who preach him in every city, being read in the synagogues every Sabbath."

The so-called New Perspective on Paul has taken hold in many places, including strong evangelical fortresses within the Reformed faith. This new perspective suggests that the dispute over justification in the Reformation was completely unnecessary because what Paul was really teaching about justification was not how somebody is saved but how someone is to be included in the visible church. In other words, Paul's teaching on justification really had nothing to do with ultimate salvation but simply with one's status in the covenant community. This issue is by no means a new one, as this portion of Acts makes clear. It was the issue that provoked the first great church council, the Council of Jerusalem. As we look at the text, we will see that Paul's mighty concern in terms of the Judaizer heresy of the first century was not about how one is included in the visible church but how one enters into the kingdom of heaven.

War on Heresy

Before we look at the text of Acts 15, we will do well to consider some of what Paul wrote to the Galatians. Paul devoted basically the entire letter of Galatians to the very issue that was being discussed at the Council of Jerusalem in Acts 15, the threat of the so-called Judaizers. Reviewing a portion of Galatians will give us some sense of the importance that Paul gave to this matter:

I marvel that you are turning away so soon from Him who called you in the grace of Christ, to a different gospel, which is not another; but there are some who trouble you and want to pervert the gospel of Christ. But even if we, or an angel from heaven, preach any other gospel to you than what we have preached to you, let him be accursed. As we have said before, so now I say again, if anyone preaches any other gospel to you than what you have received, let him be accursed. For do I now persuade men, or God? Or do I seek to please men? For if I still pleased men, I would not be a bondservant of Christ. (Gal. 1:6–10)

Then in Galatians 3 we read these words from the Apostle: "O foolish Galatians! Who has bewitched you that you should not obey the truth, before whose eyes Jesus Christ was clearly portrayed among you as crucified? This only I want to learn from you: Did you receive the Spirit by the works of the law, or by the hearing of faith? Are you so foolish? Having begun in the Spirit, are you now being made perfect by the flesh?" (vv. 1–3). The Apostle Paul had a pastor's heart. He was willing to give his life for the sake of those whom God entrusted to his pastoral care. For that reason, his harsh tone here in Galatians is uncharacteristic of the Apostle. What provoked such strong language and admonition from Paul's pen? His epistle to the Galatians was a circular letter, which means it was meant not just for one congregation but for every congregation in the area from which the Judaizing heresy had been spawned.

We learn about that heresy in Acts 15. **Certain men came down from Judea and taught the brethren, "Unless you are circumcised according to the custom of Moses, you cannot be saved"** (v. 1). Throughout our study of the book of Acts we have seen that those in the first-century church wanted to know how Gentiles, Samaritans, and the God-fearing Greeks fit into the New Testament church. Were they to be second-class citizens? Was there to be a certain secondary rung like there had been in Israel, with an outer court for the Gentiles and an inner court reserved for the Jews? As we have seen repeatedly, the overarching theme of the book of Acts is that there is no second-class citizenship in the New Testament community. Samaritan believers, God-fearing believers such as Cornelius's household, and Gentile believers such as the Ephesians, were all numbered among the people of God and had equal status in the New Testament church. There is no preference for the Jew or the Greek, the male or the female. All people are on even ground at the foot of the cross. Later Paul will labor the point that salvation through justification by faith alone is the same basis for salvation in the Old Testament as in the New Testament.

Some from among the Jews saw the Gentile conversions and how these converts were baptized, given the Spirit of God, and made members of the household of God. These messianic Jews said that the Gentiles' faith was insufficient for entry into the family of believers and that, in addition to faith, circumcision is a necessary condition for salvation. When Paul addressed this claim in his Galatians epistle, he wrote, "I could wish that those who trouble you would even cut themselves off!" (5:12). He meant that he wished God would cut them off from the kingdom of God because of the damage they were doing to the gospel by preaching this other gospel, saying that faith is not enough. Paul said that no flesh shall be justified by the works of the law, whereas the Judaizers said that apart from works of the law, no flesh shall be justified. So a serious controversy arose over what is necessary for salvation. Are believers justified by faith alone, or is it faith plus something else?

Sola Fide

Therefore, when Paul and Barnabas had no small dissension and dispute with them, they determined that Paul and Barnabas and certain others of them should go up to Jerusalem, to the apostles and elders, about this question (v. 2). For Paul and Barnabas, everything was at stake. In the sixteenth century Martin Luther said that the doctrine of justification is the article upon which the church stands or falls. That may contain a bit of hyperbole, but Luther certainly believed that the gospel of justification by faith alone was so singularly important that it was essential to the New Testament gospel itself and that to remove oneself from that gospel, to add something else to it, would be to fail as a church.

That is why by the end of the sixteenth century the Reformers believed that the Roman Catholic Church was not just another denomination but that it was no longer a church at all. It still professed faith in the Trinity and affirmed a host of doctrines that are central to historic Christianity, but on that one doctrine— justification—Rome was disqualified. Luther said that when the Catholic Church anathematized the doctrine of justification by faith alone, it anathematized the biblical gospel and ceased to be a church. Calvin used a different metaphor. He said justification by faith alone is the hinge upon which everything turns. A contemporary theologian made a different metaphor, saying that justification by faith alone is the Atlas that holds up the whole of Christian truth, and if Atlas should shrug and the gospel of justification by faith alone be cast to the ground, that would be a death blow to the heart and soul of Christianity. That is what the Reformation was all about. The church was turned upside down then and the worst schism in Christian history took place, the same battle that Paul had in the first century with the Judaizers.

So, being sent on their way by the church, they passed through Phoenicia and Samaria, describing the conversion of the Gentiles; and they caused great

**joy to all the brethren. And when they had come to Jerusalem, they were
received by the church and the apostles and the elders; and they reported all
things that God had done with them. But some of the sect of the Pharisees
who believed rose up, saying, "It is necessary to circumcise them, and to
command them to keep the law of Moses"** (vv. 3–5). If the Gentiles were
going to be part of the true church, the Pharisees said, they had to undergo
circumcision and commit themselves to the Law of Moses. Circumcision was
the sign of the old covenant. It was given first to Abraham and then repeated
under the Mosaic dispensation of the Old Testament.

When God gave the Ten Commandments through Moses, He set before the
people of Israel two options—blessings or curses:

> Now it shall come to pass, if you diligently obey the voice of the Lord your
> God, to observe carefully all His commandments which I command you today,
> that the Lord your God will set you high above all nations of the earth. . . .
> The Lord will establish you as a holy people to Himself, just as He has sworn
> to you, if you keep the commandments of the Lord your God and walk in His
> ways. . . . But it shall come to pass, if you do not obey the voice of the Lord
> your God, to observe carefully all His commandments and His statutes which
> I command you today, that all these curses will come upon you and overtake
> you. (Deut. 28:1–15)

Paul teaches us in Galatians that Christ submitted to that law and became
the curse for us, being cursed upon the tree. In bearing our sin, He bore the
negative sanctions of the Old Testament law, which were symbolized in the rite
of circumcision. The Pharisees and the Jews were just like people today who resist
change. We want to do things the way we have always done them. We want to
put new wine in old wineskins. That was not going to work, however, for the
Pharisees. They did not understand the meaning of circumcision.

When Jews came into the covenant by circumcision, they were saying, "If I
fail to keep God's law perfectly, may I be cursed." Jesus came and submitted to
the law at every point, thereby living a life of perfect obedience for all who put
their trust in Him, and when He did, He won the blessing for all who identify
with Him, and He took their curse upon Himself by going to the cross. The full
measure of God's curse was poured out upon Jesus, and then came the gospel: if
you put your trust in Jesus, the righteousness He gained by obeying the law is
yours, and the curse that belongs on your head is His—a double exchange. His
righteousness is imputed to us. The curse that we deserve is given to Him. When
we put our trust in Jesus, God pronounces us just in His sight and removes the

curse from our head, and the negative sanction of our circumcision is removed once and for all.

Those who insisted on circumcision for those Gentile converts were patently repudiating the work of Jesus, which is why Paul was so upset. The Judaizers were saying that the atonement of Jesus was not good enough, something the first-century church could not tolerate. The issue wasn't simply about who could be included in the household of faith. Yes, that was in dispute; but the Pharisees wanted the Gentiles to be circumcised for the purpose of salvation, which indicated that they had completely misunderstood the gospel. Millions do the same in our day. They trust their own behavior, their own works, and their own goodness to get them into heaven.

There is only one correct answer to the question, "If you were to die today, why should God let you into His heaven?" That only answer is this: "I have put my trust in Christ alone." The Judaizers are alive and well today, and they are everywhere. People are still told that all they have to do to get into heaven is to live a good life. Well, that is true. If you live a good life, you don't need Jesus or the gospel. The good news of the gospel is for people who don't live a good life, and the Bible tells us that, apart from Jesus, no one lives a good life. People argue, "I never murdered anybody. I never committed adultery. I never stole from anybody." Haven't we? Have we not violated the commandment against murder as Jesus interpreted it: "Whoever is angry with his brother without a cause shall be in danger of the judgment. And whoever says to his brother, 'Raca!' shall be in danger of the council. But whoever says, 'You fool!' shall be in danger of hell fire" (Matt. 5:21–22). Have we never committed adultery? Jesus said, "Whoever looks at a woman to lust for her has already committed adultery with her in his heart" (Matt. 5:28). Have we never stolen another's property? How about someone's reputation? Have we gossiped about others? Have we born false witness?

A young man approached Jesus and asked, "Good Teacher, what shall I do that I may inherit eternal life?" Jesus said to him, "Why do you call Me good? No one is good but One, that is, God. You know the commandments: 'Do not commit adultery,' 'Do not murder,' 'Do not steal,' 'Do not bear false witness,' 'Do not defraud,' 'Honor your father and your mother.'" The man said, "Teacher, all these things I have kept from my youth." Then Jesus said, "One thing you lack: Go your way, sell whatever you have and give to the poor, and you will have treasure in heaven; and come, take up the cross, and follow Me" (Mark 10:17–21). You cannot get there through your good works, because your good works aren't good enough. The best works that you have done in this world are tainted by your flesh. To the degree that you rely on your own goodness, you are saying that you do not need the Savior. That is what Paul would not and could not negotiate.

The Jerusalem Council

Paul and Barnabas came to the first great council of the church, and Peter, the Apostle to the Jews, listened. After much dispute Peter stood up and said, **"Men and brethren, you know that a good while ago God chose among us, that by my mouth the Gentiles should hear the word of the gospel and believe. So God, who knows the heart, acknowledged them by giving them the Holy Spirit, just as He did to us, and made no distinction between us and them, purifying their hearts by faith. Now therefore, why do you test God by putting a yoke on the neck of the disciples which neither our fathers nor we were able to bear? But we believe that through the grace of the Lord Jesus Christ we shall be saved in the same manner as they"** (vv. 7–11). The people were arguing about how to be saved, and Peter said that the Jews would be saved in the same manner as the Gentiles—by faith alone. Every Pharisee in the room was angry with Peter when he said that.

Then all the multitude kept silent and listened to Barnabas and Paul declaring how many miracles and wonders God had worked through them among the Gentiles (v. 12). After they became silent, James answered. James was presiding at the first ecumenical council of the church. It is astonishing that James was officiating rather than Peter or Paul. James, the brother of our Lord Jesus Christ, was the head of the church in Jerusalem. It is James who gave us the most morally inclined book of the New Testament. It is James who was nicknamed "Old Camel Knees" because he knelt in prayer so frequently. If anyone was likely to back the Judaizers, it would have been James. But what does James say? **"Men and brethren, listen to me: Simon has declared how God at the first visited the Gentiles to take out of them a people for His name. And with this the words of the prophets agree, just as it is written: 'After this I will return and will rebuild the tabernacle of David, which has fallen down; I will rebuild its ruins, and I will set it up; so that the rest of mankind may seek the LORD, even all the Gentiles who are called by My name, says the Lord who does all these things'"** (vv. 13–17). He was saying to his Jewish brothers and to the Pharisees, "Have you never read the Old Testament? You want the kingdom of Israel to be restored again, but that promise, which God gave through the prophet Amos, would include the Gentiles."

So the council answered the question definitively against the Judaizers and refused to require circumcision as a cultic rite for those converted to the Christian faith. They understood that the implication of circumcision would be a rejection of the gospel altogether, which gospel is that the just shall live by faith.

39

THE JERUSALEM DECREE

Acts 15:22–29

Then it pleased the apostles and elders, with the whole church, to send chosen men of their own company to Antioch with Paul and Barnabas, namely, Judas who was also named Barsabas, and Silas, leading men among the brethren. They wrote this letter by them:

The Apostles, the elders, and the brethren,

To the brethren who are of the Gentiles in Antioch, Syria, and Cilicia:

Greetings.

Since we have heard that some who went out from us have troubled you with words, unsettling your souls, saying, "You must be circumcised and keep the law"—to whom we gave no such commandment—it seemed good to us, being assembled with one accord, to send chosen men to you with our beloved Barnabas and Paul, men who have risked their lives for the name of our Lord Jesus Christ. We have therefore sent Judas and Silas, who will also report the same things by word of mouth. For it seemed good to the Holy Spirit, and to us, to lay upon you no greater burden than these necessary things: that you abstain from things offered to idols, from blood, from things strangled, and from sexual immorality. If you keep yourselves from these, you will do well. Farewell.

Threat the conclusions set forth at the Council of Jerusalem were put into a pastoral letter that was sent back to Asia Minor with Paul and Barnabas and their comrades. Although the conclusions seem rather straightforward, there are a couple of things about them that remain a little bit puzzling if not troubling to the contemporary reader. First, we recall that what provoked the need of an ecumenical council of this sort in the first century was the controversy that arose when a sect of the Pharisees, called Judaizers, began spreading heresy, saying that for Gentiles to become full members of the church they had to undergo circumcision and submit themselves to all the dimensions of the Old Testament law.

Necessary Things

The council's decree does not say explicitly that the Gentiles did not have to be circumcised; however, such a conclusion is manifest from what the decree does say: **For it seemed good to the Holy Spirit, and to us, to lay upon you no greater burden than these necessary things: that you abstain from things offered to idols, from blood, from things strangled, and from sexual immorality. If you keep yourselves from these, you will do well. Farewell** (vv. 28–29). The focus here is on the four things that the early church asked the Gentile converts to abstain from. Therein lies the puzzle.

The first thing that they are told to abstain from is "things offered to idols." Most commentators, if not all, agree that in view here was the problem of eating meat that had been offered as sacrifices at pagan altars. The pagans had their altars to the various false gods, and in their ritual ceremonies they took food, particularly meat, and put it in front of the statue or idol. When the ceremony was done, the meat had to be dealt with. After all, the idols were unable to swallow this perfectly good food. So, being of some commercial orientation, the priests of these pagan cults took the meat into the marketplace and sold it for a profit.

The practice was utterly scandalous to the Jews. For centuries they had been instructed concerning the ceremonial and dietary laws to be completely scrupulous about eating that which was clean as opposed to that which was unclean. In the moral law of the Decalogue, the greatest accent in the Ten Commandments is on the prohibition against idolatry and all things associated with it. The Jewish people were utterly careful to avoid the use of anything that was part and parcel of a pagan ritual, particularly the eating of meat that had been offered to idols.

This becomes problematic in the text before us because it seems that abstaining from the meat was set as a necessary obligation upon Gentile converts as they entered into the New Testament community. Just a few years later, when the Apostle Paul wrote to the churches about various issues, he addressed this very issue in the context of Christian liberty (Romans 14). There he covers the need for Christians to be sensitive to weaker brothers and sisters, but in that context he declared that the question of meat offered to idols is *adiaphorous*, which means that intrinsically it has no particular moral bearing. In other words, eating meat offered to idols is neither here nor there. There is nothing particularly sinful about it or particularly virtuous.

Years ago a college friend of mine fell in love with ping-pong. There was a ping-pong table in one of the dorms, and he spent hours each day playing. He was obsessed with it to the point that it ate into his study time and affected his grades. One day he came to me about it in an earnest state of repentance and said, "The Spirit of God has convicted me that it's a sin for me to play ping-pong." At that point in his life, playing ping-pong had become sinful for him because it was bad stewardship. However, that does not mean that there is anything inherently evil about playing ping-pong.

There are churches all over the world that have added to the law of God and bound men where God has left them free. Some people have grown up believing that wearing lipstick or playing cards or going to the movies are among the worst of sins. When I have been asked about this, I have said, "If you believe it's a sin to wear lipstick, then for you it is a sin to wear it, because you're acting against your conscience."

That is the kind of thing Paul had to deal with in the church at Corinth and in Rome and in other places where people had come to believe that partaking of meat offered to idols was sin. Paul made clear it was not a sin, but for those who believed it to be sinful, for them it was. As for those who had liberty to partake, Paul said that they should be sensitive to the weaker brother, not rubbing it in the face of people who had objections to it. At the same time, the Apostle would never allow the scruples of the weaker brother to become the law for the whole church, something people have tried to do repeatedly in church history.

Art and Idolatry

To bring this back to the problem at hand, we see the council saying abstain from the meat and elsewhere Paul saying believers do not have to abstain. Was Paul now undermining the authority of the Jerusalem council? He was not, but the fact that there is this difference indicates something we must be careful to notice in biblical texts and church history. Sometimes councils come together to enact legislation; other times they come together to give advice. There is a difference between prudence and law. The early church was saying that at such a critical moment, when the Gentiles were just coming into full communion with the church and bringing with them the baggage of eating meat offered to idols, the best piece of wisdom was to abstain. Obviously that was not meant as a perpetual obligation, placed upon the church for all ages, because we see later on Paul declaring this very action *adiaphorous.*

Some time ago Ligonier Ministries hosted a pastors' conference here in Orlando, and pastors from all over the world came. Many of the pastors were pleased to see our church building and were taking pictures of the stained-glass window and of the artwork that adorns our sanctuary. Some were overwhelmed in a positive way at the beauty, but a few, coming out of the Reformed tradition, were scratching their heads and saying, "If this church holds to the Reformed tradition, why are there crosses and stained-glass windows and art in the church?"

Thinking about that event reminds me of another time a pastor visited our church. He was absolutely aghast that we had artwork in the sanctuary. Afterward he wrote me a scathing letter accusing me of everything but killing Jimmy Hoffa. Not satisfied with that, he wrote to one of my publishers and urgently asked that publisher to cease and desist from publishing my books because I had artwork in my church. On the one hand, I understood the man's passion, because he comes from a tradition deeply entrenched within Reformed circles that is opposed to any kind of symbolism such as candles or crosses. Such symbols are considered unbiblical. Such symbols have a historic link to Romanism.

In 1521 at the Diet of Worms, after Luther took his stand before the church and the government, he was whisked away by his friends and taken to the Wartburg castle where he donned the disguise of a knight and undertook the work of translating the New Testament. While he was there, one of his chief lieutenants back in Wittenberg by the name of Andreas Karlstadt led a group into Roman Catholic churches and destroyed the stained-glass windows and artwork and crushed the icons. The group did everything it could to get rid of any images whatsoever, because Karlstadt was convinced that in order to purify the faith he had to purify the church of all art. Luther took a different view of it. He came back and fired Karlstadt for this wanton destruction and said, "We are here to reform the church, not to destroy the church."

Calvin, who certainly shared Luther's passion for justification by faith alone, was even more impassioned by the problem of idolatry. Calvin's chief concern was not simply the reformation of doctrine but the reformation of worship. The second commandment prohibits the use of images designed to reflect God or to use in the worship of Him. Such activity is idolatry, as Calvin well knew. However, he also knew that the same God who prohibited the use of images commanded the artistic shaping of the cherubim to guard the mercy seat in the temple. The artisans are the first people we find in the Old Testament who were filled with the Holy Spirit. God set them apart to create artwork for the tabernacle and the temple and for the manufacture of the garments of the priesthood. Therefore, in the Old Testament economy there is no divine opposition to art. If there were a divine objection to the use of art in the house of God, then it would have been as sinful in the Old Testament as some try to make it today.

In the sixteenth century Calvin said, "Under God and under the Word of God the use of artistic representations of historical events and historical personages is quite legitimate." If you go to the world's greatest museums—the Louvre in Paris, the Rijksmuseum in Amsterdam, the National Gallery in Washington, the Metropolitan Museum of Art in New York—you will see that a high percentage of the greatest art in Western history has a religious theme, and much of it was done for the glory of God.

While Calvin believed that there is nothing intrinsically evil in art, he counseled against allowing it in the church as a matter of prudence. Converts coming into the Christian church out of Roman Catholicism had previously worshiped with images, lighting candles and asking the images to intercede for them in prayer. Calvin believed that such actions in the church were indeed idolatrous and that those who practiced them were addicted to idolatry. In fact, Calvin said, we are by nature *fabricum idolarum*, idol factories. Given our tendency to mass-produce our idols, Calvin advised against the use of any sort of images in church.

Reformed believers in many quarters followed that counsel; some today consider it a perpetual obligation throughout the church age. However, I do not think we are in the same situation as those in the sixteenth century. Additionally, God is the one who designed art for glory, beauty, and holiness. The glory of God, the beauty of God, and the holiness of God are from everlasting to everlasting. He wants to be honored with beauty as well as with goodness and truth. We understand as Christians that God is the source and foundation and measuring rod of all that is good and true, but we, particularly Protestants, have forgotten that He is also the source and fountainhead of all that is beautiful. There is nothing particularly pious about plainness or ugliness, nor is there anything particularly virtuous about beautiful paintings. What beauty does and is supposed to do is to incline us to worship the Source and Foundation of all that is beautiful, not the objects of beauty.

Here in Acts 15 I think we have an example of decisions that were made temporarily, as a matter of prudence, which we know from the rest of the New Testament did not go on to perpetuity, other than the prohibition against immorality or fornication. We do not see later in the New Testament any lax of prohibition against sexual immorality. Later Paul writes, "Fornication and all uncleanness or covetousness, let it not even be named among you, as is fitting for saints" (Eph. 5:3). Sexual morality is not situational ethics or a question of prudence, but a question of insulting the holiness of God. We live in a culture today that exists on this side of the sexual revolution. Sexual immorality today is the norm, particularly for young people, many of whom are sexually active outside of and before marriage. Today the marriage of two virgins is almost unheard of, because the church has embraced the morality of the pagan culture. That ought not to be.

Early in my teaching career, I taught at a Baptist college. One year the students were asked to participate in a national survey designed to measure personal guilt. The results indicated that the students at this particular college—a Christian college—were in the ninety-ninth percentile of unresolved guilt. I taught these students the New Testament treatment of the sex ethic as Paul gives it to us in the Corinthian correspondence, and at that time I told them, "Our parents used to warn us about premarital sex by referencing the pending consequences. A girl's reputation could be ruined for life if an unwanted pregnancy resulted or if she caught a sexually transmitted disease." That was before the Pill and legal abortion. After the sexual revolution, known virgins on college campuses were disgraced because they weren't sophisticated, as Gael Greene's book *Sex and the College Girl* indicated.

There is one thing that the sexual revolution did not change—sexual immorality is an offense against the holy God. When I was teaching at that Baptist college, I said to my wife rather facetiously, "The kids on this campus are not allowed to dance, smoke, play cards, or go to movies, but behind every bush there's a Baptist; in fact there are two of them." These students were wracked with guilt from trying to be Christians in a neo-pagan culture. Young people take their mores from what everybody else is doing.

That is what the Gentiles had been doing in the first-century church. They lived in an immoral culture, and the Council of Jerusalem wanted to keep that out of the church. Immoral behavior has to stop when you become a Christian. It must not even be named among us as is befitting saints (Eph. 5:3). So the letter was sent to the churches of Asia Minor as they awaited the return of the Apostles.

40

AMONG THE BRETHREN

Acts 15:30–41

So when they were sent off, they came to Antioch; and when they had gathered the multitude together, they delivered the letter. When they had read it, they rejoiced over its encouragement. Now Judas and Silas, themselves being prophets also, exhorted and strengthened the brethren with many words. And after they had stayed there for a time, they were sent back with greetings from the brethren to the Apostles. However, it seemed good to Silas to remain there. Paul and Barnabas also remained in Antioch, teaching and preaching the word of the Lord, with many others also. Then after some days Paul said to Barnabas, "Let us now go back and visit our brethren in every city where we have preached the word of the Lord, and see how they are doing." Now Barnabas was determined to take with them John called Mark. But Paul insisted that they should not take with them the one who had departed from them in Pamphylia, and had not gone with them to the work. Then the contention became so sharp that they parted from one another. And so Barnabas took Mark and sailed to Cyprus; but Paul chose Silas and departed, being commended by the brethren to the grace of God. And he went through Syria and Cilicia, strengthening the churches.

Sacred Scripture does not need to be demythologized. The great heroes and heroines of the faith are described in the history of redemption with warts and all. There is no attempt to gloss over the failures, weaknesses, or even the sins of the greatest of saints. It is indeed disturbing, however, to read of a great

241

dissension that arose between two men who had served so marvelously together in the first missionary journey to the Gentiles. They had worked shoulder to shoulder, and through them God had wrought marvelous wonders and powers so that they came within a hair's breadth of being executed by angry mobs. Nothing bonds men more than being together in dangerous situations. Foxholes make for lasting male relationships. There is no doubt that a powerful affection had developed between Paul and Barnabas the encourager up until this point. Yet we read of a dispute that broke them asunder, leading Paul in one direction and Barnabas in another.

The Dispute over John Mark

The contention arose over the place in the mission of John Mark, who in some texts has been understood as being the nephew of Barnabas. Other texts indicate he was the cousin of Barnabas. The words used in the text that indicate familial relationship are somewhat ambiguous, so we are not sure whether the two were nephew and uncle or cousins. In any case, they were blood relatives.

At the beginning of the first missionary journey, John Mark was invited, at the encouragement of Barnabas, to come along as part of the team. He had an integral role to perform in the mission. However, early on in that journey, he went home. We do not know for sure why. Perhaps he feared the inevitable obstacles and opposition, or maybe a conflict arose between John Mark and Paul, perhaps a personality issue or a philosophical difference. In any case, John Mark left. Later Barnabas and Paul eventually returned to Antioch. **Then after some days Paul said to Barnabas, "Let us now go back and visit our brethren in every city where we have preached the word of the Lord, and see how they are doing." Now Barnabas was determined to take with them John called Mark. But Paul insisted that they should not take with them the one who had departed from them in Pamphylia, and had not gone with them to the work** (vv. 36–38).

Have you ever been fired from a job for one reason or another? A great many people, particularly in our nation in the last ten years, have experienced a job loss, which next to divorce can be one of the most devastating personal experiences, not simply because of the economic peril it brings but because of the psychological wounds that can come as a result. Such wounds can have lasting impact on a person's life. There is an unwritten rule that those in Christian ministry can never be fired because Christianity is based on grace, not merit. If someone fails to pull his or her weight in the workplace, that is supposedly okay.

I have told my staff at Ligonier that the mission of Ligonier is not and has never been to provide employment for Christians. We are not an employment agency; we have a mission to perform. We hope that the people who come to work at Ligonier will be gifted and fit into that mission and will be productive in whatever the ministry undertakes, but that does not always work out. That is the case in any Christian mission. It is true in the church and in parachurch ministries. It is true outside in the world. Our culture has lost the idea of vocation, something that was central to the Protestant Reformation. The word *vocation* is not synonymous with *career* or *job*. The word *vocation* comes from a Latin term that means "to call," and it is based on the idea that it is the Lord God who equips each of us with gifts and talents and then calls us to serve Him in whatever capacity pleases Him. Whether as a farmer, an accountant, a butcher, a baker, or a candlestick maker—whatever employment we are involved in—we are to see it as our vocation from God, and we are to offer our labor to His glory. Today that idea has been obscured.

One reason that the Pittsburgh Steelers won four Super Bowl championships in the 1970s was the stellar performance of their chief running back Franco Harris. Franco Harris is in the top ten ground gainers of all time, even though, when he came to the end of his career, he lost a step here or there. Near the end he was not as fast or as capable, and his yardage began to dwindle, so the coach of the Pittsburgh Steelers, Chuck Knoll, gave Franco Harris his release. The firing caused a huge uproar in the city of champions. At a press conference, Chuck Knoll was asked how he could let go of this football icon, and he said, "I released Franco Harris so that he could get on with the main business of his life." Now that I am older, I understand what the coach meant. Professional football careers last a relatively short time; players don't play much beyond the age of thirty-five. Therefore, their real life's work begins after their participation in the limelight of professional sports.

Job Loss

Why are people fired or let go? There are a host of reasons. Most of those who lose their jobs believe they have been let go unjustly. Sometimes that is true. People get fired unjustly for political reasons or because their boss feels threatened by their competence. Such are victims of bad management. The vast majority lose their jobs due to budget cuts in times of economic stress. Economics often dictate that if a company is to survive, the payroll has to be cut, which seems in many cases unfair.

When I was growing up in Pittsburgh, the city was famous for producing steel. As the greatest steel producer in the history of the world, the whole city and environs were marked by massive, smoke-belching steel mills. Today those areas are practically ghost towns, for the steel mills have been shut down. At some point the American steel mills were no longer able to compete in a global market. The steel workers began demanding higher wages, which resulted eventually in massive layoffs. The companies had no choice; they were in business to make a profit, not to provide employment. People do not always understand that.

The primary reason that people lose their jobs is that the tasks they are assigned do not match their gifts. The generic term for that is *incompetency*, as in "So-and-so was let go because he was incompetent." However, the term *incompetent* is incorrectly applied. Every person in the Christian community has a gift and is therefore competent. There are lots of things I cannot do, and if I were placed in a job that necessitated one or more of the things I cannot do, I would be deemed incompetent. That would not mean that I am totally incompetent but simply that I had not yet found a job in which my responsibilities meet my areas of ability. So, if we lose our job, it may very well be that the providence of God is indicating that we are in the wrong place at the wrong time for the wrong reason.

I have also seen people lose their job because they were stealing from the company. That is very rare, but it happens. A much more common reason for job loss has to do with morale. Some of the most productive, talented, capable people can become destructive influences of morale in the workforce. In a company with ten employees, I guarantee you there is at least one that never stops whining, complaining, gossiping, or backstabbing the rest of the workers. If a manager becomes aware of it, no matter how productive that person is, the manager has a duty to remove that destructive influence.

Losing your job is not the worst calamity that can befall you, which is what I like about this story here in Acts. Paul at first says no to the addition of John Mark. Paul had given John Mark his chance, but he had turned and run when things got tough, and Paul was not about to trust him again. The mission of the Apostles was a perilous duty, and Paul wanted people on his team who were ready to lay down their lives rather than to run at the first sign of trouble. So John Mark went on for a while to Cyprus and ministered there with Barnabas, and finally he left that job and went back home, unemployed. He sat down and wrote a book, the Gospel of Mark.

That was his vocation, and he made a tremendous contribution to the kingdom of God, not as a missionary but as a chronicler of the life of our Lord. Paul read it right: missionary journeys were not John Mark's vocation. God had something else for him to do. Paul here was like Chuck Knoll, who told Franco Harris to get on with the business of his life. I take great solace in that, because it shows that if we fail at one thing, our failure does not mean that we ourselves are a failure. It means only that we failed to find where we can be productive in the kingdom of God. We see later in Paul's epistles that the Apostle was grateful for the ministry of Mark; he even said that Mark had later proven useful to him.

Loss and God's Providence

Those who have lost employment must not allow that to envelop them in bitterness or hatred or hostility, because the providence of God is involved even here. That is what we see in this text. As humanly as Paul and Barnabas were behaving in this particular circumstance, God was moving through it. As a result of their split, instead of one missionary team, there were two, and the missionary outreach to the Gentiles was doubled because Paul and Barnabas split up. However, we do not want to bury the reality of the breakup. **Then the contention became so sharp that they parted from one another. And so Barnabas took Mark and sailed to Cyprus; but Paul chose Silas and departed** (vv. 39–40).

The contention was not a mild disagreement. From the Greek word *paraxysmos*, translated "sharp" we get the word *paroxysm*. A paroxysm is a violent explosion. Some get so angry that we refer to a paroxysm of rage being let loose. That is the word the Holy Spirit inspired Luke to use to describe the contention between Paul and Barnabas. The issue produced fury in Paul and Barnabas; a paroxysm of rage emerged. Barnabas was beside himself that his beloved associate Paul would not bend to his wishes to bring John Mark along. He could not understand that Paul was more concerned with the mission before them with all its dangers than with the feelings of Barnabas and his relative John Mark. Ahead of every other consideration Paul put faithfulness to the task God had given them.

After this episode we hear no more about Barnabas in the book of Acts, but we do hear about him later on in Paul's epistles, and there Paul speaks very highly of Barnabas. As the time passed Paul's recollection of Barnabas was much more focused on the time they had spent together shoulder to shoulder in the arena as co-laborers; he did not dwell on the dispute that led to their separation. In his older years Paul was able to speak with great respect and affection for his former comrade.

On one hand, although the Bible tells us what the Apostles did in various circumstances, this does not mean the Apostles are perfect models for our behavior. The Bible, not the Apostles themselves, is infallible. On the other hand, we cannot help but look at the Apostle Paul as the number-one model of Christian virtue, apart from Christ Himself, in the New Testament. I think it would be wrong to convict the Apostle Paul here of having a hard heart, of being insensitive, unloving, or uncaring, because he loved the mission of Christ. Paul did not feel threatened by John Mark; rather, John Mark's earlier behavior, if replicated in the future, would have placed the mission in jeopardy, and Paul would not have that.

Even unintentionally we can find ourselves in situations where we imperil the very mission of Christ. No Christian intentionally does that, but we have to be careful not to think more highly of ourselves than we ought. We must hold a sober evaluation of our gifts and talents and try to make sure that whenever possible we seek to match our work and tasks with the best of our abilities and gifts. There is a special joy when our job is a completely perfect fit for our gifts, but that happens rarely. We are exceedingly fortunate to have our abilities match our job description by a factor of 90 percent. Inevitably there will be times when our gifts will not be used in our job, and we are left with responsibilities for which we have little or no aptitude, which can hinder the overall mission of a particular ministry or company. That is why I believe that the best time to fire people is before you hire them.

If you have lost your job, see it as the providence of God. Perhaps the job was a bad fit for your particular gifts. If so, that certainly does not mean that God does not have something extremely important and significant for you to do. Winston Churchill was basically a failure till he was sixty-five years old. Douglas MacArthur was basically a failure until he reached that same age, and then he became one of the greatest heroes in American history. It took those men a long time to find their life's work, to discover their vocation, but when they got it, they set the world on fire, just as John Mark did as a result of this dispute.

41

DOCTRINE OF BAPTISM

Acts 16:1–15

Then he came to Derbe and Lystra. And behold, a certain disciple was there, named Timothy, the son of a certain Jewish woman who believed, but his father was Greek. He was well spoken of by the brethren who were at Lystra and Iconium. Paul wanted to have him go on with him. And he took him and circumcised him because of the Jews who were in that region, for they all knew that his father was Greek. And as they went through the cities, they delivered to them the decrees to keep, which were determined by the Apostles and elders at Jerusalem. So the churches were strengthened in the faith, and increased in number daily. Now when they had gone through Phrygia and the region of Galatia, they were forbidden by the Holy Spirit to preach the word in Asia. After they had come to Mysia, they tried to go into Bithynia, but the Spirit did not permit them. So passing by Mysia, they came down to Troas. And a vision appeared to Paul in the night. A man of Macedonia stood and pleaded with him, saying, "Come over to Macedonia and help us." Now after he had seen the vision, immediately we sought to go to Macedonia, concluding that the Lord had called us to preach the gospel to them. Therefore, sailing from Troas, we ran a straight course to Samothrace, and the next day came to Neapolis, and from there to Philippi, which is the foremost city of that part of Macedonia, a colony. And we were staying in that city for some days. And on the Sabbath day we went out of the city to the riverside, where prayer was customarily made; and we sat down and spoke to the women who met there. Now a certain woman named Lydia heard us. She was a seller of purple from the city of Thyatira, who worshiped God. The Lord opened her heart to heed the things spoken by Paul. And when she and her household were baptized, she begged us, saying, "If you have judged me to be faithful to the Lord, come to my house and stay." So she persuaded us.

C hapter 16 begins with a record of Paul's second missionary journey. We see that he returns to Derbe and Lystra. The two places are mentioned in reverse order from how they were presented during his first missionary journey because this time Paul approached these areas from the opposite direction. The primary feature I want to look at is the joining of a new member to the apostolic entourage, a young man who became known later as Paul's beloved child in the faith and figured prominently in Paul's life and ministry. Here for the first time we meet Timothy.

Timothy Circumcised

And he took him and circumcised him because of the Jews who were in that region, for they all knew that his father was Greek (v. 3). Initially it may seem strange that when Paul brought Timothy into partnership in the missionary cause, he subjected him to circumcision. This occurred at the same time that Paul and Silas and the others were going back to the churches of Asia Minor to deliver the decree that had come out of the Council of Jerusalem. If you recall, that council was called because there were some among the Judaizers insisting that Gentile converts had to undergo circumcision. The council decreed that the Old Testament requirement of circumcision was not binding on the early church. That is what Paul has come to announce to the public, yet he subjects his disciple Timothy to circumcision. What is going on here? The plot thickens later under similar circumstances when Titus comes along. On that occasion Paul adamantly refused to circumcise Titus. So why did he circumcise Timothy but refuse to circumcise Titus?

Earlier we noted that Paul, concerning matters such as food offered to idols, declared these things to be *adiaphorous*, which means "ethically neutral." Some people in Corinth, whom Paul called weaker brothers, had scruples about *adiaphorous* things. He counseled stronger brothers not to be insensitive to the scruples, as unfounded as they were, of the weaker with respect to meat offered to idols. Yet the same Apostle who called for sensitivity toward the weaker brother on one occasion would never permit the weaker brother to tyrannize the stronger. When the weaker brother wanted to elevate an option to the level of requirement, Paul's sensitivity stopped. There he drew a line in the sand.

Circumcising a Jew at that point in redemptive history was not a matter of theological obligation; it was *adiaphorous*. So, as soon as someone attempted to require it, as was the case with Titus, Paul would not allow it. Yet here with Timothy, Paul made a decision based not on theology or ethics but on strategy. It was strategic to circumcise Timothy because he was taking Timothy with him into a region of many Jews who were well aware of Timothy's background. They knew that Timothy's mother, Eunice, was a godly woman and a believer and that Timothy's grandmother Lois, mentioned later on in Paul's epistles to Timothy, was likewise a godly woman. Nevertheless, Eunice, the mother of Timothy, was married to a Greek, a pagan. Because Timothy had a pagan father, he was not circumcised in his youth, but now Paul, as it were, adopts Timothy as his spiritual son and gives him circumcision so as to stop any scandal among the Jews about whether Timothy was worthy to be heard. So we see that the Apostle's decision was based on prudence, not on theological necessity.

Covenant Signs

There is something else about this that relates indirectly to something that we struggle with to this present day—baptism. Beginning in the sixteenth century with the Anabaptist movement in Zürich, when and how to baptize has caused a great divide among Christians. We find in the New Testament no explicit command that the infant children of believers are to be baptized. Therein the New Testament differs from the Old Testament, because in the Old Testament the command to include infants in the sign of the covenant, circumcision, is explicitly set forth. Abraham was required to circumcise Isaac. Moses was negligent in having his son circumcised, and God sought Moses to kill him because he had failed to give the covenant sign to his infant child. The Old Testament is replete with explicit references that male children of the covenant were to receive the sign of the covenant, which was circumcision.

The New Testament has no explicit direct statement requiring the same thing. However, there is no explicit prohibition in the New Testament that states that it is wrong to baptize infants. So, with the absence of either an explicit command or an explicit prohibition, what are we to do? First, since there is no explicit teaching one way or the other, we need to be very patient and charitable with each other, acknowledging that both sides in this controversy want to do what is pleasing to God. They just differ as to what that is, and they differ about it because the New Testament is silent about it. Second, decisions about it can come only from inferences, by implications drawn from the text, since there are no explicit commandments.

I am convinced that it is proper to baptize infants, and my conviction comes from the implications of sacred Scripture, which I believe are overwhelming and not at all obscure. Having said that, I also realize that many of us, whether we are for or against infant baptism, develop our conviction based upon our love lines, which sometimes get in the way of our interpretation of Scripture. I grew up in a church that practiced infant baptism, so it is part of my tradition. My grandparents, parents, professors, and pastor all held to infant baptism. Everybody that I held dear embraced infant baptism. I have friends who hold to believers' baptism for the same reason. They are convinced on the basis of their love lines that infant baptism is wrong. At some point we have to be willing to question our love lines and let the Scripture be the final arbiter of such a dispute.

Almost everybody agrees that in the New Testament baptism was established by our Lord as the sign of the new covenant, and insofar as it is the sign of the new covenant, it parallels circumcision. Please do not misunderstand me—baptism and circumcision are not the same thing, but they are closely related. They are both signs of the covenant. From the Old Testament it is clear that circumcision was the sign of the old covenant. Likewise, it is clear from the New Testament that baptism is the sign of the new covenant. There is no dispute about that. Also, there is no question that the Old Testament sign of the covenant was the sign of God's promise of redemption, which is received only by faith. Many Jews believed they were saved by circumcision. Paul labors the point in Romans that it takes circumcision of the heart to get someone into the kingdom of God; the outward sign does not save. Nevertheless, the outward sign was significant because it indicated God's promise to all who believe. Circumcision was a sign of faith, and baptism is also a sign of faith.

When the old covenant sign of circumcision was given to an adult, a first-generation believer, that adult was required to make a profession of faith before receiving the sign. We might call it believer's circumcision. Second, that sign was to be given to one's male offspring before they came to faith. So we have a clear example in biblical history of the principle of a sign of faith—in one case, of adults, the sign coming after faith; in the other case, of infants, the sign coming before faith. Therefore, if people object in principle about giving a sign of faith to those in the new covenant community who do not yet have faith, then the objectors have to prove that the whole covenant economy of the Old Testament was principally wrong.

That is what we see happening here in Acts with Timothy. Timothy was being circumcised as an adult. He was experiencing believer's circumcision, and rightly so, because his father was not a Jew at the time of his infancy. Now, if it was automatically assumed by every Jew in Israel that children of believers were included in the covenant and were to receive the sign of the covenant, why would those in the new covenant economy assume that the principle behind that had ceased, when there is not a word to that effect in the New Testament? In fact, just the opposite is the case.

The argument that I hear most against infant baptism is one based on the narrative examples that we find in the book of Acts. In the New Testament there are twelve recorded incidents of baptisms, and every single one of those is the baptism of an adult who has come to faith. The call is to repent and believe and be baptized, and obviously infants cannot repent or believe; therefore, they should not be baptized. In the twelve occurrences of baptisms in the New Testament, three of these include household baptisms in which the believer and his or her household are baptized.

The great Swiss New Testament scholar Oscar Cullmann wrote a lengthy essay trying to prove that the word *oikos*, which is translated "family" or "household" in the New Testament, has specific reference to young children. If that could be proved beyond a shadow of a doubt, then we would have a clear record in the New Testament of infants of believers being included in baptism, and the argument would be over. But not everybody agrees with Oscar Cullmann. We have to grant the possibility that some of these households had no children in them; however, the reason Old Testament children received the covenant sign was the principle of corporate solidarity in the family covenant. When we see in the New Testament an entire household receiving baptism, it is clear that the principle of family solidarity is shown to remain intact.

I will take this another step. Every church I know of that practices infant baptism also practices believers' baptism in the case of adults. At St. Andrew's we baptize people as adults who were not baptized as infants either because they were not children of believers or they were not children of people who believed in infant baptism. Those who come to faith as adults make a profession of faith, and then they are baptized. In the book of Acts we have a record of the conversion of people who were baptized as adults, and every last one of them was a Gentile. Coming, as they did, as first-generation converts to Christianity, they were of course required to make a profession of faith as adults before receiving the sign of baptism. If we could show that any one of those baptized as an adult in the New Testament had been a child of Christian believers, then that would abolish and annihilate the doctrine of infant baptism. But no such evidence exists, and one wonders how that could even be the case since the baptisms occurred at the beginning of the Christian church, which was made up of first-generation Christians.

We find in the New Testament a statement that the Apostle Paul makes with specific reference to the children of believers. The Apostle said that the unbelieving husband is sanctified by the believing wife, and the unbelieving wife is sanctified by the believing husband (1 Cor. 7:13–14). That does not mean that people can be justified by marriage. Here, the term *sanctification* does not refer to that process by which we are conformed to the image of Christ after we are justified. It has a more primary meaning, the one used most often in the Scriptures; namely, that they are "set apart" or "consecrated." Paul gives the rationale for that: "Otherwise your children would be unclean, but now they are holy" (1 Cor. 7:14). There is no inference here. Paul made an explicit statement, an apostolic statement, that the children of even one believer are considered clean and holy in the sight of God. In the language of the Jew, to be clean meant being a full member of the covenant community that God has set apart for Himself. If that were the only text in the New Testament, that would be enough to satisfy me that our children should receive the sign of the covenant, because they are clean and holy, not strangers and foreigners to the covenant.

The author of Hebrews labors the point that the new covenant is much richer, more inclusive, than the old covenant. However, if we believe that children of believers under the old covenant received the sign of the covenant but then stopped receiving it in the new covenant, we are left with a covenant that is less inclusive rather than more inclusive, which goes against the whole weight of the thinking of the New Testament about the wider inclusion of membership in the body of Christ.

There is also a historical point. Some have argued that there is not a single reference in the New Testament to the baptism of an infant. That is true. Some also argue that there is not a single reference to infant baptism in church history until the middle of the second century. The first reference we have occurs in the middle of the second century; however, this is a reference in passing without dispute that mentions that infant baptism was the universal practice of Christendom. It is possible that there could have been within a hundred years a widespread defection from the apostolic practice of baptism into a heretical practice of baptizing infants. It does not take a long time for heresies to spread to the entire church. However, there is not a single word of controversy about such a heresy, even though for every other theological controversy that arose in the early church there is an avalanche of literature attesting to it from that same sub-apostolic period. That such a defection occurred is possible, but the odds against it are astronomical.

I just can't imagine that the church could universally depart from the apostolic practice to that degree in that period of time without any extant literature appearing. I think history is silent about any such controversy because there wasn't one, and there wasn't one was because no one was teaching that baptism saved people. In the sixteenth century the Roman Catholic Church was teaching that baptism works *ex opera operato*—"by the working of the works"—and automatically conveyed regeneration and justification. Protestants found that abhorrent. To protect against it, the Anabaptists in Switzerland decided to stop baptizing babies because people began to think that they were saved because they had been baptized, just as the Jews believed that circumcision saved them. However, an abuse cannot be corrected by disuse.

This is a debate that separates earnest believers who want to do what is pleasing to God. We have to argue, however, on implications, on inferences drawn from text—from the whole context of Scripture—and not just from a narrative or two that we find in the New Testament.

42

THE PHILIPPIAN JAILER

Acts 16:11–34

Therefore, sailing from Troas, we ran a straight course to Samothrace, and the next day came to Neapolis, and from there to Philippi, which is the foremost city of that part of Macedonia, a colony. And we were staying in that city for some days. And on the Sabbath day we went out of the city to the riverside, where prayer was customarily made; and we sat down and spoke to the women who met there. Now a certain woman named Lydia heard us. She was a seller of purple from the city of Thyatira, who worshiped God. The Lord opened her heart to heed the things spoken by Paul. And when she and her household were baptized, she begged us, saying, "If you have judged me to be faithful to the Lord, come to my house and stay." So she persuaded us. Now it happened, as we went to prayer, that a certain slave girl possessed with a spirit of divination met us, who brought her masters much profit by fortune-telling. This girl followed Paul and us, and cried out, saying, "These men are the servants of the Most High God, who proclaim to us the way of salvation." And this she did for many days. But Paul, greatly annoyed, turned and said to the spirit, "I command you in the name of Jesus Christ to come out of her." And he came out that very hour. But when her masters saw that their hope of profit was gone, they seized Paul and Silas and dragged them into the marketplace to the authorities. And they brought them to the magistrates, and said, "These men, being Jews, exceedingly trouble our city; and they teach customs which are not lawful for us, being Romans, to receive or observe." Then the multitude rose up together against them; and the magistrates tore off their clothes and commanded them to be beaten with rods. And when they had laid many stripes on them, they threw them into prison, commanding the jailer to keep them securely. Having received such a charge, he put them into the inner prison and fastened their feet in the stocks. But at midnight Paul and Silas were praying and singing hymns to God, and the prisoners were listening to them. Suddenly there was a great earthquake, so that the foundations of the prison were shaken; and immediately all the doors were opened and everyone's chains were loosed. And the keeper of the prison, awaking from sleep and seeing the prison doors open, supposing the prisoners had fled, drew his sword and was about to kill himself. But Paul called with a loud voice, saying, "Do yourself no harm, for we are all here." Then he called for a light, ran in, and fell down trembling before Paul and Silas. And he brought them out and said, "Sirs, what must I do to be saved?" So they said, "Believe on the Lord Jesus Christ, and you will be saved, you and your household." Then they spoke the word of the Lord to him and to all who were in his house. And he took them the same hour of the night and washed their stripes. And immediately he and all his family were baptized. Now when he had brought them into his house, he set food before them; and he rejoiced, having believed in God with all his household.

Earlier in Acts 16, Paul and Silas had set out on the second missionary journey and had employed Timothy to work with them. As they traveled, we read that the Holy Spirit directed their journey, prohibiting them from entering certain regions. From that we learn that one of the ways God leads His people is by closing doors. He nudges and guides us to the work and place He wants us to be in. In Paul's case, in the midst of this seemingly frustrating interruption to the progress of the missionary journey, Paul had a vision of a Macedonian appealing to him, saying, "Come over to Macedonia and help us" (v. 9). I have never seen a vision of someone pleading for me to come somewhere to help them, but I do hear the cry that comes from all over this globe of people who are in desperate need of the gospel of Christ and for the help of the church. We must have ears always to hear those cries for help that come to us. Paul was obedient to that vision, and with his friends he set out for Macedonia.

The journey took them to Macedonia, and they came to Philippi. The ancient town of Philippi in Macedonia had been resettled, rebuilt, and fortified as a military stronghold. It was King Philip of Macedon, the father of Alexander the Great, who reconstructed the city in Macedonia and lent his name to it. In the year 42 B.C. a crucial battle took place in this city between rival Roman generals that changed the course of Roman history. The united forces of Brutus and Cassius went up against the united forces of Mark Anthony and Octavian, and at the battle of Philippi in 42 B.C. Mark Anthony and Octavian soundly defeated and destroyed the forces of Cassius and Brutus. Soon afterward Octavian became emperor and took upon himself the name Caesar Augustus. Because of the historic significance of Philippi, Caesar Augustus went back and further fortified Philippi and made it a very important Roman colony in Macedonia.

Lydia

When Paul and Silas got to Macedonia, they met Lydia from Thyatira. She was distinguished as a seller of purple and dyes. In the ancient world, where dyes were rare and costly, this was a lucrative enterprise. Lydia specialized in dye that had hues of purple, a color associated with princely authority. The rulers of that age wore garments in hues of purple, the dye for which came from shellfish. Lydia was the first European convert mentioned in the New Testament.

And on the Sabbath day we went out of the city to the riverside, where prayer was customarily made; and we sat down and spoke to the women who met there (v. 13). When lacking a local synagogue, the Jewish people would meet by the river since part of worship included the use of water for cleansing rites. Paul and Silas sat down and talked to the women that they met there, and this is where we meet Lydia. **Now a certain woman named Lydia heard us. She was a seller of purple from the city of Thyatira, who worshiped God. The Lord opened her heart to heed the things spoken by Paul** (v. 14). What we see here is consistent throughout the New Testament—conversion takes place not when we open our hearts but when God intervenes and changes the dispositions of our hearts. What was true for Lydia is true for every convert in Christian history. It takes a work of God to change the soul of the human being. God intervened in the life of this woman and opened her heart to the hearing of the word of God. **And when she and her household were baptized, she begged us, saying, "If you have judged me to be faithful to the Lord, come to my house and stay." So she persuaded us** (v. 15).

The Slave Girl

Then the narrative changes. **Now it happened, as we went to prayer, that a certain slave girl possessed with a spirit of divination met us, who brought her masters much profit by fortune-telling** (v. 16). Here we have one of many "we" passages in the book of Acts. Suddenly the author of the book includes himself in the narrative; he is no longer just a recorder of what was taking place but is himself one who participates. Luke enters into the entourage at this point.

The slave girl had the spirit of divination; that is, she was involved in the occult. She was involved in sorcery and fortune-telling. Her masters kept close tabs on her since she made them a lot of money. Among those who lived in this pagan center there was great interest in hearing predictions of the future, and the slave girl would sell her predictions.

This girl followed Paul and us, and cried out, saying, "These men are the servants of the Most High God, who proclaim to us the way of salvation." And this she did for many days (vv. 17–18). The slave girl was in a sense harassing and stalking Paul and his band. Everywhere they went to preach, the slave girl, who was possessed by a demon, cried out that what Paul and Silas were preaching was the word of God. How are we to understand that? Was this done in a spirit of satire, in mockery? Was she laughing, or was she, against her own will, declaring the truth of what the Apostles were saying, much as the demons did when they encountered Jesus during His earthly ministry? In the Gospels, the first ones to recognize the identity of Jesus in His earthly ministry were the demons. "What have we to do with You, Jesus, You Son of God? Have You come here to torment us before the time?" they would ask (Matt. 8:29). Even though they could provide a backward appraisal of the true character of Christ, their acknowledgment came from them in a spirit of reluctance because they were utterly hostile to the true identity of Jesus.

So although the slave girl spoke the truth, she did so through clenched teeth as one who hated what she was hearing from the lips of Paul and Silas and their friends. **But Paul, greatly annoyed, turned and said to the spirit, "I command you in the name of Jesus Christ to come out of her." And he came out that very hour. But when her masters saw that their hope of profit was gone, they seized Paul and Silas and dragged them into the marketplace to the authorities** (vv. 18–19). The agora was not only the place where business transactions took place every day but also where court cases were frequently heard and judgments rendered. When Paul began rebuking the girl, he was no longer just preaching; he was meddling and upsetting the economics of the slave owner. Disputes over religious ideas were tolerable, but when those disputes entered the marketplace, real hostility would erupt against the truth of God.

And they brought them to the magistrates, and said, "These men, being Jews, exceedingly trouble our city; and they teach customs which are not lawful for us, being Romans, to receive or observe" (vv. 20–21). Contrary to the slave owners' complaint, the only thing Paul and Silas had done was drive one demon out of the city. It was the best thing that ever happened in that city, of course, but the people didn't see it that way, so the charges were multiplied. They charged Paul and Silas with imposing an alien religion, thereby upsetting the equilibrium of the entire city. The place was under Roman jurisdiction, and it was against Roman law to teach foreign religions there. So, in order to get a judgment against Paul and Silas, the slave owners add to their charges, which is the same thing that had happened to Jesus.

Then the multitude rose up together against them; and the magistrates tore off their clothes and commanded them to be beaten with rods (v. 22). We do not know to what degree they were stripped. They may have been stripped completely naked; such was part of prisoners' punishment in the ancient world in order to impose utter humiliation. This was also often done in combat. When one force defeated another and took prisoners, the victors would march the prisoners naked to humiliate them. Perhaps Paul and Silas were stripped only to the waist. The main desire here was to bare skin for a beating, which was administered with sticks or rods, like caning. Here, no limit was set for how many blows could be applied, such as there was in Jewish law, so we have no idea how many stripes were inflicted upon Paul and Silas. In any case, they were badly beaten.

And when they had laid many stripes on them, they threw them into prison, commanding the jailer to keep them securely (v. 23). Paul and Silas were taken into the innermost part of the prison, perhaps even down into a dungeon hewn out of the rock, but we do not know the specifics. In any case, they were put in the most secure part of the prison, and their feet were put in stocks. The purpose of the stocks was twofold. First, the stocks were used to keep the prisoners held securely so they could not get away. Second, the stocks exerted pressure on the feet and the ankles of the prisoner, which was a kind of torture. So here they are beaten within an inch of their lives, taken into the deepest part of the dungeon, put in the stocks that inflicted even more pain upon them, and left there under the watch of the jailer.

Set Free

But at midnight Paul and Silas were praying and singing hymns to God, and the prisoners were listening to them (v. 25). Here were two men with their bodies bloody and bruised and their feet held tightly, but they were praying aloud, punctuating their prayers with singing, most likely of Old Testament psalms. What were the rest of the prisoners thinking? They heard those songs of praise in the midst of abject suffering and affliction. Paul and Silas were singing glory to God.

Suddenly there was a great earthquake, so that the foundations of the prison were shaken; and immediately all the doors were opened and everyone's chains were loosed (v. 26). This earthquake was strong enough to shake the very foundation of the structure so that the whole building instantly collapsed. Not only did the building fall apart, but also all the chains and stocks securing the prisoners came loose and set them free, which created quite a problem for the jailer. **The keeper of the prison, awaking from sleep and seeing the prison doors open, supposing the prisoners had fled, drew his sword and was about to kill himself** (v. 27). Losing prisoners was the most disgraceful thing that could happen to a Roman jailer, and if he wanted to regain his honor, he could do so by falling on his sword. Such suicide was not considered to be an act of cowardice but a heroic act of personal sacrifice.

Just as the jailer was about to take his life, Paul interrupted him. He called out in a loud voice, **"Do yourself no harm, for we are all here"** (v. 28). How could that be? The doors were gone, the chains were gone, the stocks were gone. We can picture the jailer looking around and starting to count: one, two, three, four, five, six, seven—all the prisoners were still there. Nobody had taken advantage of the providential earthquake to flee from captivity. The jailer fell down trembling before Paul and Silas and asked, **"Sirs, what must I do to be saved?"** (v. 30).

What kind of salvation was he talking about? It is hard to know. The Greek word "to save" can be translated as "we were being saved," "we were saved," "we are saved," "we have been saved," "we are being saved," "we are still being saved," and "we shall be saved." Additionally, the Bible speaks of salvation in a multitude of ways. When Jesus healed people and said, "Your faith has saved you," we tend to equate that with eternal salvation. That may have been the case, but at the very least Jesus was saying that those healed had been spared from the dire consequences of their illness. When the people of Israel were spared from defeat in battle by the intervention of God, that sparing from a dire and negative circumstance was called "salvation." In the Bible, "to be saved" or "salvation" means "to be rescued from any serious calamity."

It takes on its ultimate meaning in the New Testament. When the Bible speaks of salvation in a spiritual or theological sense, it is speaking of salvation from the worst of all possible consequences. So, what was in the mind of the jailer? He might have been saying, "Look, I'm in real trouble with the Roman authorities because my prison is in shambles and my prisoners are about to escape. How can I be saved from the consequences of this? Will you prisoners tell the authorities that it wasn't my fault?" Maybe that is all he was asking, but I doubt it. This was one of those life-threatening moments when a man's whole life comes before him. He knew that he was out of reconciliation with his Creator. We must keep in mind that God reveals Himself and His character to every human being in the world. All human beings, whether they profess faith or not, know in the deepest chamber of their heart that God exists and that they will have to face Him at the end of their lives.

The analytical philosopher Antony Flew was one of the most outspoken atheists of the twentieth century, but at the age of eighty-one he said he had become convinced that the universe must have been created by a superior intelligence. He repudiated his atheism. He did not embrace Christianity, but he could not get away from the fact that the universe is directed by intelligence. Concerning the existence of God, Flew lied all his life, and in his stated change of mind, he was still lying. Flew was really no different from W.C. Fields, who on his deathbed was reading the Bible, and when someone asked him what he was doing, he said, "Looking for loopholes." As Antony Flew got close to the grave he hedged his bets, but nevertheless he knew that the "superior intelligence" he had come to believe in is the Lord God omnipotent, who held him accountable on the day of his death, just as He will hold us accountable.

I think that the fear of judgment upon death is what terrified the jailer and that he recognized in front of him two men who knew the way of salvation. How did Paul and Silas respond to him? They did not list the Ten Commandments or tell him to live a good life from then on. They told him, **"Believe on the Lord Jesus Christ, and you will be saved, you and your household"** (v. 31). They told him what was essential. That is not only what you must do, Mr. Jailer, but that is what everybody has to do to be saved. In modern evangelism, people are invited to come to Christ, but God never invites people to come; God commands people to come to Christ. An invitation is something that you can decline with impunity, but God does not issue an R.S.V.P. because our only hope in life and death is Christ.

And he took them the same hour of the night and washed their stripes. And immediately he and all his family were baptized. Now when he had brought them into his house, he set food before them; and he rejoiced, having believed in God with all his household (vv. 33–34). Hours earlier this man had believed he was experiencing the worst moment of his life, but this was his providential day. It was the day he heard the gospel. This man who had tortured and imprisoned the Apostles of Christ now bathed their wounds and gave them food. That is what happens when God changes the heart of a fallen sinner. May He in His grace do that for each one of us.

43

REASONING FROM SCRIPTURE

Acts 16:35–17:15

And when it was day, the magistrates sent the officers, saying, "Let those men go." So the keeper of the prison reported these words to Paul, saying, "The magistrates have sent to let you go. Now therefore depart, and go in peace." But Paul said to them, "They have beaten us openly, uncondemned Romans, and have thrown us into prison. And now do they put us out secretly? No indeed! Let them come themselves and get us out." And the officers told these words to the magistrates, and they were afraid when they heard that they were Romans. Then they came and pleaded with them and brought them out, and asked them to depart from the city. So they went out of the prison and entered the house of Lydia; and when they had seen the brethren, they encouraged them and departed. Now when they had passed through Amphipolis and Apollonia, they came to Thessalonica, where there was a synagogue of the Jews. Then Paul, as his custom was, went in to them, and for three Sabbaths reasoned with them from the Scriptures, explaining and demonstrating that the Christ had to suffer and rise again from the dead, and saying, "This Jesus whom I preach to you is the Christ." And some of them were persuaded; and a great multitude of the devout Greeks, and not a few of the leading women, joined Paul and Silas. But the Jews who were not persuaded, becoming envious, took some of the evil men from the marketplace, and gathering a mob, set all the city in an uproar and attacked the house of Jason, and sought to bring them out to the people. But when they did not find them, they dragged Jason and some brethren to the rulers of the city, crying out, "These who have turned the world upside down have come here too. Jason has harbored them, and these are all acting contrary to the decrees of Caesar, saying there is another king—Jesus."

And they troubled the crowd and the rulers of the city when they heard these things. So when they had taken security from Jason and the rest, they let them go. Then the brethren immediately sent Paul and Silas away by night to Berea. When they arrived, they went into the synagogue of the Jews. These were more fair-minded than those in Thessalonica, in that they received the word with all readiness, and searched the Scriptures daily to find out whether these things were so. Therefore many of them believed, and also not a few of the Greeks, prominent women as well as men. But when the Jews from Thessalonica learned that the word of God was preached by Paul at Berea, they came there also and stirred up the crowds. Then immediately the brethren sent Paul away, to go to the sea; but both Silas and Timothy remained there. So those who conducted Paul brought him to Athens; and receiving a command for Silas and Timothy to come to him with all speed, they departed.

As we look at this section of the second missionary journey, it seems like déjà vu. There is a pattern manifested in the way in which the apostolic enterprise was carried out. Upon entering a city, Paul and his entourage would go into the synagogue and declare the Scriptures, and a few people would be converted, yet among those who remained unconverted, some would rise up in protest, stir up the people against Paul and his friends, and have them beaten and imprisoned. We would think that by now Paul would have learned that publicly proclaiming the gospel of Christ without compromise was going to bring hostility and result in much pain and affliction to those preaching the gospel. It is incorrect to assume that Paul, as brilliant as he was, was slow of mind to learn that particular lesson. He did not care what the consequences were; he was happy to participate in the humiliation of Jesus. He was happy to fill up that which was lacking in the afflictions of Christ (Col. 1:24).

False Peace

The spirit that so characterized the preaching and ministry of the Apostle Paul and of all the great saints of Christian history is sorely lacking in our own day. I hear complaints from people all over America that they cannot find a church with bold and accurate preaching. What they find instead are exercises in entertainment, pop psychology, or something about contemporary social ethics. The gospel is not heard with clarity. One reason for this is that when ministers do proclaim the Word of God without compromise, it always creates division. We want peace when there is no peace. We do not want to offend people, so we have learned to remove the offense from the gospel in order to keep the peace.

We do it in such subtle ways. During a recent Christmas season, my daughter ordered pizza, and when the delivery man came to the door, he wished my daughter a merry Christmas. Sherry said to him, "Thank you for saying 'Merry Christmas' instead of 'Happy Holidays.'" The deliveryman beamed and said, "I say 'Merry Christmas' because Jesus is the reason for the season." He was not willing to remove Christ from the holiday. I say "Merry Christmas" to everybody. If I see a Muslim, I say, "Merry Christmas." I hope he has a lousy Ramadan, because I know that Ramadan is an affront to the holiness of God, and I know the only way that a Muslim is going to have a merry Christmas is if he is converted to Christ. There is nothing like Christmas for the Christian, and it is my hope that every person will be able to share in that true joy. All too often, however, we back away from such an open testimony. We surrender to political correctness when the danger before us may be a little bit of social intimidation; as of yet, no one is throwing us in jail. The culture is getting more militant against all things specifically Christian, but we must remember our heritage. We would not have the freedom we do if not for people like Paul and Silas and Timothy and Luke who went from town to town in the ancient world being beaten with rods and stoned within an inch of their lives and cast into prison.

And when it was day, the magistrates sent the officers, saying, "Let those men go." So the keeper of the prison reported these words to Paul, saying, "The magistrates have sent to let you go. Now therefore depart, and go in peace" (vv. 35–36). At this point Paul did not pack up and leave town. Paul said to them, **"They have beaten us openly, uncondemned Romans, and have thrown us into prison. And now do they put us out secretly? No indeed! Let them come themselves and get us out"** (v. 37). All the rights established in the Roman law code, even before the Caesars came into authority, were violated in Paul's beating and imprisonment, and Paul wanted a public apology. The authorities had violated his rights as a Roman. Of course, they did not know that Paul was a Roman citizen; they did not bother to find out. When news got back to the magistrates that they had beaten and imprisoned a Roman citizen who was asking for a personal and public apology, they came with their hats in their hands. **Then they came and pleaded with them and brought them out, and asked them to depart from the city** (v. 39). God vindicates His people.

So Paul left and went on to Thessalonica. Thessalonica was the most important city in Macedonia and became its capital city. The name Thessalonica was borrowed from the sister of Alexander the Great. Her husband renamed this ancient city in honor of his wife, Thessali. Her name was given to her by her father, Philip of Macedon, after he won a very important military battle in that area. **Then Paul, as his custom was, went in to them, and for three Sabbaths reasoned with them from the Scriptures, explaining and demonstrating that**

the Christ had to suffer and rise again from the dead, and saying, "This Jesus whom I preach to you is the Christ" (17:2–3).

I once asked someone how many numbers one has to get right in the lottery to win the big prize. He told me that six numbers must be given correctly. How much money do you suppose someone would get if they won the big prize ten times—untold riches? No, the winner would likely get nothing but a long sentence in a penitentiary because the only way anybody could get six correct numbers ten different times is if he is crooked. The odds are just too astronomical. In the same way, no one can predict in advance with exact precision what will happen to our world in the future or in the life of a human being. Yet it is an indisputable fact that over a thousand specific prophecies from antiquity regarding the Messiah were fulfilled—specifically, particularly, and perfectly—in the person of Jesus. If skeptics would take time to look at those prophecies, their mouths would be shut forever about any doubt of the divine origin of the Scriptures and of Jesus.

Opening the Scriptures

That was Paul's approach. He went to the Thessalonians, even as he had done with the Philippians, and later on with the Bereans, and he debated them publicly in the market square. He opened up the Scriptures of the Old Testament and showed them text after text, just as Jesus had done on the road to Emmaus. He showed those people that the Messiah had to suffer and die, which was something that the Jews of that day had utterly forgotten. Paul did not argue in the abstract; he reasoned to the people from the Bible using all the prophecies about the Messiah in the Old Testament. Would you be able to do that? I would not. I wouldn't be able to come up with all those prophecies off the top of my head, but Paul could. He was the most educated Jew in Palestine. Paul had mastered the Word of God, and the more people were aware of the Word of God, the greater the response to the preaching. Biblical preaching is what turned the world upside down—expository preaching, not just topical preaching.

My academic background—my education and teaching career—has been in the fields of systematic theology and philosophy. I am not a biblical scholar, technically. I have to pay attention to what biblical scholars write. If I had to do it over again, I would be a biblical scholar rather than a theologian, because there is nothing more I would rather do than give expository preaching of the Scriptures themselves. I love to learn from Augustine, Calvin, Luther, and Edwards, but that is nothing like searching the Scriptures, because faith comes by hearing and hearing by the Word of God (Rom. 10:17).

Then the brethren immediately sent Paul and Silas away by night to Berea. When they arrived, they went into the synagogue of the Jews. These were more fair-minded than those in Thessalonica, in that they received the word with all readiness, and searched the Scriptures daily to find out whether these things were so. Therefore many of them believed, and also not a few of the Greeks, prominent women as well as men. But when the Jews from Thessalonica learned that the word of God was preached by Paul at Berea, they came there also and stirred up the crowds (vv. 10–13). What was Paul doing in Berea? He was doing the same thing he had done in Thessalonica and in Philippi—opening the Scriptures to the people.

I preach expository sermons, going word for word through whole books of the Bible. That way, I cannot pick and choose what I want to preach about, because I am required to preach what is there in the text. If a subject comes before me that I am not comfortable with, I cannot skip over it, because I am committed to setting forth the Word in its entirety. That sort of preaching is what people need because it is through the hearing of the Word that Christ is made manifest.

As Paul showed the people at Thessalonica, the message is Jesus in all His fullness. When the Word is rightly preached, people will learn about Jesus, whether from the Old Testament or the New Testament. All of it is about Jesus. If we do this faithfully, maybe the next generation will look back at us and say, "They were the ones who turned the world upside down," because that is what the Word of God can do.

44

PAUL AT MARS HILL, PART 1

Acts 17:16–23

Now while Paul waited for them at Athens, his spirit was provoked within him when he saw that the city was given over to idols. Therefore he reasoned in the synagogue with the Jews and with the Gentile worshipers, and in the marketplace daily with those who happened to be there. Then certain Epicurean and Stoic philosophers encountered him. And some said, "What does this babbler want to say?" Others said, "He seems to be a proclaimer of foreign gods," because he preached to them Jesus and the resurrection. And they took him and brought him to the Areopagus, saying, "May we know what this new doctrine is of which you speak? For you are bringing some strange things to our ears. Therefore we want to know what these things mean." For all the Athenians and the foreigners who were there spent their time in nothing else but either to tell or to hear some new thing. Then Paul stood in the midst of the Areopagus and said, "Men of Athens, I perceive that in all things you are very religious; for as I was passing through and considering the objects of your worship, I even found an altar with this inscription: TO THE UNKNOWN GOD. Therefore, the One whom you worship without knowing, Him I proclaim to you.

I n every ancient Greek city, the highest point of elevation housed a temple to some god or goddess, usually the patron deity of the particular city. Such locations were called the "high places," which, all the way back in antiquity, we read about in the Old Testament. Pagans built altars there for use in worship because the high places, the places of highest elevation, were considered closest to heaven and were therefore the point of supremacy for all who dwelt in the area. In Greece, that high place or high city was called the acropolis. From *acro*, which means "height," we get words such as "acrobatics" and "acrophobia," and *polis* is the word for "city." The high city was the place where the chief deity resided. If you were to go today to Athens, the first thing you would see upon entering the city would be the elevated position of the acropolis that boasts the remains of the temple of Athena, known in Roman terms as Minerva, housed in the Parthenon, which is the center of the city of Athens.

In the text before us, the Apostle Paul comes to Athens and beholds the city for the first time. He went there on business, not as a tourist, yet the city was flooded with tourists from all over the world. Athens was perceived as the cultural center of antiquity. It was the city that housed the greatest contributors to knowledge, art, science, and political theory. It was the city of Plato, of Aristotle, of Pericles, and of Solon. The average tourist upon entering Athens was surely overwhelmed by the magnificent beauty of the architecture and the numerous temples. It was said sarcastically by one visitor to Athens that it was easier to find a god in the city of Athens than it was to find a man.

That was not the reaction of the Apostle Paul. When Paul came to Athens for this first time and saw this city, he did not see a city of culture. He did not see a focal point of wisdom or of the high age of art. He saw the world's greatest monument to idolatry. **Now while Paul waited for them at Athens, his spirit was provoked within him when he saw that the city was given over to idols** (v. 16). Luke tells us that when Paul saw this city that was given over to idols, he had a visceral reaction. He wasn't just a little bit peeved or annoyed; his heart was in turmoil. His insides were in a paroxysm of distress as he looked across this city noted for its brilliance but drowning in evil.

Therefore he reasoned in the synagogue with the Jews and with the Gentile worshipers, and in the marketplace daily with those who happened to be there (v. 17). Paul reasoned. He was not simply Paul the missionary or Paul the preacher, but Paul the chief apologist of the Christian church. He went to the heart of the intellectual center of the ancient world to reason with its people about ultimate truth.

Age of Skepticism

Then certain Epicurean and Stoic philosophers encountered him. And some said, "What does this babbler want to say?" Others said, "He seems to be a proclaimer of foreign gods," because he preached to them Jesus and the resurrection (v. 18). I find it striking that these two schools of philosophical thought—the Stoics and the Epicureans—are the only two schools of philosophy ever mentioned in the sacred Scripture. The fact that they were flourishing when Paul came to Athens is something of a commentary on what had taken place in the academic world of the first century, something that has taken place in every culture throughout the history of the Western world. It is all the more relevant to us today because, at the beginning of the twenty-first century, we are living in almost the exact intellectual climate that Paul encountered in Athens on that occasion.

Prior to this time in the history of Athens, even before Socrates appeared in the city, the two great giants of philosophy were Heraclitus and Parmenides. They were titans in terms of the quest for the ultimate truth of their day, yet they came out in radical disagreement as to what constitutes ultimate truth. Because these two giants of philosophy could not agree on what constitutes ultimate truth, the people who came after them abandoned the quest for truth altogether, saying that truth is something beyond man's ability to penetrate. They cast off the quest for truth in search of practical understanding.

A seminary student in one of my theology classes once approached me after a class in which we had been going over the doctrine of God. He was bored to tears and said, "I need news I can use. I'm a pragmatist." I tried to get him to understand that nothing was more practical than to understand the character of God. If he cannot use that, then the rest of his knowledge is utterly useless altogether.

Such a spirit followed the impasse between Parmenides and Heraclitus, and Greek philosophy degenerated into cynicism and skepticism, which is how it was when Socrates appeared on the scene. The one who rescued Greek philosophy and culture from pure cynicism and nihilism was Plato. He revived the quest for ultimate truth and created the most profound system of truth that the world had ever seen up until that time. But his success was short-lived because his most famous student, Aristotle, disagreed with him and created an alternate view of ultimate reality that clashed with Plato's. After that, the man on the street said that if Plato and Aristotle could not agree on ultimate truth, then obviously ultimate truth could not be discovered, and with that, a new period of skepticism was ushered in.

We are right now living in an age of skepticism, which always follows the impasse between rationalism and empiricism. When those two could not be resolved, we went into a period of skepticism that continues into this day. People have abandoned the pursuit of higher knowledge and truth and are now concerned only with the *hic et nunc*, the "here and now." So it was with both the Stoics and the Epicureans. Both virtually abandoned the quest for ultimate truth and instead pursued what happiness there is to be enjoyed in the brief period man has in this world.

They were both seeking the same thing, but they came at it in radically different ways. The Epicureans developed the philosophy that we call *hedonism*. We apply the term *epicurean* to gourmets who like the finest food and wines. The philosophy of hedonism defines truth this way: truth is found in the achieving of pleasure and the avoidance of pain. In simple terms the creed was, "If it feels good, it is good." There has probably never been a more hedonistic culture on the face of the earth than contemporary America. We work ourselves to death to satisfy every feeling or lust for pleasure that we can have.

We ought not to confuse the Epicureans with a more crass type of hedonist that preceded them, the Cyrenaics, the group often depicted in Hollywood versions of the bacchanalia. The Cyrenaics involved themselves in orgies, gorging themselves on food and drink, and when they could eat and drink no more, they would vomit so that they could go back and gorge themselves some more. They experienced the dreadful consequence of overindulgence in physical pleasure. The Epicureans were more refined and sophisticated. Their philosophy was to seek pleasure in moderation, just the right amount of drink or food or adultery. Excess has dire consequences and leaves one with the hedonistic paradox that every hedonist faces sooner or later: if you seek physical pleasure as the single purpose of life but you fail to achieve it, you will be constantly frustrated. On the other hand, if you search for physical pleasure and achieve it, you will be bored. Those who seek physical pleasure as their ultimate goal lose both ways. The Epicureans tried to come up with a formula, a calculus of pleasure and pain, that would be so balanced that they could avoid this paradox.

The Stoics, on the other hand, believed that everything in this world happens according to fixed mechanistic causes. There is no such thing as human freedom except at a very limited point. They believed man has no power to influence his life—*que sera, sera*, "what will be will be." However, man can control his attitude about what happens. He can be bitter or discouraged or defeated by what life throws his way, or he can develop the philosophical attitude of imperturbability, or what they called *philosophical ataraxia*. Today that word is the name given to a form of Valium. *Philosophical ataraxia* means that nothing gets you down. You keep a stiff upper lip and remain cool no matter what happens. Life is meaningless, but don't let it get you down. That is the ultimate skepticism of stoicism, which is slightly warmed over in the nihilism of a Nietzsche, a Camus, or a Sartre in our day.

Such thinking is pervasive today. People are saying that all anyone can really know is the here and now. This is the way the vast majority of people in America live their lives. They never think about ultimate reality or truth. They do not think about the meaning of their existence. They think only about today and tomorrow and how they feel right now. Very few ask where they will be and what they will be doing one hundred years from today.

So the philosophers came together in Athens and skeptically wondered what Paul, the babbler, would have to say. The word translated "babbler" literally means "seed gatherer." It had reference to those who gathered little pieces of cloth to sell in the marketplace at cheap prices, much like people today who collect bottles and try to make a living selling them for a few cents. That is how they considered Paul, this ragtag fellow. **And they took him and brought him to the Areopagus, saying, "May we know what this new doctrine is of which you speak? For you are bringing some strange things to our ears. Therefore we want to know what these things mean"** (vv. 19–20). About 50 yards out from the Parthenon is a little butte that comes up out of the ground. It is about 50 feet high and 150 yards long. On that butte was a temple to the god Ares, the Greek counterpart to the Roman god of war, Mars. That is why this hill in Athens was called the Areopagus, the hill of Ares, or, to the Romans, Mars Hill. People went to Mars Hill to dispute and debate and on occasion hold trials. On this occasion Paul was not put on trial. He was invited to join in the debates and disputes of the philosophers.

Then Luke gives a footnote: **For all the Athenians and the foreigners who were there spent their time in nothing else but either to tell or to hear some new thing** (v. 21). Does that sound familiar? "What is new?" "How is the world treating you?" We glorify that in popular music. We get the paper in the morning to find what is new. The academic world is intoxicated with this. The world of science is constantly seeking new information, new discoveries, and new insights, which is good, but in the social sciences, most of the innovations are destructive. Where I went to school, in order to get a doctoral dissertation approved a student had to come up with something new—the newer, the better; the more novel, the more acceptable, even though we were studying a book that has been around for two thousand years in its latest edition (four thousand years in its totality). A man at the University of Manchester got his PhD in New Testament studies with the thesis that Jesus was really the founder of a phallic mushroom cult. That is new, but it is also ridiculous. We have a tendency to give credibility to people if they come up with something new and different.

One of the rages in theology today is the so-called New Perspective on Paul. A British theologian wrote a book that claimed he knew what Paul was really teaching. He claims he is the first one to understand Paul's teaching in two thousand years—nonsense! But it is new, and since it is new, it has a following. The same thinking led those in Athens to be interested in what Paul might say.

God Made Known

Then Paul stood in the midst of the Areopagus and said, "Men of Athens, I perceive that in all things you are very religious; for as I was passing through and considering the objects of your worship, I even found an altar with this inscription: TO THE UNKNOWN GOD. Therefore, the One whom you worship without knowing, Him I proclaim to you" (vv. 22–23). This was before Paul wrote Romans 1, where he said that God has so clearly manifested Himself to every human being as to leave no one without excuse (vv. 18–20). Psalm 19 proclaims that there is no place to which the language of God has not gone (v. 3). God reveals Himself plainly through nature, outwardly, but He also reveals Himself in the soul of every creature that bears His image. God has revealed Himself, as Paul tells us in Romans 2 (vv. 5–6).

I do not argue with atheists. I simply say, "You know very well that God exists. Your problem isn't that you don't know that God exists; your problem is that you can't stand Him." The sin of man is not atheism; it is religion, which is how we distort God's revelation of Himself. We shape a deity in our own image and make houses for Him with our own hands, and serve and worship the creature rather than the Creator, exchanging the glory of God for a lie (Rom. 1:25). Paul told the Romans that God so manifests Himself that every human being knows God, and knowing God, we refuse to worship Him as God, neither are we grateful, and we turn ourselves to idols (Rom. 1:21). That is what religion is—the substitution of a false god for the true God. Even Christianity can become a religion when we substitute the God of Scripture for a god of our own making.

To hedge their bets, the Greeks involved in this idolatry set up a little monument off to the side. It had nothing of the splendor of the three statues that adorned the Parthenon of Athena in gold and ivory. The monument was dedicated "To the Unknown God." They knew nothing about this god. Why in the world would they build an altar to an unknown god? Modern sociology and anthropology have found that man is incurably religious, *homo religiosos*. No matter where we go, we find people practicing religion, most of which is animistic and idolatrous. Yet when scholars go into these primitive places and begin to probe, people will talk about the big God who lives on the other side of the mountain. They cannot erase from their consciousness the knowledge of the Most High God. That was as true in Athens as it is among the aborigines today.

We do it too. "Oh, I believe in some higher power, something greater than myself." Higher powers do not go around saying, "Thou shalt . . ." and "Thou shalt not . . ." A higher power will not hold us accountable at the end of our lives to a standard of holiness. Everyone knows that people are accountable for how they live. We are creatures, and we know that we did not make ourselves. We were made by Almighty God, and at some point we are going to have to answer for every single thing we have done and said and thought. People hedge their bets and build an altar off in a corner to an unknown God. Paul did not believe for a moment that they did not know who God is, and he used that altar publicly to expose the folly of their godless religion.

45

PAUL AT MARS HILL, PART 2

Acts 17:25–33

"Nor is He worshiped with men's hands, as though He needed anything, since He gives to all life, breath, and all things. And He has made from one blood every nation of men to dwell on all the face of the earth, and has determined their preappointed times and the boundaries of their dwellings, so that they should seek the Lord, in the hope that they might grope for Him and find Him, though He is not far from each one of us; for in Him we live and move and have our being, as also some of your own poets have said, 'For we are also His offspring.' Therefore, since we are the offspring of God, we ought not to think that the Divine Nature is like gold or silver or stone, something shaped by art and man's devising. Truly, these times of ignorance God overlooked, but now commands all men everywhere to repent, because He has appointed a day on which He will judge the world in righteousness by the Man whom He has ordained. He has given assurance of this to all by raising Him from the dead." And when they heard of the resurrection of the dead, some mocked, while others said, "We will hear you again on this matter." So Paul departed from among them.

When my teaching career began some forty years ago, I taught philosophy in the university, not theology in the seminary. One course I taught was ancient philosophy, beginning before Socrates and continuing up through Aristotle. Perhaps because of that time of concentration on the thinking of the ancient Greeks, I have a hard time getting past the profundity of what the Apostle Paul declared to the philosophers in Athens.

In our last study we saw that Paul was deeply concerned about the total giving over of the populace of Athens to idolatry. The city that had been the high cultural watershed of the ancient world had reached no higher than the depths of crass idolatry. Throughout the city were statues of stone and wood and silver and gold at the feet of which the people routinely worshiped. Paul reminded the people that God does not dwell in temples made with hands, **"nor is He worshiped with men's hands, as though He needed anything, since He gives to all life, breath, and all things. And He has made from one blood every nation of men to dwell on all the face of the earth, and has determined their preappointed times and the boundaries of their dwellings"** (vv. 25–26).

Life in God Alone

Paul does away with this notion of polytheism. The people had a god for this and a goddess for that, and each deity in the pantheon had a particularized sphere of authority over which it reigned. There is only one God, Paul said, and that one God has made all things and all people. That one God determines the boundaries and limits of every nation, **"so that they should seek the Lord, in the hope that they might grope for Him and find Him, though He is not far from each one of us; for in Him we live and move and have our being, as also some of your own poets have said, 'For we are also His offspring'"** (vv. 27–28).

This single sentence is the most profound sentence found anywhere in sacred Scripture. It addresses the three greatest intellectual issues of both ancient and contemporary philosophy. The quest for ultimate truth throughout history has always focused on three basic issues. First is the question of life. What is life? Where does it come from? How does it happen? What keeps it going? What causes it to stop? In other words, the question of the mystery of life is rooted and grounded in its source. The source of life as we experience it today is perhaps the single greatest intellectual crisis and collision between Christianity and paganism.

Children in the public schools are taught routinely, almost daily, that their life is the result of a cosmic accident, that human life emerged fortuitously through the chance collision of atoms and is moving relentlessly towards the abyss of nothingness at the end. The two poles of our existence start and end in meaninglessness; this is the grand folly of humanism, which philosophy I say does not deserve an intelligent response; it basically deserves nothing but ridicule. Humanists, who steal their capital from Christianity, tell us that we are creatures of great dignity, and yet they say our origin and destiny are in meaninglessness. This is a roller coaster with no brakes, and yet it is what our children are taught.

This is the point of human life that Paul addresses in Athens. Life is rooted and grounded in God. That is the first assertion of biblical Christianity, that we are creatures who have come into being by the creative act of an intelligent, eternal being. Not only does God wind us up and start us off in life, but He sustains that life as long as we have it. I recoil in horror when I hear that on the cross of Calvary, God died. If God had died on the cross, every living thing, not only in Jerusalem but in the whole world, would have died that same moment, because without the life of God, there is no life possible. No, the God-man died, and the divine nature that had been perfectly united to a living, breathing human nature was then united to a corpse. The deity of Christ did not perish on the cross because all of life is in God.

The practical significance of that is not just that the life of all things in general is based and grounded in the life of God, but that your life and my life are based in God. We fear for our lives. We are easily frightened about what the latest doctor's report is going to tell us about the state of our health. If I am nothing more than a grown-up germ on the way to nothingness, the report I am waiting for is simply going to tell me when I am going to get there. As a Christian, I understand that no matter what that pathological report is, my life right now—today and tomorrow—is in the hands of God, and there is no better or safer place for it to be.

Not only do I live in Him, but I move in Him. Once when I was watching a football game, one of the teams punted to the other team, and the ball was downed on the one-yard line, pressed close to the goal line. The team was in danger of suffering a safety. As the team came up to the ball at the line of scrimmage on first down and prepared to snap the ball, there was motion in the backfield, and a penalty flag was thrown. The penalty was half the distance to the goal line, so the referee took the ball and marked it on the eighteen-inch line. On the very next play, the team came up to the ball, the quarterback started the signal, and again somebody moved, the flag was thrown, and the team was penalized half the distance to the goal line. So the ball was moved to the nine-inch line. I'd never seen that happen, two consecutive penalties inside the one-yard line. The fellow with whom I was watching the game said, "They'd better be careful. If they have a couple more penalties like that, they are going to be in the end zone, and there will be a safety." I said, "No, they could have one hundred more motion penalties in a row and still not have a safety because it is half the distance. The distance on the playing field is infinitely divisible. They could have an infinite number of half-the-distance penalties and still not end up in the goal, over the goal line." My friend hadn't considered that. It is an ancient problem in philosophy.

That is the problem that Zeno the Skeptic wrestled with when he looked at what he considered to be the illusory character of matter. He said if matter is real, it has to be endlessly divisible. This was before we split the atom, which we thought was the smallest possible particle. Now we know better. Zeno told the story of the race between Achilles and the tortoise. To make it fair, he gave the tortoise a bit of a head start. The race began, and Achilles ran as fast as he could to catch up with the tortoise. He reached that spot, but in the meantime the tortoise had moved forward, so Achilles had to catch him again. Now the distance between them was shorter, but before Achilles could catch up, the tortoise had again moved forward. In this scenario, Achilles could never catch up with the tortoise.

Motion for the ancient Greek was not just a question of acceleration or of speed or of moving from one physical spot to another, but all change was considered to be a kind of motion. Aging is a kind of motion. Our bodies change, and some people find it very difficult to adjust to that process. As we get older, the changes become more significant, the pains become worse, and our abilities become more challenged. Yet that motion or change is in God, who is the source of all motion. In Him, Paul said, we live and move, or, in Him we live and change. As we go through these changes, God is still there. He is sovereign over those changes. He is no more or less our sovereign Lord when we are eighty-five than when we are twenty-five or fifteen. We find our comfort in the fact that our lives and changes are in Him, and they are for Him, and they are being used by Him for His eternal changeless purposes.

Our kids are taught that once upon a time, all matter was comprised into one tiny, infinitesimal point, and for eternity that point remained in a state of absolute inertia. The law of inertia states that bodies at rest tend to remain at rest unless acted upon by an outside force, and bodies that are in motion tend to remain in motion unless acted upon by an outside force. It is because of inertia that we can play golf—and why playing golf is so hard. When I tee off, I want to hit the ball as far as I can. The ball is at rest until I hit it, and after I do, it is acted upon by gravity and the friction of the wind. Forces work to thwart my desire to make that ball go far. However, without those outside forces, I could hit the ball only once. If there was nothing to resist its forward motion, the ball would continue through the green and just keep on going until it was in orbit. Golf would not be very much fun. People say that from all eternity matter and energy were in a singular state of inertia, and then one day it blew up and moved from organization toward disorganization, all without any outside source. If any theory of origins ever screamed for and demanded the idea of a self-existent eternal being, it is the Big Bang theory. Without God, the Big Bang theory is absolute folly, pure nonsense, yet that is what our kids are taught every day.

"In Him we live and move and have our being," Paul said. Our being is creaturely being. It is very much involved with life and change, but our existence is nothing we could have brought about on our own. Apart from a being that is not derived, dependent, or contingent but has the power within Himself eternally to be—without that none of us would exist. This was what Paul addressed when he spoke to the ancient philosophers at Mars Hill. His speech answered the three biggest questions they struggled with—life, motion, and being. The God who made them does not dwell in temples made with hands. He cannot be reduced to ivory, silver, gold, or wood. In this God, man lives and moves and has his being. It is in the biblical God that we find the answer of the one and the many. We find the answer to ultimate reality. All the philosophical problems that vex us find their solution ultimately in the being and character of God, and any attempt to explain reality apart from that ends in manifest and manifold ignorance, the shadows on Plato's cave.

Repentance Commanded

Paul calls it what it is—ignorance. "**Truly, these times of ignorance God overlooked**" (v. 30). Up till this point in history, Paul is saying to the Athenians, God has been unbelievably patient. He has been patient while they have built altars and temples to gods and goddesses that do not exist. He knows that they have exchanged His glory for a lie, and that every one of the statues slanders the living God. God has been putting up with their boasting in their glorious philosophy and culture, a culture smothered in idolatry, "**but now commands all men everywhere to repent**" (v. 30). Something has changed dramatically in the course of human history, something that is not just for Jews but for Athenians and Romans and Philippians and every person in the world. Now God commands all men everywhere to repent.

When God commands us to do something, it is not an invitation. It is a divine subpoena. It is every human's duty to come to Jesus and bow before the King of kings. Those who refuse will receive the everlasting judgment of Almighty God. God does not give us the right to choose what religion we want to follow. The United States government may give you that right, but God does not. He commands all men everywhere to repent.

Why does he do that now? Why the change? "**Because He has appointed a day on which He will judge the world in righteousness by the Man whom He has ordained. He has given assurance of this to all by raising Him from**

the dead" (v. 31). God made this command because He has marked on the calendar a day that we call "judgment day." On that day, He is going to judge the whole world with a righteous judgment by the Man whom He has ordained. God has ordained a man to be the judge on judgment day, and His name is not Muhammad, Moses, or Buddha. The Man that God has chosen to judge the world in righteousness is His only begotten Son, the identity of whom He has proved to the world by raising Him from the dead. Muhammad, Moses, and Buddha are dead, but Jesus is alive because He is the one appointed by God, the judge of all of the earth.

Paul came to that outcropping of rock fifty yards from the Parthenon and stood on the Areopagus and announced the greatest crisis that any human being will ever face. What do you do with Jesus? That is the greatest question you and I will ever deal with. It is the question that determines ultimately where we live, where we move, and where we will have our being. It is not an optional matter. God simply will not tolerate our rejection of His only begotten Son. That truth is on a collision course with what we hear every day in secular America, which tells us there are many ways to God: it does not matter to God which one you choose, so long as you are religious. If that is true, then what the Bible teaches is false. If all religions are equally good, then one stands out as terribly bad, and that is Christianity, because Christianity has no time for pluralism. It sees one way only. Now, that is downright un-American. Sometime you have to make a decision where your allegiance is going to be—with the secular culture or with the One whom God sent into the world as your Redeemer.

46

PAUL AT CORINTH

Acts 18:1–17

After these things Paul departed from Athens and went to Corinth. And he found a certain Jew named Aquila, born in Pontus, who had recently come from Italy with his wife Priscilla (because Claudius had commanded all the Jews to depart from Rome); and he came to them. So, because he was of the same trade, he stayed with them and worked; for by occupation they were tentmakers. And he reasoned in the synagogue every Sabbath, and persuaded both Jews and Greeks. When Silas and Timothy had come from Macedonia, Paul was compelled by the Spirit, and testified to the Jews that Jesus is the Christ. But when they opposed him and blasphemed, he shook his garments and said to them, "Your blood be upon your own heads; I am clean. From now on I will go to the Gentiles." And he departed from there and entered the house of a certain man named Justus, one who worshiped God, whose house was next door to the synagogue. Then Crispus, the ruler of the synagogue, believed on the Lord with all his household. And many of the Corinthians, hearing, believed and were baptized. Now the Lord spoke to Paul in the night by a vision, Do not be afraid, but speak, and do not keep silent; for I am with you, and no one will attack you to hurt you; for I have many people in this city. And he continued there a year and six months, teaching the word of God among them. When Gallio was proconsul of Achaia, the Jews with one accord rose up against Paul and brought him to the judgment seat, saying, This fellow persuades men to worship God contrary to the law. And when Paul was about to open his mouth, Gallio said to the Jews, "If it were a matter of wrongdoing or wicked crimes, O Jews, there would be reason why I should bear with you. But if it is a question of words and names and your own law, look to it yourselves; for I do not want to be a judge of such matters." And he drove them from the judgment seat. Then all the Greeks took Sosthenes, the ruler of the synagogue, and beat him before the judgment seat. But Gallio took no notice of these things.

I t is evident from biblical history that Paul did not spend a long time in Athens. He stayed just a few weeks and then departed from that cultural center of the ancient world, where he had debated their intellectual elite with very little fruit. Later Paul said, "God has chosen the foolish things of the world to put to shame the wise, and God has chosen the weak things of the world to put to shame the things which are mighty" (1 Cor. 1:27). By the leading of the Spirit, Paul shook the dust from Athens off his feet and made his way to Corinth.

From Athens, Corinth was a two-day journey by land. If the journey was made by sea with favorable winds, it could be accomplished in as little as four hours. Corinth at this time was a relatively new city. It had been destroyed over one hundred years prior to Paul's visit, but at the time of the early church it had been recently rebuilt by the Romans and had become a significant center of Roman trade. It was populated mostly by Greeks and Romans with some Jews also. Corinth was known for its luxury. It was a city of great affluence because of the commerce that took place there. It was also known for its wild and extravagant immorality. Here Paul went and labored in the preaching of the gospel and the establishing of the church for at least a year and a half, possibly longer.

The affluence of Corinth is manifested in the decorative style of its architecture, a style that indicates a penchant for ornamentation and ostentation. Of the ancient cities of the world, particularly of the biblical world, the one whose ruins are most intact today are those in the town of Ephesus in Turkey. The second-most intact city with ruins from the ancient world is Corinth. The structures we find in this text in Acts are still intact. The synagogue is there, as is the home of Justus. The plain or court where Gallio judged Paul and gave him his hearing is also still visible to this day.

Aquila and Priscilla

So Paul left Athens and went to Corinth. **And he found a certain Jew named Aquila, born in Pontus, who had recently come from Italy with his wife Priscilla (because Claudius had commanded all the Jews to depart from Rome); and he came to them** (v. 2). The reason, we are told, why they had just come from Italy to Greece and to Corinth was because of an edict that had been delivered by Caesar Claudius, the emperor of Rome at the time. Claudius issued a decree that expelled the Jews from Rome in the year A.D. 52. The decree came about because of disruption and upheaval going on in the city of Rome in the middle of the first century due to the teachings of one Jewish person named Chrestus. It is rare to find outside of the New Testament any reference from the ancient world that mentions Jesus. But here in the writing of Suetonius is a mention of Jesus. His name is misspelled, which reflects the pagan pronunciation of the name Christus, the Greek name for Jesus. This was certainly a reference to Jesus. That the edict took place in A.D. 52 was also attested by the historian Tacitus. That is important for placing the time that Paul spent in Corinth.

Paul met Priscilla and Aquila very shortly after their arrival, coming as a result of the expulsion mandated by Claudius. **So, because he was of the same trade, he stayed with them and worked; for by occupation they were tentmakers** (v. 3). Tentmaking was very important at this time in the ancient world because many people lived in tents, particularly Jews who remained semi-nomadic in their lifestyle. Tentmaking was a rather lucrative business. Jewish fathers were obliged to teach their sons a trade. The adage was that if a father failed to teach his son a trade, he taught his son to be a thief. It is obvious that the Apostle Paul had learned the trade of tentmaking as a young boy before his vast education in the rabbinic schools, and he maintained this trade as his livelihood through much of his adult life. Given the shared trade with Aquila and Priscilla, he dwelt with them at this time in Corinth.

To the Gentiles

And he reasoned in the synagogue every Sabbath, and persuaded both Jews and Greeks. When Silas and Timothy had come from Macedonia, Paul was compelled by the Spirit, and testified to the Jews that Jesus is the Christ. But when they opposed him and blasphemed, he shook his garments and said to them, "Your blood be upon your own heads; I am clean. From now on I will go to the Gentiles" (vv. 4–7). We have seen this same pattern again and again in our study of Acts. Paul preaches in a particular synagogue, and some believe while the rest get hostile. Here Paul gave them a lesson reminiscent of the Old Testament prophets. In the Old Testament, the prophets communicated not only verbally but with certain behaviors. We find prophets eating scrolls, running naked through the streets, and using a plumb line to illustrate the truth of God. When the Jews in this synagogue rose up and blasphemed against Christ, Paul took off his garment and shook it to indicate that he was shaking the filth of the blasphemers off his body. His conscience was clear, he had proclaimed the word of God to them, and they had despised it. From now on, Paul said, he was going to the Gentiles.

How reminiscent this is of our Lord's behavior on the way to the cross. When Jesus was led to His crucifixion, the women along the way were weeping in commiseration for Him, and He said to them, "Daughters of Jerusalem, do not weep for Me, but weep for yourselves and for your children" (Luke 23:28). Our Lord said those words because He understood that those who were rejecting Him were calling down the judgment of God upon their own heads. Paul did not waste his time with people who would not respond to the gospel.

So Paul left the synagogue, and he went right next door to the home of a Gentile named Justus. He started holding meetings there and preaching to the Gentiles. **Then Crispus, the ruler of the synagogue, believed on the Lord with all his household. And many of the Corinthians, hearing, believed and were baptized** (v. 8). First Justus believed in Christ followed by Crispus, the head of the synagogue. This calls to mind Nicodemus, a member of the Sanhedrin, who became a secret disciple, as it were, of Jesus. While the rest of the Sanhedrin rejected Jesus, Nicodemus became His disciple. Not everybody in the synagogue rejected the gospel.

Now the Lord spoke to Paul in the night by a vision, "Do not be afraid, but speak, and do not keep silent; for I am with you, and no one will attack you to hurt you; for I have many people in this city" (vv. 9–10). If ever there was a preacher in the history of the world that did not need to be instructed in this manner by God, it was the Apostle Paul. Nobody appears to us more fearless or faithful in the bold proclamation of the truth of Christ then Paul, but Paul was a human being. He was not a masochist. Preachers do not love to provoke people to hate them. When I was first converted, I told my friends about Christ. I just assumed that because I was happy about my discovery of Jesus that they would be happy too. I took every opportunity to communicate the gospel to my friends, but one by one they walked away. They thought I had lost my mind, and they became hostile. So I started toning it down. I started keeping my mouth shut because I did not want to lose more friends. Nobody was throwing me in jail or beating me with rods; it was solely the rejection of my contemporaries that made me timid about proclaiming Christ. Do we not all go through that in one way or another in our Christian experience? Even Paul was beginning to lose his nerve, as it were, until God appeared to him in a vision and told him not to be afraid.

And he continued there a year and six months, teaching the word of God among them. When Gallio was proconsul of Achaia, the Jews with one accord rose up against Paul and brought him to the judgment seat, saying, "This fellow persuades men to worship God contrary to the law" (vv. 11–12). This may seem to be an insignificant incident in the overall life and ministry of Paul, but what happened here in a sense freed Paul to preach the gospel for more than an additional ten years. That is because the Jews appealed to the Roman proconsul Gallio, and they dragged Paul to the judgment place. Suddenly Paul was on trial, not before the Jews but before the Roman authorities.

Gallio had just recently been appointed proconsul, probably in conjunction with Claudius's activity. Gallio's brother Seneca was one of the most famous writers of the Roman world. Seneca was famous as a moralist and a sage in his day; he was celebrated for his wisdom. Seneca dedicated two of his books to his brother Gallio. They shared a common commitment to wisdom and justice, even as pagans. In fact, their commitment to a high standard of justice and morality got them in deep trouble more than a decade later with the wicked Roman emperor Nero. Nero executed Seneca and Gallio. So the man who intervened here in Corinth to save Paul's life and to preserve the legitimacy of his ministry in the Roman provinces was later martyred by Nero, who also killed Paul.

So the Jews rose up against Paul and brought him to this judgment seat. **And when Paul was about to open his mouth, Gallio said to the Jews, "If it were a matter of wrongdoing or wicked crimes, O Jews, there would be reason why I should bear with you. But if it is a question of words and names and your own law, look to it yourselves; for I do not want to be a judge of such matters." And he drove them from the judgment seat. Then all the Greeks took Sosthenes, the ruler of the synagogue, and beat him before the judgment seat. But Gallio took no notice of these things** (vv. 14–17). What basically happened here is that the Roman proconsul gave Paul a safe-conduct pass because of his Roman citizenship. This intervention of Gallio paved the way for Paul to be able to continue preaching and planting churches throughout various parts of the Roman Empire, which is why this was a decisive moment in Paul's ministry of building churches in the ancient world. With the intervention of Gallio, the words that had occurred to Paul in the vision were fulfilled: "Do not be afraid, but speak, and do not keep silent; for I am with you, and no one will attack you to hurt you."

When that prophecy from Paul's vision seemed to fail and he was dragged into the judgment place, along came the Roman proconsul, a tool in the hand of God who protected Paul and allowed the preaching of the gospel to go on and the church at Corinth to flourish.

47

PAUL AT EPHESUS

Acts 19:1–20

And it happened, while Apollos was at Corinth, that Paul, having passed through the upper regions, came to Ephesus. And finding some disciples he said to them, "Did you receive the Holy Spirit when you believed?" So they said to him, "We have not so much as heard whether there is a Holy Spirit." And he said to them, "Into what then were you baptized?" So they said, "Into John's baptism." Then Paul said, 'John indeed baptized with a baptism of repentance, saying to the people that they should believe on Him who would come after him, that is, on Christ Jesus." When they heard this, they were baptized in the name of the Lord Jesus. And when Paul had laid hands on them, the Holy Spirit came upon them, and they spoke with tongues and prophesied. Now the men were about twelve in all. And he went into the synagogue and spoke boldly for three months, reasoning and persuading concerning the things of the kingdom of God. But when some were hardened and did not believe, but spoke evil of the Way before the multitude, he departed from them and withdrew the disciples, reasoning daily in the school of Tyrannus. And this continued for two years, so that all who dwelt in Asia heard the word of the Lord Jesus, both Jews and Greeks. Now God worked unusual miracles by the hands of Paul, so that even handkerchiefs or aprons were brought from his body to the sick, and the diseases left them and the evil spirits went out of them. Then some of the itinerant Jewish exorcists took it upon themselves to call the name of the Lord Jesus over those who had evil spirits, saying, "We exorcise you by the Jesus whom Paul preaches." Also there were seven sons of Sceva, a Jewish chief priest, who did so. And the evil spirit answered and said, "Jesus I know, and Paul I know; but who are you?" Then the man in whom the evil spirit was leaped on them, overpowered them, and prevailed against them, so that they fled out of that house naked and wounded. This became known both to all Jews and Greeks dwelling in Ephesus; and fear fell on them all, and the name of the Lord Jesus was magnified. And many who had believed came confessing and telling their deeds. Also, many of those who had practiced magic brought their books together and burned them in the sight of all. And they counted up the value of them, and it totaled fifty thousand pieces of silver. So the word of the Lord grew mightily and prevailed.

At the conclusion of our last study, we were still with the Apostle Paul in Corinth where he had been defended by the Roman procurator Gallio. As a result of that, Paul had the freedom to continue to preach and teach openly in Corinth. After that, Paul took leave of his friends in Corinth and went to Syria, along with Priscilla and Aquila, and came for the first time to Ephesus. There he entered the synagogue and stayed briefly, preaching to the Ephesians. He was not there for a long time because he was impelled to return to Jerusalem to celebrate one of the major feasts of the Jews, perhaps Passover or the Feast of Tabernacles. After taking leave of his friends in Ephesus, he sailed from there and landed in Caesarea and then made his way to Jerusalem. This indicates the end of Paul's second missionary journey.

In the interlude between the end of the second missionary journey and the beginning of the third, we are introduced at the end of Acts 18 to an eloquent Greek-speaking Jew, probably from Alexandria, named Apollos. He distinguished himself by coming to the Corinthian community and showing a tremendous knowledge of the Scriptures and ability to communicate them, supplementing his knowledge with what he learned from Priscilla and Aquila. After that we read that Paul, accompanied by Priscilla and Aquila, returned to Jerusalem.

Baptized into Christ

Acts 19 is the starting point of Paul's third missionary journey. **And it happened, while Apollos was at Corinth, that Paul, having passed through the upper regions, came to Ephesus. And finding some disciples he said to them, "Did you receive the Holy Spirit when you believed?"** (vv. 1–2). Throughout the book of Acts we have seen the empowerment of the Holy Spirit upon the Christian community. On the day of Pentecost God had poured out His Spirit as He had promised in the Old Testament, and those who received the baptism of the Holy Spirit manifested it by speaking in tongues. Those assembled were all Jewish believers, and all who were there received the baptism. When we studied that, I mentioned that Luke follows the outline of the Great Commission, in which Jesus had said that the disciples should tarry in Jerusalem until they received the Holy Spirit. Afterward they were to be His witnesses in Jerusalem, Judea, Samaria, and the uttermost parts of the earth. We have followed the Apostle Paul on the missionary enterprise set forth by Jesus. All told, we have seen four separate occasions in which the Spirit was poured out—first to the Jews, then to the God-fearers in Cornelius's household, then to the Samaritans, and now to the Gentiles in Ephesus. The membership in the body of Christ of all four groups was questioned in the first century, and each individually received the outpouring of the Spirit.

By this time, the Samaritans were approved as full citizens in the kingdom. The God-fearers were in the kingdom. The Jewish believers were in the kingdom and in the New Testament church. Then Paul came to Ephesus and found twelve believers there. He asked them if they had received the Holy Spirit, but they didn't know anything about the Holy Spirit and obviously had not received the baptism of the Spirit. Paul asked them an interesting question: **"Into what then were you baptized?"** (v. 3). The implication was that had they been baptized into Christ, they would have received the baptism of the Holy Spirit already. They responded, **"Into John's baptism"** (v. 3). The only baptism they had received to date had been the baptism of John the Baptist.

There is a clear difference between the baptism of John the Baptist and the baptism of Jesus. Although John the Baptist appears in the New Testament, he lived and died before the new covenant was inaugurated. The New Testament period did not begin until Jesus inaugurated it in the upper room on the night before His death, when He spoke of the new covenant shed in His blood. The new covenant was ratified the next day by His blood on the cross. All of history up to that point belonged to the old covenant of redemption, so John's baptism must not be confused with the sign of the new covenant, which was inaugurated by Christ. John's baptism was directed to the Jews and those who heard of John's message. John had disciples who went around baptizing, and their message was one of repentance because of the historical crisis then at hand. John's message was this: "The Messiah is coming. Your Savior is at the door, and you are not ready. You are still unclean, so you need to undergo a rite of cleansing to prepare yourself for the coming of the king, and after He comes, He will baptize you with the Spirit." John pointed ahead to one whose baptism was superior to his own.

All of that is involved here in Paul's discussion with those who had come to Christ as a result of John's witness but had not yet undergone New Testament baptism. **When they heard this, they were baptized in the name of the Lord Jesus. And when Paul had laid hands on them, the Holy Spirit came upon them, and they spoke with tongues and prophesied** (vv. 5–6). So we see

Pentecost coming in full measure to the Gentiles. The loop is complete. That is why the modern revival of Pentecostalism that seeks a new baptism and tongues represents, in my view, a low view of Pentecost, not a high view. It postulates the idea that there are Christians who have received the Spirit and regeneration but who have not received the Spirit in terms of baptism. It is a complete antithesis of what Acts teaches about Spirit baptism and what Paul himself teaches in 1 Corinthians about the Spirit's being distributed to every Christian. So even though there was a time in church history, at the very beginning, when there may have been a gap between conversion and Spirit baptism, that time had passed. Once the baptism was established in church history, it then accompanied conversion for every Christian. Every true believer has received the Holy Spirit and has been empowered from on high to be a participant in the ministry of Christ.

Ministry in Ephesus

Then Paul went into the synagogue and spoke boldly for three months. The same pattern we have seen in city after city occurred here in Ephesus: **But when some were hardened and did not believe, but spoke evil of the Way before the multitude, he departed from them and withdrew the disciples, reasoning daily in the school of Tyrannus** (v. 9). Just as Paul had moved next door from the synagogue in Corinth, now he moved down the street in Ephesus to the school of Tyrannus, who was obviously a professional teacher of philosophy or rhetoric with his own school building. Paul used it in the off-hours to instruct the people in the things of God.

Ephesus is the most heavily reconstructed city from antiquity. If you go to Turkey and visit the ancient city of Ephesus, you can walk down the streets and see the buildings almost as they were, an exact replica of the time in which the Apostle Paul ministered there, with one notable exception. The center point of the city of Ephesus in the ancient world was its magnificent temple dedicated to the goddess Diana, or Artemus. This temple was one of the seven wonders of the ancient world. The city of Ephesus was one of the five largest cities in the Roman Empire at that time, being the capital of the province of Asia under Roman government. It was also a very important commercial center for the Roman Empire. Due to Paul's ministry there, it later superseded Antioch as the center for Christian expansion into the Gentile world. Also, the city of Ephesus boasted one of the three largest libraries in the ancient world, the largest one, of course, being in Alexandria in Egypt. We do not want to think that Ephesus at that time was only a tiny village or a remote outpost of Asia; it was the intellectual center of Asia.

Now God worked unusual miracles by the hands of Paul, so that even

handkerchiefs or aprons were brought from his body to the sick, and the diseases left them and the evil spirits went out of them (vv. 11–12). These miracles were extraordinary but not magical. Today there are charlatans on Christian television who appeal for funds and tell viewers that if they send in money, they will receive a blessed handkerchief and power from the Holy Spirit and healing. I heard a televangelist tell viewers that if they would just send him sixty dollars, he could guarantee that God would pour out a blessing upon them. If they would double the amount of their gift, he could guarantee a double portion of this blessing. It is tragic the way people take the truth and power of God and turn it into a sideshow.

That is what happened next in Ephesus. **Then some of the itinerant Jewish exorcists took it upon themselves to call the name of the Lord Jesus over those who had evil spirits, saying, "We exorcise you by the Jesus whom Paul preaches." Also there were seven sons of Sceva, a Jewish chief priest, who did so** (vv. 13–14). After the exorcists had witnessed the miracles, they tried to co-opt Paul's power for their own work. They approached a man who was sorely distressed and possessed by a demon, and in the name of Jesus they adjured the demon to come out of the man. And the evil spirit answered and said, **"Jesus I know, and Paul I know; but who are you?"** (v. 15).

The demons were the first to recognize the true identity of Jesus during his earthly ministry. Jesus said that the exorcism of demons was the one sign that should have convinced everybody of His origin and of the significance of redemptive history: "If I cast out demons with the finger of God, surely the kingdom of God has come upon you" (Luke 11:20). Jesus attached singular importance to the miracle of exorcising evil spirits as a sign and manifestation of the breakthrough of the supernatural kingdom.

Then the man in whom the evil spirit was leaped on them, overpowered them, and prevailed against them, so that they fled out of that house naked and wounded (v. 16). The seven sons of Sceva were absolutely powerless before the forces of hell. One of the great dangers in our day is the intrusion into Christian experience of magic. Pervasive today are commitments to arcane practices of manipulating our environment, and so much of that has made its way into the Christian church, where people confuse the occult with the kingdom of God. The kingdom of Christ is a kingdom of power. We do not need any more power than what we have right now in the person and work of the Holy Spirit, who always works according to Scripture and never against it. We need to be discerning, not being deceived by magic in the name of God; magic practiced in the name of Christ is the occult. It is blasphemous, and from such you should run for your lives.

Can you imagine Jesus healing a deaf person and making a show of it before a large crowd? "Can you hear me now?" Jesus asks repeatedly, lowering His voice each time until He is merely whispering so that the crowd will be amazed at His healing ability. Jesus would never do that, but we see it on television all the time. How that cheapens the power of Christ. Jesus really healed people and never made a circus out of it; He never called attention to Himself in the process. The church has to be discerning in this day.

This became known both to all Jews and Greeks dwelling in Ephesus; and fear fell on them all, and the name of the Lord Jesus was magnified. And many who had believed came confessing and telling their deeds. Also, many of those who had practiced magic brought their books together and burned them in the sight of all. And they counted up the value of them, and it totaled fifty thousand pieces of silver (vv. 17–19). Books were very expensive in the ancient world. The library of ancient Ephesus is still standing; it is a magnificent edifice that was richly endowed with books. Most of the books that filled that library pertained to the occult, books that promised power over nature and diseases. Yet the people were so stricken in their conscience by the truth of the power of the Holy Spirit that they saw immediately the difference between the real and the counterfeit, and they went and got the books for which they had spent much money and burned them.

Satan does have power. He does not have the power of God, and whatever power he has is forbidden altogether for the Christian. Once we are committed to the things of God, we are to turn our backs completely on the things of darkness and the kingdom of Satan. If you want true power that will edify, come to the power of the cross.

48

RIOT AT EPHESUS

Acts 19:21–41

When these things were accomplished, Paul purposed in the Spirit, when he had passed through Macedonia and Achaia, to go to Jerusalem, saying, "After I have been there, I must also see Rome." So he sent into Macedonia two of those who ministered to him, Timothy and Erastus, but he himself stayed in Asia for a time. And about that time there arose a great commotion about the Way. For a certain man named Demetrius, a silversmith, who made silver shrines of Diana, brought no small profit to the craftsmen. He called them together with the workers of similar occupation, and said: "Men, you know that we have our prosperity by this trade. Moreover you see and hear that not only at Ephesus, but throughout almost all Asia, this Paul has persuaded and turned away many people, saying that they are not gods which are made with hands. So not only is this trade of ours in danger of falling into disrepute, but also the temple of the great goddess Diana may be despised and her magnificence destroyed, whom all Asia and the world worship." Now when they heard this, they were full of wrath and cried out, saying, "Great is Diana of the Ephesians!" So the whole city was filled with confusion, and rushed into the theater with one accord, having seized Gaius and Aristarchus, Macedonians, Paul's travel companions. And when Paul wanted to go in to the people, the disciples would not allow him. Then some of the officials of Asia, who were his friends, sent to him pleading that he would not venture into the theater. Some therefore cried one thing and some another, for the assembly was confused, and most of them did not know why they had come together. And they drew Alexander out of the multitude, the Jews putting him forward. And Alexander motioned with his hand, and wanted to make his defense to the people. But when they found out that he was a Jew, all with one voice cried out for about two hours, "Great is Diana of the Ephesians!" And when the city clerk had quieted the crowd, he said: "Men of Ephesus, what man is there who does not know that the city of the Ephesians is temple guardian of the great goddess Diana, and of the image which fell down from Zeus? Therefore, since these things cannot be denied, you ought to be quiet and do nothing rashly. For you have brought these men here who are neither robbers of temples nor blasphemers of your goddess. Therefore, if Demetrius and his fellow craftsmen have a case against anyone, the courts are open and there are proconsuls. Let them bring charges against one another. But if you have any other inquiry to make, it shall be determined in the lawful assembly. For we are in danger of being called in question for today's uproar, there being no reason which we may give to account for this disorderly gathering." And when he had said these things, he dismissed the assembly.

As we follow in the footsteps of the Apostle Paul during his missionary journeys, we see controversy, hostility, violence, uproar, and dissension spread throughout the land. It is only by the grace of God's protective providence that the Apostle has survived even this long. Throughout his journeys he has been rescued time and time again by the intervention of God. Yet we must understand that the record of Acts, this record of the birth of the church, is, of course, the testimony of the martyrs' blood. It is the testimony of the nature of the church of Jesus Christ as the church militant. We look forward to heaven, where the church on high is called "the church triumphant," but there can be no church triumphant unless there is first a church militant. In our day, with the rigors of political correctness, the idea of confrontation and bold critique of forms of paganism and idolatry are politically incorrect. We have become in many cases, at least in America, the church quiescent as we just stand by and watch our own generation give themselves, as the people of the ancient world did, to idolatry.

Conflict with Idolatry

We see another pattern throughout the book of Acts. When Paul preached the gospel, a conflict always arose from the confrontation between the truth of Christ and the false doctrine of idolatry. John Calvin tells us in the *Institutes* that the heart of every human being is an idol factory, a *fabricum idolarum*. We are by nature inventors, craftsmen who create for ourselves idols as substitutes for the living God. In his letter to the Romans, Paul said that God's wrath is revealed against the whole world, not because there are isolated incidents of idolatry but because the penchant toward idolatry is universal. It is foundational to everyone.

Every human being knows the living God because God has clearly revealed His character to everyone. Yet every person by nature represses that knowledge of the true God and exchanges it for a lie by creating idols as substitutes for the true God (Rom. 1:18–23). That propensity does not end with conversion. That strong drive within us to replace the living God with something more palatable to us remains even in the hearts and minds of the converted. Today we do not fashion idols from stone, but we do fashion idols from ideas.

There was probably no place in the ancient world where this conflict with idolatry was more severe than in Ephesus. The temple of Diana in Ephesus, one of the seven wonders of the ancient world, was four times larger than the Parthenon in Athens. It was constructed of 127 pillars, and each pillar was 60 feet high. The walls of the temple were adorned by the ancient sculptor Praxiteles, the Michelangelo of his time. The grandeur of the temple of Diana was known throughout the entire world. In fact, the cult of religion that focused on Diana, or Artemis, was one of the largest religions of that time worldwide. There were thirty-three shrines to the goddess Diana in the ancient world spread out across different cities. She was a fertility goddess and was also known as the goddess of the hunt. Worshipers built little household shrines in their backyards dedicated to Diana before which they would bow and pray. Additionally, a large economy was established on the worship of Diana.

Naturally, conflict arose when Paul began to preach the uniqueness of Christ. God is not made with hands of wood or stone. How blasphemous to substitute wood and stone for God Himself. The gospel began to expose false religion, as it always does when it is preached clearly, accurately, and boldly. One who got very upset with Paul was the silversmith Demetrius. He gathered together his fellow craftsmen and said, **"Men, you know that we have our prosperity by this trade. Moreover you see and hear that not only at Ephesus, but throughout almost all Asia, this Paul has persuaded and turned away many people, saying that they are not gods which are made with hands. So not only is this trade of ours in danger of falling into disrepute, but also the temple of the great goddess Diana may be despised and her magnificence destroyed, whom all Asia and the world worship"** (vv. 25–27). Paul was undermining their business. The silversmiths made images and souvenirs for visitors who came from all over the world to see this great temple, and outside the temple they had booths for displaying and selling Diana-related paraphernalia.

Demetrius was also concerned that Paul was going to ruin the magnificent reputation that Diana enjoyed throughout the world. Demetrius and his comrades considered themselves temple wardens of this great goddess whose image had supposedly fallen from the sky from the hand of Zeus. In the ancient world, when a meteorite fell to the earth people thought that it was a sign from heaven, and they would see in the figures of these meteorites some kind of form that they could imagine represented a particular deity. Whenever a meteorite fell intact into their laps, they would enshrine it. They saw it as a gift from heaven, and they took responsibility to oversee it. They built a shrine to beat all shrines for the meteorite that fell in Ephesus, as they dedicated the entire temple to the goddess Diana.

Now when they heard this, they were full of wrath and cried out, saying, "Great is Diana of the Ephesians!" (v. 28). It was common in the ancient world to pray and offer praise and honor to a deity with repetitious chants, a practice the New Testament warns us against. Luke tells us that the whole city was filled with confusion and frenzy, and they stormed the theater and seized Paul's traveling companions. Inside the theater the crowd seized Alexander and put him before all the people. **But when they found out that he was a Jew, all with one voice cried out for about two hours, "Great is Diana of the Ephesians!"** (v. 34).

Ancient Ephesus has been greatly reconstructed and much of the old city restored, but the theater needed no restoration because it was carved out of the rock of a mountain in Ephesus on the edge of the city. This amphitheater held 25,000 people, and the structure remains to this day. That is where this incident took place. The disciples of Paul were brought into this theater, and the mob screamed for their blood, yelling and screaming for two hours.

But again an intervention came, just as had happened in Corinth, at the hands of the local magistrates. The proconsul came forward represented by the city clerk, and he quieted the crowd and said, **"Men of Ephesus, what man is there who does not know that the city of the Ephesians is temple guardian of the great goddess Diana, and of the image which fell down from Zeus? Therefore, since these things cannot be denied, you ought to be quiet and do nothing rashly"** (vv. 35–36). The clerk said that the whole world knew about Diana, so a few preachers were not going to be able to destroy that religion by a couple of sermons. He counseled the crowd to allow Demetrius and the silversmiths to make their complaint legally, in open court, where reasonable defenses could be given. He told the mob to disband, and once again the preaching of the gospel was able to continue.

Religion Collision

That is not always the way it turns out. Many times, those who dare to preach in such environments pay for it with their lives. That is happening today all over the world. We see every night on television what happens when world religions collide, and the conclusion is that religion divides so we do not want to be associated with that. "Jesus is the Prince of peace," we say, "so we should seek to be at peace with all people." We have to remember that our Lord said, "Do not think that I came to bring peace on earth. I did not come to bring peace but a sword" (Matt. 10:34). The sword Jesus had in mind wasn't the sword of Islamic jihad. Jesus said, "For I have come to 'set a man against his father, a daughter against her mother, and a daughter-in-law against her mother-in-law'" (Matt. 10:35). What is at stake with respect to Christianity is not religion; it is human life—human life as defined by the Creator of human life. At stake is truth that is rooted and grounded in the character of God himself, which is worth dying for.

We claim to love peace and personal rights, but how will that hold up on the day of judgment? We sit back and allow millions of unborn babies to be destroyed in the wombs of women in the name of freedom and personal preference. Why aren't we being killed in fighting against that? That is what God will ask us on judgment day. No woman has been given a right by God to do what is wrong, and no human being has ever been given the right by God to murder another human being. A woman's rights end where a baby's rights begin. For two thousand years, the Christian church has been monolithic on this point. There was no debate or dissension. One of the most basic principles of Christianity is the sanctity of human life, yet we have been willing to see that traded in for the sanctity of human peace and comfort. That is why we are not being dragged into the amphitheater. Nobody is yelling at us, because they do not have any reason to. That is not right, and we should be willing to be completely dedicated to the truth of God for the welfare of people, not for religion. The truth of God is for you, and it is for your neighbor. It is for the unbeliever down the street who breathes every breath of life by the grace of God. When God's sanctity is besmirched, human sanctity goes with it.

We are living not just in a post-Christian or neo-pagan era; we are also living in a neo-barbarian culture. It is every bit as barbarian as it was in Asia Minor when Paul took the gospel there in his day. That is why we need Christians today who are sold out, who believe the Christian faith and are committed to the truth of Christ and will say, "Great is Jesus of Nazareth, the son of God!" and compromise that with no one.

49

THE MINISTRY OF TROAS

Acts 20:1–12

⟨⟨⟨⟨⟩⟩⟩⟩

After the uproar had ceased, Paul called the disciples to himself, embraced them, and departed to go to Macedonia. Now when he had gone over that region and encouraged them with many words, he came to Greece and stayed three months. And when the Jews plotted against him as he was about to sail to Syria, he decided to return through Macedonia. And Sopater of Berea accompanied him to Asia—also Aristarchus and Secundus of the Thessalonians, and Gaius of Derbe, and Timothy, and Tychicus and Trophimus of Asia. These men, going ahead, waited for us at Troas. But we sailed away from Philippi after the Days of Unleavened Bread, and in five days joined them at Troas, where we stayed seven days. Now on the first day of the week, when the disciples came together to break bread, Paul, ready to depart the next day, spoke to them and continued his message until midnight. There were many lamps in the upper room where they were gathered together. And in a window sat a certain young man named Eutychus, who was sinking into a deep sleep. He was overcome by sleep; and as Paul continued speaking, he fell down from the third story and was taken up dead. But Paul went down, fell on him, and embracing him said, "Do not trouble yourselves, for his life is in him." Now when he had come up, had broken bread and eaten, and talked a long while, even till daybreak, he departed. And they brought the young man in alive, and they were not a little comforted.

S eventh-day Adventists assemble for worship on Saturday. They hold to the conviction that the true Sabbath is that which God established in creation on the seventh day of the week. The Jewish nation has held to that throughout its history, and there are many Christians who believe that the Sabbath remains the seventh day of the week rather than the first day of the week. Those who hold to it believe that the church is in violation of the law of God by worshiping on Sunday rather than on Saturday. It would take nothing less than the Word of God to authenticate a shift in the day by which Christians assemble for worship, and that Word was delivered historically through God's prophets in the Old Testament and through His Apostles in the New Testament. Is there an apostolic sanction for changing the day of solemn assembly from Saturday to Sunday?

The term *sabbath* means "seventh," not so much "seventh in a series" but "seventh in a sequence." According to the Hebrew concept, the day could be Wednesday or Thursday just as easily. In the Old Testament the seventh day that was observed was Saturday. However, Justin Martyr noted that by the early decades of the second century, the practice of Christians meeting weekly occurred on Sunday rather than Saturday. This was virtually universal in every city and village. The question is whether this was second-century innovation, unwarranted in the departure from the biblical mandate, or whether it was established by the first-century church with apostolic warrant.

The Lord's Day

We come to this in Acts 20. **Now on the first day of the week [Sunday], when the disciples came together to break bread, Paul, ready to depart the next day, spoke to them and continued his message until midnight** (v. 7). Throughout the New Testament we see that the early Christian church came together weekly to celebrate the breaking of bread and the sacrament of the Lord's Supper. This breaking of bread and celebration of the Lord's Supper were at the heart of the regular corporate worship of the Christian community. The church came together on Sunday because at the heart of the new covenant was the celebration of the resurrection of Jesus. Sunday was known from the beginning as the Lord's Day. So here we see in apostolic time the church coming together for the preaching of the Word and the celebrating of the sacrament on the first day of the week.

This gathering on Sunday did not necessarily preclude their also observing the Jewish Sabbath on Saturday. We have observed that as Paul went from place to place to proclaim the gospel, he went first into the synagogue. There was no clear, decisive, immediate break between the Christian community and the

Jewish community. In Corinth, the magistrates gave Paul a certain amount of freedom because Judaism was protected under Roman law. Since the Christian community was seen as a subset of Judaism, certain rights and privileges were accorded to Christians.

All that had changed by the end of the first century. The watershed moment in church history was A.D. 70, when the judgment of God fell upon Israel. Jesus had warned the Jews time after time that the stone that the builders had rejected was to be the cornerstone of the new covenant. And in A.D. 70 Jerusalem was destroyed by the Roman armies, and the temple was destroyed as well. The Jews fled from Jerusalem and dispersed to nations all over the world. After that momentous occasion, the Christian community had a clearly separate identity from the Jewish religion. Yet even before A.D. 70 we see the Christians coming together to worship and to celebrate the Lord's Supper on the first day of the week.

On this occasion Luke tells us that Paul had taken his leave from the Ephesian Christians and had traveled to Troas. On the first day of the week the disciples came together to break bread. Paul, being ready to depart the next day, spoke to them and continued his message until midnight. Paul's message was interrupted, and they celebrated the sacrament; then he resumed his preaching until daybreak. This was the way the church was committed to worship and to learning in the early days.

Sleepy Saints

Luke gives us this detail: **There were many lamps in the upper room where they were gathered together** (v. 8). The lamps were basically torches used to illumine the room so that people could see. The burning lamps, along with the people, used a lot of oxygen. As a result, a man named Eutychus was seated at a window, probably seeking a greater source of fresh air. The word *window* today usually refers to panes of glass that start three or four feet off the floor and then continue upward. We use windows so that we can see outside. However, windows originally got their name because they were wind doors. They were a means of allowing fresh air into a building. Therefore, the windows of antiquity began at floor level and went up very high. Poor Eutychus was sitting on the edge of the window. The torches were sucking out the oxygen as Paul preached, and Eutychus grew sleepy. He finally nodded off and fell out the window, and when he hit the ground three floors below, he was dead.

When someone in the congregation falls asleep during the sermon, the preacher sees it. It is understandable when the ill or the elderly fall asleep during the service. However, if you are healthy and youthful, there are two things you should know. First, if you fall off your chair and break your neck and die, the best the preacher can do for you is call the undertaker. Preachers today do not have powers that the Apostle Paul had. Second, and more serious, is the implication of nodding off when God's Word is being proclaimed. Why does the mind begin to engage in woolgathering? That rarely happens when we attend football games or other events attended with great excitement.

John Calvin, in his great work on prayer, talked about how we as sinners are prone to fall asleep, even while we are praying. We fall asleep not only when we listen to the Word of God but when we speak directly to Him. Once when I was a guest at the home of some friends, I dozed off while my host was talking. Thirty-five years later I am still teased about it because it was so offensive and insulting. What are we communicating when we fall asleep when someone is speaking to us? We are saying that we really are not interested in what the other has to say. Calvin said this is our lot as sinners, that we fall asleep even while having a conversation with Almighty God.

There is something difficult about listening to someone speak for a lengthy time. It can become almost hypnotic and force us into dreamland. It happens from time to time, and surely preachers own some of the responsibility for it, but if you are prone to fall asleep on a regular basis when the Word of God is being preached, you need to ask yourself why you are so disinterested in the things of God that, when you hear them, they put you to sleep. Is the Word of God so boring that your only recourse is to flee to the arms of Morpheus and enter into dreamland? If that is the case, you need to ask yourself about the state of your soul.

A Great Awakening

It is no accident that the greatest revival that ever came to America came to New England in the eighteenth century under the preaching of John Wesley and George Whitefield and Jonathan Edwards. That revival was called the Great Awakening. Souls that had been dormant, in slumber for years and years, were suddenly made alive. We are awakened by the power of God, and when that awakening comes to pass in our souls, the things of God can never again be boring to us because they are the stuff of which life is formed and made mature.

Some sit in church for a lifetime and are never awakened by the power of the Holy Spirit. They are like fetuses carried for several months in a mother's womb that afterward are stillborn. God forbid that we should arrive at the end of our lives spiritually stillborn. The Word of God is designed to wake us up. The Word of God is that which brings life to the soul, now and forevermore. That is why we should hunger and thirst as Christians to hear every word that comes from the mouth of God.

When Eutychus fell out the window and broke his neck and died, Paul ran downstairs and, like Elisha in the Old Testament, embraced him and raised him from the dead. Then Paul continued to preach until dawn. **And they brought the young man in alive, and they were not a little comforted** (v. 12). What Paul did brought great comfort to the people there. God again authenticated His Apostle by using him as His instrument to raise this man from the dead.

50

MESSAGE TO THE ELDERS

Acts 20:17–38

From Miletus he sent to Ephesus and called for the elders of the church. And when they had come to him, he said to them: "You know, from the first day that I came to Asia, in what manner I always lived among you, serving the Lord with all humility, with many tears and trials which happened to me by the plotting of the Jews; how I kept back nothing that was helpful, but proclaimed it to you, and taught you publicly and from house to house, testifying to Jews, and also to Greeks, repentance toward God and faith toward our Lord Jesus Christ. And see, now I go bound in the spirit to Jerusalem, not knowing the things that will happen to me there, except that the Holy Spirit testifies in every city, saying that chains and tribulations await me. But none of these things move me; nor do I count my life dear to myself, so that I may finish my race with joy, and the ministry which I received from the Lord Jesus, to testify to the gospel of the grace of God. "And indeed, now I know that you all, among whom I have gone preaching the kingdom of God, will see my face no more. Therefore I testify to you this day that I am innocent of the blood of all men. For I have not shunned to declare to you the whole counsel of God. Therefore take heed to yourselves and to all the flock, among which the Holy Spirit has made you overseers, to shepherd the church of God which He purchased with His own blood. For I know this, that after my departure savage wolves will come in among you, not sparing the flock. Also from among yourselves men will rise up. speaking perverse things, to draw away the disciples after themselves. Therefore watch, and remember that for three years I did not cease to warn everyone night and day with tears. "So now, brethren, I commend you to God and to the word of His grace, which is able to build you up and give you an inheritance among all those who are sanctified. I have coveted no one's silver or gold or apparel. Yes, you yourselves know that these hands have provided for my necessities, and for those who were with me. I have shown you in every way, by laboring like this, that you must support the weak. And remember the words of the Lord Jesus, that He said, 'It is more blessed to give than to receive.'" And when he had said these things, he knelt down and prayed with them all. Then they all wept freely, and fell on Paul's neck and kissed him, sorrowing most of all for the words which he spoke, that they would see his face no more. And they accompanied him to the ship.

After Paul left Ephesus, he made his way by ship ultimately toward Jerusalem. The ship pulled into Miletus for a few days, which was thirty miles south of Ephesus. While Paul had this brief layover, he sent messengers to Ephesus asking that those who had been consecrated as elders in that church would come and meet with him in Miletus, and when they arrived, he gave the discourse in the passage before us now.

This discourse occurs in one of those "we" passages found in the book of Acts in which Luke, the author of Acts, includes himself in the narrative. On this occasion Luke had been present, so he was writing directly from what he heard on the shores of Miletus. Also, this is the only one of Paul's sermons in Acts that was delivered to Christians. All the rest of his sermons were preached to Jews, to Greeks, or to the authorities, but here we have a sermon given specifically to believers.

Elders

From Miletus he sent to Ephesus and called for the elders of the church (v. 17). Paul called for the elders of the church; that is, he called for the *presbuteroi*, which is the Greek word translated as "elders." This immediately raises the question of what the New Testament teaches about the structure of church government. Some today follow a Presbyterian system of government, which means "rule by elders." St. Andrew's holds to that form of government, not by way of denominational affiliation but by eldership. That is what it means to be Presbyterian. Other churches are governed by bishops, such as Episcopal and Methodist churches. The Catholic Church is governed by mono-episcopacy, which means that in addition to bishops there are also cardinals, and ultimately, at the top, the vicar of Christ on earth, the pope of Rome. Other churches are ruled by the congregation as a whole. Why are some congregational whereas others are Presbyterian, or Episcopal, or mono-Episcopal? All seek to follow the way in which the church was established biblically, and yet there are these ongoing disagreements among Christians, as they search the Scriptures to try to find out the pattern of church government.

The elders whom Paul assembled here at Miletus were not what we call "ruling elders"; they were teaching elders, described here as pastors who had been left behind. In the early church, the church was ruled by Apostles, but those Apostles transferred authority to the next generation by ordaining men whom they called to be pastors and shepherds of the flock, which is what these elders were. The English text here is problematic. There is absolutely no grammatical or theological justification for the English translation. At the beginning of this text Paul speaks about assembled elders. Later on, he calls them to pay attention to the tasks to which they have been delivered as guardians and shepherds of the flock. The English translations have "guardians" or "overseers" or "shepherds" of the flock, when the word in Greek is *episcopos*, the very word from which we get the word *Episcopalian*, which everywhere else in the Bible is translated by the English word "bishop." The difficulty of discerning the biblical structure of church government occurs because in the same context Paul calls those assembled here "elders" and "bishops," indicating that, at least at that stage in church history, the titles "elder" and "bishop" were used interchangeably. Both called attention to the same function, which is most clearly seen if we examine the word *episcopos*.

The root word *scope* simply has to do with vision, but an *episcopos* or *episcopas* is some particular kind of scope. The prefix *epi-* simply takes the root word scope and intensifies it. So the task of the bishop is to look at things with intense care. That is why Paul reminded the elders, who were also the bishops of the flock in Ephesus, to pay close attention to the welfare of those congregations that were by then many throughout the Asia Minor region.

Paul told them that he was leaving Asia Minor. He had completed his missionary activity there and was entrusting the future of the church at Ephesus to the bishops and elders, the pastors and shepherds of the people there, and he gave them various instructions. At this time, Paul's heart was heavy, as were the hearts of all assembled, because they recognized this as Paul's farewell address. It is amazing how many parallels there are between Paul's message here to the Ephesians and Jesus' message in the upper room to His disciples when He announced that in just a short while they would see Him no more although His departure would ultimately be to their benefit. In that regard, Paul echoed those words of Christ to His disciples.

Paul's Defense

The first part of Paul's sermon here is a defense of his ministry. **"You know, from the first day that I came to Asia, in what manner I always lived among**

you, serving the Lord with all humility, with many tears and trials" (vv. 18–19). That was Paul's record. To the Corinthian congregation he wrote that he had been with them in tears, in their sufferings and afflictions (2 Cor. 2:4). Paul did not go to people simply as a scholar instructing them in theology; his heart was with them. He wept and prayed with them and endured all manner of attacks and suffering from hostile hands for their sakes.

"I kept back nothing that was helpful, but proclaimed it to you, and taught you publicly and from house to house, testifying to Jews, and also to Greeks, repentance toward God and faith toward our Lord Jesus Christ" (vv. 20–21), and a few moments later he said, **"I have not shunned to declare to you the whole counsel of God"** (v. 27). I worry that when I stand before Christ at His judgment seat, He is going to say, "R.C. what did you keep back? What were you afraid to preach? How much of My counsel did you declare to the people under your care? It was your task when I consecrated you to hold nothing back, to proclaim the whole counsel of God." I try to be sure to hold nothing back by doing expository preaching, the setting forth of the text of Scripture. Expository preaching puts inhibitions on the pastor from riding his own hobbyhorse, and it has its foundation in apostolic preaching. Paul preached it all. He didn't just preach the love of God. He also preached God's mercy, grace, and wrath. He called people to repentance.

Paul reminded them how he had acted as their pastor over the years, and then he said, **"Now I go bound in the spirit to Jerusalem, not knowing the things that will happen to me there, except that the Holy Spirit testifies in every city, saying that chains and tribulations await me"** (vv. 22–23). This reminds us of a conversation Jesus had with His disciples:

> From that time Jesus began to show to His disciples that He must go to Jerusalem, and suffer many things from the elders and chief priests and scribes, and be killed, and be raised the third day. Then Peter took Him aside and began to rebuke Him, saying, "Far be it from You, Lord; this shall not happen to You!" But He turned and said to Peter, "Get behind Me, Satan! You are an offense to Me, for you are not mindful of the things of God, but the things of men." (Matt. 16:21–23)

Similarly, the Apostle Paul knew that he had been called to fill up what was lacking in the ministry of Christ in his own body and to be prepared to pour out his life on behalf of the gospel. He knew what was ahead of him, not all the details but that it would involve suffering and death.

"But none of these things move me; nor do I count my life dear to myself, so that I may finish my race with joy, and the ministry which I received

from the Lord Jesus, to testify to the gospel of the grace of God" (v. 24). The Apostle was telling his friends that he was not afraid. What lay ahead of him was his call. It is what the Lord Jesus Christ had set him aside to do. Paul did not guard his life. I cannot say that. I guard my life. I do not volunteer to go to Jerusalem in chains to be beheaded. I worry when people get hostile, but not the Apostle. What mattered to him was finishing the race. Paul found joy in doing what the Lord had set before him to do.

That calls attention to Paul's last statements to Timothy: "For I am already being poured out as a drink offering, and the time of my departure is at hand. I have fought the good fight, I have finished the race, I have kept the faith" (2 Tim. 4:6–7). What a man the Apostle Paul was. All he cared about was completing the course. We sing, "Let goods and kindred go, this mortal life also," and that passion beats in the heart of every godly person. **"And indeed, now I know that you all, among whom I have gone preaching the kingdom of God, will see my face no more. Therefore I testify to you this day that I am innocent of the blood of all men"** (vv. 25–26).

Sheep and Wolves

Then Paul said, **"Therefore take heed to yourselves and to all the flock, among which the Holy Spirit has made you overseers, to shepherd the church of God which He purchased with His own blood"** (v. 28). The church is God's. He bought it, not with silver and gold but with the blood price of his own life. **"For I know this, that after my departure savage wolves will come in among you, not sparing the flock. Also from among yourselves men will rise up, speaking perverse things, to draw away the disciples after themselves. Therefore watch, and remember that for three years I did not cease to warn everyone night and day with tears"** (vv. 29–31). Harvard, Princeton, Yale—the most prestigious secular universities in America were started as evangelical Christian seminaries, totally committed to the inerrancy of sacred Scripture. Those who hold that view today need safe-conduct passage to walk on those campuses. If a Christian institution lasts fifty years in its commitment to the Scriptures, that is an extraordinary thing. At the request of the session, I have drawn up a list of nonnegotiable qualifications for future pastors of St. Andrew's, but as tight as I draw that list, it will not be enough to keep ravenous wolves dressed in sheep's clothing from invading this church and corrupting its mission at some time in the future. It happens again and again.

Paul was not concerned about sheep dressed in wolves' clothing but about wolves dressed as sheep. In this concern he echoed Jesus, who warned, "Beware of false prophets, who come to you in sheep's clothing, but inwardly they are ravenous wolves" (Matt. 7:15). The secular people are not the concern. We know where they stand. It is the clergy who have to be watched. It has always been the clergy. The greatest threat to the nation of Israel was not the Philistines or the Syrians or the Babylonians but the false prophets in the midst of the people who took the truth of God and twisted it and distorted it and carried away the people to idolatry. Jesus' greatest enemies were the clergy of his day, the Pharisees and the Sadducees. Church history bears witness to the fact that those who bring unbelief into the church are not the secular professors; they are the seminary professors who deny the resurrection and the cross and train ministers of a new generation to deny the very essence of biblical truth. The church lives out the drama of *Little Red Riding Hood* every day.

When Paul wrote to Timothy while he was in jail awaiting his execution, he said, "Demas has forsaken me, having loved this present world, and has departed for Thessalonica—Crescens for Galatia, Titus for Dalmatia. Only Luke is with me" (2 Tim. 4:9–11). What a temptation that is, that we start loving this world more than the things of God. Where were the Ephesians? Paul was all alone. Later, we hear Jesus instructing John to write to the seven churches of Asia Minor. Included among that list is the church at Ephesus. The Lord Jesus rebuked that church for leaving its first love (Rev. 2:4). In spite of that message, the wolves came and devoured the sheep, and the Ephesian church was corrupted.

Blessed to Give

Nevertheless, in the second century Ignatius wrote that later there was a revival, and the Ephesian church was restored. That is rare in the history of Christianity, but it happened at Ephesus. Perhaps it was because, under the direction of the Holy Spirit, these words were preserved in sacred Scripture: **"So now, brethren, I commend you to God and to the word of His grace, which is able to build you up and give you an inheritance among all those who are sanctified. I have coveted no one's silver or gold or apparel. Yes, you yourselves know that these hands have provided for my necessities, and for those who were with me. I have shown you in every way, by laboring like this, that you must support the weak. And remember the words of the Lord Jesus, that He said, 'It is more blessed to give than to receive'"** (vv. 32–35). These words of the Lord are found nowhere in the Gospels. Paul was aware of one of the *logia*, a saying of Jesus' that had been preserved in the early church but not included in the Gospels. The people were obviously aware of these words already since Paul told them to remember.

And when he had said these things, he knelt down and prayed with them all. Then they all wept freely, and fell on Paul's neck and kissed him, sorrowing

most of all for the words which he spoke, that they would see his face no more. And they accompanied him to the ship (vv. 36–38). As the disciples stood on the Mount of Transfiguration, gazing into heaven, watching the ascended Christ leave this earth, so they stood on the shores of Miletus and watched the ship depart, knowing they would never again in this world see the face of the beloved Apostle who had given them their greatest treasure, the word of God. May we see that Word with the same love and passion that they did.

51

THY WILL BE DONE

Acts 21:1–14

Now it came to pass, that when we had departed from them and set sail, running a straight course we came to Cos, the following day to Rhodes, and from there to Patara. And finding a ship sailing over to Phoenicia, we went aboard and set sail. When we had sighted Cyprus, we passed it on the left, sailed to Syria, and landed at Tyre; for there the ship was to unload her cargo. And finding disciples, we stayed there seven days. They told Paul through the Spirit not to go up to Jerusalem. When we had come to the end of those days, we departed and went on our way; and they all accompanied us, with wives and children, till we were out of the city. And we knelt down on the shore and prayed. When we had taken our leave of one another, we boarded the ship, and they returned home. And when we had finished our voyage from Tyre, we came to Ptolemais, greeted the brethren, and stayed with them one day. On the next day we who were Paul's companions departed and came to Caesarea, and entered the house of Philip the evangelist, who was one of the seven, and stayed with him. Now this man had four virgin daughters who prophesied. And as we stayed many days, a certain prophet named Agabus came down from Judea. When he had come to us, he took Paul's belt, bound his own hands and feet, and said, "Thus says the Holy Spirit, 'So shall the Jews at Jerusalem bind the man who owns this belt, and deliver him into the hands of the Gentiles. Now when we heard these things, both we and those from that place pleaded with him not to go up to Jerusalem. Then Paul answered, "What do you mean by weeping and breaking my heart? For I am ready not only to be bound, but also to die at Jerusalem for the name of the Lord Jesus." So when he would not be persuaded, we ceased, saying, "The will of the Lord be done."

A s Luke tells of points of transition from one city to another during the apostolic missionary journeys, he gives a brief travelogue, citing the places that are visited or passed during this trip. Chapter 21 is no different, as he tells how the apostolic entourage made its way from Miletus down to Caesarea. They began their journey on a small ship, which was called a coasting ship because it was not sufficiently large or strong to be sailed in the open seas. Coasting ships hugged the coast, staying very close to the shore as they made their way along. While they were on such a vessel, they stopped at Cos, a city that housed one of the most prestigious medical schools in the ancient world. It was the school founded by Hippocrates, from whom we get the name of the Hippocratic Oath.

From Cos they went on to Rhodes, where the Colossus of Rhodes, one of the seven wonders of the ancient world, was located. By the time Paul made his way to Rhodes, the Colossus was not so colossal anymore, because an earthquake had brought it crashing down into many pieces. From there, they traveled on to Patara, where there lived an oracle who had some degree of rivalry with the famous Oracle of Delphi. They finally boarded a seagoing vessel loaded with cargo and sailed down to Phoenicia. They sighted Cyprus on the way, sailing to Syria and landing at Tyre. We are told that there the ship would unload her cargo. Finding disciples, they remained there seven days, and Luke notes that they told Paul through the Spirit not to go up to Jerusalem. After seven days they left after praying with the believers and their families, and they boarded a ship and returned home. When they had finished their voyage from Tyre, they came to Ptolemais, where they stayed one day.

On the next day we who were Paul's companions departed and came to Caesarea, and entered the house of Philip the evangelist, who was one of the seven, and stayed with him (v. 8). We met Philip back in Acts 8. He was one of those set apart and used of God for outreach and missions. He had traveled on his journeys to Caesarea, and there he settled. Twenty years had elapsed since the time of his consecration. Paul and Luke and their party met up with Philip and surely had a wonderful time hearing all that had transpired among the Christians there in Caesarea.

Luke tells us that in that interim Philip and his wife had had four daughters who had grown up and remained unmarried, and all four had the gift of prophecy. At least three of those daughters lived into their nineties and became a rich source of information for the early church fathers, who wanted to research everything that had transpired in the apostolic church. The church historian Papias and also Eusebius make mention of these daughters from whom they gleaned wonderful information from the past.

Polycarp, the bishop of Smyrna who was martyred in his late eighties, reminisced in his old age. As a boy, Polycarp had been taught in Ephesus by the Apostle John when John was an old man. This is how these traditions were passed on from generation to generation, the ultimate tradition of which the New Testament speaks, the *paradisus*, the tradition of God and the Apostles. We benefit from it every day in the Scriptures, because the Scriptures contain the inspired record of the divine apostolic tradition. Even to this day we are indebted to the daughters of Philip, who were gifted with prophecy.

The Prophecy of Agabus

And as we stayed many days, a certain prophet named Agabus came down from Judea (v. 10). We met Agabus earlier in the book of Acts as well. He came down from Judea. **When he had come to us, he took Paul's belt, bound his own hands and feet, and said, "Thus says the Holy Spirit, 'So shall the Jews at Jerusalem bind the man who owns this belt, and deliver him into the hands of the Gentiles'"** (v. 11). Agabus at that moment was following a tradition rich in Old Testament history. Even in the New Testament, prophets not only delivered the oracles of God with their lips but with object lessons, dramatizing the word God had given to them. In the Old Testament Ahijah tore his garments, symbolizing that the united kingdom of Israel would be torn asunder with the death of Solomon. Isaiah shocked everybody when he became the first-recorded streaker in biblical history. He took all his clothes off, including his sandals, and walked down the street barefoot, giving the message of how God was going to deal with the Egyptians. He would strip them naked and humiliate them and drive them away. Ezekiel built a replica of Jerusalem and used it to show the people what God was going to do when He visited His wrath upon the city.

In the revolution of worship that we have seen over the past century, skits are performed at church services on Sunday mornings. Someone has pointed out that if we want visible drama in church on Sunday morning, why not use the drama that our Lord himself gave in the institution of the sacraments of baptism and the Lord's Supper? In those sacraments we not only hear the Word of God, but we see it, and we act out the drama that was won for us in Christ, in which Jesus said, "Do this in remembrance of Me" (Luke 22:19). Agabus used drama to show as well as to speak the divine word. In this case, the word is ominous. It was not an oracle of weal but of woe. After hearing this, Luke was inspired to include a record of his own shame: **Now when we heard these things, both we and those from that place pleaded with him not to go up to Jerusalem**

(v. 12). Luke confesses that when Agabus gave this prophecy, they pleaded with Paul not to go up to Jerusalem.

On December 7, 1941, the United States of America was attacked, and war was declared the following day by the president of the United States, who said that that date would live forever as a day of infamy. On December 8, 1941, the recruiting office of the United States military had the highest number of volunteers in American history. At that time my father was too old to be drafted, so he was asked to chair our local draft board, which job he accepted. After a few months of making decisions as to which men would go to war and which would not, he shocked everybody in our house when one day he appeared at the back door of the kitchen dressed in an Army uniform. He said to my mother, "Honey, there is no way I could keep sending those kids to war and not go myself. I am constrained to go." My mother cried and asked him not to go. It is interesting that when people are called to do their duty, and when that duty involves danger and peril and risk, it is their closest friends and family who inevitably try to talk them out of it. People who should be supporting those who are seeking to do their duty become impediments to it. Think of Jesus, who told the disciples that He was going to suffer and die. Peter said, "Far be it from You, Lord; this shall not happen to You!" (Matt. 16:22). Jesus, who had just given Peter the name *Petras*, "rock," then gave him another name: "Get behind Me, Satan! You are an offense to Me, for you are not mindful of the things of God, but the things of men" (Matt. 16:23).

I became a Christian during my freshman year in college. I was filled with zeal. I met regularly with Christians for prayer and Bible study and hymn singing. When we sang, my soul was flooded with joy. My eyes would mist over and fill with tears as I sang, "Where He leads me, I will follow. I can hear my Savior calling." When I sang that, I meant it. Of course, then I matured in the Christian faith and found out that some places are far less desirable than others. Many times in my life I have said, "Most of the places that you lead me, Lord, I'll follow, but please don't lead me over there." If the Lord came and asked you to go somewhere with little or no appeal, how soon would you pack? Would you pack your bags filled with joy in your soul that He asked you to go for Him? Paul had a vocation, and he knew what lay ahead.

Ready to Die

Then Paul answered, "What do you mean by weeping and breaking my heart? For I am ready not only to be bound, but also to die at Jerusalem for the name of the Lord Jesus" (v. 13). Back on the shores of Miletus, Paul had said, "I go bound in the spirit to Jerusalem, not knowing the things that will happen to me there, except that the Holy Spirit testifies in every city, saying that chains and tribulations await me" (Acts 20:22–23). Agabus's prophecy wasn't news to the Apostle, and he was distressed by the others' reaction to it. He was trying to be faithful to his vocation, but his friends were standing in the way. Paul was ready. He had been ready since that day in the desert when Christ had called him. That day on the road to Damascus, he said to Jesus, "Lord, what do You want me to do?" (Acts 9:6).

So when he would not be persuaded, we ceased, saying, "The will of the Lord be done" (v. 14). That was a profound theological insight. Of course, the will of the Lord was going to be done, and Paul knew that, just as Jesus knew the will of God when He wrestled in the garden and prayed, "Take this cup away from Me; nevertheless not My will, but Yours, be done" (Luke 22:42). The original author of "Where He Leads Me, I Will Follow" was Jesus. Wherever You send Me, Father, I will go. Whatever cup You give Me, I will drink, for My meat and My drink is to do the will of the Father. It is as if Paul said to them, "Do you hear it? I can hear my Savior calling from Jerusalem, and where He leads me, I will follow." May we all be true to our vocation, whatever it costs us, wherever it takes us, that we may be ready to run the race until it is over.

52

PAUL'S ARREST IN JERUSALEM

Acts 21:23–40

"Therefore do what we tell you: We have four men who have taken a vow. Take them and be purified with them, and pay their expenses so that they may shave their heads, and that all may know that those things of which they were informed concerning you are nothing, but that you yourself also walk orderly and keep the law. But concerning the Gentiles who believe, we have written and decided that they should observe no such thing, except that they should keep themselves from things offered to idols, from blood, from things strangled, and from sexual immorality." Then Paul took the men, and the next day, having been purified with them, entered the temple to announce the expiration of the days of purification, at which time an offering should be made for each one of them. Now when the seven days were almost ended, the Jews from Asia, seeing him in the temple, stirred up the whole crowd and laid hands on him, crying out, "Men of Israel, help! This is the man who teaches all men everywhere against the people, the law, and this place; and furthermore he also brought Greeks into the temple and has defiled this holy place." (For they had previously seen Trophimus the Ephesian with him in the city, whom they supposed that Paul had brought into the temple.) And all the city was disturbed; and the people ran together, seized Paul, and dragged him out of the temple; and immediately the doors were shut. Now as they were seeking to kill him, news came to the commander of the garrison that all Jerusalem was in an uproar. He immediately took soldiers and centurions, and ran down to them. And when they saw the commander and the soldiers, they stopped beating Paul. Then the commander came near and took him, and commanded him to be bound with two chains; and he asked who he was and what he had done. And some among the multitude cried one thing and some another. So when he could not ascertain the truth because of the tumult, he commanded him to be taken into the barracks. When he reached the stairs, he had to be carried by the soldiers because of the violence of the mob. For the multitude of the people followed after, crying out, "Away with him!" Then as Paul was about to be led into the barracks, he said to the commander, "May I speak to you?" He replied, "Can you speak Greek? Are you not the Egyptian who some time ago stirred up a rebellion and led the four thousand assassins out into the wilderness?" But Paul said, "I am a Jew from Tarsus, in Cilicia, a citizen of no mean city; and I implore you, permit me to speak to the people." So when he had given him permission, Paul stood on the stairs and motioned with his hand to the people. And when there was a great silence, he spoke to them in the Hebrew language.

Accelerated crisis" is a literary device commonly used by writers of fiction, particularly in mystery or adventure novels. The protagonist is faced with a severe crisis from which there seems to be no possible way of escape. This technique was used in old film serials such as *The Perils of Pauline*. A damsel tied to the railroad tracks had no hope of escape as a fast-moving train bore down upon her. At that moment, the screen would fade to black with an invitation to tune in next week to see what happened. Inevitably there was a literary *deus ex machina*, a device by which the hero or heroine was miraculously rescued from certain destruction. A short time later, however, the hero or heroine fell into an even greater crisis. In creating an accelerated crisis, a writer plays with the emotions of the reader as the hero or heroine goes from the frying pan into the fire.

We could easily think that this literary device had been invented by Luke when he wrote the history of Paul's missionary journeys. From place to place, Paul faced one crisis after another. He was beaten with rods in one town and stoned in another. In still another he was cast into prison. He always managed somehow to escape at the last possible second, only to go to the next town and find himself in a worse crisis than before. Paul had just been warned by the prophet Agabus not to go to Jerusalem because chains and imprisonment awaited him there. Paul refused to be persuaded by these dire warnings, and, like Jesus before him, he set his face as a flint to go.

Paul in Jerusalem

Agabus was right. Paul came to Jerusalem, and what happened is something that typically takes place in the lives of great heroes. Earlier in Acts 21 we see that Paul did go up to Jerusalem. Some of the disciples from Caesarea went along and brought with them Mnason of Cyprus, an early disciple, with whom they were to lodge. Luke writes that when they arrived in Jerusalem, the brethren received them gladly. The next day, Paul and his entourage went and visited James, presumably James the brother of Jesus, and the elders of the community and gave an account of all that had taken place on the missionary journeys. The Jewish Christians, who now numbered in the thousands, were beside themselves with joy, and they began to celebrate for the work God had accomplished through the missionary enterprise of Paul and his comrades.

In the midst of the jubilation, Luke tells us, a rumor had begun to circulate among the Christians from the Jewish community. People were saying that Paul had taught Jewish converts to forget about the law of God, to despise the temple, and to do away with all the sacred traditions and rituals. This was patently false; Paul had told the Gentile converts that they had freedom in adiaphorous matters, issues of indifference. Yet because there was a desire among some in the church to bring Paul down, he was told that he had to deal with these rumors.

"Therefore do what we tell you. We have four men who have taken a vow" (v. 23). These four men had taken a Nazarite vow, which required that they spend thirty days without touching strong drink or wine and let their hair grow. At the end of that thirty days, they would cut their hair and burn it along with the sacrifices, a purification ritual that lasted seven days in accordance with the feast of Pentecost. Thousands of Jews from all over the empire flocked into Jerusalem to celebrate the festival and to go through all of the sacrifices and rites of purification. **Take them and be purified with them, and pay their expenses so that they may shave their heads, and that all may know that those things of which they were informed concerning you are nothing, but that you yourself also walk orderly and keep the law** (v. 24). They wanted Paul to go with these Nazarites and participate in the purification rites and pay for their sacrifices. Paul agreed to go, and he went with the four men and was purified with them in order to stop the mouths of the slanderous critics who were spreading the rumors.

Now when the seven days were almost ended, the Jews from Asia, seeing him in the temple, stirred up the whole crowd and laid hands on him, crying out, "Men of Israel, help! This is the man who teaches all men everywhere against the people, the law, and this place; and furthermore he also brought Greeks into the temple and has defiled this holy place" (vv. 27–28). These Jews were not Christian Jews. They were Jews from Asia Minor who had rejected Paul during his missionary journeys. They were Jews from the Jewish community in Ephesus, the Jews of the Diaspora, who had come close to killing him earlier. Paul had been rescued at the last moment by the civil magistrates there, and then he shipped out and escaped from the clutches of his enemies in Ephesus. Now these Jews had come to Jerusalem to celebrate Pentecost, and as soon as they got to the city they saw Paul. They recognized him immediately. They were infuriated by the presence of Paul in the Holy City. A mob formed, and they grabbed Paul and dragged him violently out of the confines of the temple, which in itself was a violation of Jewish law and of behavior within the holy place.

To make matters worse, they stirred up the rest of the crowd by saying that Paul had taken Trophimus, a Gentile convert, with him into the temple. The temple was constructed so that Gentiles were barred from admittance into certain portions. The Holy of Holies was the inner sanctum where only the high priest could go on the Day of Atonement. Then there was the Holy Place, where only Jews could go. The outer court, or the court of the Gentiles, was the only portion of the temple permitted to Gentiles. At the entrance to the Holy Place there was a sign written in both Greek and Latin warning all who were not Jews from passing that point and entering. Gentiles caught entering the holy place were condemned to execution. Josephus testifies that the Roman occupiers were so careful not to stir up the Jews about their religious conviction that the Romans would carry out the execution of Gentiles who violated this particular sacred principle.

Paul and the Angry Mob

The fact was that Paul had never taken a Gentile into the Holy Place, but we know how rumors circulate. The mob was convinced that Paul had committed the ultimate sacrilege. **And all the city was disturbed, and the people ran together, seized Paul, and dragged him out of the temple; and immediately the doors were shut. Now as they were seeking to kill him, news came to the commander of the garrison that all Jerusalem was in an uproar** (vv. 30–31). Luke gives the impression that if the mob was not interrupted, Paul's life would not last another five minutes.

All the screaming and yelling came to the attention of the commander of the Roman garrison that was housed at the Antonia Fortress in Jerusalem. The Antonia Fortress was adjacent to the temple, connected by some stairways, and it was in that area that Jesus Himself had participated in part of His trial before His execution. The Roman garrison was commanded by a *chiliarchos*, a man in charge of one thousand troops. There were one thousand Roman soldiers at the Antonia Fortress. Seven hundred and sixty were foot soldiers; 240 were cavalry. The commander heard what was going on and got his centurions and their soldiers to rush to the front of the temple to put a stop to the mob. When the people saw the Roman soldiers coming, they stopped beating Paul.

Then the commander came near and took him, and commanded him to be bound with two chains; and he asked who he was and what he had done. And some among the multitude cried one thing and some another. So when he could not ascertain the truth because of the tumult, he commanded him to be taken into the barracks. When he reached the stairs, he had to be carried by the soldiers because of the violence of the mob. For the multitude of the people followed after, crying out, "Away with him!" (vv. 33–36). To get into the safety of the barracks, the soldiers had to surround Paul and carry him over their heads to keep him away from the people who were reaching out to hit him with whatever they had.

When Jesus entered into Jerusalem on Palm Sunday, the Pharisees and the Sadducees required that Jesus' disciples stop the praise. Jesus said, "If these should keep silent, the stones would immediately cry out" (Luke 19:40). Those stones were passive pieces of nature bearing witness to the screams of the crowd shouting, "Crucify him!" In that exact same spot twenty-seven years later, those stones heard the echo of the same words directed at Christ's most gifted Apostle.

Then as Paul was about to be led into the barracks, he said to the commander, "May I speak to you?" (v. 37). The commander came to attention. Before him stood Paul, his hair matted from the blood and gashes on his face, bruised and beaten. The commander was surprised that Paul spoke Greek. A few years prior, an Egyptian had come along and led thousands out into the wilderness in a plot to overthrow the Romans. Could Paul be that man, he wondered? Josephus tells us that a battle ensued where many thousands who followed this Egyptian prophet were killed, but the prophet himself escaped. He was like the Osama bin Laden of the ancient world; they looked everywhere for him with no success.

But Paul said, "I am a Jew from Tarsus, in Cilicia, a citizen of no mean city; and I implore you, permit me to speak to the people" (v. 39). The commander gave Paul permission to speak to the crowd, and he put him on the stairs in front of those who were screaming and yelling for Paul's blood. The power of the Holy Spirit came upon the Apostle, and with a mere gesture of his hand the screaming mob was silenced. What followed is one of the most important defenses of Paul's life and ministry.

53

PAUL'S DEFENSE IN JERUSALEM

Acts 22:1–21

"Brethren and fathers, hear my defense before you now." And when they heard that he spoke to them in the Hebrew language, they kept all the more silent. Then he said: "I am indeed a Jew, born in Tarsus of Cilicia, but brought up in this city at the feet of Gamaliel, taught according to the strictness of our fathers' law, and was zealous toward God as you all are today. I persecuted this Way to the death, binding and delivering into prisons both men and women, as also the high priest bears me witness, and all the council of the elders, from whom I also received letters to the brethren, and went to Damascus to bring in chains even those who were there to Jerusalem to be punished. Now it happened, as I journeyed and came near Damascus at about noon, suddenly a great light from heaven shone around me. And I fell to the ground and heard a voice saying to me, 'Saul, Saul, why are you persecuting Me?' So I answered, 'Who are You, Lord?' And He said to me, 'I am Jesus of Nazareth, whom you are persecuting.' And those who were with me indeed saw the light and were afraid, but they did not hear the voice of Him who spoke to me. So I said, 'What shall I do, Lord? And the Lord said to me, 'Arise and go into Damascus, and there you will be told all things which are appointed for you to do.' And since I could not see for the glory of that light, being led by the hand of those who were with me, I came into Damascus. Then a certain Ananias, a devout man according to the law, having a good testimony with all the Jews who dwelt there, came to me; and he stood and said to me, 'Brother Saul, receive your sight.' And at that same hour I looked up at him. Then he said, 'The God of our fathers has chosen you that you should know His will, and see the Just One, and hear the voice of His mouth. For you will be His witness to all men of what you have seen and heard. And now why are you waiting? Arise and be baptized, and wash away your sins, calling on the name of the Lord.' Now it happened, when I returned to Jerusalem and was praying in the temple, that I was in a trance and saw Him saying to me, 'Make haste and get out of Jerusalem quickly, for they will not receive your testimony concerning Me.' So I said, 'Lord, they know that in every synagogue I imprisoned and beat those who believe on You. And when the blood of Your martyr Stephen was shed, I also was standing by consenting to his death, and guarding the clothes of those who were killing him.' Then He said to me, 'Depart, for I will send you far from here to the Gentiles.'"

The Book of Acts is really quite a short book, so it is extraordinary that a book of this length would repeat the same incident three times. We are told three times of the circumstances of the conversion of Saul of Tarsus on the road to Damascus. The first time, it is a third-person narrative reported to us by Luke. The next two occurrences are Paul's recalling those events in times of his defense, first here in Jerusalem and then before King Herod Agrippa. Why did Luke tell the same story three times? We can only guess at the reason. Luke was a punctilious historian. He is noted as the most accurate historian of all antiquity, and he kept himself clearly close to the facts. I think Luke did it not only because Acts is a historical narrative of what took place in the early church but because Luke's primary concern is to give a defense of the authenticity of Paul's apostleship. As we know, Paul was not numbered among the original Twelve, yet when we look at the early history of the church, we see that, apart from Jesus, the single most important leader was Paul the Apostle, who wrote thirteen of the books of the New Testament. No theologian since has surpassed his excellence. Luke underscores the importance of Paul in Christian history and in the life of the church even today.

Paul's Testimony

At the conclusion of our last study, Paul was in front of an angry mob in Jerusalem. He had waved them into silence after being given permission to defend himself. Paul then spoke to them in the Hebrew language. The fact that he addressed them in their own tongue was a sign of respect. He did not retreat to academic jargon. Paul began with the same words Stephen had used so many years earlier when he addressed the mob in Jerusalem. **"Brethren and fathers, hear my defense before you now." And when they heard that he spoke to them in the Hebrew language, they kept all the more silent. Then he said: "I am indeed a Jew, born in Tarsus of Cilicia, but brought up in this city**

at the feet of Gamaliel, taught according to the strictness of our fathers' law, and was zealous toward God as you all are today" (vv. 1–3). The three most celebrated rabbis of antiquity were Hillel, Akiba, and Gamaliel. Of those three, without question the most celebrated was Gamaliel. So Paul in his defense reminds his hearers that he had studied under the best.

Gamaliel had gained a reputation not only for brilliance but also for a kind, gentle, and tolerant spirit. Many students of great teachers become brash and impetuous. Filled up with the knowledge they have learned, they seek to impose it on everyone else. Saul had been no different; he had learned a love for the law from Gamaliel, and he had a passion to get rid of anybody who disagreed with this Jewish tradition. The young theologian Saul had believed that the great threat to the purity of Israel was the emerging sect called the Way, people who claimed that Jesus was the Messiah. Saul would have none of it, and he did everything in his power to stamp it out. He testified here that he had gone from house to house dragging not only men but women into the prison to be flogged or killed.

"Now it happened, as I journeyed and came near Damascus at about noon, suddenly a great light from heaven shone around me. And I fell to the ground and heard a voice saying to me, 'Saul, Saul, why are you persecuting Me?' So I answered, 'Who are You, Lord?' And He said to me, 'I am Jesus of Nazareth, whom you are persecuting'" (vv. 6–8). Jesus had long ago been executed, twenty-seven years before Saul recounted his conversion here. He had been raised from the dead and had ascended into heaven. He was beyond the reach of the savagery of Saul. Saul couldn't do anything to hurt Jesus personally, and yet Jesus had said, "Why are you persecuting *Me*?" Saul in his fury had been persecuting Jesus' people—His body, the church. Earlier Jesus had said, "Assuredly, I say to you, inasmuch as you did not do it to one of the least of these, you did not do it to Me" (Matt. 25:45). Saul's persecution of Jesus' people was persecution of Jesus Himself.

Paul recounts that he had been struck blind. **"So, I said, 'What shall I do, Lord?' And the Lord said to me, 'Arise and go into Damascus, and there you will be told all things which are appointed for you to do.' And since I could not see for the glory of that light, being led by the hand of those who were with me, I came into Damascus"** (vv. 10–11). Rather than coming into Damascus in chariots and power, Saul was led groping in the dark as somebody held his hand and led him through the alleys and the streets, taking him to the house of Ananias. When Saul arrived at the home of this devout man, who was also known to the audience here in Jerusalem, he said that Ananias welcomed him and called him Brother Saul. Immediately Saul's eyes were opened and he could see.

Then Ananias said, "'**The God of our fathers has chosen you that you should know His will, and see the Just One, and hear the voice of His mouth. For you will be His witness to all men of what you have seen and heard. And now why are you waiting? Arise and be baptized, and wash away your sins, calling on the name of the Lord'**" (vv. 14–16). It is a rare thing in the theological world for somebody who militantly embraces a particular theological position for a period of years to suddenly switch and go to the other side of the aisle. It happens, but not very often. It usually takes some kind of dramatic crisis to provoke such a change.

Saul was told that he had been chosen by God to know His will. If you look carefully at the terms of this account, you see that Luke is jealous to communicate the circumstances of Paul's call to be an Apostle. In the Old Testament many went who had not been sent. As we noted earlier, to be a true prophet one had to be called directly and immediately by God and anointed by His Spirit to be an agent of His revelation. So what we have here is another record of the call of Paul to be an Apostle. He had not been numbered among the original Twelve, but he had the most important credential he could have—a direct and immediate call by Christ. That is what Ananias was confirming.

If you look at Peter's sermon in Acts 3 and at Stephen's speech in Acts 7, or at Ezekiel and Isaiah in the Old Testament, you will see that the promised Messiah was given extraordinary titles. The Messiah is called the Holy One of Israel and the Righteous One. So when Paul self-consciously recounts the story of his conversion, he says that Ananias had told him that God had chosen him to preach and teach the words of the Righteous One. The crowd all understood what Paul was saying—the one that the Jews had killed, including Paul, the one to whom Stephen bore witness—was the Messiah, the Righteous One of Israel.

Paul went on, **"When I had returned to Jerusalem and was praying in the temple . . . I was in a trance"** (v. 17). The Greek word for *trance* is the word from which we get "ecstasy." In the Latin, it is translated in *stupora mentus*, "in a mental stupor." There is a mystical element that we cannot deny in the life of the Apostle Paul. We find the same thing in Peter when he was in Cornelius's house and had the vision of the sheets from heaven. It is the same concept that we find in Revelation when the Apostle John said, "I was in the Spirit on the Lord's Day" (Rev. 1:10). Paul said that he had been praying and the Lord had moved him to ecstasy, and in that ecstasy Paul had seen and heard him again.

Many see an allusion here to the similarities between the call of Paul and the call of Isaiah in the temple. In Isaiah's vision the Lord said, "Whom shall I send, and who will go for Us?" And Isaiah replied, "Here am I! Send me" (Isa. 6:8). And then God told him to go preach to the people, even though God would close the ears and eyes of the people lest they hear and see and be converted. What kind of missionary job was that? Isaiah cried out in despair, "Lord, how long?" (v. 11). God told him to preach "until the cities are laid waste and without inhabitant, the houses are without a man, [and] the land is utterly desolate" (v. 11). Isaiah was simply to do what God had told him and to let God worry about who would respond. What we see is that God told Isaiah to stay and speak to Israel, which is just the opposite of what he told Paul: **"Make haste and get out of Jerusalem quickly, for they will not receive your testimony concerning Me. . . . Depart, for I will send you far from here to the Gentiles"** (vv. 18–21). That is what Paul had done. He had gone out as Christ's witness as the Apostle to the Gentiles.

Paul's closing arguments on his own behalf at this kangaroo court converted few if any, because the response of the crowd was the same as that given to Stephen all those years earlier. Nevertheless, the mission still goes on today. The testimony of Paul reaches every corner of the world today, because God chose him to be the one to speak his word as the Apostle to the Gentiles. Never before has the church needed more desperately to listen again to this Apostle.

54

A HOUSE DIVIDED

Acts 22:22–23:9

And they listened to him until this word, and then they raised their voices and said, "Away with such a fellow from the earth, for he is not fit to live!" Then, as they cried out and tore off their clothes and threw dust into the air, the commander ordered him to be brought into the barracks, and said that he should be examined under scourging, so that he might know why they shouted so against him. And as they bound him with thongs, Paul said to the centurion who stood by, "Is it lawful for you to scourge a man who is a Roman, and uncondemned?" When the centurion heard that, he went and told the commander, saying, "Take care what you do, for this man is a Roman." Then the commander came and said to him, "Tell me, are you a Roman?" He said, "Yes." The commander answered, "With a large sum I obtained this citizenship." And Paul said, "But I was born a citizen." Then immediately those who were about to examine him withdrew from him: and the commander was also afraid after he found out that he was a Roman, and because he had bound him. The next day, because he wanted to know for certain why he was accused by the Jews, he released him from his bonds, and commanded the chief priests and all their council to appear, and brought Paul down and set him before them. Then Paul, looking earnestly at the council, said, "Men and brethren, I have lived in all good conscience before God until this day." And the high priest Ananias commanded those who stood by him to strike him on the mouth. Then Paul said to him, "God will strike you, you whitewashed wall! For you sit to judge me according to the law, and do you command me to be struck contrary to the law?" And those who stood by said, "Do you revile God's high priest?" Then Paul said, "I did not know, brethren, that he was the high priest; for it is written, 'You shall not speak evil of a ruler of your people.'" But when Paul perceived that one part were Sadducees and the other Pharisees, he cried out in the council, "Men and brethren, I am a Pharisee, the son of a Pharisee; concerning the hope and resurrection of the dead I am being judged!" And when he had said this, a dissension arose between the Pharisees and the Sadducees; and the assembly was divided. For Sadducees say that there is no resurrection—and no angel or spirit; but the Pharisees confess both. Then there arose a loud outcry. And the scribes of the Pharisees' party arose and protested, saying, "We find no evil in this man; but if a spirit or an angel has spoken to him, let us not fight against God."

P aul has had to defend himself before the Jews, then before the Romans, and then again before the Jews, and then again before the Romans. It is as though musical chairs were being played with the Apostle's life. Paul has just given a personal defense in which he recounted his conversion on the Damascus road and that in a trance Christ had appeared to him and verified his call as the Apostle to the Gentiles. The defense was supposed to calm the crowd, but instead it incited them to even more hostility. **And they listened to him until this word, and then they raised their voices and said, "Away with such a fellow from the earth, for he is not fit to live!"** (v. 22).

When the Roman commander saw all this, he was puzzled as to the cause of the depth of hostility being manifested against Paul, so **as they cried out and tore off their clothes and threw dust into the air, the commander ordered him to be brought into the barracks, and said that he should be examined under scourging, so that he might know why they shouted so against him** (vv. 23–24). No longer was the commander satisfied simply to interrogate Paul; he wanted to get to the bottom of the turmoil.

Paul the Roman

Paul had already endured beatings and stoning and imprisonment, and he had been beaten by the Jews on more than one occasion. Yet up until now, Paul had never been subjected to the Roman form of scourging. The Roman scourging made use of flagellum, leather thongs attached to the ends of which were metal pieces. Many victims of this type of scourge died, and if they did not die, they were left with scars. That was the kind of torture the commander is advocating here as a means to get to the truth of the matter.

As they prepared him for this whipping, Paul asked the centurion, **"Is it lawful for you to scourge a man who is a Roman, and uncondemned?" When the centurion heard that, he went and told the commander, saying, "Take care**

what you do, for this man is a Roman." Then the commander came and said to him, "Tell me, are you a Roman?" He said, "Yes." The commander answered, "With a large sum I obtained this citizenship." And Paul said, "But I was born a citizen" (vv. 25–28). Today people are automatically a citizen of the country in which they are born, but that was not the case in Rome. To be a citizen of the city of Rome was to be numbered among the elite. It was a high privilege accorded, for the most part, only to the patricians of society. Roman citizenship could be achieved in basically two ways: by achieving a high level of service to the Roman Empire or by purchasing it with a large sum of money. Since Paul was born a Roman citizen, either his father or his grandfather had gained citizenship, perhaps without ever setting foot in Rome, through one of those two means. Paul's father or grandfather was therefore likely extremely wealthy. There are other reasons to believe that Paul came from a wealthy family, not the least of which was his ability to come to Jerusalem and study at the feet of Gamaliel.

We do not know with certainty when the practice of purchasing citizenship began in the Roman Empire. We do know that when Emperor Claudius needed to fill the general coffers, of which Julius Caesar had spoken or had accomplished according to his funeral oration, he sold citizenships to various wealthy individuals or whoever could gather enough money together. We find here that the commander had paid a large sum to get his citizenship papers. We do not know when he did it, but his name, as we will see, was Claudius, which hints at the possibility that he purchased his citizenship under the reign of Claudius and took the name Claudius in gratitude for this citizenship and to honor the emperor. Whatever the case, this man was impressed that Paul was a Roman citizen.

There were two things at stake here. First, if someone punished a Roman citizen without due legal process, he exposed himself to the death penalty. Had Claudius scourged Paul without a trial, he could have been executed. Second, if a prisoner at his trial claimed falsely to be a Roman citizen, that person could be put to death. This is how highly Roman citizenship was prized at this time in history and why the issue of Paul's credentials as a Roman is very much at the fore in the discussion.

Then immediately those who were about to examine him withdrew from him; and the commander was also afraid after he found out that he was a Roman, and because he had bound him (v. 29). He had not scourged Paul, but he had tied him up and hindered him to this degree, not knowing that Paul was a Roman. He could get in trouble just for that. So he loosed Paul as fast as he could and brought Paul before the council of the Jews.

A Good Conscience

So again Paul addressed the council and said, **"Men and brethren, I have lived in all good conscience before God until this day"** (23:1). I don't know about you, but when I read that, I do a double take. Isn't Paul the man who had stood holding the clothes of the people who were killing Stephen? Wasn't he the one who had gone from house to house dragging away men and women and putting them in prison and having them executed? How can he say that he has lived with a good conscience before God all his days? Maybe Paul was speaking in the context of his former address, and what he simply meant to suggest is that his conscience has been clear since his conversion. I don't think so, however, because when Paul stood by at the execution of Stephen and when he carried on his crusade to stamp out Christians, he was convinced that he was doing the right thing.

When Luther was commanded at the Diet of Worms to revoke his convictions, he could not. He addressed Emperor Charles and the delegation from Rome and said, "Unless I am convinced by sacred Scripture or by evident reason, I cannot recant. For my conscience is held captive by the Word of God, and to act against conscience is neither right nor safe." I believe Luther's conscience was held captive by the Word of God, and I agree with the principle that he expressed, that to act against conscience is not right. It is certainly not safe. The Bible tells us that that which is not of faith is sin (Rom. 14:23). There are people who believe that certain things are wrong and sinful, even though the Bible leaves people free at that point, and if their conscience is persuaded that something is evil but they go ahead and do it anyway, then they have sinned. On the other hand, if someone is totally convinced that a certain activity is just and virtuous even though in God's sight it is a sin, does the fact that he acts according to conscience exonerate him? No, not if his conscience has been calloused by repetitive sin and by a slothful neglect of the Word of God, which is what captures the conscience.

We all have had our conscience influenced by things apart from God, for better or worse. We have a tendency to live not by the mandates of Scripture but by Jiminy Cricket theology, which says, "Let your conscience be your guide." If you commit sin in good conscience, it is still sin. When I took violin lessons, my teacher would ask. "Did you practice this week?" I'd say, "Yes, teacher." But she did not take my word for it. She would take my hand and run her fingers across the tips of my fingers to see if they were calloused. If they were calloused, then she would know I had practiced, but if they were not calloused, she would know I had lied.

We get calloused from repeated practice. The first time we commit a sin, we may abhor ourselves. We may be stricken with a guilty conscience. If we do it again, our conscience is less strident. If we do it repeatedly, we will eventually feel no remorse at all. We live in a culture that has lost its conscience. We are like the people Jeremiah described who had the forehead of a harlot who had lost her capacity to blush. We live in a culture that practices sin day after day, and nobody says anything about it. We had better be careful that if and when we follow our conscience, it has been informed by the Word of God.

Paul and the High Priest

When Paul made mention of his conscience, the high priest Ananias commanded those who stood by him to strike him on the mouth, and they did. Paul responded. **"God will strike you, you whitewashed wall! For you sit to judge me according to the law, and do you command me to be struck contrary to the law?"** (v. 3). That does not sound like a Christian response, but it does sound like Jesus talking to the Pharisees. They were whitewashed tombs on the outside—beautiful, clean, pure—but on the inside they were filled with dead men's bone. So Paul rebuked the high priest for his hypocrisy. Those who heard Paul said to him, **"Do you revile God's high priest?"** (v. 4).

Then Paul said something very puzzling: **"I did not know, brethren, that he was the high priest; for it is written, 'You shall not speak evil of a ruler of your people'"** (v. 5). That principle has never been abrogated; we are called to speak respectfully of our leaders. How are we to understand Paul's words? Scholars have gone through all sorts of gymnastics to try to explain why Paul spoke so harshly against the high priest and then claimed he did not know he was the high priest. One excuse offered is that Paul was troubled with his vision so he was unable to distinguish among those who were speaking to him. That is possible. Others exonerate Paul with the excuse that since he had been away from Jerusalem for twenty years, he did not recognize Ananias. Others argue that, according to Josephus, Ananias was not the high priest at this time, and there was some confusion in the crowd there about who this Ananias actually was. Another option, which is somewhat imaginative, is that Paul was speaking ironically, saying something such as, "I never thought a high priest would order a prisoner to be slapped without due process, so I assumed he couldn't be the high priest."

Paul perceived that part of the group were Sadducees and the other Pharisees. These two Jewish parties were constantly warring both doctrinally and theologically, despite the fact that they stood together here. Today the neo-orthodox get along with each other because they do not care about truth, and as much as they debate about some things, they close ranks in the face of orthodoxy. The same sort of thing was happening here before Paul. The Pharisees and the Sadducees, traditional adversaries, came together in a common bond to stop the ministry of the Apostle Paul.

Paul was nobody's fool. He knew the most ancient stratagem of warfare—divide and conquer. He told them that the underlying reason for the uproar was the fact that he was witnessing to the resurrection of Jesus Christ. The foundation of everything he taught was based on the resurrection. He wrote to the Corinthians, "If Christ is not risen, then our preaching is empty and your faith is also empty" (1 Cor. 15:14). The whole truth claim of Christianity stands or falls on the resurrection.

The Sadducees did not believe in resurrection, in life after death, but the Pharisees did, so all of a sudden they were at each other's throats. One of the Pharisees said, **"We find no evil in this man; but if a spirit or an angel has spoken to him, let us not fight against God"** (v. 9). Then the dissension became so riotous that the Roman commander told the soldiers to take Paul by force to the barracks.

Again Paul has been faithful to the resurrection of Christ.

55

PAUL SENT TO FELIX

Acts 23:11–35

But the following night the Lord stood by him and said, "Be of good cheer, Paul; for as you have testified for Me in Jerusalem, so you must also bear witness at Rome." And when it was day, some of the Jews banded together and bound themselves under an oath, saving that they would neither eat nor drink till they had killed Paul. Now there were more than forty who had formed this conspiracy. They came to the chief priests and elders, and said, "We have bound ourselves under a great oath that we will eat nothing until we have killed Paul. Now you, therefore, together with the council, suggest to the commander that he be brought down to you tomorrow, as though you were going to make further inquiries concerning him; but we are ready to kill him before he comes near." So when Paul's sister's son heard of their ambush, he went and entered the barracks and told Paul. Then Paul called one of the centurions to him and said, "Take this young man to the commander, for he has something to tell him." So he took him and brought him to the commander and said, Paul the prisoner called me to him and asked me to bring this young man to you. He has something to say to you." Then the commander took him by the hand, went aside, and asked privately, "What is it that you have to tell me. And he said, "The Jews have agreed to ask that you bring Paul down to the council tomorrow; as though they were going to inquire more fully about him. But do not yield to them, for more than forty of them lie in wait for him, men who have bound themselves by an oath that they will neither eat nor drink till they have killed him; and now they are ready, waiting for the promise from you." So the commander let the young man depart, and commanded him, "Tell no one that you have revealed these things to me." And he called for two centurions, saying, "Prepare two hundred soldiers, seventy horsemen, and two hundred spearmen to go to Caesarea at the third hour of the night; and provide mounts to set Paul on, and bring him safely to Felix the governor." He wrote a letter in the following manner:

> Claudius Lysias,
>
> To the most excellent governor Felix:
>
> Greetings.

This man was seized by the Jews and was about to be killed by them. Coming with the troops I rescued him, having learned that he was a Roman. And when I wanted to know the reason they accused him, I brought him before their council. I found out that he was accused concerning questions of their law, but had nothing charged against him deserving of death or chains. And when it was told me that the Jews lay in wait for the man, I sent him immediately to you, and also commanded his accusers to state before you the charges against him.

> Farewell.

Then the soldiers, as they were commanded, took Paul and brought him by night to Antipatris. The next day they left the horsemen to go on with him, and returned to the barracks. When they came to Caesarea and had delivered the letter to the governor, they also presented Paul to him. And when the governor had read it, he asked what province he was from. And when he understood that he was from Cilicia, he said, "I will hear you when your accusers also have come." And he commanded him to be kept in Herod's Praetorium.

As we have followed Paul through all his missionary journeys, he has testified about Christ to the Gentiles, the Jews, and to lesser magistrates, but nowhere before kings or the upper echelon of government. Even though Paul's freedom was over, his ministry was not. As he languished in the prison at the barracks by the Antonia Fortress, he had to wonder whether his ministry was over and whether there would be any fruit from his labors. Do you ever feel like that?

When Calvin was banished from Geneva and sent to Strasbourg, where he ministered to a congregation of three hundred, he called it his "little church in Strasbourg." As he was preaching and teaching there, who could have imagined that five hundred years later people would still be translating those sermons and lectures to feed the whole church of the twenty-first century? Jonathan Edwards, after many years of faithful service to his congregation in Northampton, was fired on the basis of false reports and slander and exiled from the town. He went to work among the Indians, and while he was in Stockbridge, he took that occasion to sit down and write *The Freedom of the Will*, one of the ten most important classics in all of Christian history. Who knows when God is finished with you? Who knows how much impact your life and testimony will have?

Some time ago Sinclair Ferguson came to St. Andrew's, and he told a bit about his conversion. He was led to Christ by a man who, in turn, had been converted by the witness of a woman typist. He had listened to the clickety-clack of her typewriter and thought, *Why is it that that typist seems to be so much more consistent than everyone else?* He found out that she was a Christian who dedicated her typing to the kingdom of God and to the glory of Christ. What would that woman think if she realized that as a result of her typing, another man was led to Christ, who in turn had led Sinclair Ferguson to Christ, who in turn has taught the whole world of the gospel? All because she was faithful at a typewriter. Nevertheless, we are human, and we struggle and wonder whether it is worth it.

Suffering Servants

After recovering from a painful illness, a member of our congregation returned to church, and she told me that her suffering made her feel somewhat like Samson. She pointed out that even though Samson's eyes had been gouged out, his mission wasn't over yet. At the time I thought, *How wonderful that somebody in our midst uses a biblical narrative from the Old Testament to help herself understand her affliction.* She went on to tell me that she had learned a lot through her illness. She said, "I think the Lord was trying to show me that I need to have more sensitivity and compassion for others who are in pain, and I hope God will use my pain to make me more faithful in intercession."

That is the way Paul was. Despite his being discouraged, he still had work to do. **The following night the Lord stood by him and said, "Be of good cheer, Paul; for as you have testified for Me in Jerusalem, so you must also bear witness at Rome"** (v. 11). We remember again the Great Commission given at the day of Jesus' ascension into heaven. When He left His disciples He said, "You shall be witnesses to Me in Jerusalem, and in all Judea and Samaria, and to the end of the earth" (Acts 1:8). That commission was then given to Paul and continued here with encouragement.

The English translation of Jesus' words here doesn't really grasp the force of what happened. First, it says that Jesus "stood by" him. That is weak. The Greek words indicate that Jesus came and in a sense overshadowed Paul. His presence was enormous. There was Paul cringing in his cell, and suddenly the risen Christ came and hovered over him and said, "Be of good cheer."

The Latin translation uses a word that is the foundation for the English word *constancy.* This was no glib "Cheer up!" Jesus was saying, "Paul, be constant. Be consistent. Stay with the ministry you have had through all these years, day in and day out." That is a message we all need to hear. This is how Jesus encouraged His Apostle. If anybody had ever been constant in ministry from the day he was called, it was Paul; yet Jesus had to come to him personally and shore him up.

And when it was day, some of the Jews banded together and bound themselves under an oath, saying that they would neither eat nor drink till they had killed Paul (v. 12). Luke tells us three times that they were so convinced that Paul had to die that these forty-plus men gathered together and took a sacred vow to go on a hunger strike. They would neither eat nor drink until Paul was dead. They were zealots, the terrorists of the first century. They were infuriated by Roman occupation. They hated the Sanhedrin. They hated the scribes and the Pharisees because they were convinced that the Jewish authorities had betrayed them. Nevertheless, they would use the authorities whenever it was expedient for their goals. Their goal in this case was to kill Paul.

Every day we read about people who tie explosives to their bodies and become human suicide bombs. The Kamikaze pilots of World War II did the same sort of thing. Perhaps one or two of the Twelve had been numbered among this group of assassins and terrorists. Simon was a zealot, and there is good reason to believe that the meaning of the name Judas Iscariot is not just "Judas from a place called Iscariot," but "Judas from the Sicarii," the assassins, one of the zealots. It makes sense that Judas joined the band of Jesus' disciples with the hope of throwing over the Romans, but when he saw that Jesus did not come with a sword he decided to trade that in for some money and find another messiah. These people meant business. Their zeal was a zeal without knowledge; they wanted to kill the Anointed One of God.

So they set a trap. **"Now you, therefore, together with the council, suggest to the commander that he be brought down to you tomorrow, as though you were going to make further inquiries concerning him; but we are ready to kill him before he comes near"** (v. 15). "Set the ambush," they were saying, "and when Paul comes, we will fall upon him and kill him. We know that to take on the Romans in that situation will mean heavy casualties for us, but we are committed to wiping out the influence of Christianity and this Apostle." So they banded together and called on the Sanhedrin, and the Sanhedrin agreed to the chicanery. But Paul escaped.

Escape

So when Paul's sister's son heard of their ambush, he went and entered the barracks and told Paul (v. 16). This is the first time we have heard anything about Paul's family. Obviously, he had at least one sister, and that sister had a son, Paul's nephew. We do not know how Paul's nephew heard about this plot to kill Paul. His family may have disowned him upon his conversion, but it is apparent that Paul's sister and nephew had remained loyal to him.

A minister friend and his family have a motto: "We stick with the stuck." It means they hang together as a family. That is what we see here with Paul's family. This is the only time we hear of this nephew. Paul told him to go to the commander, and he did and told the commander of the plot to kill Paul, so Paul's life was spared. The commander sent 470 troops as an armed guard to whisk Paul out of Jerusalem and to take him 60 miles north to Caesarea where the regional governor, Felix, was headquartered. So the soldiers did as they were commanded. They traveled 35 miles with the entourage, and when they saw that the group was safe, the infantry went back, and the cavalry took Paul the rest of the way to Caesarea.

Felix

The commander wrote a letter to Felix the governor and said: **Claudius Lysias, to the most excellent governor Felix: Greetings** (v. 26). In Roman society there were clearly defined levels of social order. At the apex of the social order was the emperor himself, on the first tier were members of the senate, and on the second tier were the equestrian knights. The equestrian order, second only to the senate, and regional governors were given the honorific title "Most Excellent," so when Claudius Lysias sent Paul to Felix, he was sending him to somebody very high up in the Roman hierarchy.

The letter continues: **This man was seized by the Jews and was about to be killed by them. Coming with the troops I rescued him, having learned that he was a Roman. And when I wanted to know the reason they accused him, I brought him before their council. I found out that he was accused concerning questions of their law, but had nothing charged against him deserving of death or chains** (vv. 27–29). Claudius did not mention that before he had realized Paul was a Roman, he had put him in chains and had prepared to flog him. **And when it was told me that the Jews lay in wait for the man, I sent him immediately to you, and also commanded his accusers to state before you the charges against him** (v. 30).

Then we are told how Paul was delivered to Felix, the governor situated in Caesarea, a representative of Emperor Claudius of Rome. He had great credentials.

Some time ago I heard a woman on television say, "I don't know whether Jesus ever existed because there is no mention of Him in any historical record apart from the Bible"—as if the Bible were not an important historical record. Of course, she was wrong about that because there are references in Suetonius and in Tacitus, however brief, to Christ. Of the four most important historians of antiquity—Suetonius, Tacitus, Josephus, and Luke the physician—all four wrote about Felix.

We are told that Felix was born into slavery but later was given his freedom, either by the mother of Claudius, according to Tacitus, or by Claudius himself, according to Josephus. Both historians agreed that Felix was born a slave and then elevated to the level of governor. His brother Pallas was also born into slavery. He rose so high in the Roman hierarchy that he became in charge of all the civil servants in Rome, much like holding a cabinet position in the United States government. So both Felix and Pallas were very high up in the Roman hierarchy. Felix had three wives. His first wife was the granddaughter of Antony and Cleopatra. His third wife was Drusilla, the daughter of King Herod Agrippa I. At the time of Paul, Felix, who had begun as a slave, was married to royalty, surrounded by royalty, and holding the honorific titles of royalty.

We are told by Tacitus, however, that Felix was known for his brutal and ruthless quelling of insurrections in his territory. When the Jews stood against the Romans, Felix wiped them out. Tacitus said that Felix had the power of a king but the mind of a slave, yet he went down in history, and the most important thing that ever happened to him was this encounter with Paul the Apostle.

When Felix got the letter and Paul came before him, he said, **"I will hear you when your accusers also have come." And he commanded him to be kept in Herod's Praetorium** (v. 35). He was willing to hear Paul's case but not until the Sanhedrin had sent representatives up from Jerusalem and his accusers had stated their case. This is one aspect of Roman law that is still used today, even in the laws that govern the church—the accused has the right to confront his accusers. This does not always work in the business world today where there are disgruntled employees complaining anonymously to the authorities. I do not pay attention to anonymous complaints, because issuing a complaint in that manner is wrong. Even the Romans understood that principle, and Paul was given that right for his trial.

56

PAUL'S DEFENSE BEFORE FELIX

Acts 24:1–21

Now after five days Ananias the high priest came down with the elders and a certain orator named Tertullus. These gave evidence to the governor against Paul. And when he was called upon, Tertullus began his accusation, saying: "Seeing that through you we enjoy great peace, and prosperity is being brought to this nation by your foresight, we accept it always and in all places, most noble Felix, with all thankfulness. Nevertheless, not to be tedious to you any further, I beg you to hear, by your courtesy, a few words from us. For we have found this man a plague, a creator of dissension among all the Jews throughout the world, and a ringleader of the sect of the Nazarenes. He even tried to profane the temple, and we seized him, and wanted to judge him according to our law. But the commander Lysias came by and with great violence took him out of our hands, commanding his accusers to come to you. By examining him yourself you may ascertain all these things of which we accuse him." And the Jews also assented, maintaining that these things were so. Then Paul, after the governor had nodded to him to speak, answered: "Inasmuch as I know that you have been for many years a judge of this nation, I do the more cheerfully answer for myself, because you may ascertain that it is no more than twelve days since I went up to Jerusalem to worship. And they neither found me in the temple disputing with anyone nor inciting the crowd, either in the synagogues or in the city. Nor can they prove the things of which they now accuse me. But this I confess to you, that according to the Way which they call a sect, so I worship the God of my fathers, believing all things which are written in the Law and in the Prophets. I have hope in God, which they themselves also accept, that there will be a resurrection of the dead, both of the just and the unjust. This being so, I myself always strive to have a conscience without offense toward God and men. Now after many years I came to bring alms and offerings to my nation, in the midst of which some Jews from Asia found me purified in the temple, neither with a mob nor with tumult. They ought to have been here before you to object if they had anything against me. Or else let those who are here themselves say if they found any wrongdoing in me while I stood before the council, unless it is for this one statement which I cried out, standing among them, 'Concerning the resurrection of the dead I am being judged by you this day.'"

Paul had been rescued from an angry mob. The Roman governor Claudius Lysias had interceded and brought Paul into custody. Claudius had discovered that Paul was a Roman citizen and had sent him under cover of night with an entourage of four hundred and seventy soldiers to a hearing before Felix, the governor of the whole land. Then Felix had ordered Paul's accusers to come the sixty miles to Caesarea to give their testimony in person. That is where we left off in our last study, so now we read of the arrival of Ananias with his entourage for the occasion of bearing witness against Paul.

Accused

After five days Ananias the high priest came down with the elders and a certain orator named Tertullus. These gave evidence to the governor against Paul (v. 1). Although Tertullus had a Greek name, he was a Jewish attorney. The Sanhedrin had enlisted him as the prosecuting attorney in the case against Paul, and he proceeded to give his evidence to the governor. **And when he was called upon, Tertullus began his accusation, saying: "Seeing that through you we enjoy great peace, and prosperity is being brought to this nation by your foresight, we accept it always and in all places, most noble Felix, with all thankfulness"** (vv. 2–3). Hypocrisy dripped from the tongue of this attorney. He began by praising the Roman governor as the agent of peace in Israel. The *pax Romana* had come. Of course, the Jews hated the fact that they were a nation occupied by foreign troops. They knew peace only at the cost of Roman domination.

The Roman historian Tacitus said of Felix and his cohorts that everywhere they went, they brought a desert and called it peace. The land was basically a desert region, but through the centuries of agricultural labor, the Jewish people had transformed the desert into a beautiful agrarian setting with trees and gardens. When the Romans invaded Israel in the latter years of the decade of the sixties, which culminated in the destruction of Jerusalem in the year A.D. 70, they completely denuded the land; their way of battle was to lay siege to the walled cities. While the city was besieged, the Roman soldiers camped outside the walls until food and water became so scarce that the inhabitants of the city were weakened and ready for conquest. While the soldiers waited, they cut down every tree in sight and used the wood to cook and to keep themselves warm at night. On the night of Jesus' agony in the garden of Gethsemane, that slope of Mount Gethsemane had been covered by huge olive trees, three or four hundred years old. When Jerusalem was destroyed in A.D. 70, not a single olive tree was left on the Mount of Olives. It had been stripped bare like a desert. Tacitus had it right when he said that the Romans made the place a desert and called it peace.

Felix was ruthless in putting down Jewish disputes. Later, after the death of Claudius, Felix was recalled to Rome when a new emperor came to the throne. The new emperor was concerned that Felix was too brutal. The extent of Felix's brutality can be measured by the fact that this new emperor was none other than Nero, the cruelest ruler of the time.

The English text translates Tertullus's words in verse 2 as "by your foresight," but the Greek word used is *providence*. Tertullus was a Jew and therefore someone who supposedly understood that it is only by God's providence that prosperity comes to a land and that any benefit enjoyed in this world comes from God's goodness and mercy. This Jewish attorney betrayed his Judaism by heaping praise upon the Roman government, saying, "We acknowledge your providence as the cause of our prosperity."

Finally the orator said, **"Nevertheless, not to be tedious to you any further, I beg you to hear, by your courtesy, a few words from us"** (v. 4). Then he gave his testimony regarding Paul. **"We have found this man a plague"** (v. 5). Some translations have "pest," but that translation is far too weak. The word "plague" is much better because Tertullus was saying that Paul was a pestilence on the earth. Everywhere he went, dissension occurred, and the people were sick of it.

Some time ago I saw James Dobson being interviewed on television. He had been distressed about a compromise in the U.S. Senate and had been soundly criticized for his views. When told during the interview some of the rancorous things being said about him, he handled himself with great dignity. People were calling him an anti-American extremist, but he was not angry or bitter because, he said, that is just name-calling and does not get to the substance of the issues. We live in an era in which anybody can voice an opinion in the public square except for an evangelical Christian. If we are faithful to Christ in the public square, we will be regarded as the plague. We have enjoyed a tremendous measure of freedom and protection in this country for centuries, but the day is coming when those protections will go away. We need to be ready for it, because whenever people are faithful to the gospel, the world sees them first as pests and then as a plague, which was the charge brought against Paul.

Tertullus said Paul was a plague because he had created dissension among all the Jews throughout the world and had been a ringleader of that sect called the Nazarenes. **"He even tried to profane the temple, and we seized him, and wanted to judge him according to our law. But the commander Lysias came by and with great violence took him out of our hands, commanding his accusers to come to you. By examining him yourself you may ascertain all these things of which we accuse him." And the Jews also assented, maintaining that these things were so** (vv. 6–9). There is a shift here in the accusation. When Paul was brought before Claudius Lysias in Jerusalem, the charge was that he *did* defile the temple, that he had taken a Gentile into the inner chamber. That was not true. Since nobody could back up the charge, Tertullus said that Paul had "tried" to defile the temple but had been stopped. Tertullus said nothing about the mob that had tried to kill Paul.

Tertullus claimed that Claudius Lysias had grabbed Paul away from them, which is the exact opposite of what had happened. Tertullus did not know how to tell the truth, even part of the truth, so he said everything but the truth and bore false witness against the Apostle Paul. Finally all the Jews agreed with the charges Tertullus brought, and then Paul gave his reply. It is often said that a person who defends himself has a fool for a client and that it is therefore wise to be defended by someone else. In this case, the Sanhedrin hired the best lawyer they could find as prosecutor, but Paul was left to defend himself without help from another. He had no advocate. I wonder if on that day he remembered the occasion of a similar tribunal, when Stephen was martyred and looked up and saw his advocate, Jesus Christ, standing in his defense. Stephen had had no one on earth to defend him, but from heaven Christ came to do so. Christ has promised to be Paul's advocate, so though Paul gave the defense, he did so in the power and presence of the Holy Spirit, the best defense attorney there could be.

Paul's Defense

"Inasmuch as I know that you have been for many years a judge of this nation, I do the more cheerfully answer for myself" (v. 10). He gave a slight tip of the hat to the magistrate, which was customary in antiquity and even throughout the ages. When John Calvin wrote his *Institutes of the Christian Religion*, he wrote a dedication to the king of France. In the dedication he appealed to the king's sense of justice to stop the persecution of innocent Christians. Paul was saying, "I am glad that I can speak here, because you are not a stranger. You have been around for a long time and understand the Jewish people. You have some knowledge about our affairs, and so you are likely to understand my defense."

Paul said that no more than twelve days had passed since he had gone up to Jerusalem to worship. He hadn't had enough time in Jerusalem to cause all the trouble he was accused of. He hadn't preached once or addressed the multitude. Seven of those days had been dedicated to offering his sacrifices in the temple, where he had gone for purification. He was in the midst of being purified when they had come in and arrested him. No Gentiles had been there with him, nor had he done anything to defile the temple.

Paul explained that the charges about dissension and his being a plague came from the people in Ephesus who had come to Jerusalem. About them he said, **"They ought to have been here before you to object if they had anything against me"** (v. 19).

Paul continued, **"Or else let those who are here themselves say if they found any wrongdoing in me while I stood before the council, unless it is for this one statement which I cried out, standing among them, 'Concerning the resurrection of the dead I am being judged by you this day'"** (vv. 20–21). We cannot help but see the parallel here between the trial of Paul and the trial of Jesus. The unbridled hostility that the Jewish leaders were exhibiting toward Paul contained the same venom and hatred that they had expressed toward Jesus, and it concerned who understood the Bible correctly. Jesus was tried as a heretic, according to Jewish law. Paul was charged with not being faithful to the Bible. He stated that he had been committed to God's Word throughout his life. He had never swayed from his commitment to the Law and the Prophets.

The problem was what the Old Testament said about the Messiah. Jesus said that He was the Messiah; Paul said that Jesus was the Messiah; but Ananias, the Sanhedrin, and the Pharisees said that Jesus was not the Messiah. The issue between Jesus and the Pharisees was who believed in the Old Testament. The Jews told Jesus that they believed in the Old Testament and were the ones following Moses. "We are the children of Abraham, not you," they told Jesus, but Jesus answered:

If I honor Myself, My honor is nothing. It is My Father who honors Me, of whom you say that He is your God. Yet you have not known Him, but I know Him. And if I say, "I do not know Him," I shall be a liar like you; but I do know Him and keep His word. Your father Abraham rejoiced to see My day, and he saw it and was glad. (John 8:54–56)

Jesus had claimed to be the true Israel, and Paul was making this same claim. He had preached only pure, unvarnished, historic Judaism in its fulfillment in the Messiah.

No Compromise

A Jewish friend of mine has said to me, "I wish there'd never been a Jesus so that we wouldn't have to be divided over religion. What difference does it make?" Her comment was somewhat prophetic about where our society is today. Our society claims that it doesn't make any difference, and if you say it does make a difference, you are anti-Semitic. No Christian is ever to be involved in the persecution of a Jew, a Muslim, a Hindu, a Buddhist, or anybody else; we are called to treat everyone as a neighbor and to show love to all. However, we are not to say that there is no difference. What difference does it make if we say Jesus is the Messiah while others say He is not? If you say Jesus is not the Messiah and I say Jesus is the Messiah, one of us is wrong; one of us is against God at that point. If Jesus is not the Messiah, we who worship Him are idolaters in the extreme. If Jesus is the Messiah, those who reject Him are rejecting the only Son of God and calling Him a false prophet, and the consequences of that are eternal. We live in a culture that says it doesn't matter what you believe so long as you are sincere, but the Devil is sincere. He sincerely hates Christ and everything Christ stands for. You cannot embrace Christ and at the same time embrace every pretender to the kingdom of God. At some point, you have got to be a pest to the world. At some point, you must take a stand.

I once heard a series of lectures on the life of the Apostle Paul, and the teacher used the name of Paul as an acrostic to describe the Apostle's character. *P* was for polluted, because Paul was the chief of sinners and he saw himself as polluted by his sin. *A* represented his apostolic task and ministry. *U* represented the character of the Apostle as being uncompromising. Even here before this hostile group, Paul again bore witness to Christ without compromise. *L* stood for loving. Paul was the most loving Christian who ever walked the face of the earth. He took an oath saying that he would trade his salvation for that of his kinsmen according to the flesh, Israel (Rom. 9:3–4). He preached Christ to his Jewish neighbors, kinsmen, and friends, not because he hated them but because he loved them. The teacher of the acrostic pointed out that many will say that Paul was uncompromising *but* he was also loving, but the truth is that Paul was uncompromising with the truth of God and *therefore* loving.

If you love Christ and if you love people, then you will never compromise His gospel. Let Paul be an example for us in our own day.

57

PAUL TRIED BEFORE FESTUS

Acts 24:22–25:12

But when Felix heard these things, having more accurate knowledge of the Way, he adjourned the proceedings and said, "When Lysias the commander comes down, I will make a decision on your case." So he commanded the centurion to keep Paul and to let him have liberty, and told him not to forbid any of his friends to provide for or visit him. And after some days, when Felix came with his wife Drusilla, who was Jewish, he sent for Paul and heard him concerning the faith in Christ. Now as he reasoned about righteousness, self-control, and the judgment to come, Felix was afraid and answered, "Go away for now; when I have a convenient time I will call for you." Meanwhile he also hoped that money would be given him by Paul, that he might release him. Therefore he sent for him more often and conversed with him. But after two years Porcius Festus succeeded Felix; and Felix, wanting to do the Jews a favor, left Paul bound. Now when Festus had come to the province, after three days he went up from Caesarea to Jerusalem. Then the high priest and the chief men of the Jews informed him against Paul; and they petitioned him, asking a favor against him, that he would summon him to Jerusalem—while they lay in ambush along the road to kill him. But Festus answered that Paul should be kept at Caesarea, and that he himself was going there shortly. "Therefore," he said, "let those who have authority among you go down with me and accuse this man, to see if there is any fault in him." And when he had remained among them more than ten days, he went down to Caesarea. And the next day, sitting on the judgment seat, he commanded Paul to be brought. When he had come, the Jews who had come down from Jerusalem stood about and laid many serious complaints against Paul, which they could not prove, while he answered for himself, "Neither against the law of the Jews, nor against the temple, nor against Caesar have I offended in anything at all." But Festus, wanting to do the Jews a favor, answered Paul and said, "Are you willing to go up to Jerusalem and there be judged before me concerning these things?" So Paul said, "I stand at Caesar's judgment seat, where I ought to be judged. To the Jews I have done no wrong, as you very well know. For if I am an offender, or have committed anything deserving of death, I do not object to dying; but if there is nothing in these things of which these men accuse me, no one can deliver me to them. I appeal to Caesar." Then Festus, when he had conferred with the council, answered, "You have appealed to Caesar? To Caesar you shall go!"

You might be thinking, *Oh, not again. Do we have to go through another hearing of the Apostle Paul?* You might even come to the conclusion that at this point the narrative of Acts is getting boring. Let me remind you that God has never uttered a boring word in all of eternity, and if it pleases the Holy Spirit to include all these accounts for our edification, there must be something profitable for us in this record.

But when Felix heard these things, having more accurate knowledge of the Way, he adjourned the proceedings and said, "When Lysias the commander comes down, I will make a decision on your case" (v. 22). Here Felix invoked the Roman principle known as *amplius*, the formal delay or reservation of a final judgment. Paul was not convicted in front of Felix, but Felix delayed a final decision on the matter and ordered that Paul be bound over to prison to await further examination by Lysias and then a final decision by Felix.

Politics as Usual

Luke does not tell us if Lysias ever came and brought the testimony that Felix had asked for. Whether he did or didn't, Felix still did not render a verdict, and he kept Paul in captivity for two years. Paul was held in a liberal prison. Felix gave him permission to interact with his friends and relatives. Some church historians speculate that during these two years Luke amassed much of the material that he incorporated both into his Gospel and into Acts.

Paul did not waste time while in prison. Even so, justice delayed is justice denied, and Paul was clearly denied justice under the procrastination of Felix. Why did Felix put Paul in prison even though he knew Paul was not guilty of the charges? The answer comes a little bit later in the text: **But after two years Porcius Festus succeeded Felix; and Felix, wanting to do the Jews a favor, left Paul bound** (v. 27). It was a political decision. Paul was kept in prison as a matter of political expediency. This Roman magistrate knew that under the law

Paul was innocent, but in order to appease the Jews, who were screaming for the blood of the Apostle Paul, and to seek some measure of peace among the people, he judged not by principle but by expediency.

That was no different in the trial of Jesus. After saying publicly, "I find no fault in this Man," Pontius Pilate washed his hands but could not remove the blood of Christ from them because he had compromised for political reasons to mollify the crowd (Luke 23:4). On those occasions lady justice took the blindfold off to see which way the wind was blowing before she reached a verdict. We should not be too hard on Felix or Pontius Pilate because this has been the way of rulers of all generations. Rulers always keep one eye on public opinion, and when they are torn between justice and expediency it is a rare ruler who will keep his eyes on justice. The idea of political expediency is a temptation that comes to everyone in a position of leadership or power, and we face it and feed it ourselves in our own culture.

Paul and Felix

Felix was at least impressed enough by Paul to want to learn something from him. Felix's third wife was Drusilla, and she is mentioned here in the text. When this conversation between Paul and Felix took place, Drusilla was not yet twenty years old. Felix was her second husband. She had broken one engagement because the man to whom she was engaged did not embrace Judaism. After she had broken that engagement, she married a lesser monarch from Syria, to whom she had remained married for just a short time. When she was sixteen years old, Felix found her and persuaded her to leave her husband and come and live with him. Even though she came and inquired about Jesus and the Christian faith, she was no paragon of virtue. Drusilla and Felix had a son named Agrippa. Both Agrippa and his mother, Drusilla, died in the year A.D. 79, buried by the ashes of an eruption of Mount Vesuvius of Pompeii and Herculaneum fame.

Luke tells us that they came and inquired about Jesus, and Paul explained to them what it means to have faith. **Now as he reasoned about righteousness, self-control, and the judgment to come, Felix was afraid and answered, "Go away for now; when I have a convenient time I will call for you"** (v. 25). Luke does not include everything that they discussed, but he emphasizes what Paul emphasized, which first was righteousness. In his whole life Felix, who was supposed to govern according to justice and righteousness, had never been so thoroughly tutored in the concept of righteousness. Before Paul gave the gospel, he gave the law, because before the good news comes, there has to be an understanding of the bad news. He addressed Felix at the point of Felix's sin—his unrighteousness. He also gave him a lecture on self-control, which Felix certainly hadn't exercised when he took Drusilla from her previous husband.

The coup de grâce is when Paul focused attention on the last judgment. Here was Paul speaking to his captor about the last judgment and about righteousness. What would happen if the Apostle Paul came and talked to you about righteousness, self-control, and the last judgment? We like to make plans. We plan what we are going to do tomorrow, next week, and next month. We have plans for our children and grandchildren. We think about what our lives will be like ten or twenty years from now. Where will you be and what will you be doing one hundred years from now? I hope the consideration of that provokes in your soul nothing but absolute joy—the idea of being in heaven with your Savior and departed loved ones, your brothers and sisters in Christ. Statistically, some of you reading this book will one hundred years from now be in hell because you will fail on the day of judgment. I can think of nothing more terrifying than that.

What happened to Felix? He became terrified. The last thing he wanted to think about was facing God at the last judgment. However, he did not ask Paul about the remedy—the gospel. He told Paul to stop talking. He did not want to hear another word. But it nagged at him. The text says he kept coming back for further conversations with the Apostle. Surely Paul never changed his tune, but we can put callouses on our consciences. We can do everything in our power to suppress and repress the Word of God, but we cannot destroy it. We can flee from it. We can silence those who deliver it, but as Shakespeare's Hamlet understood, "Conscience doth make cowards of us all." Felix had much to be afraid of, but what a tragedy. Felix had the world's greatest theologian and evangelist explaining to him the things of Christ, yet he said, "Go away; I don't want to hear any more."

After two years of waiting in hope that Paul would give him a bribe to be let out of jail, Felix was recalled to Rome. The brother Pallas, who had protected him, was no longer in power. Nero was now sitting on the throne of Rome. Even though Pallas was no longer the head of civic affairs in Rome, he still was a man of unbelievable wealth and influence, and we are told from the historians that when Felix was recalled, he was not punished for his failures to rule well in Israel.

Festus

In his place came Porcius Festus, who seemed just the opposite of Felix. Felix was known for his procrastination—"One of these days I'll render a verdict, but in the meantime Paul can rot in jail." Three days after Festus arrived, he went to Jerusalem. That was wisdom and good diplomacy. If he was going to govern the

Jews, he realized he had better get to know the Jewish officials and authorities. No sooner had he arrived in Jerusalem than the leaders there petitioned Festus to send Paul to Jerusalem so that they could ambush and kill him. **But Festus answered that Paul should be kept at Caesarea, and that he himself was going there shortly (25:4).**

After three days he went up from Caesarea, and the high priest and the chief rulers of the Jews informed him against Paul. All the same charges that had been leveled during the hearings before Felix were brought up again, and Paul gave his own defense. None of the charges could be proven against him, so he said, **"Neither against the law of the Jews, nor against the temple, nor against Caesar have I offended in anything at all." But Festus, wanting to do the Jews a favor, answered Paul and said, "Are you willing to go up to Jerusalem and there be judged before me concerning these things?" (vv. 8–9).** One hand washes the other—that is politics. Festus wanted a compromise. He agreed to judge Paul, but instead of doing it in Caesarea, he decided to hold Paul's trial in Jerusalem.

Appeal to Caesar

There was a principle in Roman jurisprudence called the *provocation*, which granted the right of a citizen to appeal his case to Caesar. Paul invoked it: **"I stand at Caesar's judgment seat, where I ought to be judged. To the Jews I have done no wrong, as you very well know. For if I am an offender, or have committed anything deserving of death, I do not object to dying; but if there is nothing in these things of which these men accuse me, no one can deliver me to them. I appeal to Caesar" (vv. 10–11).** Paul knew that if he went down to Jerusalem, he would probably never get there alive, and if he did, there would be a multitude clamoring with false charges. The Roman seat was there in Caesarea, and Paul wanted to be judged there. If he was refused, he would appeal to Caesar. We can almost feel the relief of Festus at that point. He finally had a way to get Paul off his hands. **Then Festus, when he had conferred with the council, answered, "You have appealed to Caesar? To Caesar you shall go!" (v. 12).**

The Caesar that Paul was asking to hear his case was none other than Nero, known as the Wild Beast in the first century. Nero came to power in the year A.D. 54, and we are told by both Josephus and Tacitus that between A.D. 54 and A.D. 59 Nero was tutored by the stoic philosopher Seneca, whose works are read and studied still today. Seneca instructed Nero how to judge and rule, and, for the first five years of Nero's reign, he was a model emperor. Then, for reasons we do not know, he became the bloodiest, most ruthless, most corrupt emperor in the history of Rome. At this time his corruption had not yet been manifested, so Paul did a very intelligent thing by appealing to Nero to hear his case. He did not know that Nero was waiting for him with a sword.

Paul was dismissed, at least temporarily, from the jurisdiction of Festus. Though Festus would subject Paul to one more hearing before a neighboring king, Agrippa, he delivered Paul to the hands of Caesar, and Paul had to wait again for his case to be decided. History shows that the church and the world are judged politically rather than by principle. We all do it; we all have it done to us; but we ought not to be like that.

58

PAUL'S DEFENSE

Acts 25:23–26:18

So the next day, when Agrippa and Bernice had come with great pomp, and had entered the auditorium with the commanders and the prominent men of the city, at Festus' command Paul was brought in. And Festus said: "King Agrippa and all the men who are here present with us, you see this man about whom the whole assembly of the Jews petitioned me, both at Jerusalem and here, crying out that he was not fit to live any longer. But when I found that he had committed nothing deserving of death, and that he himself had appealed to Augustus, I decided to send him. I have nothing certain to write to my lord concerning him. Therefore I have brought him out before you, and especially before you, King Agrippa, so that after the examination has taken place I may have something to write. For it seems to me unreasonable to send a prisoner and not to specify the charges against him." Then Agrippa said to Paul, "You are permitted to speak for yourself." So Paul stretched out his hand and answered for himself: "I think myself happy, King Agrippa, because today I shall answer for myself before you concerning all the things of which I am accused by the Jews, especially because you are expert in all customs and questions which have to do with the Jews. Therefore I beg you to hear me patiently. My manner of life from my youth, which was spent from the beginning among my own nation at Jerusalem, all the Jews know. They knew me from the first, if they were willing to testify, that according to the strictest sect of our religion I lived a Pharisee. And now I stand and am judged for the hope of the promise made by God to our fathers. To this promise our twelve tribes, earnestly serving God night and day, hope to attain. For this hope's sake, King Agrippa, I am accused by the Jews. Why should it be thought incredible by you that God raises the dead? Indeed, I myself thought I must do many things contrary to the name of Jesus of Nazareth. This I also did in Jerusalem, and many of the saints I shut up in prison, having received authority from the chief priests; and when they were put to death, I cast my vote against them. And I punished them often in every synagogue and compelled them to blaspheme; and being exceedingly enraged against them, I persecuted them even to foreign cities. While thus occupied, as I journeyed to Damascus with authority and commission from the chief priests, at midday, O king, along the road I saw a light from heaven, brighter than the sun, shining around me and those who journeyed with me. And when we all had fallen to the ground, I heard a voice speaking to me and saying in the Hebrew language, 'Saul, Saul, why are you persecuting Me? It is hard for you to kick against the goads.' So I said, 'Who are You, Lord?' And He said, 'I am Jesus, whom you are persecuting. But rise and stand on your feet; for I have appeared to you for this purpose, to make you a minister and a witness both of the things which you have seen and of the things which I will yet reveal to you. I will deliver you from the Jewish people, as well as from the Gentiles, to whom I now send you, to open their eyes, in order to turn them from darkness to light, and from the power of Satan to God, that they may receive forgiveness of sins and an inheritance among those who are sanctified by faith in Me.'"

In our last study we saw that Festus was relieved to be off the hook when Paul appealed to Rome. He said, "You have appealed to Caesar? To Caesar you shall go!" (Acts 25:12). We would therefore expect that the next chapter in the book of Acts would be about Paul's journey to Rome to give his defense there, yet what we find is Paul giving another defense before a Jewish magistrate. Between the words of Festus that we ended with last time and where we begin now, in Acts 26, a few things have happened to Paul.

Agrippa and Bernice

After Festus had said to Paul, "To Caesar you shall go!" the local Jewish king, Agrippa II, and his consort Bernice came to visit Festus to offer congratulations to the newly appointed Roman governor. While Agrippa and Bernice were there, Festus told them he was sending his prisoner Paul, a Jewish Roman citizen, to Rome for a trial and a hearing, but he did not know what to say in the documents he was preparing to send in advance. Festus hoped that Agrippa, being something of an expert in Jewish customs, could explain to him who Paul was and what the issue was all about.

Agrippa II was the grandson of Herod the Great. The son of Herod the Great was the one who had had Peter arrested and James executed. He died in A.D.

44, and at the time of his death his son Agrippa II was only seventeen years old, and Rome did not think it appropriate to transfer to him the authority of his father. For a period of six years or so, the authority in that Jewish region was placed under a Roman procurator. Later on, when Agrippa II was twenty-three, Claudius appointed him as king over this Jewish region, although with not as much territory as his father had governed. A little later, Claudius enlarged his region, and even after Claudius was gone, the new emperor, Nero, gave even greater authority to Agrippa II, who came on the scene in A.D. 50 and lived until almost the end of the century.

Bernice was Agrippa II's sister. Her first marriage had been to her uncle, and when he died she came to live with her brother in an incestuous relationship. That was interrupted briefly when she married another man for a short time and then left him and came back to Agrippa II. Together with her brother, she pleaded with the Jews not to be involved with a rebellion against the Romans in the year A.D. 66, but their pleas fell on deaf ears. The Jews revolted. The Romans came in to conquer the land, which culminated in the destruction of Jerusalem under Titus in A.D. 70. Later, Titus succeeded his father as the emperor of Rome. Bernice left her brother again later and became the mistress of Titus, the general who led the expedition against Jerusalem, but Titus finally decided not to marry her; he did not think that the marriage would go over well with his constituents back in Rome. Historians say that Herod Agrippa II was not as cruel or as violent as his father and grandfather, but he was not a paragon of virtue from a moral standpoint.

So the next day, when Agrippa and Bernice had come with great pomp, and had entered the auditorium with the commanders and the prominent men of the city, at Festus' command Paul was brought in (v. 23). We are told that Agrippa and Bernice arrived in the city with great pomp, which means they came with their flags waving, their swords gleaming, and their horses prancing. Luke uses the Greek word *phantasias*, which the English translates as *pomp*. However, the word is typically translated as *fantasy*. All their pomp was really just fantasy because the real power was in the Jewish prisoner. There was no fantasy about the Apostle Paul. He spoke the sober truth, not fantastic imaginations.

Paul before Agrippa

They assembled the leading businessmen of the city for the interview, and finally Paul was brought before Agrippa, who permitted Paul to speak for himself. Paul stretched out his hand, not to quiet the crowd as he had done earlier but to give honor to the king. Paul said, **"I think myself happy, King Agrippa, because today I shall answer for myself before you concerning all the things of which**

I am accused by the Jews, especially because you are expert in all customs and questions which have to do with the Jews. Therefore I beg you to hear me patiently" (26:2–3). When I read this, I cannot help but think of Luther and the anguish he went through between 1517 and 1521. After he had tacked up the Ninety-five Theses on the church door of Wittenberg, word of it got back to Rome. When people accused Luther of being a heretic, he wanted to discuss the matters at hand as allowed for by church law. Year after year he was denied any real opportunity to defend himself. Finally the Diet of Worms was called, and Luther was excited that at last he would have an opportunity to explain his position biblically and historically. When he arrived, there was no debate. His accusers wanted only to hear him revoke his convictions.

The same sort of thing happened to Paul here. Finally he got a chance to explain his position before a king who knew Jewish law and tradition, and he expressed his happiness at the opportunity and begged him to listen patiently. **"My manner of life from my youth, which was spent from the beginning among my own nation at Jerusalem, all the Jews know"** (v. 4). Paul explained that according to the strictest sect of the Jewish religion, he had lived as a Pharisee. The Pharisees were those who, after the return from captivity, were very upset by the decadence of the new generation. The people had become secularized and turned their hearts away from the religion of their fathers. They forgot the covenant that God had made with Abraham. They forgot the law of God. The Pharisees wanted a revival to call people back to the foundation of the faith. They were the reformers of their day. However, even though they defended the truths of the ancient religion, they did not truly embrace them. Paul said that he had been one of them.

"Now I stand and am judged for the hope of the promise made by God to our fathers. To this promise our twelve tribes, earnestly serving God night and day, hope to attain. For this hope's sake, King Agrippa, I am accused by the Jews" (vv. 6–7). Before I agreed to start Ligonier Ministries in 1971, I sought permission from the local presbytery to undertake the pursuit. At that time I was a minister in a liberal mainline denomination. When I went before that presbytery to be examined, they were rather hostile. The church had adopted The Confession of 1967, which, while not repudiating earlier church confessions, attempted to neutralize them by making them one of many, thereby allowing those ordained into the denomination the freedom to pick and choose personal convictions from among the various creeds. When I told the presbytery that I hold to the Westminster Confession, they did not like it, and they asked me to leave the room while they considered my request. Before I left the room I said, "I only hope that if you judge me unfit for your presbytery that it is not because I am loyal to the confession under which I was ordained and, by the way, under which you were ordained and which you swore to uphold." I had put them in a difficult position. If they condemned me, they would condemn themselves. So with great reluctance they gave their okay for Ligonier Ministries to begin. Because of that experience, I can understand a bit of what the Apostle Paul was feeling here. Paul said that people were trying to kill him in the name of orthodoxy, when he was the orthodox one. He was under attack because he believed and taught the resurrection as set forth in the Old Testament in the fulfillment of the covenant that God had made with Abraham, Isaac, Jacob, David, Jeremiah, Daniel, and Ezekiel.

He Is Risen

"Why should it be thought incredible by you that God raises the dead?" (v. 8). We all today have been raised in a generation controlled by naturalism, a worldview that says there is no intelligent author of nature. Teaching the doctrine of creation in public schools is not allowed in this country, because ours is a godless country. Our culture is committed to naturalism, whereas Christians have been saying for centuries that man cannot understand nature apart from the light of super nature. Man cannot understand clouds or mathematics unless he first understands the author of clouds and mathematics. When naturalism prevails, people think life after death defies credibility. This is an intellectual war, not a question of religion. It is a question of truth. It is a question of life itself. I agree with Paul's words to the Corinthians: "If Christ is not risen, your faith is futile . . . if in this life only we have hope in Christ, we are of all men the most pitiable" (1 Cor. 15:17–19). Human beings did not pop from the head of Zeus or ooze from slime. There is an eternal, intelligent, almighty, sovereign God who breathed into us the breath of life. That is the Christian's view of life, and that is our view of death and resurrection. It is not something that should be seen as incredible.

After this exchange Paul recounted how he had persecuted believers, and for the third time in Acts we see his conversion experience on the road to Damascus. We find here a couple of details not mentioned in the earlier accounts. As we noted in an earlier study, there are several places in Scripture where we encounter someone being addressed by the repetition of his or her name. God stopped Abraham from plunging the dagger into his son Isaac at the last moment, saying, "Abraham, Abraham! . . . Do not lay your hand on the lad" (Gen. 22:11–12). God later addressed Jacob in the same terms. We see it again with Elisha when the chariots of fire came for Elijah. When Samuel was in the temple at the tutelage of Eli, he heard a voice calling him, "Samuel! Samuel!" and Samuel answered,

"Speak, for Your servant hears" (1 Sam. 3:10). When David got the news of the death of his rebellious son, he tore his garments and cried in agony, "O my son Absalom—my son, my son Absalom" (2 Sam. 18:33). Jesus used it on more than one occasion: "Martha, Martha" (Luke 10:41); "Simon, Simon! Indeed, Satan has asked for you, that he may sift you as wheat" (Luke 22:31); "My God, My God, why have You forsaken Me?" (Matt. 27:46). Sprinkled throughout the Scriptures we have this form of personal address.

Here in Acts we read that Jesus stopped Paul and addressed him by name in the most tender and intimate terms: **"Saul, Saul, why are you persecuting Me?"** and immediately after He said something that we see only here: **"It is hard for you to kick against the goads"** (v. 14). This was a reference to the manner in which oxcarts were driven. At the front of the oxcart was a plate with spikes jutting out. When a stubborn ox refused to move, the driver would hit the ox with a switch, and the ox in anger would kick back, driving its feet right into those spikes. Just so, Paul had once fought against Jesus. Many today do the same thing. They fight and kick against Christ and the gospel all their days in an effort to resist Him.

Paul continued with the story of his conversion. Jesus had said to him, **"But rise and stand on your feet; for I have appeared to you for this purpose, to make you a minister and a witness both of the things which you have seen and of the things which I will yet reveal to you. I will deliver you from the Jewish people, as well as from the Gentiles, to whom I now send you, to open their eyes, in order to turn them from darkness to light, and from the power of Satan to God, that they may receive forgiveness of sins and an inheritance among those who are sanctified by faith in Me"** (vv. 16–18). Why would anybody want to stay in the darkness? We get the answer from John. The darkness is our natural habitat. "Men loved darkness rather than light, because their deeds were evil" (John 3:19). The light exposes this.

Paul was saying, "King Agrippa, what do you do with your sin? Don't you want to receive forgiveness and by faith be sanctified and made holy in the sight of God? Are you listening, King?" The people who were standing there that day chose the darkness. They did not want their eyes opened. They preferred the power of Satan to the power of God, so they lived and died in their fantasy. God forbid that that should happen to any of us.

59

ALMOST PERSUADED

Acts 26:19–32

"Therefore, King Agrippa, I was not disobedient to the heavenly vision, but declared first to those in Damascus and in Jerusalem, and throughout all the region of Judea, and then to the Gentiles, that they should repent, turn to God, and do works befitting repentance. For these reasons the Jews seized me in the temple and tried to kill me. Therefore, having obtained help from God, to this day I stand, witnessing both to small and great, saying no other things than those which the prophets and Moses said would come—that the Christ would suffer, that He would be the first to rise from the dead, and would proclaim light to the Jewish people and to the Gentiles." Now as he thus made his defense, Festus said with a loud voice, "Paul, you are beside yourself! Much learning is driving you mad!" But he said, "I am not mad, most noble Festus, but speak the words of truth and reason. For the king, before whom I also speak freely, knows these things: for I am convinced that none of these things escapes his attention, since this thing was not done in a corner. King Agrippa, do you believe the prophets? I know that you do believe." Then Agrippa said to Paul, "You almost persuade me to become a Christian." And Paul said, "I would to God that not only you, but also all who hear me today, might become both almost and altogether such as I am, except for these chains." When he had said these things, the king stood up, as well as the governor and Bernice and those who sat with them; and when they had gone aside, they talked among themselves, saying, "This man is doing nothing deserving of death or chains." Then Agrippa said to Festus, "This man might have been set free if he had not appealed to Caesar."

We have been looking at Paul's defense before King Agrippa, where, for the third time in the book of Acts, we had related to us the circumstances of Paul's dramatic conversion on the desert road to Damascus. He saw a light that was brighter than the noonday sun and heard the voice of Jesus speaking to him in Hebrew and calling him to his mission. After reciting the events of his conversion, Paul said, **"Therefore, King Agrippa, I was not disobedient to the heavenly vision"** (v. 19).

Paul's Obedience

I have never seen a light brighter than the noonday sun. I have never had a visual experience of the risen Christ. I have not seen Him face-to-face, nor have I heard the sound of His voice in my ear. I trust that is true for you as well. Biblical conversion is the immediate supernatural work upon the soul of a sinner who has heretofore lived in darkness but now, through a divine and supernatural light, is brought out into the kingdom of light. Therefore, in a very real sense, though not sensory, we also have experienced the *visio Dei*, or the vision of God, in our soul. However, unlike Paul, we cannot say that we have never been disobedient to that heavenly vision. We may excuse ourselves by saying, "But who is? Who is completely faithful to the end?" Paul was. Paul was not bragging; he was speaking the truth before the king. He had not been disobedient to the vision that Christ had given him.

Paul went on to say that he had kept the Great Commission. He had preached first in Jerusalem to the Jews, then in Judea, and then to the Gentiles. He had stood before little and great proclaiming the word of God and calling people to repent. Paul was not here articulating a doctrine of justification by works; in fact, there has never been a clearer advocate of justification by faith alone. Paul understood that our works do nothing to make us right in the sight of God; but once we have been converted, our faith is supposed to produce works of obedience and righteousness in our lives. That is the message Paul had preached in all those places, and it is why people had tried so hard to kill him.

"Therefore, having obtained help from God, to this day I stand, witnessing both to small and great, saying no other things than those which the prophets and Moses said would come—that the Christ would suffer, that He would be the first to rise from the dead, and would proclaim light to the Jewish people and to the Gentiles" (vv. 22–23). The Bible teaches that the servant of Israel would suffer, die, and be raised from the grave, and He would be a light to the nations. Here Paul talks about the Messiah, the baby fulfilling the Old Testament prophecy of bringing the light of God to the Gentiles.

The king and the governor had both agreed to let Paul speak, but Festus couldn't stand anymore, so he finally interrupted Paul in a loud voice and said, **"Paul, you are beside yourself! Much learning is driving you mad!"** (v. 24). In other words, "Paul, I understand that you are learned, but I'm afraid you have been educated beyond your intelligence. They say there's a thin line between genius and insanity, and I think you've skated over the line, Paul." The Greek word "mad" here is the word from which we get the English word *maniac*. Festus was saying that Paul was a maniac. From the Latin translation of the word, we get the English term *insane*. Festus was telling Paul that he had to be crazy to believe this sort of thing.

Paul was not ruffled; he listened to the charge. This wasn't the first time somebody had called him crazy. He responded, **"I am not mad, most noble Festus, but speak the words of truth and reason"** (v. 25). Paul did not care about religion. Christianity is not about religion; it is about truth, sober truth. It is not about finding a purpose for your life but coming to a saving knowledge of Christ and understanding the whole world around you in light of the truth of God. It is a sobering truth.

Truth Rejected

Paul included Agrippa in his response to Festus: **"For the king, before whom I also speak freely, knows these things; for I am convinced that none of these things escapes his attention, since this thing was not done in a corner. King Agrippa, do you believe the prophets? I know that you do believe"** (vv. 26–27). Christianity did not begin as a mystery religion with secret rites and rituals that only the initiates knew about. It did not begin like the Mormon religion in Palmyra, New York, when Joseph Smith said he had received special revelation on golden tablets hidden from others' view. The manifestation of the Son of God was a public matter. It was not secret or private. There is a pernicious cliché uttered in the church today. Likely you have heard it; maybe you have said it, and if so, you had best get on your knees and ask God to forgive you. It is this: "My faith is personal and private." If your faith is private, the faith you have is not Christian faith, because a Christian who trusts Christ is commanded to declare Him before others. Yet that is what the world tells us we ought to be like. "Oh, you can have your religion; just keep it in your closet. Don't mention it in the workplace. Don't mention it in the school. Don't mention it in the public square. Make sure it's personal and private, and we'll all get along." Jesus said, "For whoever is ashamed of Me and My words, of him the Son of Man will be ashamed when He comes in His own glory, and in His Father's, and of the holy angels" (Luke 9:26). Jesus was killed publicly. He was raised from the dead and did not appear to just a few disciples in the upper room, but He appeared to over five hundred people at one time. It is a public matter, and God has declared that this truth is to be made known to the whole world.

Agrippa replied with agonizingly pathetic words: **"You almost persuade me to become a Christian"** (v. 28). These were the most tragic words Agrippa uttered in his life. The Apostle of Christ was standing before him, preaching Christ to him, and Agrippa said that he was almost persuaded, but not quite. Some time ago a conversation between two professional golfers was told to me. Following a tournament, one of the golfers said, "The difference between winning a tournament and not winning a tournament is one stroke." The other countered, "The difference of one stroke is not a tournament; it's a career. One stroke better and my life changes dramatically." This pro had almost won the tournament. Everybody has those "almost" moments in their lives. At times we think, *If I had just done this one other thing, what a difference it would have made in my life.* Or, *If I just hadn't done that one thing, how different my life would be.*

In my living room over the mantle hangs a painting of the Apostle Paul standing before Agrippa. The first time I saw that painting, I wanted it because it so beautifully depicts the words that Paul said next to Agrippa: **"I would to God that not only you, but also all who hear me today, might become both almost and altogether such as I am, except for these chains"** (v. 29). That is my plea also, that no one would turn away from the gospel and spend eternity in regret.

When he had said these things, the king stood up, as well as the governor and Bernice and those who sat with them; and when they had gone aside, they talked among themselves, saying, "This man is doing nothing deserving of death or chains" (vv. 30–31). They were persuaded enough to be nice to Paul. It is too bad that he had appealed to Caesar; otherwise he would have been set free. Yet the Apostle was not thinking at that moment about his freedom. His heart was burdened by their chains, not by his.

60

PAUL IN THE TEMPEST

Acts 27:1–38

And when it was decided that we should sail to Italy, they delivered Paul and some other prisoners to one named Julius, a centurion of the Augustan Regiment. So, entering a ship of Adramyttium, we put to sea, meaning to sail along the coasts of Asia. Aristarchus, a Macedonian of Thessalonica, was with us. And the next day we landed at Sidon. And Julius treated Paul kindly and gave him liberty to go to his friends and receive care. When we had put to sea from there, we sailed under the shelter of Cyprus, because the winds were contrary. And when we had sailed over the sea which is off Cilicia and Pamphylia, we came to Myra, a city of Lycia. There the centurion found an Alexandrian ship sailing to Italy, and he put us on board. When we had sailed slowly many days, and arrived with difficulty off Cnidus, the wind not permitting us to proceed, we sailed under the shelter of Crete off Salmone. Passing it with difficulty, we came to a place called Fair Havens, near the city of Lasea. Now when much time had been spent, and sailing was now dangerous because the Fast was already over, Paul advised them, saying, "Men, I perceive that this voyage will end with disaster and much loss, not only of the cargo and ship, but also our lives." Nevertheless the centurion was more persuaded by the helmsman and the owner of the ship than by the things spoken by Paul. And because the harbor was not suitable to winter in, the majority advised to set sail from there also, if by any means they could reach Phoenix, a harbor of Crete opening toward the southwest and northwest, and winter there. When the south wind blew softly, supposing that they had obtained their desire, putting out to sea, they sailed close by Crete. But not long after, a tempestuous head wind arose, called Euroclydon. So when the ship was caught, and could not head into the wind, we let her drive. And running under the shelter of an island called Clauda, we secured the skiff with difficulty. When they had taken it on board, they used cables to undergird the ship; and fearing lest they should run aground on the Syrtis Sands, they struck sail and so were driven. And because we were exceedingly tempest-tossed, the next day they lightened the ship. On the third day we threw the ship's tackle overboard with our own hands. Now when neither sun nor stars appeared for many days, and no small tempest beat on us, all hope that we would be saved was finally given up. But after long abstinence from food, then Paul stood in the midst of them and said, "Men, you should have listened to me, and not have sailed from Crete and incurred this disaster and loss. And now I urge you to take heart, for there will be no loss of life among you, but only of the ship. For there stood by me this night an angel of the God to whom I belong and whom I serve, saying, 'Do not be afraid, Paul; you must be brought before Caesar; and indeed God has granted you all those who sail with you.' Therefore take heart, men, for I believe God that it will be just as it was told me. However, we must run aground on a certain island." Now when the fourteenth night had come, as we were driven up and down in the Adriatic Sea, about midnight the sailors sensed that they were drawing near some land. And they took soundings and found it to be twenty fathoms; and when they had gone a little farther, they took soundings again and found it to be fifteen fathoms. Then, fearing lest we should run aground on the rocks, they dropped four anchors from the stern, and prayed for day to come. And as the sailors were seeking to escape from the ship, when they had let down the skiff into the sea, under pretense of putting out anchors from the prow, Paul said to the centurion and the soldiers, "Unless these men stay in the ship, you cannot be saved." Then the soldiers cut away the ropes of the skiff and let it fall off. And as day was about to dawn, Paul implored them all to take food, saying, "Today is the fourteenth day you have waited and continued without food, and eaten nothing. Therefore I urge you to take nourishment, for this is for your survival, since not a hair will fall from the head of any of you." And when he had said these things, he took bread and gave thanks to God in the presence of them all; and when he had broken it he began to eat. Then they were all encouraged, and also took food themselves. And in all we were two hundred and seventy-six persons on the ship. So when they had eaten enough, they lightened the ship and threw out the wheat into the sea.

William Foxwell Albright was to twentieth-century archaeology what Albert Einstein was to physics. Albright was in a class by himself. He was the first one to date the Dead Sea Scrolls. The last thing he wrote before he died was an academic introduction to the Gospel of Matthew in the scholarly Anchor Bible Series. In that introduction Albright took his fellow scholars to task for their unbridled and unwarranted skepticism of the historical reliability of the Scriptures. He criticized the scholars of his generation for basing too much of their criticism on pure speculation, on a biased approach to Scriptures, and on what Albright called the "baleful influence of existential philosophy." He chided them for their lack of scientific integrity. There are certain principles of historiography that sober scientists should follow, and he reminded them that the most significant test of historical reliability comes through empirical research, such as that found in archaeology.

To Albright's remarks I would add that there has been no time in the history of the church since the first century with less reason to affirm without reservation the historical accuracy of the New Testament. The ongoing criticism and assault against the Bible in our day is based on gratuitous hostility, not on science. Of course, there are only so many things that can be verified or falsified through the science of archaeology. Some of the supernatural events recorded in the New Testament, such as the appearance of the angel Gabriel to Mary announcing the Nativity, cannot be proven or disproven by archaeology. However, there is much in the Scripture of a historical nature that can be subjected to the objective verification or falsification of such historiographical methods.

One of the most remarkable sections of the New Testament is Acts 27. Luke was not a professional mariner or a member of the royal navy, yet historians have said that Acts 27 contains a masterful presentation of what took place in tempests on the Mediterranean Sea in the ancient world of shipping. Luke's account outdoes the graphic descriptions of Homer in the *Odyssey* and even the book of Jonah in the Old Testament. Indeed, the trip is described from a layperson's point of view but with amazing accuracy concerning the exact techniques that were used by sailors to guard against shipwreck. The dragging anchors, the use of cables to wrap around a ship's hull, and dealing with the wind are all described according to ancient practice. The details found in Acts 27 are exactly the way ancient mariners dealt with storms at sea. The storm we find here could qualify for the sequel to Sebastian Junger's *The Perfect Storm*.

Out to Sea

We left off our study of the life of Paul looking at his hearing before King Agrippa and Festus. After that we read, **When it was decided that we should sail to Italy, they delivered Paul and some other prisoners to one named Julius, a centurion of the Augustan Regiment** (v. 1). Paul was put under arrest and kept under the guard of a member of the imperial police named Julius. Paul, Aristarchus, Luke, and other prisoners were put onboard a ship from Caesarea, and they sailed first north to Sidon. The ship they were on initially was a coastal ship; that is, it was not a ship built for the open seas. It hugged the coast of the land as much as possible so as to avoid capsizing.

At the end of Paul's second letter to Timothy, Paul asked Timothy to come to Rome and visit him before winter and to bring his cloak and parchments (2 Tim. 4:13). The reason for the plea to come before winter was that by the middle of October, ships stopped sailing in the Mediterranean. During the months of November, December, and January, the waters were so treacherous that to sail then was to risk one's life.

At this point in their journey, Paul issued a warning: **"Men, I perceive that this voyage will end with disaster and much loss, not only of the cargo and ship, but also our lives"** (v. 10). In other words, the crew would do well to winter on land because if they were to head out to open sea at that time of year, they would never make it to Rome. However, the mariners had cargo to deliver, and there was money to be made. **Nevertheless the centurion was more persuaded by the helmsman and the owner of the ship than by the things spoken by Paul. And because the harbor was not suitable to winter in, the majority advised to set sail from there also, if by any means they could reach Phoenix, a harbor of Crete opening toward the southwest and northwest, and winter there** (vv. 11–12). They did not listen to Paul. The ship was large, carrying 276 people, so the mariners thought they could survive the winter weather.

They started out, and the winds were favorable at first. **But not long after, a tempestuous head wind arose, called Euroclydon. So when the ship was caught, and could not head into the wind, we let her drive. And running under the shelter of an island called Clauda, we secured the skiff with difficulty. When they had taken it on board, they used cables to undergird the ship; and fearing lest they should run aground on the Syrtis Sands, they struck sail and so were driven** (vv. 14–17). They used all the tricks they knew. They lightened the ship and threw the ballast overboard. After a while they threw over their important equipment, and after that they tossed the wheat in order to insure their survival. Nevertheless, conditions continued to deteriorate until finally, **when neither sun nor stars appeared for many days, and no small tempest beat on us, all hope that we would be saved was finally given up** (v. 20).

Spared

These professional sailors had done everything they knew to make the ship safe, but it all failed, and they had given up hope. After enduring a long abstinence from food, Paul stood in the midst of them and said, **"Men, you should have listened to me"** (v. 21). I do not think this was a case of "I told you so," some of the cruelest words that can be uttered to someone. Rather, Paul was telling them that his earlier words had been a prophetic warning from God. Paul was reminding them that what he had said would come to pass had indeed come to pass, and it is likely that he did so because he was about to make another prophetic announcement: **"And now I urge you to take heart, for there will be no loss of life among you, but only of the ship. For there stood by me this night an angel of the God to whom I belong and whom I serve, saying, 'Do not be afraid, Paul; you must be brought before Caesar; and indeed God has granted you all those who sail with you'"** (vv. 22–24).

Paul did not speak of the God of heaven and earth, or of the God of providence, or of the God who rules over the seas. He said that he had heard directly from the God to whom he belongs. This was so typical of Paul. Throughout his epistles he wrote about divine ownership, such as we see in the Old Testament: "The earth is the LORD's, and all its fullness" (Ps. 24:1). From the standpoint of creation God owns it all, but beyond that Paul spoke of redemption in a special sense of ownership: "You were bought at a price" (1 Cor. 6:20). Paul began his letter to the Romans, "Paul, a bondservant of Jesus Christ, called to be an apostle" (1:1). I do not like an older translation that has, "Paul, a *servant* of the Lord Jesus Christ, called to be an apostle," because a servant gets wages and can come and go at will. That is not true of a *doulos*, a bondservant or slave. The word *church* comes from the Greek word *kyriaki*, which means "Those who are the possession of the kyrios," or, "Those who belong to the Lord." That is what the true church is—the possession of God, the possession of the Lord Jesus Christ.

At the end of the Sermon on the Mount Jesus said, "Many will say to Me in that day, 'Lord, Lord, have we not prophesied in Your name, cast out demons in Your name, and done many wonders in Your name?' And then I will declare to them, 'I never knew you; depart from Me, you who practice lawlessness!'" (Matt. 7:22–23). In Christian jargon we ask each other, "Do you know the Lord? Do you know Jesus?" What we need to be asking is, "Does Jesus know you?" The issue is not whether we possess Christ but whether He possesses us.

Another metaphor Jesus used often was that of the shepherd and the sheep. Jesus is not a hireling contracted to watch over someone else's sheep; rather, the Good Shepherd knows the sheep because they belong to Him. They are His sheep, and they became His possession. "All that the Father gives Me will come to Me" (John 6:37). The sheep of Christ first belong to the Father, and then the Father in His electing grace gives those sheep to His Son. The only reason I can give for why I am in the kingdom of God today is that the Father gave me to the Son that He might see the travail of His soul and be satisfied. He gave to His Son an inheritance. He gave to His Son a possession, and that possession is His people. We are His sheep. We belong to Him.

So Paul was given a message from the "angel of the God to whom I belong and whom I serve." This is almost a redundancy. How can someone belong to Jesus and not serve Him? That is something we need to stop and look at. Are you serving Christ in your life? Honestly, do you serve Him? If you do not, then you do not belong to Him, because you cannot belong to Christ unless you serve Him with your life. What Paul describes here was not unique to him. It is the situation of all genuine Christians.

The angel told Paul, "Do not be afraid, Paul; you must be brought before Caesar." This is what Paul had told them in the first place. He knew that he would get to Rome because the Lord Jesus Christ had told Paul that he had a mission to perform there. The angel had told Paul that he would be brought before Caesar and that all onboard the ship would make it to land. None of the sailors on that ship had any claim to redemption. The only reason those sailors survived that storm was that God in His mercy granted them rescue for Paul's sake.

Salvation is salvation from God, from His judgment and wrath. We are not saved because we have led a good life. We are saved only for Christ's sake. God saves us for the sake of His Son. God honored Mephibosheth, the lame son of Jonathan, not because Mephibosheth was righteous but because David loved Jonathan; so for Jonathan's sake Mephibosheth was saved. For Jesus' sake, we are saved. That is what happened here in the providence of God. God's mercy extended beyond the individual to those who were part of his family or entourage. God spared the whole crew on that ship.

"Therefore take heart, men, for I believe God that it will be just as it was told me" (v. 25). It is easy to believe in the existence of God. God makes His existence so manifest that anyone who denies it is a liar. In the United States, we now have National Atheist's Day on the calendar. It fittingly falls on April Fool's Day; the Bible says, "The fool has said in his heart 'There is no God'" (Ps. 14:1). Anybody can believe that God exists. Believing in God isn't hard; what is difficult is *believing* God. Paul told the sailors that not one of them would perish. He believed that God would do exactly what He said He would do.

Christian, do you believe that about your life? God has never said that you will not go through the valley of the shadow of death, but He has said that He will go with you. Our Lord Jesus said to His friends, "Let not your heart be troubled. . . . In My Father's house are many mansions; if it were not so, I would have told you. I go to prepare a place for you" (John 14:1–2). He always does what He says he will do, and what happened with the sailors was exactly as God had said. Not a hair on their heads was harmed.

Not everybody believed him. Some of the men took the skiff and started to lower it over the side, but Paul stopped them. If they were to get in the lifeboat, they would never make it. So the centurion cut the lifeboat adrift and trusted in the word of God, who alone could save them.

And as day was about to dawn, Paul implored them all to take food, saying, "Today is the fourteenth day you have waited and continued without food, and eaten nothing. Therefore I urge you to take nourishment, for this is for your survival, since not a hair will fall from the head of any of you." And when he had said these things, he took bread and gave thanks to God in the presence of them all; and when he had broken it he began to eat. Then they were all encouraged, and also took food themselves (vv. 33–36). I do not believe that Paul celebrated the Lord's Supper on the deck of that ship—not with unbelievers—but he did share a meal. When Jesus shared a meal in the upper room with His disciples for the very last time, He took bread, and when He blessed it He broke it and said, "'This is My body which is given for you; do this in remembrance of Me.' Likewise He also took the cup after supper, saying, 'This cup is the new covenant in My blood, which is shed for you'" (Luke 22:19–20). When we participate in the Supper, we show forth the Lord's death, even though the Lord is alive and He is here. He does what He says He will do, so He is here.

61

PAUL AT MALTA

Acts 28:1–15

Now when they had escaped, they then found out that the island was called Malta. And the natives showed us unusual kindness; for they kindled a fire and made us all welcome, because of the rain that was falling and because of the cold. But when Paul had gathered a bundle of sticks and laid them on the fire, a viper came out because of the heat, and fastened on his hand. So when the natives saw the creature hanging from his hand, they said to one another, "No doubt this man is a murderer, whom, though he has escaped the sea, yet justice does not allow to live." But he shook off the creature into the fire and suffered no harm. However, they were expecting that he would swell up or suddenly fall down dead. But after they had looked for a long time and saw no harm come to him, they changed their minds and said that he was a god. In that region there was an estate of the leading citizen of the island, whose name was Publius, who received us and entertained us courteously for three days. And it happened that the father of Publius lay sick of a fever and dysentery. Paul went in to him and prayed, and he laid his hands on him and healed him. So when this was done, the rest of those on the island who had diseases also came and were healed. They also honored us in many ways; and when we departed, they provided such things as were necessary. After three months we sailed in an Alexandrian ship whose figurehead was the Twin Brothers, which had wintered at the island. And landing at Syracuse, we stayed three days. From there we circled round and reached Rhegium. And after one day the south wind blew; and the next day we came to Puteoli, where we found brethren, and were invited to stay with them seven days. And so we went toward Rome. And from there, when the brethren heard about us, they came to meet us as far as Appii Forum and Three Inns. When Paul saw them, he thanked God and took courage.

Acts 27 ends by telling what happened after the ship carrying 276 passengers floundered. When the ship broke up, those who could swim made it to shore on their own. Those who could not swim held onto pieces of wood from the broken ship until they washed up on shore. Just as Paul had prophesied, not a single person onboard the ship lost his life; they all reached the beach alive, if utterly exhausted, cold, and wet. It was November, a very cold time of year on Malta. The natives of Malta were called Barbarians by the Greeks because the Greeks considered anybody who wasn't Greek or Jewish to be barbarian. We discover, however, that they hardly acted like vicious barbarians but were extremely hospitable toward the shipwrecked men. They dragged them out of the water and brought them safely to shore. They built a bonfire to warm them and cooked food to feed them.

As was typical for Paul, he did not simply stand around and watch. He participated in this ministry of mercy. He gathered twigs and threw them on the fire, and at that point an extraordinary event took place. A viper was quickened by the heat of the fire and fastened onto Paul's hand. A snakebite in winter? During the summer in Florida, it is not safe to go into the woods, but in December and January one can tromp around among the palmettos without fear of snakes because at that time of year, they are either asleep or very torpid. This incident has been the target of certain critics throughout church history. One criticism is that there are no snakes on the island of Malta. However, we have records from antiquity that indicate snakes once inhabited certain places that they no longer inhabit because those places became too heavily populated by humans.

Snakebite

Another criticism is that a viper does not strike and hold onto its victim; it strikes suddenly and then pulls back its fangs. Therefore, they say, Luke was incorrect about a viper biting Paul and holding on. However, there are numerous examples of vipers that get their fangs caught on clothing or boots and cannot let go. I know a man who was struck by a six-foot diamondback rattlesnake, but fortunately he was wearing boots. The boots prevented the snake's fangs from penetrating too deeply into his foot; however, the fangs stuck in the boot, and the man could not get rid of the snake, as much as he tried to shake it loose. So it is very possible that the snake in Luke's account got caught on Paul's sleeve while it was striking him.

Yet another criticism is that the natives wrongly identified the snake as a viper. These critics know nothing about the ancient flora and fauna of Malta, yet they doubt the word of the eyewitnesses.

The reason they struggle so much with the story is obvious: it was a miracle.

Luke records it as such, the truth of what happened by the intervention of Almighty God.

Although the natives were kind and generous, they were, like many of us, swift to make incorrect judgments. **So when the natives saw the creature hanging from his hand, they said to one another, "No doubt this man is a murderer, whom, though he has escaped the sea, yet justice does not allow to live"** (v. 4). How else could they explain that Paul first survived a shipwreck and then a deadly snakebite? This they attributed to Nemesis, the mythological god of vengeance. That god is how the word *nemesis* came into our language. Somebody who constantly gives us a hard time and makes our lives miserable we refer to as our "nemesis." The natives attributed this work to the god Nemesis, whose job it was to bring justice to people where other attempts to bring justice had failed. That was their first assumption, so they prepared for Paul's imminent demise. They watched and waited for Paul to swell up and drop over dead. When Paul did not swell or die, they realized that they had made a mistake. Paul wasn't a murderer at all, but a god. They were wrong again. Paul was neither a murderer nor a god. Rather, he was an Apostle of Jesus Christ fulfilling the mission that Christ had given to him.

Jesus said, "Go into all the world and preach the gospel to every creature. He who believes and is baptized will be saved; but he who does not believe will be condemned. And these signs will follow those who believe: In My name they will cast out demons; they will speak with new tongues; they will take up serpents; and if they drink anything deadly, it will by no means hurt them; they will lay hands on the sick, and they will recover" (Mark 16:15–18). Virtually every one of those signs took place in the life and mission of the Apostle Paul. In passing, I will mention that the incident here is the text that religious snake handlers use as a proof text for their practices.

Publius's Father Cured

In that region there was an estate of the leading citizen of the island, whose name was Publius, who received us and entertained us courteously for three days. And it happened that the father of Publius lay sick of a fever and dysentery. Paul went in to him and prayed, and he laid his hands on him and healed him (vv. 7–8). The father of Publius had Maltese Fever, a recurring illness caused by bacteria that was common to the goats on the island. Luke correctly diagnosed the problem. In some respects it was like malaria. There was an acute phase, when the afflicted one would be desperately ill. This phase was followed by a recovery that lasted six months to a year, after which the acute phase would occur again. One afflicted with this malady would suffer recurring bouts of the illness throughout his lifetime.

Luke diagnosed it, and Paul cured it. Paul came to the father of Publius and laid his hands on him and cured him of this dreadful disease. When the word of the healing spread around the countryside, people with all kinds of diseases came, and Paul laid his hands on them, and they were healed. Even while he was a prisoner and even though his missionary journeys were over, Paul was still being used of Christ in the ministry of the apostolic faith.

Winter Voyage

After this follows a description of the rest of the voyage. **After three months we sailed in an Alexandrian ship whose figurehead was the Twin Brothers, which had wintered at the island** (v. 11). Every ship from that time had a name derived from the decoration or adornment carved on its prow. This particular ship had in its prow the decorative carving of the mythical twins Casper and Pollux whose correspondence was in the constellation called Gemini. Today, only those who follow horoscopes believe that the constellation Gemini has any influence over the lives of people, but ancient mariners believed that Gemini had particular jurisdiction over the sea and mariners. In any case, Paul got onboard this Alexandrian ship named after the twins, and it set sail for Italy.

And landing at Syracuse, we stayed three days (v. 12). Syracuse was the major city of Sicily. **From there we circled round and reached Rhegium** (v. 13), which is on the toe of the boot of Italy. So they sailed from Syracuse in Sicily to Rhegium. In order to make that journey by sea, they had to pass through the Strait of Messina, which was a very narrow passageway famous at that time for its treacherous waters.

The treacherousness of that portion of the sea has been immortalized for all time in Greek literature and on into English history through the work of Homer. In *The Odyssey*, Odysseus has to sail his ship through the Strait of Messina between Scylla and Charybdis. Anytime someone faces a dangerous voyage or a difficult decision, they say they are "between a rock and a hard place." Well, the ancient people would say they were between Scylla and Charybdis. Scylla was a mythological monster dog who was said to live in a cave by the shore of the Strait of Messina. If a ship unawares sailed too close to that shore, then Scylla would jump from the cave and snatch one or two sailors from the ship, take them back into his cave, and devour them. Charybdis was a whirlpool that appeared three times every day. It was a violent whirlpool such that if a ship sailed near and got caught up in the eddy, it was taken down to the bottom of the sea. Odysseus was very careful when he sailed through that strait to favor the side of Scylla rather than Charybdis, because the worst that could happen on the

Scylla side was that he might lose one or two sailors, but if he got too close to Charybdis, all hands would go to the bottom of the sea. Of course, there really was no Scylla or Charybdis—just treacherous sea that on this occasion carried the cargo of Paul the Apostle.

From there we circled round and reached Rhegium. And after one day the south wind blew; and the next day we came to Puteoli, where we found brethren, and were invited to stay with them seven days. And so we went toward Rome (vv. 13–14). Finally, after all these hardships, the ship bearing Paul finally arrived in Italy. The rest of the trip would be on land.

Paul on Roman Soil

When Paul arrived in Italy, those who greeted him were Christians. This was Paul's first visit to those to whom he had written three years earlier, saying, "I make mention of you always in my prayers, making request if, by some means, now at last I may find a way in the will of God to come to you. For I long to see you, that I may impart to you some spiritual gift, so that you may be established" (Rom. 1:9–11). He was clearly passionate to get to the believers in Rome, and now, by the invisible hand of providence, the means had been found.

After staying a few days on the coast, they began the overland journey to the city of Rome. We are told that on the way they got as far as the Appii Forum and the Three Inns. Rome was founded in the same year that Isaiah saw the Lord high and lifted up (Isa. 6:1). The Roman Empire lasted over a thousand years, so Rome was basically the central city of the world for over a millennium. To this day, structures from those glory days remain. The Circus Maximus, the coliseum, the ruins of the temples and of the forum, and the Mamertine Prison where Paul spent his last hours—all are still there. The Romans were famous not for their art but for their engineering and architectural skills. The saying "All roads lead to Rome" came about as a result of the city's well-built transportation system. The roads they built did not need to be replaced every two or three years like ours do. If you go to Rome today, you can still make your way along portions of the Appian Way.

At long last, Paul arrived at this destination, and he arrived there by the providence of God. What can we learn from this? All who are in Christ have a manifest destiny, and God will bring each one to it. As Christians we do not believe that our ultimate destiny is in the hands of blind fate or of the furies or of arbitrary promiscuous deities. This is our Father's world, and we are His children; He has appointed for every one of us a final point, and He will bring us there. In the midst of storm, shipwreck, beatings, and pain, when we start to lose courage and give up hope and think that the invisible hand of God has let us go, we need only remember His servant Paul, who took courage when his feet landed safely on Roman soil. That is the God we worship, who has each one of His people in the hollow of His hand. He will not let us go.

62

PAUL AT ROME

Acts 28:16–31

Now when we came to Rome, the centurion delivered the prisoners to the captain of the guard; but Paul was permitted to dwell by himself with the soldier who guarded him. And it came to pass after three days that Paul called the leaders of the Jews together. So when they had come together, he said to them: "Men and brethren, though I have done nothing against our people or the customs of our fathers, yet I was delivered as a prisoner from Jerusalem into the hands of the Romans, who, when they had examined me, wanted to let me go, because there was no cause for putting me to death. But when the Jews spoke against it, I was compelled to appeal to Caesar, not that I had anything of which to accuse my nation. For this reason therefore I have called for you, to see you and speak with you, because for the hope of Israel I am bound with this chain." Then they said to him, "We neither received letters from Judea concerning you, nor have any of the brethren who came reported or spoken any evil of you. But we desire to hear from you what you think; for concerning this sect, we know that it is spoken against everywhere." So when they had appointed him a day, many came to him at his lodging, to whom he explained and solemnly testified of the kingdom of God, persuading them concerning Jesus from both the Law of Moses and the Prophets, from morning till evening. And some were persuaded by the things which were spoken, and some disbelieved. So when they did not agree among themselves, they departed after Paul had said one word: "The Holy Spirit spoke rightly through Isaiah the prophet to our fathers, saying, 'Go to this people and say:

"Hearing you will hear, and shall not understand;
And seeing you will see, and not perceive;
For the hearts of this people have grown dull.
Their ears are hard of hearing,
And their eyes they have closed,
Lest they should see with their eyes and hear with their ears,
Lest they should understand with their hearts and turn,
So that I should heal them.'"

"Therefore let it be known to you that the salvation of God has been sent to the Gentiles, and they will hear it!" And when he had said these words, the Jews departed and had a great dispute among themselves. Then Paul dwelt two whole years in his own rented house, and received all who came to him, preaching the kingdom of God and teaching the things which concern the Lord Jesus Christ with all confidence, no one forbidding him.

Luke tells us that when Paul and his entourage finally came into the city of Rome, the centurion turned over all the prisoners, except for one, to the one in charge of the fortress prison in the Roman barracks.

House Arrest

Paul was not incarcerated in the Roman jail but was put on house arrest. House arrest meant that Paul could enjoy the company of his friends even though he was kept under guard twenty-four hours a day, chained by his wrist to one of the guards. The guards changed shifts every four hours, so in a twenty-four-hour period, six different guards were chained to the Apostle Paul. Surely they did not appreciate that guard duty because by it they were restricted to Paul's activities and company. Yet there were no more blessed prison guards in the history of the world than those six men who had the unspeakable privilege of being cuffed to the wrist of the world's greatest preacher of all time. We can only imagine their situation at the judgment day if they ignored the teaching they heard while they were guarding God's anointed.

The closest thing I have witnessed to a house arrest occurred while I was teaching at Gordon-Conwell Seminary during the administration of President Gerald Ford. Ford's son was enrolled in the seminary and preparing for the ministry. Although he was the son of the president of the United States, most of the time he felt like a prisoner. Everywhere he went, he was accompanied by two members of the Secret Service. When he arrived at my class, which was held in a large amphitheater, the Secret Service agents escorted him to his chair and then went out of the room to stand guard by the doors. Sometime about the third day of lectures, the Secret Service agents no longer waited outside the doors but remained in the room to listen to the lecture. They began taking notes and continued to do so for the duration of the course. The agents seem to have been influenced by him while he was under their protection so that they had taken an interest in the things of God. In the same way, I cannot help but wonder what happened to those guards who were with Paul day and night during his two years of house arrest in Rome.

After three days, Paul summoned the leaders of the Jewish community in Rome to visit him. He did not go to the synagogue, as was his custom, because he was under arrest, but he sent a message to the leaders and invited them to come. Many of them took up the invitation, and when they came together he gave them his story in brief. **"Men and brethren, though I have done nothing against our people or the customs of our fathers, yet I was delivered as a prisoner from Jerusalem into the hands of the Romans, who, when they had examined me, wanted to let me go, because there was no cause for putting me to death. But when the Jews spoke against it, I was compelled to appeal to Caesar, not that I had anything of which to accuse my nation"** (vv. 17–19). There was no spirit of vengeance or vindictiveness in the heart of Paul. These are the people to whom he had written three years earlier that he would be willing, basically, to lose his salvation if it would mean the conversion of his fellow Jews. So even now in chains Paul is pouring out his heart to the Jewish leaders.

"For this reason therefore I have called for you, to see you and speak with you, because for the hope of Israel I am bound with this chain" (v. 20). Luke tells us that they responded to Paul's announcement by saying that they had heard nothing from the leaders in Jerusalem or received any letters. No one had come to Rome to bear witness against Paul. They wanted to hear, however, about this sect that was being spoken of everywhere. Why no one had sent messages yet from Jerusalem is a bit of a puzzle, because Rome required that anybody bringing charges against another was compelled to present evidence of the charges in the Roman court. So far, no one from Jerusalem had shown up, not because his adversaries had lost their zeal but because of the bad weather at that time of year. Paul barely made it to Rome due to the winter conditions, so probably the elders in Jerusalem were waiting for better weather before coming to Rome to present their case against Paul.

The Kingdom of God

In any case, the delay gave Paul an opportunity to bear witness to the Jewish leaders about the Christian faith. **So when they had appointed him a day, many came to him at his lodging, to whom he explained and solemnly testified of the kingdom of God, persuading them concerning Jesus from both the Law of Moses and the Prophets, from morning till evening** (v. 23). Paul's first point of explanation was the kingdom of God. If there is any motif that connects the Old Testament to the New Testament, it is the kingdom of God. The content of the gospel has to do with the person of Jesus and the work of Christ, but before we hear this gospel of Jesus Christ, the first reference to the gospel is to the gospel of the kingdom.

When John the Baptist appeared on the scene, he called for the nation of Israel to repent: "Repent, for the kingdom of heaven is at hand!" (Matt. 3:2). When Jesus began His public ministry, His message was exactly the same: "Repent, for the kingdom of heaven is at hand" (Matt. 4:17). Throughout His earthly ministry, particularly in His parables, Jesus explained the idea of the kingdom of God to His hearers: "The kingdom of God is like . . ." At the center of Jesus' preaching was the idea of the kingdom of God. All through the pages of the Old Testament God promises His people that He will make His sovereign authority manifest in sending His anointed Messiah into the world; the Old Testament is all about the promised King of the kingdom of God.

So that is where Paul starts. He said that the Jews for centuries had been waiting for their king. He went back to the patriarchs and to the prophets because that single chord was sounded there again and again, that the King of kings was coming. By going to the Jewish Scriptures, he set forth Christ and the gospel of Christ. This was no three-minute salvation message, because it would take Paul from morning until evening to expound all the content of the Word of God that had driven history to that point of the coming King.

Hard Hearts

And some were persuaded by the things which were spoken, and some disbelieved (v. 24). Hasn't that always been the case wherever the gospel is proclaimed? Some are persuaded while others remain in unbelief. That is what happened here under the preaching of Paul. **So when they did not agree among themselves, they departed after Paul had said one word: "The Holy Spirit spoke rightly through Isaiah the prophet to our fathers, saying, 'Go to this people and say: "Hearing you will hear, and shall not understand; And seeing you will see, and not perceive; for the hearts of this people**

have grown dull. Their ears are hard of hearing, and their eyes they have closed, lest they should see with their eyes and hear with their ears, lest they should understand with their hearts and turn, so that I should heal them'" (vv. 25–27). Paul was not given to redundancies or to a waste of breath when he lectured or preached, but if there ever was a redundancy in the apostolic proclamation, it is here, when he used Isaiah's words to show that the Holy Spirit had spoken rightly. When the Holy Spirit speaks, He always speaks rightly. The Holy Spirit does not know how to speak wrongly. Paul, in a sense, was rebuking them. They believed that the Scriptures of the Old Testament were inspired by the Holy Spirit, so when these people left in unbelief, Paul told them that the Holy Spirit had been right. He had spoken through the prophet Isaiah saying exactly what these people would do.

There is a parallel between Isaiah's experience in the temple and Paul's experience on the road to Damascus, and here Paul reminded them of the call of Isaiah. After Isaiah volunteered for the mission, God told him to go, even though God would make the heart of the people fat, their ears deaf, and their eyes blind, lest they see and understand, lest they hear and embrace and become converted (Isa. 6:9–10). Isaiah's mission was to be a mission impossible, because he was going to preach to spiritually dead people who did not want to hear his message. Yet in the end, God had said to Isaiah, "A tenth will be in it, and will return and be for consuming, as a terebinth tree or as an oak, whose stump remains when it is cut down. So the holy seed shall be its stump" (Isa. 6:13).

We are coming to the end of the record of the apostolic testimony of the first century. Have you heard it? Have you seen it? Or have you become calloused to the Word of God? Have you heard it so often you do not want to hear it anymore? Are you turning a deaf ear to the Word of God? It is impossible to hear the Word of God and remain neutral. It is impossible to hear the Word of God and be unchanged. When you hear the Word of God, you are moved either toward sanctification or toward hardness of heart. That is what Paul said to these people who were familiar with the Scriptures, who knew the Scriptures, who had listened to the great expositor of the Scriptures. Isaiah had been telling the truth, because the Holy Spirit through Isaiah spoke rightly.

Some say that it doesn't seem fair. Why would God close ears and shut eyes and then punish for not hearing and seeing? He does so because the closing of the ears and the eyes is God's judgment upon people who, in the first place, did not want to hear and did not want to see. That is the way He operates. In His judgment He said, "He who is unjust, let him be unjust still; he who is filthy, let him be filthy still; he who is righteous, let him be righteous still; he who is holy, let him be holy still" (Rev. 22:11). If you hear the Word of God again and again, and it continues to fall upon a stony, recalcitrant heart, God may give you over to that heart forever. That is the warning Paul gave these people.

"Therefore let it be known to you that the salvation of God has been sent to the Gentiles, and they will hear it!" (v. 28). We know Christ today because those people in the first century refused to hear the gospel, and God grafted us in as a wild olive tree. Where sin abounded, grace even more abounded (Rom. 5:20).

Then Paul dwelt two whole years in his own rented house, and received all who came to him, preaching the kingdom of God and teaching the things which concern the Lord Jesus Christ with all confidence, no one forbidding him (vv. 30–31). If I were to purchase a novel and find after reading to the end of it that I am not told what happens to the hero, I am going to complain to the publisher. We have followed the Apostle through the known world of his day. We finally see him in Rome, but there is no word of his trial. Luke ends his book saying that Paul was under house arrest in Rome for two years, presumably in A.D. 60. There are abundant references from early church history that tell us what happened afterward. Paul came before Caesar and had his trial, and was exonerated and set free. He resumed his missionary travels and continued freely in his apostolic ministry for two or three years.

In July of the year A.D. 64, a calamity befell Rome. The city was virtually burned to the ground, and, of course, legend has it that Nero himself set fire to Rome and fiddled the violin while the city was in flames. At the end of this disaster, somebody had to be blamed, and since Nero certainly was not going to step forward, he publicly accused Christians for setting the fire that all but destroyed the city of Rome.

We noted earlier that at the beginning of his tenure Nero was known for justice and fairness and his good administration, but somewhere along the way he became the beast of the ancient world. In A.D. 64 we see Nero as the beast he had become. Most citizens of Rome by this time were not hostile toward the Christian community, as we are told by Tacitus, but Nero had a personal hatred for Christianity. We are told that in A.D. 65 both Peter and Paul were martyred under the cruelty of Nero. They died in different ways. Peter was crucified, and, according to tradition, he asked to be crucified upside down because he did not feel worthy to die in exactly the same manner as his Savior had died. Paul, unlike Peter, was a Roman citizen, and Roman citizens convicted of capital crimes were not executed by crucifixion. They were beheaded with the sword. Tradition holds that under Nero in A.D. 65, Paul, once again a prisoner, was taken out of jail and publicly executed by a guard who took his sword and cut Paul's head from his body.

What went on in the few days and weeks before his last moments on earth are not told to us in the book of Acts, which ends with the Apostle free and the gospel continuing to spread throughout the known world.

EPILOGUE

2 Timothy 4:6–22

For I am already being poured out as a drink offering, and the time of my departure is at hand. I have fought the good fight, I have finished the race, I have kept the faith. Finally, there is laid up for me the crown of righteousness, which the Lord, the righteous Judge, will give to me on that Day, and not to me only but also to all who have loved His appearing. Be diligent to come to me quickly; for Demas has forsaken me, having loved this present world, and has departed for Thessalonica—Crescens for Galatia, Titus for Dalmatia. Only Luke is with me. Get Mark and bring him with you, for he is useful to me for ministry. And Tychicus I have sent to Ephesus. Bring the cloak that I left with Carpus at Troas when you come—and the books, especially the parchments. Alexander the coppersmith did me much harm. May the Lord repay him according to his works. You also must beware of him, for he has greatly resisted our words. At my first defense no one stood with me, but all forsook me. May it not be charged against them. But the Lord stood with me and strengthened me, so that the message might be preached fully through me, and that all the Gentiles might hear. Also I was delivered out of the mouth of the lion. And the Lord will deliver me from every evil work and preserve me for His heavenly kingdom. To Him be glory forever and ever. Amen! Greet Prisca and Aquila, and the household of Onesiphorus. Erastus stayed in Corinth, but Trophimus I have left in Miletus sick. Do your utmost to come before winter. Eubulus greets you, as well as Pudens, Linus, Claudia, and all the brethren. The Lord Jesus Christ be with your spirit. Grace be with you. Amen.

The first time I went to Rome, I told our professional tour guide that I wanted to see the Lateran Church. In 1511 on the stairs of that church Martin Luther had a spiritual crisis. He had joined other monks on those stairs as they knelt on each step in prayer in an effort to win indulgences for their souls and for the souls of departed relatives. When Luther got to the top of those stairs, he wondered aloud, "Who knows if this is true?" The seeds of disquiet began right then to assail his soul, and the disquiet continued until he was awakened to the gospel of justification by faith alone, and the Reformation was underway.

On that first trip to Rome, our tour group also went down into what originally had been used as a place to gather water, a cistern carved out of solid rock. It was a chamber about fifteen feet wide, fifteen feet deep, and eight feet high. The cavern was cold, dark, and dank. It was the Mamertine Prison, where the Apostle Paul was held captive while awaiting execution. From the steps of that prison one can look across the street and see the ruins of the forum where the Romans legislated their law. As a man in prison looks out the window of his cell and sees the scaffold being erected for his hanging, so the Apostle Paul waited his last moments when his head would be placed upon the executioner's block. No one knows how long Paul was held prisoner in that cistern. Whether several months or several weeks, we just do not know. As I stepped down into that old cistern, I could imagine Paul there in that dank, desperate place writing his final letter to Timothy. I thought in wonder, *This is where it happened. This is where Paul wrote to his beloved disciple and gave his last words.*

Poured Out

Paul wrote some poignant words. **For I am already being poured out as a drink offering, and the time of my departure is at hand** (v. 6). He was making a reference to the Old Testament sacrifice system. When animals were offered in sacrifice, blood was poured out on the altar. The sacrifice of Christ was a perfect sacrifice offered once for all, and Paul knew that he could not possibly add anything of merit to it; nevertheless, he was acutely aware that it is every Christian's task to bear witness to the perfect sacrifice of Christ by offering to Christ the sacrifice of his or her own life. At the end of Romans, after spelling out the doctrines of the gospel, Paul wrote, "I appeal to you therefore, brothers, by the mercies of God, to present your bodies as a living sacrifice, holy and acceptable to God, which is your spiritual worship" (Rom. 12:1). It was in this vein that Paul told Timothy that he was already being poured out as an oblation to honor his Lord.

Paul's death was very close, yet the words he used were "my departure is at hand." The Greek word translated "departure" is the word *analusis*, from which we get the English word *analysis*. So a more literal translation might be "the time of my analysis is near." If Paul were to write that today, we would think that he had an appointment with a psychiatrist or a tax attorney. When the term *analysis* was first coined, it was closer to the original Greek meaning. To analyze something was to parse it, to make close and careful distinctions as one part of something was separated from another. Paul was saying that in a very short time his body was going to be separated from his soul. He would still be alive, and his soul would enter into the presence of Christ, though his body would be put into a grave.

From the Latin translation of that same word, we get the word *disillusion* or, even better, *resolution*. Therefore, we could also translate it this way: "For the time of my resolution is at hand." The type of resolution in mind here concerns resolving tension or conflict. Those who love music know that when the music gets away from the tonic foundation, the tension of dissonance occurs and the ear longs for the music to be resolved. Great musicians know that the tension is resolved by bringing the melody back home. That is what Paul was saying to Timothy. His entire life had been one of stress and tension. Rather than giving Luke's work the title "Acts of the Apostles" it could just as easily have been called "The Tensions and Distress of the Life of Paul." But that is all done now. The time of his resolution is at hand. All his problems and pains will shortly be resolved. Paul was not writing with a discouraged soul. He was ready to go home and was already beginning the oblation of the final sacrifice.

The Good Fight

Paul died a martyr. The word *martyr* comes from the Greek word *martyrea*, but the word *martyrea* in Greek does not mean "martyr"; it means "witness." *Martyr* got its English meaning because those in the early church showed their witness so consistently that their witness often ended in death. So the word *martyrdom*, which originally was synonymous with *witnessing*, came to mean "those who witness to the ultimate degree of paying with their lives."

Then Paul borrowed three metaphors to describe his witness that was about to be resolved: **I have fought the good fight, I have finished the race, I have kept the faith** (v. 7). As a seventeen-year-old boy I watched my father die a day at a time. I would drag him to the dining room table and then back to his bedroom every night. One night as I was dragging him across the living room floor, he said to me, "Stop and put me down for a second on the sofa." Once he was seated, he said to me, "Son, I have fought the good fight, I have finished the race, and I have kept the faith." At that time I had never read the Bible. I wasn't a Christian, so I had no idea where those words came from, but I knew exactly what my father was saying to me—he was telling me that he was ready to die. Those were the last words he ever spoke to me. My last words to him, to my everlasting shame, were, "Don't say that, Dad." I did not realize that in his words was a tremendous testimony of confidence about where he was going. I carried him to his bed, and that night he had his final stroke and went into a coma. He never awoke again here, but he was awake there instantly.

Paul said he had fought the good fight. The contemporary view of Christianity is that Christians should never be engaged in combat or conflict of any kind. We are supposed to be peacekeepers always, never engaged in arguing or debate. The New Testament tells us we are not to be quarrelsome. We are not supposed to be belligerent or bellicose in our personality. However, there is a fight out there, and it is a good fight. It is a spiritual war that all Christians are called to be engaged in. Every Christian is supposed to believe the things of God, and every Christian is supposed to defend the truths of God, but let me take that one step further. It is not enough to hold the faith or even to defend the faith; we are called to *contend* for the faith. Was that not the example of the Apostle Paul? Everywhere he went, he didn't just preach Christianity; he defended it.

In *On the Waterfront* Marlon Brando said to his brother, "I could have been a contender." What does it take to be a contender? Anybody can become a professional boxer; Bob Hope tried it in an undistinguished way. To be a contender, you have to win, and you have to win enough that you become ranked. You must become recognized as one of the top ten fighters in your weight division to even be considered as a contender. Then you have to fight your way up the ladder until finally you get a championship bout, a shot at the title. The challenger is not the champion until he defeats the champion, but he is a contender. Paul was a contender. In fact, Paul was a champion. Apart from Christ, Paul was the supreme champion of the kingdom of God in that day. The fight Paul had fought was "the good fight." There is a good fight, and we are all called to be enlisted in that battle.

The Race Finished

Then he changed the metaphor from the boxer to the runner: "I have finished the race." Paul was not writing about the 100-yard dash. It is easy, in one sense, to be a sprinter, to work hard for the kingdom over the short haul, but Paul wasn't interested in a 100-yard dash; he was in a marathon, one that went a lot longer than twenty-six miles. He was engaged in that race for his entire life. I struggle with patience and pray for it all the time. I tend to have two speeds— fast and off. Yet patience is what it takes to be a marathoner, to endure, not to just run for one hundred yards. Merely finishing a 100-yard dash is not much of an accomplishment compared to completing a marathon, which is what Paul was saying to Timothy. He hadn't just started the race and sprinted through it.

He had run and run and kept on running. His legs had burned with fire, but he had kept moving for the hope in front of him. Now his race was over, and he had kept the faith the whole time.

Then Paul gave a military illustration. Throughout military history the responsibility of every soldier is fidelity to his general and to his country. When the shooting starts, the faithful soldier does not run. He does not quit. He goes forward. That is what Paul said about his life. Like a first-century Marine, his motto was *semper fidelis*, "always faithful." He had been faithful to the doctrine that the Lord had given to him. He had not changed his theology every time someone disapproved of it. He had not negotiated or compromised the truth when people were angered by it. He had stayed the course and remained faithful to his Lord. Could anybody have a better epitaph than that?

Paul's Crown

Finally, there is laid up for me the crown of righteousness, which the Lord, the righteous Judge, will give to me on that Day, and not to me only but also to all who have loved His appearing (v. 8). In the ancient world winners of the Olympic Games did not get a gold medal hung around their neck. Rather, the victor was adorned with a laurel wreath. The crown Paul was writing about, however, was the crown of righteousness that Christ had put aside with Paul's name on it. He was now ready to receive that crown, one which all who have loved His coming will also receive.

Even though in the rest of the closing lines of the letter Paul mentioned those who had betrayed him, he ended with a doxology. He thanked God for His mercy and grace: **The Lord Jesus Christ be with your spirit. Grace be with you. Amen** (v. 22). How did Timothy react when he received that parchment of this letter? If we had been there, we most likely would have seen tears roll down Timothy's cheeks when he discovered that Paul was about to die. Yet, at the same time, we would have seen his chest start to swell. Paul had been his mentor, the Apostle, praying for grace for him and for his people.

INDEX OF NAMES

ABOUT THE AUTHOR

Dr. R.C. Sproul was founder of Ligonier Ministries, founding pastor of Saint Andrew's Chapel in Sanford, Fla., first president of Reformation Bible College, and executive editor of *Tabletalk* magazine. His radio program, *Renewing Your Mind*, is still broadcast daily on hundreds of radio stations around the world and can also be heard online. He was author of more than one hundred books, including *The Holiness of God*, *Chosen by God*, and *Everyone's a Theologian*. He was recognized throughout the world for his articulate defense of the inerrancy of Scripture and the need for God's people to stand with conviction upon His Word.